NEW PATHWAYS TO JOB CREATION
AND DEVELOPMENT IN AFRICA

NEW PATHWAYS TO JOB CREATION AND DEVELOPMENT IN AFRICA

The Promise of Industries without Smokestacks

EDITED BY

**HAROON BHORAT,
BRAHIMA S. COULIBALY,
RICHARD NEWFARMER,**
AND
JOHN PAGE

Brookings Institution Press
Washington, DC

This is a study prepared for the Brookings Institution's Africa Growth Initiative.

Published by Brookings Institution Press®
1775 Massachusetts Avenue, NW
Washington, DC 20036
www.brookings.edu/bipress

Co-published by Rowman & Littlefield
Bloomsbury Publishing Inc, 1385 Broadway, New York, NY 10018, USA
Bloomsbury Publishing Plc, 50 Bedford Square, London, WC1B 3DP, UK
Bloomsbury Publishing Ireland, 29 Earlsfort Terrace, Dublin 2, D02 AY28, Ireland
https://www.bloomsbury.com

Typeset in Janson Text
Composition by Circle Graphics
Printed and bound in the United States of America

The Brookings Institution is a nonprofit organization devoted to research, education, and publication on important issues of domestic and foreign policy. Its principal purpose is to bring the highest quality independent research and analysis to bear on current and emerging policy problems. Brookings' publications represent the sole views of their author(s).

Library of Congress Control Number: 2024950880

ISBN: 978-0-8157-4016-2 (cloth : alk. paper)
ISBN: 978-0-8157-4017-9 (pbk. : alk. paper)
ISBN: 978-0-8157-4018-6 (ebook)
ISBN: 978-0-8157-4131-2 (ePDF)

For product safety related questions contact productsafety@bloomsbury.com.

The paper used in this publication meets the minimum requirements of American National Standard for Information Sciences—Permanence of Paper for Printed Library Materials, ANSI/NISO Z39.48-1992

Contents

Foreword

Countries across Sub-Saharan Africa need to overcome two important challenges to achieve economic development. The first is the creation of large-scale jobs, particularly for its burgeoning number of youth entering the labor market every year. The second is a sustained increase in productivity to raise standards of living and break the poverty cycle for millions of people. In other parts of the world, both these challenges have been historically achieved through the development of the industrial sector. The relatively high labor intensity of industry has made it a viable destination for labor moving out of agriculture at the start of the economic development journey. Also, because productivity tends to be higher in industry than in agriculture, the movement of labor from agriculture to industry has raised the economy-wide productivity and accelerated structural transformation.

However, the traditional industrial sector has been less dynamic in Africa, certainly in comparison with fast-growing East Asia. Industrial activity and employment in African countries have tended to peak at lower shares of gross domestic product in earlier stages of economic development—a phenomenon known as *premature deindustrialization*. Even though manufacturing was expanding in Africa, other sectors have been expanding much more quickly. In part, this reflects technological progress in communication, expansion of the internet, and new forms of business organization including global value chains. Given these trends, how can Africa create productive jobs for its large and growing youth population and achieve structural transformation if the well-trodden path of industrial development has become difficult to replicate?

To answer this question, Brookings' Africa Growth Initiative initiated research—in collaboration with several partner think tanks across Africa—which has revealed the emergence of modern services sectors with characteristics similar to traditional industry. We find that these "industries without smokestacks"—including tourism, horticulture, agro-processing, financial and business services, and information and communications technology—are tradable, relatively labor-intensive, and amenable to technological upgrading, much like manufacturing. They exhibit higher productivity than traditional agriculture, and thus they have the potential to spur Africa's structural transformation.

This book synthesizes the results of this research and provides key policy recommendations for industries without smokestacks to play an important role in job creation and structural transformation. The book pushes the global knowledge frontier in this field, and I am hopeful that it serves as a useful resource for academics, policymakers, scholars, and all other stakeholders.

I am very grateful to the contributors: Our think tank partners across Africa, which provided regional insights and expertise—including UNU-WIDER, the International Growth Centre, and Finn Tarp—for their partnership on the early research agenda, as well as to our think tank partners across the region and my fellow editors—Haroon Bhorat, Richard Newfarmer, and John Page—for their analytical and editorial contributions.

—Brahima S. Coulibaly
Vice President, Global Economy and Development, Brookings

Acknowledgments

This study was initiated from 2018 to 2020 by the Africa Growth Initiative at Brookings. It was a collaborative project involving several African think tanks and research institutions. The study is a follow-up to Brookings' and UNU-WIDER's joint research project, Industries Without Smokestacks: Industrialization in Africa Reconsidered.

We gratefully acknowledge the partnership of African think tanks and research institutions that participated in this collaborative study, including the Development Policy Research Institute at the University of Cape Town, the Kenya Institute for Public Policy Research and Analysis (KIPPRA), the International Growth Centre (University of Oxford and London School of Economics and Political Science), Laboratoire d'Analyse des Politiques de Développement at the University Cheikh Anta Diop, the Economic Policy Research Centre (Makerere University), the Policy Studies Institute, and the University of Ghana.

The study benefited from comments and suggestions from several experts who reviewed the book manuscript, including Shanta Devarajan, Mary Hallward-Driemeier, Celestin Monga, and Finn Tarp. This study also benefited from useful feedback from workshop participants at Brookings, as well as a workshop in Nairobi cohosted by the Brookings Africa Growth

Initiative, the Africa Economic Research Consortium (AERC), and KIPPRA. We thank former AERC executive director Njuguna Ndung'u and KIPPRA executive director Rose Lingui.

Wafa Abedin provided excellent research and editorial assistance throughout the work. Andrew Hayes, Chris Heitzig, and Dhruv Ghandi also provided valuable research and coordination support. We also thank Christina Golubski and Molly Sugrue for project management and development support, respectively.

The publication of the book was managed by Brookings Institution Press and Rowman & Littlefield. The editors would like to thank Alfred Imhoff, Yelba Quinn, and the team at Circle Graphics of Reisterstown, Maryland, for their support in the production of this volume.

The conclusions and recommendations of Brookings publications are solely those of its author(s), and do not reflect the views or policies of the institution, its management, its other scholars, or the funders acknowledged below.

Brookings gratefully acknowledges the support of the International Development Research Centre, Ottawa; the Mastercard Foundation; and an anonymous donor.

Brookings recognizes that the value it provides is in its absolute commitment to quality, independence, and impact. Activities supported by its donors reflect this commitment.

A Special Acknowledgment

To John Page, at the end of an illustrious professional career as an insightful and committed development economist, who inspired all those who worked with him on issues of economic development in Africa and around the world, we convey a special word of thanks.

—Haroon Bhorat, Brahima S. Coulibaly, and Richard Newfamer

Contributors

CAITLIN ALLEN   former Junior Researcher, Development Policy Research Unit, University of Cape Town (South Africa case study).

ERNEST ARYEETEY   secretary-general, African Research Universities Alliance and professor of economics, University of Ghana (Ghana case study).

ZAAKHIR ASMAL   former senior research officer, Development Policy Research Unit, University of Cape Town (South Africa case study).

ASSANE BEYE   researcher, Laboratoire d'Analyse des Politiques de Développement, Cheikh Anta Diop University (Senegal case study).

HAROON BHORAT   professor of economics and director, Development Policy Research Unit, University of Cape Town, and nonresident senior fellow, Africa Growth Initiative, Global Economy and Development, Brookings (coeditor; South Africa case study).

DENNIS CHIWELE   former country manager for Zambia, International Growth Centre (Zambia case study).

BRAHIMA S. COULIBALY   vice president and director, Global Economy and Development, Brookings (coeditor).

ABDOU KHADIR DIA   statistician, Laboratoire d'Analyse des Politiques de Développement, Cheikh Anta Diop University, and research assistant, Université du Québec à Trois-Rivières (Senegal case study).

LOUISE FOX   nonresident senior fellow, Africa Growth Initiative, Global Economy and Development, Brookings (labor markets).

DHRUV GANDHI   consultant, World Bank; former senior research analyst, Global Economy and Development, Brookings (labor markets).

FATOU GUEYE   (deceased) former director, Laboratoire d'Analyse des Politiques de Développement, Cheikh Anta Diop University (Senegal case study).

MADINA M. GULOBA   senior research fellow, Economic Policy Research Centre (Uganda case study).

CHRIS HEITZIG   former senior research analyst and project manager, Africa Growth Initiative, Global Economy and Development, Brookings.

ROBERT HILL   junior research fellow, Development Policy Research Unit, University of Cape Town (South Africa case study).

MEDARD KAKURU   research analyst, Economic Policy Research Centre (Uganda case study).

NANCY LAIBUNI   former policy analyst, Kenya Institute for Public Policy Research and Analysis (Kenya case study).

SAMANTHA LUSENO   former young professional, Kenya Institute for Public Policy Research and Analysis (Kenya case study).

AHMADOU ALY MBAYE   vice chancellor, Cheikh Anta Diop University (Senegal case study).

MASSAER MBAYE   researcher, Laboratoire d'Analyse des Politiques de Développement, Cheikh Anta Diop University, and research assistant, Université du Québec à Montréal (Senegal case study).

JABULILE MONNAKGOTLKA   junior research fellow, Development Policy Research Unit, University of Cape Town (South Africa case study).

BOAZ MUNGA   senior policy analyst, Kenya Institute for Public Policy Research and Analysis (Kenya case study).

RICHARD NEWFARMER   country director for Uganda and Rwanda, International Growth Centre (coeditor; Rwanda case study).

HUMPHREY NJOGU   principal policy analyst, Kenya Institute for Public Policy Research and Analysis (Kenya case study).

ELDAH ONSOMU   director of economic management, Kenya Institute for Public Policy Research and Analysis (Kenya case study).

MORNÉ OOSTHUIZEN   chief research officer and deputy director, Development Policy Research Unit, University of Cape Town (South Africa case study).

JOHN PAGE   former senior fellow, Africa Growth Initiative, Global Economy and Development, Brookings, and nonresident senior fellow, UNU-WIDER (coeditor).

MWANDA PHIRI   Africa lead, Charter Cities Institute, and former research fellow, Zambia Institute for Policy Analysis and Research (Zambia case study).

ANAND RAJARAM   former country director for Zambia, International Growth Centre (Zambia case study).

JAKOB RAUSCHENDORFER   former country economist, International Growth Centre (Uganda case study).

CHRISTOPHER ROONEY   former junior researcher, Development Policy Research Unit, University of Cape Town (South Africa case study).

ADAN SHIBIA   senior policy analyst, Kenya Institute for Public Policy Research and Analysis (Kenya case study).

SARAH N. SSEWANYANA   executive director, Economic Policy Research Centre (Uganda case study).

TSEGAY G. TEKLESELASSIE   lead researcher, Policy Studies Institute, and visiting lecturer, Wellesley College (Ethiopia case study).

FESTUS EBO TURKSON associate professor of economics, Department of Economics, University of Ghana (Ghana case study).

ANNA TWUM economist, macroeconomics, trade, and investment, World Bank, and former country economist, International Growth Centre (Rwanda case study).

PRISCILLA TWUMASI-BAFFOUR senior lecturer, Department of Economics, University of Ghana (Ghana case study).

List of Abbreviations

1D1F	One District One Factory (Ghana)
AfDB	African Development Bank
AGI	Africa Growth Initiative (Brookings)
AGR	agriculture
ANSD	Agence Nationale de Statistique et de la Démographie (Senegal)
AU	African Union
BPO	business process outsourcing
BTS	Brevet de Technicien Supérieur (Superior Technician Certificate) (Senegal)
CAGR	compound annual growth rate
CCM	cool chain management
CON	construction
CSA	Central Statistical Agency (Ethiopia)
CSP	community, social, and personal services
CSS	Senegalese Sugar Corporation (Compagnie Sucrière Sénégalaise)
DAFF	Department of Agriculture, Forestry, and Fisheries (South Africa)

DBSA	Development Bank of Southern Africa
DFZ	Dakar Free Zone
DPRU	Development Policy Research Unit
DRC	Democratic Republic of Congo
EAC	East African Community
ECOWAS	Economic Community of West African States
EPZ	export-processing zone
ERSWEC	Economic Recovery Strategy for Wealth and Employment Creation (Kenya)
ETB	Ethiopian birr
ETD	Economic Transformation Database
EU	European Union
FCFA	Central African franc
FDI	foreign direct investment
FDRE	Federal Democratic Republic of Ethiopia
FFV	fresh fruits and vegetables
FIN	financial and business services
FTA	free trade agreement
GDP	gross domestic product
GGDC	Groningen Growth and Development Centre
GHS	Ghanaian cedi
GLSS	Ghana Living Standards Survey
GNI	gross national income
GSS	Ghana Statistical Service
GTP	Growth and Transformation Policy (Ethiopia)
GVA	gross value added
HEI	higher education institutions
HS	Harmonized System
IAIP	Integrated Agro-Processing Industrial Parks (Ethiopia)
IATA	International Air Transport Association
IBES	Integrated Business Establishments Survey (Ghana)
ICT	information and communications technology
IGC	International Growth Centre
ILO	International Labor Organization
IMF	International Monetary Fund
ISIC	International Standard Industrial Classification of All Economic Activities

IT	information technology
ITC	International Trade Centre
IWSS	industries without smokestacks
KES	Kenyan shilling
KIHBS	Kenya Integrated Household Budget Survey
KIPPRA	Kenya Institute for Public Policy Research and Analysis
KNBS	Kenya National Bureau of Statistics
LFPR	labor force participation rate
LIC	low-income country
LMIC	lower-middle-income country
LPI	Logistics Performance Indicator
LTE	long-term evolution
MCC	Millennium Challenge Corporation
MoCT	Ministry of Culture and Tourism (Ethiopia)
MoTAC	Ministry of Tourism, Arts, and Culture (Ghana)
NAEB	National Agricultural Export Development Board (Rwanda)
NBE	National Bank of Ethiopia
NDP III	National Development Plan III (Uganda)
NEPAD	New Partnership for Africa's Development
NES	National Export Strategy (Rwanda)
NISR	National Institute for Statistics of Rwanda
NSDEPS	National Skills Development and Employment Protection Strategy (Rwanda)
OECD	Organization for Economic Cooperation and Development
O*NET	Occupational Network Database
PASDEP	Plan for Accelerated and Sustained Development to End Poverty (Ethiopia)
PAYE	pay-as-you-earn
PHH	private households
PSE	Emerging Senegal Plan (Plan Sénégal Emergent)
RLFS	Rwanda Labor Force Survey
ROW	rest of the world
RR	resource-rich
RSA	Republic of South Africa
RTC	Rural Transformation Centre (Ethiopia)

RWF   Rwandan franc
SEZ   special economic zone
SIC   Standard Industrial Classification
SMEs   small and medium-sized enterprises
SSA   Sub-Saharan Africa
STEM   science, technology, engineering, and mathematics
STEP   systematic tracking of exchanges in procurement
TRA   transportation
TSA   Tourism Satellite Account
TVET   technical and vocational education and training
UBOS   Uganda Bureau of Statistics
UGX   Ugandan shilling
UHT   ultra-high temperature (milk)
UMIC   upper-middle-income country
UNCTAD   UN Commission on Trade and Development
UNECA   UN Economic Commission for Africa
UNHS   Uganda National Household Survey
UNICEF   UN International Children's Emergency Fund
UNU-WIDER   United Nations University–World Institute for
                        Development Economics Research
URA   Uganda Revenue Agency
UTI   utilities
VAT   value-added tax
WBES   World Bank Enterprise Survey
WRT   wholesale and retail trade
WTO   World Trade Organization
XOF   West African franc
ZAR   South African rand
ZEGA   Zambia Export Growers Association
ZMW   Zambian kwacha

ONE

From Deindustrialization to Job Creation

New Perspectives on African Growth

CHRIS HEITZIG, RICHARD NEWFARMER, AND JOHN PAGE

After a tumultuous few years since the onset of the COVID-19 pandemic, African policymakers are turning their attention to promoting economic recovery with structural measures that build in resilience to external shocks. These imply undertaking macro- and microeconomic policies that propel increases in productivity while diversifying the base of economic activity and exports to achieve economic transformation. At its heart, achieving structural transformation and overall economic development requires increasing within-sector productivity as well as progressively increasing the share of labor, investment, and technology allocated to activities with relatively higher productivity.[1]

In contrast to the conventional path of transformation—agriculture to industry to services—Africa's growth has relied less on manufacturing and instead has featured sectors such as horticulture, agro-processing, business services, activities based on information and communications technology (ICT), and tourism. A previous study indicated that these activities share many of the same characteristics as manufacturing—they have higher labor productivity relative to traditional agriculture, they are amenable to technology-induced and scale-induced productivity growth, they are tradable and hence can propel export growth and benefit from import competition, and, importantly, they are labor intensive (Newfarmer, Page, and Tarp 2018). As a result, they have the potential to create productive jobs with higher worker earnings. We call these activities—somewhat metaphorically—"industries without smokestacks" (IWSS).[2]

Africa's pattern of economic transformation prompts important questions for the continent's policymakers: Can the growth of these sectors generate a sufficient number of new jobs to employ people productively without relying mainly on manufacturing growth? Can these new jobs incorporate women, youth, and unskilled workers? Will these new jobs be sufficiently productive to power growth and raise incomes? In other words, if well supported, can these sectors, in tandem with manufacturing, drive Africa's economic development?

The purpose of this volume is to provide answers to these questions by undertaking case studies of eight Sub-Saharan African countries: Ethiopia, Rwanda, Uganda, Ghana, Kenya, Senegal, Zambia, and South Africa. The studies highlight three to four most-promising IWSS sectors in each country, assess their potential to create productive jobs, examine the constraints holding back their growth, and suggest policy recommendations to address these constraints.

By focusing on IWSS, the studies in this volume turn the analytical prism in a way different from the lens crafted from the conventional trichotomy of agriculture, industry, and services. Identifying activities that have relatively high productivity, are amenable to the adoption of new technologies, and are tradable is designed to focus attention on potential sources of growth that fall below the radar screen of policymakers as they design industrial policies. The aggregation of IWSS highlights activities in Africa that collectively power growth in ways different from more traditional paths followed in other regions. Whether agro-processing, horticulture, tourism, other business services, or other tradable activities, these could have as easily—if less elegantly—been dubbed "modern" sectors or "high-performing" sectors. They are modern industries that have traditionally been services oriented, boast scalable production, and, owing to recent innovations, have become tradable across borders.[3] Collectively, these IWSS sectors as prospective drivers of growth present a rather more optimistic view of the potential for structural transformation in Africa than a narrow focus on manufacturing (figure 1-1).

FIGURE 1-1. **Labor Moves from Agriculture into Services in Sub-Saharan Africa**

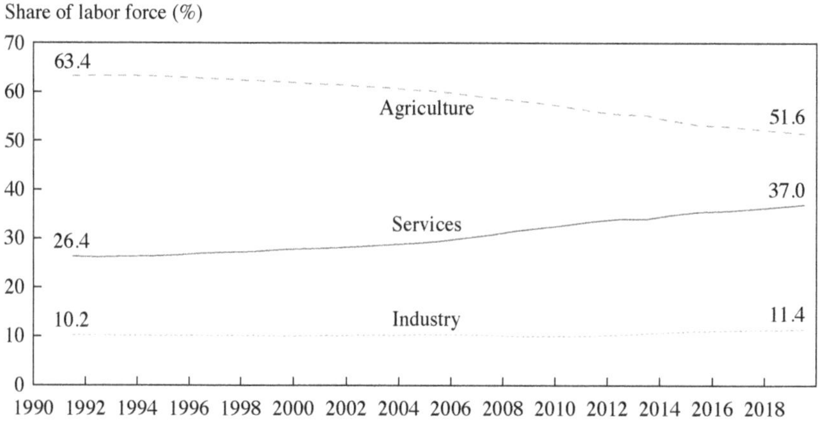

Share of labor force (%)

To elaborate on these ideas, this chapter utilizes an analytical framework emerging from the literature on structural transformation and that synthesizes data from all eight case studies. The opening section reviews the recent literature on the roles of manufacturing, agriculture, and services in contributing to unconditional convergence in labor productivity growth rates between low- and high-income countries. It highlights activities that have the potential to drive income convergence and analyzes ways Africa's pattern of transformation differ from those of other regions. The second section drills down on the many activities within sectors in Africa beyond manufacturing that hold the promise of higher productivity, and then sketches the role of these IWSS activities in a comparative analytic framework for the eight countries in this study. It reviews their growth, employment, and export performance. The third section elaborates on the role of IWSS activities for productivity growth. The analysis underscores that productivity gains within IWSS sectors are an essential part of Africa's transformation.

The Context: Africa's Transformation and Employment Challenges

Trends in employment, as seen through the lens of conventional economic sectors—agriculture, industry, and services—across Sub-Saharan Africa, indicate that average employment shares in agriculture have been consistently declining for the past decades, from 64 percent to 52 percent (figure 1-1).

Meanwhile, the share of industry—conventionally subsuming mining, construction, and manufacturing—has been relatively stagnant. In contrast, the share of employment in services has risen from 26 percent to 37 percent. These patterns reinforce the puzzling observations that labor in Africa has been migrating from agriculture directly into services, seemingly bypassing the industrial sector.

Rodrik (2014) and McMillian, Rodrik, and Sepúlveda (2016) focused centrally on the slow shift of resources out of agriculture into industry—notably manufacturing—asserting that this process of structural transformation was inadequate to power growth. Manufacturing was seen to be special because it was subject to rapid technological change, economies of scale, and exporting, and low-income countries with manufacturing sectors on average have tended to have more rapid growth in labor productivity irrespective of other constraints on growth. These writings pointed out that Africa's growth, even though recently comparable to rapid growth in other regions, was not the result of a fast-growing manufacturing sector, but rather growth within agriculture. A big reason why manufacturing has been so special in propelling economic growth is that it has exhibited "unconditional convergence"—that is, its productivity converges to the global frontier, irrespective of conventional determinants of growth. A country with a booming manufacturing sector would likely have high growth rates—even when its institutions, demographics, and geography put it at a relative disadvantage. Since agriculture and services were seen not to provide drivers of high productivity, this pattern would likely foredoom Africa to slow growth. Moreover, manufacturing as a share of gross domestic product ceased to expand in the course of development, which led scholars to conclude that Africa was afflicted by "premature de-industrialization."

Other studies have questioned the assertion that agriculture and services hold little promise for rapid technological change and productivity growth. Several studies of African agriculture show that deploying modern technology can raise productivity substantially. In Uganda, for example, several studies show that farmers' low productivity is associated with the underutilization of modern seeds and fertilizer, in part because counterfeit products reduce their adoption (Bold et al. 2017) or mismanaged supply chains undercut the power of new technology (Barriga and Fiala 2018). Lagakos and Shu (2021, 4) cite studies that show that agricultural productivity in rich countries is 78 times higher than in poor countries, a fact that suggests that the potential for improvements in productivity are enormous.

Similarly, for services, Baccini and others (2021) argue that services can play a role similar to manufacturing because of changes in the organization of international production, the reduction in transportation costs, and opportunities associated with new technologies, especially in communications. The authors emphasize the heterogeneity in services and hence widely differing levels of productivity. Indeed, they show that, within services, higher-skilled services such as finance, health, and education are associated with higher levels of development, while lower-skilled services, including trade and transportation, tend to decrease with levels of development.[4]

Nayyar, Hallward-Dreimeirer, and Davies (2021) have undertaken arguably the most ambitious study of services in development. Using the traditional trichotomy of economic classifications, they found that labor productivity growth in services over the period 1995–2018 was the same or greater than in industry in four of the six main developing regions.[5] That is, services productivity growth was about the same in Latin America, but exceeded industry in the Middle East and North Africa, South Asia, and Sub-Saharan Africa. Only in Eastern Europe and East Asia did manufacturing productivity grow more rapidly than in services. Moreover, in Sub-Saharan Africa, within-sector productivity growth in services was four times that of industry. Finally, they conclude: "Although the literature has emphasized structural transformation from agriculture to manufacturing as the central dynamic to understanding productivity growth in LMICs, we find that the increasing share of services in total employment accounts for the bulk of the contribution of structural change in each region" (Nayyar, Hallward-Dreimeirer, and Davies 2021, 11).

Noting the heterogeneity of services in their degree of complexity and productivity levels, Nayyar, Hallward-Dreimeirer, and Davies (2021) created four subgroupings of services: low-skill domestic services (e.g., retail trade, administrative services, arts and recreation, etc.); low-skilled tradable services (e.g., wholesale trade, transportation, hotels, and restaurants); skill-intensive social services (e.g., education and health); and what they termed "global innovators" (e.g., financial services, ICT, and professional services). They found that domestic services growth was inversely associated with national income levels, while global innovator services were positively associated with country income. Low-skilled tradable services were uncorrelated.

For many countries around the world, the pattern of structural transformation took on different characteristics after about the 1990s, and these accelerated into the 2000s. This new form of structural transformation favors formal sector companies that offer tradable products and services that are both high in productivity and potent job creators. Diao, McMillan, and Rodrik (2021) and Rodrik (2022) generalized their model to allow the inclusion of other activities beyond manufacturing by referring to the "modern sectors." This could include formal manufacturing but presumably also services sectors and other activities, though it is unspecified in their work.[6]

While unconditional convergence is evident in formal manufacturing and, as Nayyar, Hallward-Dreimeirer, and Davies (2021) call them, "global innovator services," analysis with more recent shows it is also found in other so-called modern sectors, including construction, wholesale and retail trade, and transportation services. For four categories of activities, figure 1-2 shows three decades of country labor productivity, with the horizontal axis being labor productivity in 1990 and the vertical axis showing the growth of labor productivity over the three decades. A line with a negative slope can be interpreted as the speed of sectoral convergence in closing the gap of labor productivity between the lowest and highest rates of initial productivity. From the figure, it is apparent that unconditional convergence is found not only in manufacturing but also in the group of sectors we have labeled "modern sectors" (for lack of a better term). These include business services, construction, financial services, real estate, trade services, and transportation services (see the annex). Agriculture shows only a weak tendency toward convergence, while conventional activities—including government, mining, and utilities—also show convergent tendencies. The rate of unconditional convergence, referred to in the literature as "beta convergence," is strongest, however, in the "modern sectors" (–2.11), and somewhat greater than in manufacturing (–1.01) (figure 1-2). When the analysis excludes Africa from the sample, the beta convergence is marginally weaker in the modern sectors and manufacturing—indicating that these sectors are a powerful productivity-equalizing force for African economies.

Patterns of Structural Transformation: What Sets Africa Apart?

So how does the pattern of structural transformation in Africa over the last two decades compare with those of other regions? To analyze this, we decompose productivity growth into *within-sector* growth—the benefits of sectors more productively using their labor inputs—and *between-sector* growth—the benefits of reallocating labor from less productive sectors to more productive ones. This follows the methodology developed by

FIGURE 1-2. Unconditional Convergence in Labor Productivity by Sectoral Grouping

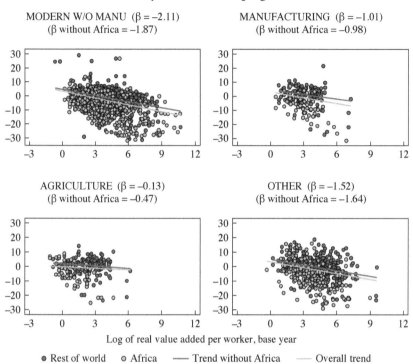

MODERN W/O MANU ($\beta = -2.11$)
(β without Africa = -1.87)

MANUFACTURING ($\beta = -1.01$)
(β without Africa = -0.98)

AGRICULTURE ($\beta = -0.13$)
(β without Africa = -0.47)

OTHER ($\beta = -1.52$)
(β without Africa = -1.64)

Log of real value added per worker, base year

● Rest of world   ○ Africa   —— Trend without Africa   —— Overall trend

Sources: Authors' calculations, using GGDC/UNU-WIDER's Economic Transformation Database and the OECD's Structural Analysis Database.

Note: The vertical axis shows the compound annual growth in real value added per worker for one-digit ISIC sectors by country using these three periods: 1990–2000, 2000–10, and 2010–18. The horizontal axis shows baseline labor productivity values in the given base year (1990, 2000, or 2010). The β coefficient is the slope of the regression of the vertical axis on the x axis, controlling for sector, decade, and sector-decade fixed effects. Modern sectors include business services, construction, financial services, real estate, trade services, and transportation services. Other sectors include government, mining, and utilities.

Fabricant (1942) and subsequently popularized by de Vries, Timmer, and De Vries (2015), Diao and others (2019), Nayyar and others (2021), and others. The analysis uses the Economic Transformation Database, a newly released data set that contains data for employment and value added for 12 sectors for 1990 to 2018, jointly produced by the Groningen Growth and Development Centre and UNU-WIDER. The database covers the eight-case study countries presented in this book as well as Botswana,

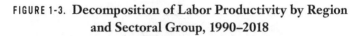

FIGURE 1-3. Decomposition of Labor Productivity by Region and Sectoral Group, 1990–2018

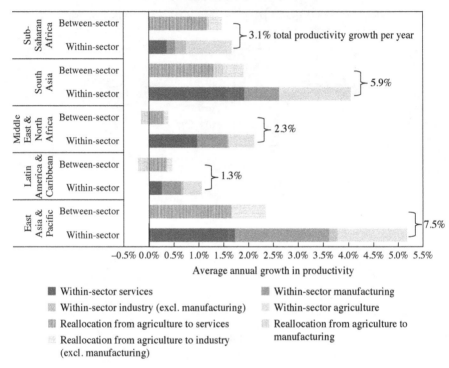

Source: Economic Transformation Database, Groningen Growth and Development Centre and UNU-WIDER. Design inspired by Nayyar, Hallward-Driemeier, and Davies (2021).

Note: Sectors from the Economic Transformation Database were divided as follows: Construction, mining, and utilities are classified under "industry"; and trade services, transportation services, business services, financial services, real estate, government services, and other services are classified under "services." Agriculture and manufacturing are defined by their ISIC Rev. 4 codes "A" and "C," respectively.

Burkina Faso, Cameroon, Lesotho, Malawi, Mauritius, Mozambique, Namibia, Nigeria, and Tanzania (see the annex to this chapter for details).

Over the period 1990–2018, the overall growth rate of productivity in Africa was notably lower than fast-growing East and South Asia, if somewhat higher than the Middle East and North Africa and in Latin America and the Caribbean. This is evident from the summation of the two bars for each region shown in figure 1-3. But the pattern of productivity growth in Sub-Saharan Africa is unique for the pace of structural transformation. Contrary to some of the earlier literature, between-sector productivity growth is nearly an almost equal share of overall productivity growth as within-sector growth. Increasing agricultural productivity has been a key driver of this pattern, but all the major sectors also contributed. Most remarkably, calculations using 2000–2018 data show that services played a more prominent role than manufacturing in both within-sector growth and between-sector growth in every region, suggesting that the services-led growth discussed at length in this book is not unique to Sub-Saharan Africa.

The composition of Sub-Saharan Africa's productivity growth has changed over time as well. The 1990s favored within-sector growth, which was led in nearly equal shares by services, industry, manufacturing, and agriculture. Since 2000, however, between-sector productivity growth has played a more significant role, led by a rising employment share in services. Services also accounted for about 40 percent of within-sector growth between 2000 and 2009, but the sector did not keep pace with the rising employment in the decade that followed.

This pattern prompts several observations. First, overall productivity growth in Sub-Saharan Africa, at 3.1 percent over the three decades, has lagged behind the fast-growing regions of East Asia and South Asia but exceeded that for the Middle East and Latin America. Still, these numbers do highlight the challenge facing the region to catch up to regions with higher incomes. Second, much like the Asian countries, the largest contributors to productivity growth in Africa have been reallocation of workers from low-productivity agriculture to services, as well as productivity growth within agriculture itself. Third, as with fast-growing South Asia, African productivity growth within agriculture has contributed more than within manufacturing growth. Fourth, productivity growth within African services has exceeded that of manufacturing. These patterns raise provocative questions: what activities within agriculture and within services are most promising, how do they fit into Africa's growth pattern, and what policies can be adopted to promote them—questions to which we now turn.

Potential New Sources of Transformation: Industries without Smokestacks

Both the recent evidence on the unconditional convergence of the "modern sectors" and the pattern of structural transformation suggest there are new sources of economic growth and structural transformation in Africa.

The natural question to ask is therefore: *what collections of economic activities are driving Africa's growth in output and employment?*

Identifying IWSS

To look beneath the surface of conventional sectoral definitions and identify new economic activities defining the economic transformation process in Africa, we selected activities that provide significant employment of workers; that can apply new technologies and indeed drive technological progress, and benefit from scale and other economies; that are tradable, either as export activities or providing productivity-increasing import competition, or sometimes both; and that tend to be associated with agglomeration economies that accompany urbanization.

To measure these activities requires applying these criteria to conventional economic margin when drawing boundaries and assigning activities to the IWSS sectors. Most troublesome was the allocation of services. Retail trade, for example, has a modern sector with relatively high productivity (think Shoprite, Pick 'N Pay, or Massmart Holdings for retailing) and a large informal sector; we have adopted the convention (where possible) of including employment in tax-paying formal firms as IWSS and the remainder in non-IWSS. No less difficult is trying to distinguish employment in higher value added, commercial agriculture (including horticulture) from traditional, even subsistence, agriculture using rudimentary technology; we have generally adopted the convention of using export agriculture as a proxy where more crop-level disaggregation was not available. Similarly, to apply the tradability criterion in selecting sub-sectoral activities, the analysis relied on the World Trade Organization's definitions—notably "trans-border service provision" (Mode 1) for transportation (e.g., Ethiopian airlines, Imperial Holdings, or numerous trucking activities) and "commercial presence" (Mode 3) for construction (e.g., WBHO) or telecommunications (e.g., MTN).

The result of this classification produces an employment array across three broad categories for analysis: IWSS, manufacturing, and non-IWSS. In the analysis that follows, we include agro-processing, construction, export crops and horticulture, finance and business services, ICT and digital services, tourism, formal trade, and transportation. The country studies in this volume zoom in on four high-value-added subsectors of IWSS because of their leading-edge characteristics. Agro-processing is included in IWSS as one the featured sectors, along with horticulture and other high-value-added agriculture. Among the service sectors, tourism, another featured sector, is a central economic driver in many African countries. ICT and digital services, and business and financial services, are comparatively new in most African countries, but they are sprouting new shoots of growth worthy of analysis.

Eight Countries with IWSS

The eight countries in this study allow for a close-up look at IWSS. While selected on the basis of available data rather than representative sampling techniques, the countries do capture well the diversity of Africa—both regionally and across income groupings. They range in population size from Rwanda, at 12 million inhabitants, to Ethiopia, with 109 million in 2018 (table 1-1). They vary in levels of per capita income. A common characteristic is the relatively high percentage of youth in the labor force, though female participation varies markedly from Senegal's low of 35 percent to Rwanda's high, at almost 84 percent. Unemployment rates are more correlated with income levels.

The countries analyzed in this volume have generally not followed the East Asian path of agriculture-to-industry development led by manufacturing growth. Rather, their trends mirror those shown in figure 1-1. In Ghana, for example, employment has transitioned from agriculture into services, which has been the leading employer since 2014, but many services are low-productivity, informal activities. The structure of employment in Zambia has shifted from agriculture to informal work, such that in 2014 4.9 million of 5.8 million workers (84.5 percent) were employed in the informal sector, mainly in services. In Senegal, the growing working age population has been almost entirely absorbed into the informal sector in urban areas. Employment is mainly characterized by low wages, underemployment, and limited social protection (box 1-1).

Employment in IWSS Sectors

For the eight country studies, IWSS, on average, accounts for about one-quarter of total employment, if with considerable variance associated with per capita income (table 1-2). In the low-income countries of Ethiopia, Uganda, and Rwanda, IWSS averaged about 16.6 percent. Their role was more important in middle-income countries—Senegal, Kenya, Ghana, and Zambia—at about 25.3 percent. Zambia, because mineral exports inflate its per capita income, is an outlier that lowers the average in this

Table 1-1. Labor Characteristics of the Case Study Countries, 2018

| Indicator | Low-income | | | | Lower-middle-income | | | | | Upper-middle-income |
	Ethiopia	Rwanda	Uganda	*Avg.*	Ghana	Kenya	Senegal	Zambia	*Avg.*	South Africa
Population (millions)	109.2	12.3	42.7	54.8	29.8	51.4	15.9	17.4	28.6	57.8
Gross domestic product per capita (current $)	772	784	770	775	2,194	1,708	1,458	1,516	1,719	6,373
Labor force (millions)	51.4	6.2	15.9	24.5	12.6	23.1	4.1	7.1	11.7	22.9
Share of youth in labor force (%)	34.1	25	28.9	29.3	19	20	21.3	26.3	21.7	10.9
Female labor force participation (%)	73.3	83.9	66.9	74.7	63.8	71.9	35	70.4	60.3	48.4
Unemployment rate (%)	2.1	1.0	1.8	1.6	4.2	2.6	6.5	12.0	6.3	26.9

Sources: Case study data; World Development Indicators.

Box 1-1. Through a Glass Darkly: Limitations in Analyzing IWSS

Assembling data with standardized definitions comparable across countries is not straightforward and poses some limitations. Once assignments are made, national statistics do not always allow for clear definitions; national surveys often change methodologies diminishing the comparability of benchmark periods. So, at times, the studies' authors have had to rely on estimations and assumptions (which can be found in notes). The estimations typically relied on nationally representative surveys. Because such surveys are only available for select years, the years are not necessarily the same across all case studies.

This chapter makes a number of departures from the case studies in order to standardize sector definitions for purposes of comparison. Case studies have slight differences in categorization and terminology in their data. In order to standardize across case studies, we subsume "finance, business, and professional services," "financial and insurance," and "real estate" under "financial and business services." In Ghana, we subsume "other crops," "cocoa," "livestock," "forestry and logging," and "fishing" under "traditional agriculture." We place transit trade in the "trade and repairs" sector. We subsume maintenance and repairs into the sector "other IWSS services."

There are a few cases for which sectors in certain countries are defined more broadly or narrowly than they are in other countries. In Ghana, for example, horticulture is contained within the agro-processing sector rather than "export crops and horticulture." In South Africa, government data include only those employees working in national, provincial, or local governments. In such cases, case study authors use household survey data and export data to estimate figures that permit comparison across all case studies.

Ethiopia, Ghana, and South Africa do not distinguish between informal and formal trade. To resolve this, we use ratios of countries that separate formal and informal trade to estimate the respective share in these countries. We follow a similar procedure when case studies were missing data for a single observation. In Ethiopia, information and communications technology (ICT) was originally

(*continued*)

Box 1-1. (continued)

categorized in transportation but was extracted using the average ratio between transportation and ICT found in the other case studies. Export crops was originally categorized in "traditional agriculture," but was extracted using the average ratio between traditional agriculture and export crops and horticulture found in the other case studies. In Zambia, export crops and horticulture value-added data were approximated using World Integrated Trade Solution data. We used a similar procedure as in Ethiopia to extract ICT value-added data.

To check the validity of the sector reclassification and data estimation, we apply our same methodology to the Groningen Growth and Development Centre and UNU-WIDER's Economic Transformation Database, which contains employment and value-added data for 12 sectors. Sectors from the Economic Transformation Database were divided as follows: construction, trade, transportation, business, finance, and real estate were classified as IWSS; agriculture, mining, utilities, government, and other were classified as non-IWSS. We analyze the data for 18 Sub-Saharan African countries that include the eight nations featured in this volume as well as Botswana, Burkina Faso, Cameroon, Lesotho, Malawi, Mauritius, Mozambique, Namibia, Nigeria, and Tanzania.

A final note: Because of the importance of level of income as an indicator of economic structure, we have classified the eight country studies into low-income, lower-middle-income, and high-income countries (see chapter 2 in this volume). This typology is heuristically useful, but it goes without saying that the sample size is too small to generalize for all countries in those categories.

volume's narrow sample. In South Africa, the highest-income country in this volume, IWSS amounted to 54.6 percent.

In the eight country studies, IWSS were roughly correlated with their per capita income levels (figure 1-4). IWSS activities generally figure more prominently at higher levels of income—largely but not solely because of the role of services. For its part, manufacturing employment shares also shows some correlation among our (unrepresentative) sample countries.

Table 1-2. Percentage Share in Total Employment, 2017–18

Sector	Low-income				Lower-middle-income						Upper-middle-income
	Ethiopia (2017)	Rwanda (2017)	Uganda (2017)	Average	Ghana (2017)	Kenya (2018)	Senegal (2017)	Zambia (2018)	Average		South Africa (2018)
Total	100	100	100	100	100	100	100	100	100		100
IWSS	14.2	15.8	19.3	16.4	40.1	23.7	25.1	12.8	25.4		54.6
Agro-processing	1.1	0.6	1.9	1.2	6.5	7.0	6.7	1.9	5.5		5.0
Construction	3.2	4.4	2.7	3.4	4.2	4.7	2.5	2.3	3.4		8.3
Export crops & horticulture	0.3	2.4	2.2	1.7	9.4	2.2	3.8	0.6	4.0		5.1
Financial & business services	1.5	0.8	2.8	1.7	1.6	0.6	0.2	2.5	1.3		15.1
Information & communications technology	0.2	0.2	0.2	0.2	0.4	0.8	0.6	0.2	0.5		0.5
Tourism	6.1	2.7	2.3	3.7	3.8	1.3	8.2	1.9	3.8		7.0
Trade (formal)	0.8	1.5	3.3	1.9	10.7	2.7	0.7	1.7	4.0		8.8
Transportation	1.0	2.6	3.2	2.3	3.4	3.4	0.6	1.6	2.2		4.9
Other IWSS services		0.6	0.7	0.7		0.8	1.7		1.3		

(continued)

Table 1-2. (continued)

Sector	Low-income				Lower-middle-income					Upper-middle-income
	Ethiopia (2017)	Rwanda (2017)	Uganda (2017)	Average	Ghana (2017)	Kenya (2018)	Senegal (2017)	Zambia (2018)	Average	South Africa (2018)
Manufacturing	4.1	1.5	4.7	3.4	11.4	3.7	6.0	2.0	5.8	11.3
non-IWSS	81.7	82.7	76.0	80.2	48.5	72.6	68.9	85.3	68.8	34.1
Traditional agriculture	63.7	67.4	58.3	63.1	22.2	42.2	40.1	55.5	40.0	1.7
Government	3.6	3.5	3.8	3.6	0.6	1.6	1.1	1.2	1.1	16.3
Mining	0.5	0.9	0.5	0.7	1.5	0.8	1.1	1.3	1.2	2.7
Trade (informal)	5.4	5.1	9.4	6.6	17.5	12.7	12.9	8.1	12.8	6.8
Utilities	0.5	0.2	0.2	0.3	0.4	0.3	0.7	0.4	0.4	0.8
Other non-IWSS	8.1	5.7	3.7	5.8	6.3	15.1	13.0	18.8	13.3	5.8

Sources: Country case studies; authors' calculations.

FIGURE 1-4. **IWSS and Manufacturing Employment Correlated with Higher Income Levels**

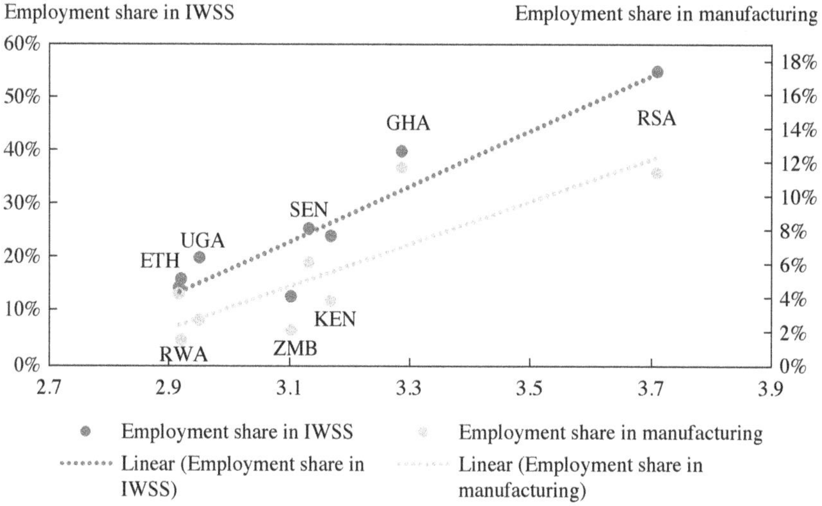

Employment share in IWSS

Employment share in manufacturing

Source: Authors' calculations.

The average employment share in non-IWSS sectors is just under 70 percent of total employment. However, the big reductions with income, as one might expect, are traditional agriculture. Within the non-IWSS sectors, aside from the huge residual employment in agriculture, informal trade, and personal services (within "other non-IWSS services) are prominent.

Within the IWSS category, the largest share of employment varies across country. In the three lowest-income countries, the top three subsectors in average share of employment are tourism, construction, and formal retail trade. In the four middle-income countries, agro-processing replaces construction in the top three, but trade and tourism remain large. In South Africa, the only upper-middle-income country in our study, financial services emerge as an important employer.

IWSS Value Added Exceeds Employment

In the eight country studies, when the IWSS subsectors are totaled up, they tended to provide greater employment than manufacturing (shown in the higher line relative to the averages in table 1-2). The fact that both are correlated with income levels highlights the implicit linkages between the

IWSS sectors and manufacturing. For example, as economies grow and become more complex, firms in the service sectors expand to provide financial, telecommunications accounting, legal, and other services to the rest of the economy, and wider markets create new opportunities for diverse agricultural and manufactured consumer goods.

Even though IWSS activities collectively employ only about a quarter of the workforce, they tend to produce a much higher share of national output—in fact, just under half in the eight-country average (table 1-3). This is substantially more than manufacturing and about equal to or somewhat greater than the non-IWSS sectors, depending on the income group. Despite differing levels of employment shares in IWSS across income groups, IWSS seems to play a relatively similar role in low-income and lower-middle-income countries in output, accounting for roughly half the value added in each grouping and little variation across countries (a range of only 6.7 percentage points). In South Africa, the only upper-middle-income country included in our sample, the share of IWSS in value added is 63.8 percent. Within IWSS, financial and business services are typically as important or more so than construction, export agriculture, and formal trade sectors. Tourism, agro-processing, and ICT are also important—though, in Rwanda, Zambia, and Senegal, tourism outpaces manufacturing. The role of high-value-added services is worth underscoring as leading sectors within these economies; summing financial, ICT, and other IWSS services and tourism indicates that these service sectors employ on average nearly 10 percent of the labor force in these eight countries.

Among non-IWSS sectors, aside from low-value-added traditional agriculture, informal trade and government are important. Natural resources, namely mining and petroleum, are important in Zambia and Ghana, but do not figure prominently in the other countries. Lower-middle-income countries have lower shares in non-IWSS sectors than do low-income countries. A smaller role for traditional agriculture explains most of the difference: in lower-middle-income countries, traditional agriculture's share in value added is 11.5 percent, whereas in low-income countries it is more than double (25.4 percent).

The correlation of income levels with employment in both the IWSS sectors and manufacturing is striking (figure 1-4). It stands to reason that as countries grow, they become more diversified, more complex, and technologically sophisticated. This underscores the interrelation of development among sectors of the economy—particularly that services are

Table 1-3. Percentage Share in Total Value Added, 2017–18

Sector	Low-income				Lower-middle-income					Upper-middle-income
	Ethiopia (2017)	Rwanda (2017)	Uganda (2017)	Average	Ghana (2017)	Kenya (2018)	Senegal (2017)	Zambia (2018)	Average	South Africa (2018)
Total	100	100	100	100	100	100	100	100	100	100
IWSS	48.0	48.5	48.5	48.3	48.8	46.9	52.1	53.8	50.4	63.8
Agro-processing	2.1	3.4	3.9	3.1	3.3	7.2	7.9	2.8	5.3	1.2
Construction	17.9	7.1	7.2	10.7	7.7	5.9	2.8	10.6	6.8	3.2
Export crops & horticulture	4.2	2.9	2.6	3.2	7.2	9.9	6.7	1.5	6.3	1.6
Financial & business services	7.3	19.3	11.5	12.7	9.0	6.8	2.3	9.8	7.0	21.6
Information & communications technology	2.5	1.7	10.6	5.0	3.7	1.4	4.6	4.3	3.5	3.0
Tourism	4.8	4.8	2.9	4.2	3.7	0.8	8.4	5.9	4.7	2.4
Trade (formal)	6.6	4.6	6.0	5.7	13.0	5.3	3.3	8.9	7.6	8.7
Transportation	2.5	4.2	3.1	3.3	1.1	8.8	2.2	3.5	3.9	5.2
Other IWSS services		0.4	0.6	0.5		0.9	13.8	6.5	7.1	16.9

(continued)

Table 1-3. (continued)

Sector	Low-income				Lower-middle-income					Upper-middle-income
	Ethiopia (2017)	Rwanda (2017)	Uganda (2017)	Average	Ghana (2017)	Kenya (2018)	Senegal (2017)	Zambia (2018)	Average	South Africa (2018)
Manufacturing	4.9	2.7	4.3	4.0	10.7	8.4	8.4	5.1	8.1	11.1
non-IWSS	47.1	48.8	47.2	47.7	40.5	44.7	39.5	41.1	41.5	25.1
Traditional agriculture	28.9	25.6	20.8	25.1	11.3	19.7	8.7	6.4	11.5	0.2
Government	9.2	10.2	5.0	8.1	1.5	4.6	5.4	4.9	4.1	8.0
Mining	0.3	2.9	1.5	1.6	10.3	0.8	2.7	10.4	6.1	5.0
Trade (informal)	6.9	3.0	5.4	5.1	6.8	1.8	10.0	11.8	7.6	3.7
Utilities	0.8	1.5	3.2	1.8	2.3	2.6	2.2	2.0	2.3	2.4
Other non-IWSS	1.0	5.5	11.3	5.9	8.3	15.1	10.6	5.6	9.9	5.7

Sources: Country case studies; authors' calculations.

integral to manufacturing development and vice versa. These sectors also tend to develop in a complementary fashion as economies become more urban and with a higher degree of business organization and formality. All these forces are obviously at work in the eight country case studies.

IWSS as Leading Growth and Employment—Along with Manufacturing

Though IWSS are leading growth sectors on average in the countries included in this study, the patterns differ from country to country. In Rwanda, for example, IWSS have grown more rapidly than non-IWSS but somewhat less rapidly than manufacturing—partly because of the small base of manufacturing in Rwanda. In Uganda, IWSS accounted for about a fifth of total employment. Value added grew more rapidly in IWSS sectors than in non-IWSS sectors during the periods covered by the case studies. This trend held true for low-income countries and South Africa. In low-income countries, this gap between IWSS and non-IWSS sectors was particularly profound: the valued-added compound annual growth rate was nearly twice as high in IWSS (9.5 percent) than in non-IWSS sectors (5.8 percent). In lower-middle-income countries, however, IWSS grew more slowly than manufacturing and non-IWSS, but grew rapidly nonetheless (9.1 percent) (tables 1-4 and 1-5).

Similarly, employment in IWSS sectors has grown at nearly twice the pace of economy-wide job creation. Leading sectors within IWSS are financial and business services, trade, construction, and tourism. Analogous to value added, low-income countries experienced significantly higher IWSS job growth relative to non-IWSS sectors (7.6 percent vs. 2.6 percent). In the middle-income countries in our sample, however, employment growth in IWSS sectors was effectively indistinguishable from that in non-IWSS sectors.

On average, across the eight countries in this study, the IWSS sectors are growing more rapidly and are employing more Africans in the process (figure 1-5). The graphs in figure 1-5 show the pace of job creation along the vertical axis and increase in value added across the horizontal axis, while the bubble size indicates the relative size of job creation in each of the broad sectors. Within the IWSS sectors, the most rapidly growing are financial and business services, formal trade, and construction (see annex). Within the non-IWSS category, informal trade is a principal driver, along with mining and domestic services (in other). Across countries, IWSS growth was particularly rapid in Ethiopia, Ghana, and Rwanda.

Table 1-4. Percentage Value-Added Compound Annual Growth Rate

Sector	Low-income countries				Lower-middle-income countries					Upper-middle-income countries
	Ethiopia 2000–17	Rwanda 2001–17	Uganda 2013–17	Average	Ghana 2013–17	Kenya 2001–18	Senegal 2001–17	Zambia 2005–18	Average	South Africa 2010–18
Total	8.0	8.0	4.7	6.9	4.7	9.5	5.4	5.1	6.2	1.7
IWSS	10.4	8.6	5.5	8.2	5.3	7.2	6.0	4.5	5.8	2.1
Manufacturing	11.9	9.8	4.0	8.6	4.0	9.0	4.6	18.4	9.0	0.4
Non-IWSS	6.1	7.4	3.9	5.8	4.3	13.5	4.9	5.1	6.9	1.5

Sources: Country case studies; authors' calculations.

Table 1-5. Employment Compound Annual Growth Rate, in Percent

Sector	Low-income countries				Lower-middle-income countries					Upper-middle-income countries
	Ethiopia (2000–17)	Rwanda (2001–17)	Uganda (2013–17)	Average	Ghana (2013–17)	Kenya (2001–18)	Senegal (2001–17)	Zambia (2005-18)	Average	South Africa (2010–18)
Total	3.6	2.7	4.3	3.5	6.4	6.1	3.1	4.0	4.9	2.6
IWSS	5.5	9.8	10.8	8.7	5.4	5.6	4.5	9.8	6.3	2.9
Manufacturing	4.3	7.9	8.7	7.0	9.4	5.4	3.4	8.2	6.6	0.1
Non–IWSS	3.3	1.9	2.7	2.6	6.6	6.3	2.6	3.4	4.7	3.2

Sources: Country case studies; authors' calculations.

FIGURE 1-5. **IWSS Activities Are Growing Rapidly and Are Creating Jobs**

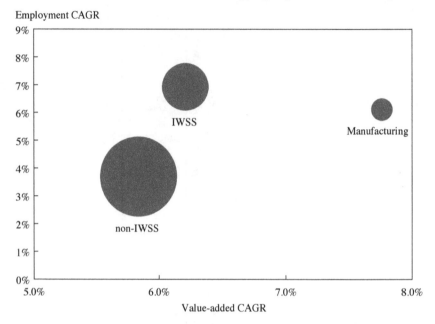

Source: Eight-country average, from tables 1-4 and 1-5, covering the available periods.

Note: CAGR = compound annual growth rate.

The results of the country studies suggest that while IWSS sectors create more jobs, the types of jobs created in each of the four focus IWSS sectors—agri-business and horticulture, tourism, IT-enabled services, and transportation and logistics, among others—are varied and may cater to different segments of the youth labor force. While the tourism and horticulture industries provide the most scope for absorbing low-skilled individuals, the agri-business/horticulture and logistics industries offer higher-skilled individuals prospects for increased employment. One important finding of the country studies is that the IWSS sectors on average are growing more rapidly than the economy as a whole in all three income categories of countries. This implies that on the demand side of the labor market, opportunities exist in IWSS for both young workers and women to find productive jobs.

In general, the IWSS sectors have a higher employment elasticity than manufacturing and the non-IWSS sectors (table 1-6). Overall, there do not seem to be significant differences between low-income countries and

Table 1-6. Employment Elasticities, IWSS versus Other Sectors

Sector	Low-income countries				Lower-middle-income countries					Upper-middle-income countries
	Ethiopia (2000–17)	Rwanda (2001–17)	Uganda (2013–17)	Average	Ghana (2013–17)	Kenya (2001–18)	Senegal (2001–17)	Zambia (2005–18)	Average	South Africa (2010–18)
IWSS	0.53	1.15	1.96	*1.21*	1.03	0.77	0.75	2.17	*1.18*	1.38
Manufacturing	0.37	0.81	2.15	*1.11*	2.34	0.60	0.74	0.45	*1.03*	0.33
Non-IWSS	0.54	0.26	0.68	*0.49*	1.53	0.47	0.53	0.67	*0.80*	2.13

Note: Elasticities are calculated by dividing the employment compound annual growth rate by the output employment compound annual growth rate.

lower-middle-income countries with respect to employment elasticity and productivity. In both groups, IWSS sectors have an employment elasticity around twice as high as the non-IWSS sectors and significantly higher productivity. In South Africa, IWSS sectors have a lower employment elasticity than non-IWSS sectors but are more productive.

The picture is far from uniform and muddied by differing periods of data. Nonetheless, IWSS sectors have demonstrated a greater employment elasticity with respect to growth than in manufacturing in all countries except Uganda and Ghana and compared with non-IWSS in all countries except Ghana.

This is not to say that low-productivity, traditional agriculture, or informal labor markets in urban areas will cease to be important. But this analysis does imply that many formal, wage-paying jobs are being created, and at a pace more rapid than in the rest of the economy. In fact, the next chapter in this volume points out the wage employment share rose in all categories of income group in Africa over the 2000–18 period. That said, wage employment growth is still very low—less than 20 percent for African low-income countries in 2018 and lower than comparable countries in the same income category.

IWSS and Exports

Like manufacturing, the IWSS sectors tend to be leading export sectors. This, of course, reflects the selection criteria for designation as IWSS. For many activities—such as tourism, agro-industry, horticulture, and transportation—this is obvious. What is less obvious is the collective importance of these activities in the export portfolio of African countries generally. In fact, for our eight-country sample in 2019, IWSS accounted for more than 38 percent of total exports and an even higher share—48 percent—of nonmineral exports (table 1-7). The largest sectors, aside from agro-processing, include financial and business services, and other services.

Over the last decade, the IWSS share of nonmineral exports had actually increased. The trend increases have fluctuated inversely to metal and petroleum prices—and rose sharply as a share of total exports after 2013–15, when price declines reduced the earnings of metal and petroleum. But the growing importance of IWSS, and particularly services, is an unmistakable trend. This reflects the epoch in which economic transformation is occurring in Africa. In contrast to previous decades, services have become among the most buoyant sectors of the global economy, despite having

Table 1-7. IWSS Activities Are Leading Export Growth: Average Composition of Exports for Eight Countries, 2010 and 2019

	2010			2019		
	Exports ('000s dollars)	Share (%)	Nonmining share (%)	Exports ('000s dollars)	Share (%)	Nonmining share (%)
Total	16,460,901	100		21,517,938	100	
IWSS	5,723,143	34.8	42.0	8,261,216	38.4	47.5
Agro-processing	1,526,016	9.3	11.2	1,870,262	8.7	10.8
Export crops & horticulture	15,329	0.1	0.1	99,015	0.5	0.6
Construction	1,119,062	6.8	8.2	1,682,858	7.8	9.7
Financial & business services	484,158	2.9	3.6	1,383,627	6.4	8.0
Information & communications technology	149,930	0.9	1.1	211,754	1.0	1.2
Transportation	4,907	0.0	0.0	90,593	0.4	0.5
Travel (including tourism)	806,661	4.9	5.9	1,123,132	5.2	6.5
Other IWSS Services	1,619,609	9.8	11.9	1,823,677	8.5	10.5
Manufacturing	7,629,586	46.3	56.0	8,717,696	40.5	50.2
Non-IWSS	3,108,173	18.9	2.0	4,539,026	21.1	2.3
Education, health & other services	18,265	0.1	0.1	84,857	0.4	0.5
Government	256,815	1.6	1.9	289,831	1.3	1.7
Mining	2,829,823	17.2	0.0	4,142,439	19.3	
Other non-IWSS	6,347	0.0	0.0	37,150	0.2	0.2

Note: Authors' categorization using HS 2-digit codes for goods exports; IMF, balance-of-payments categorization for services.

FIGURE 1-6. **Movement Out of Traditional Agriculture into IWSS**

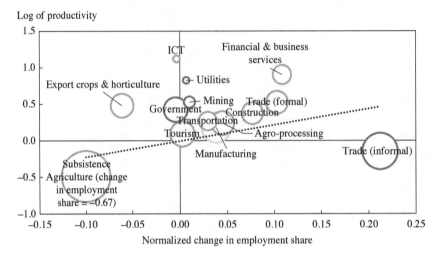

Sources: Authors' calculations based on data from the annex. Productivity is normalized with respect to the productivity of the overall economy to make it comparable across countries. Other IWSS services and non-IWSS services are not displayed. The bubble size corresponds to the average share of employment in the base year.

suffered a setback in the post 2020 pandemic years, so it is logical that Africa should be a dynamic participant in market growth.

IWSS Tends to Provide Higher-Productivity Jobs

The IWSS sectors on average tend to have higher labor productivity compared with other sectors. While this is to be expected on definitional grounds, the point is that the IWSS sectors collectively offer a path to productivity growth than a mere reliance on manufacturing would otherwise dictate.

The good news for Africa—generalizing from our eight-country sample—is that labor in traditional agriculture is declining in importance while the higher-productivity IWSS and other sectors are increasing (figure 1-6). The exception is in informal trade, where productivity is below average. In figure 1-6, the size of the bubble corresponds to the eight-country average employment share in the base year. This is important because higher productivity is usually accompanied by higher wages, absent distortions in labor markets.

The main IWSS sectors driving this high productivity include ICT, financial and business services, formal trade, construction, and tourism. The major employment-intensive sectors—agro-processing and tourism—also have relatively high labor productivity. Among the eight countries analyzed in this volume, productivity differentials, such as that between IWSS and manufacturing, are particularly great in Ethiopia and Rwanda (table 1-8). Taken together, this would indicate that economic transformation—the declining share of low productivity jobs, particularly in agriculture and to a lesser extent in informal services, and the increasing prominence of high-productivity jobs – is occurring in these African countries.

In 2017, for example, the labor productivity for IWSS sectors in Rwanda was almost five times higher than that in non-IWSS sectors and 60 percent higher than that of manufacturing. IWSS sectors are around twice as productive as the economy. Similarly, in Uganda, IWSS sectors have a significantly higher average labor productivity than manufacturing and non-IWSS sectors. Formal trade, agro-processing, and ICT have a higher labor productivity than any subsector in the non-IWSS group.

The Big Picture: The Economic Transformation of Africa and the Role of IWSS

In summary, the country case studies that follow bear out the analysis presented in this chapter. They show that the economies at hand are experiencing consistent growth in overall productivity. They also reveal how the economic transformation of Africa is following a unique path. Data from the eight country studies indicate that these IWSS activities collectively are a dynamic source of employment and productivity growth in Africa. As with manufacturing, IWSS sectors tend to grow as incomes rise, if at varying paces, depending on the country.

On average, for the eight countries studied in this volume, IWSS sectors are seven times larger as a share of total employment and employ five times more workers than manufacturing. Moreover, the IWSS sectors exhibit greater productivity and labor intensity than both the manufacturing and non-IWSS sectors in both resource-poor and resource-rich countries alike and irrespective of income levels. Trends indicate they are collectively creating twice as many jobs as conventional manufacturing—and have the potential to remain leading sectors in coming years. Though it will become

Table 1-8. Relative Productivity, IWSS versus Other Sectors

Sector	Low-income				Lower-middle-income					Upper-middle-income
	Ethiopia (2000–17)	Rwanda (2001–17)	Uganda (2013–17)	Average	Ghana (2013–17)	Kenya (2001–18)	Senegal (2001–17)	Zambia (2005–18)	Average	South Africa (2010–18)
IWSS	3.38	3.07	2.50	2.99	1.22	1.98	2.07	4.21	2.37	1.17
Manufacturing	1.20	1.86	0.93	1.33	0.94	2.24	1.41	2.58	1.79	0.99
Non-IWSS	0.58	0.59	0.62	0.60	0.84	0.62	0.57	0.48	0.63	0.73

Note: Productivity values are the ratio between the share in output and the share in employment.

clearer in the case studies that follow, IWSS tend to employ more women than manufacturing, and several IWSS subsectors employ more women than other sectors in the economy. Moreover, some IWSS sectors—notably agro-processing, horticulture, and tourism—tend to employ a relatively higher share of young workers compared with non-IWSS sectors. Finally, IWSS activities, like manufacturing, are skill-intensive compared with agriculture, and both sectors are more skill-intensive than the average for non-IWSS activities.

How do these patterns play out in individual countries? How have the external shocks in the COVID-19 pandemic and from the war in Ukraine affected the development of these sectors? What policies can governments adopt to harness the potential of IWSS and other sectors? These questions are addressed in the chapters that follow.

Annex: Technical Details

Technical Details for Productivity Decomposition

This book showcases findings from eight Sub-Saharan African countries. To expand data coverage to eighteen countries, we use the Groningen Growth and Development Centre and UNU-WIDER's Economic Transformation Database, a 12-sector database that includes the eight countries featured in this book and Botswana, Burkina Faso, Cameroon, Lesotho, Malawi, Mauritius, Mozambique, Namibia, Nigeria, and Tanzania. The expanded coverage provides us with a more accurate picture of employment and the dynamics of structural transformation across the region.

Unfortunately, the Economic Transformation Database (ETD) does not provide sectoral data at a granular enough level to organize neatly into the definitions used by the eight case studies. For this reason, we aggregate sectors into traditional groups such as industry, services, and agriculture, or into non-traditional groups such as "modern sectors" (business services, construction, financial services, real estate, trade services, and transport services) or "other" (government, utilities, and mining). An additional benefit of the ETD is that it covers 33 countries from other world regions in addition to the eighteen Sub-Saharan African economies. We apply the canonical productivity decomposition developed by Fabricant (1942)—and subsequently applied by Gaurav and others (2021), de Vries and others (2015), Diao and others (2019), Dieppe and Matsuoka (2021), and others—to the ETD to understand how the drivers of productivity growth in Sub-Saharan Africa compare with those in economies from other regions. Specifically, we define the change in productivity Δy^t as

$$\Delta y^t = \sum_i^m \theta_i^{t-k} \Delta y_i^t + \sum_i^m y_i^t \Delta \theta_i^t$$

where θ_i^t is the employment share of sectoral group i (e.g., IWSS, manufacturing, non-IWSS, etc.) at time t, m is the number of sectoral groupings, and a base period measuring k years before t. The term $\sum_i^m \theta_i^{t-k} \Delta y_i^t$ can be thought of as the share of productivity change derived from within-sector changes, while $\sum_i^m y_i^t \Delta \theta_i^t$ is the share derived from between-sector reallocation of labor. Because structural transformation in Sub-Saharan Africa, like predecessor economies, has begun with a shrinking employment share in agriculture, it is helpful to reformulate the rightmost term in terms of the gains with respect to agriculture (making use of the fact that $\Delta \theta_\alpha^t + \Delta \theta_i^t + \Delta \theta_\mu^t + \Delta \theta_\eta^t = 0$).

$$\Delta y^t = \sum_i^m \theta_i^{t-k} \Delta y_i^t + \sum_i^m y_i^t \Delta \theta_i^t$$

$$\Delta y^t = \sum_i^m \theta_i^{t-k} \Delta y_i^t + y_i^t \Delta \theta_i^t + y_\mu^t \Delta \theta_\mu^t + y_\eta^t \Delta \theta_\eta^t + y_\alpha^t \Delta \theta_\alpha^t$$

$$\Delta y^t = \sum_i^m \theta_i^{t-k} \Delta y_i^t + y_i^t \Delta \theta_i^t + y_\mu^t \Delta \theta_\mu^t + y_\eta^t \Delta \theta_\eta^t + y_\alpha^t \left(-\Delta \theta_i^t - \Delta \theta_\mu^t - \Delta \theta_\eta^t \right)$$

$$\Delta y^t = \sum_i^m \theta_i^{t-k} \Delta y_i^t + \Delta \theta_i^t \left(y_i^t - y_\alpha^t \right) + \Delta \theta_\mu^t \left(y_\mu^t - y_\alpha^t \right) + \Delta \theta_\eta^t \left(y_\eta^t - y_\alpha^t \right)$$

To find average annual productivity gains, divide both sides of the equation by $(t - k) \, y^{t-k}$. This step will allow us to measure what share of the productivity growth over the period is due to within-sector growth in services, industry, manufacturing, and agriculture, and which is due to labor reallocation from agriculture to services, industry, and manufacturing.

Technical Details for Measuring Labor Productivity Convergence

The analysis on convergence that appears in the text utilizes a sample that combines the ETD with sectoral value-added and employment data from the OECD's Structural Analysis Database. The resulting sample used for analysis is comprised of 80 countries that represent all world regions and all income groups. There are many ways to measure unconditional convergence in the literature. This book uses the following regression to calculate beta convergence (β):

$$\tilde{y}_{ic} = \beta_0 + \beta_1 \log y_{ic} + \beta_2 D_{ic} + \beta_3 S_{ic} + \beta_4 D_{ic} * S_{ic} + \varepsilon_{ic}$$

where $\tilde{y}_{ic}$ is the compound annual growth in value added per worker (y_{ic}) for sector i in country c over the previous decade and the predicted values of β_1 indicate the speed of convergence by sector. D_{ic} is a vector of binary controls for each decade in the dataset, S_{ic} is a vector of binary controls for each sector in the database. The predicted values of $\tilde{y}_{ic}$ represent the orthogonal component of growth.

Note that because the ETD has data from 1990 to 2018, the final decade included in the analysis is only eight years: 2010 to 2018. The first two decades used in the analysis are from 1990 to 2000 and 2000 to 2010. In the main body of the chapter, we look at convergence within four groups of sectors: modern, manufacturing, agriculture, and others. Here we include the results by individual sector (figure 1-A1). Note that we used the same formulation above, but since there is only one sector, the S_{ic} and $D_{ic} * S_{ic}$ are dropped from the regression.

FIGURE 1-A1. Unconditional Convergence in Labor Productivity by Sector

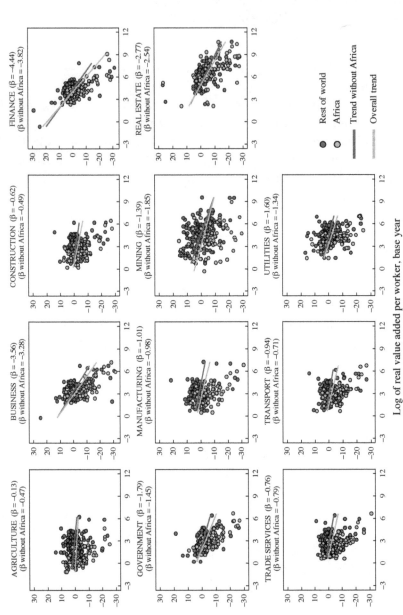

Log of real value added per worker, base year

Source: Authors' calculations using GGDC/UNU-WIDER's Economic Transformation Database and the OECD's Structural Analysis Database.

Note: The vertical axis shows the compound annual growth in real value added per worker for one-digit ISIC sectors by country using the three periods 1990–2000, 2000–2010, and 2010–18. These data control for decade fixed effects. The horizontal axis shows baseline labor productivity values in the given base year (1990, 2000, or 2010). The β coefficient is the slope of the regression of the vertical axis on the x-axis.

NOTES

1. While the early literature emphasized the evolution from agriculture to more modern productive activities (Kuznets 1971), recent charting of the broad aggregates has focused on aggregate structural shifts from agriculture to industry to services (e.g., McMillan and Rodrik 2011; Rodrik 2014; McMillain et al. 2016). Lagakos and Shu (2021, 1) have used a broader definition to mean "the movement of factors of production, including labour, human capital, physical capital, and land, from less productive activities to more productive ones." This formulation recognizes that the process of structural transformation can be intrasectoral and well as cross- sectoral. In this chapter, we use the term "economic transformation" to subsume both intra- and cross-sectoral productivity gains. In both cases, "movement" is not confined to workers actual leaving one activity and entering another but can comprise incremental increases in the relative share of labor, capital, and technology in the high-productivity sectors.

2. This term is not meant to be taken literally—many IWSS sectors like agro-processing can create pollution much as do steel or chemical manufactures. The environmental consequences of IWSS sector growth vis-à-vis other sectors of the economy, though important, are beyond the scope of this book.

3. For services, Nayyar et al. (2021) develop this point in some detail.

4. The authors cleverly use luminosity data taken from satellites to proxy level of economic development at the 1,546 subnational level of political administration in 13 countries.

5. As is customary, Nayyar, Hallward-Dreimeirer, and Davis (2021) include manufacturing, mining, utilities, and construction in "industry."

6. Rodrik (2022), in his lecture, formulated these notions of modern growth in three primary mechanisms: (1) the accumulation of societal fundamentals such as human capital and institutions, factors driving conditional convergence; (2) unconditional convergence in the modern sector; and (3) structural change in labor patterns from the traditional to modern sector

REFERENCES

Baccini, L., et al. 2021. *Global Value Chains and Deep Integration*. Policy Research Working Paper 9598. Washington: World Bank.

Barriga, A., and N. Fiala. 2018. *The Supply Chain for Seed in Uganda: Where Does It All Go Wrong?* London: International Growth Centre.

Barro, Robert J., and Xavier Sala-i-Martin. 1991. ''Convergence across States and Regions." *Brookings Papers on Economic Activity* 1: 107–58.

Bhorat, H., and K. Naidoo. 2017. "Drivers of Inequality in the Context of the Growth-Poverty-Inequality Nexus in Africa: Overview of key issues." In *Income Inequality Trends in Sub-Saharan Africa: Divergence, Determinants and Consequences*, ed. A. Odusola et al. New York: United Nations Development Program.

Bold, T. et al. 2017. "Lemon Technologies and Adoption: Measurement, Theory and Evidence from Agricultural Markets in Uganda." *Quarterly Journal of Economics.*

Chancel, Lucas, Denis Cogneau, Amory Gethin, and Alix Myczkowski, et al. 2019. "How Large Are African Inequalities? Towards Distributional National Accounts in Africa, 1990–2017." Working Paper 2019/13. World Inequality Database.

Coulibaly, B., D. Gandhi, and A. Mbaye. 2019. *Job Creation for Youth in Africa: Assessing the Potential of Industries without Smokestacks.* Africa Growth Initiative Paper 22. Brookings.

de Vries, Gaaitzen, Linda Arfelt, Dorothea Drees, Mareike Godemann, Calumn Hamilton, Bente Jessen-Thiesen, Ahmet Ihsan Kaya, Hagen Kruse, Emmanuel Mensah, and Pieter Woltjer. 2021. "The Economic Transformation Database (ETD): Content, Sources, and Methods." WIDER Technical Note 2/2021.

de Vries, G., M. Timmer, and K. De Vries. 2015. "Structural Transformation in Africa: Static Gains, Dynamic Losses." *Journal of Development Studies* 51: 674–88.

Diao, X., M. McMillan, and D. Rodrik. 2019. "The Recent Growth Boom in Developing Economies: A Structural-Change Perspective." In *The Palgrave Handbook of Development Economics.* New York: Palgrave Macmillan.

———. 2021. *Africa's Manufacturing Puzzle: Evidence from Tanzanian and Ethiopian Firms.* NBER Working Paper 28344. Cambridge, MA: National Bureau of Economic Research.

Dieppe, A., and H. Matsuoka. 2021. "Sectoral Decomposition of Convergence in Labor Productivity." Unpublished paper.

English, Philip. 2018. *How Can Tourism Become a Driver of Economic Growth in Uganda?* London: International Growth Centre.

Fabricant, S. 1942. *Employment in Manufacturing, 1899–1939.* New York: National Bureau of Economic Research.

Filmer, D., and L. Fox. 2014. *Youth Employment in Sub-Saharan Africa.* Washington: World Bank.

Fox, Louise, and Dhruv Ghandi, 2021 "A Survey of African Employment Outcomes and Implications for Youth" Unpublished paper, Brookings.

Hallward-Driemeier, Mary, and Gaurav Gaurav Nayyar. 2017. *Trouble in the Making? The Future of Manufacturing-Led Development.* Washington: World Bank.

Hausmann, R., U. Panizza, and R. Rigobon. 2004. *The Long-Run Volatility Puzzle of the Real Exchange Rate.* NBER Working Paper 10751. Cambridge, MA: National Bureau of Economic Research.

Hausmann, R., D. Rodrik, and C. Sabel. 2008. "Reconfiguring Industrial Policy: A Framework with an Application to South Africa." Harvard

University Center for International Development Working Paper 168 and Harvard Kennedy School Faculty Research Working Paper RWP08-031.

Kuznets, S. 1971. *Economic Growth of Nations: Total Output and Production Structure*. Cambridge, MA: Harvard University Press.

Lagakos, D., and M. Shu. 2021. "The Role of Micro Data in Understanding Structural Transformation." Structural Transformation and Economic Growth.

Lea, Nick. 2023. "Africa's Foreign Exchange Constraint." FCDO Internal Paper, London, March 23.

Lustig, N. 2018. "Fiscal Policy, Income Redistribution, and Poverty Reduction in Low- and Middle-Income Countries." Commitment to Equality Institute, Tulane University, New Orleans.

Maloney, W., et al. 2021. "Bridging the Technological Divide: Firm-level Adoption of Technology in the Post-COVID World." Unpublished paper, World Bank.

McMillan, M., and D. Rodrik. 2011. *Globalization, Structural Change, and Productivity Growth*. NBER Working Paper 17143. Cambridge, MA: National Bureau of Economic Research.

McMillan, M., D. Rodrik, and C. Sepúlveda. 2016. "Structural Change, Fundamental, and Growth." International Food Policy Research Institute, World Bank.

McMillan M., D. Rodrik, and I. Verduzco-Gallo. 2014. "Globalization, Structural Change, and Productivty Growth, with an Update on Africa." World Development 63: 11–32.

Nayyar, G., M. Hallward-Driemeier, and E. Davies. 2021. *At Your Service? The Promise of Services-Led Development*. Washington: World Bank.

NEPAD (New Partnership for Africa's Development), AU (African Union), and AfDB (African Development Bank). 2011. *Program for Development of Infrastructure in Africa*. Tunis: African Development Bank.

Newfarmer, R., J. Page, and F. Tarp. 2018. *Industries Without Smokestacks: Industrialization in Africa Reconsidered*. Oxford: Oxford University Press.

Odusola, A. 2017. "Fiscal Policy, Redistribution and Inequality in Africa." In *Income Inequality Trends in Sub-Saharan Africa: Divergence, Determinants, and Consequences*, ed. A. Odusola, Giovanni Andrea Cornia, Haroon Bhorat, and Pedro Conceição. New York: United Nations Development Program.

Rodrik, D. 2008. "The Real Exchange Rate and Economic Growth." *Brookings Papers on Economic Activity* 2: 365–412.

———. 2016. "Premature Industrialization." *Journal of Economic Growth* 21: 1–33.

———. 2022. "STEG Special Lecture 2022: Growth Miracles and Disappointments through the Lens of Structural Change." Structural Transformation and Economic Growth."

Rodrik D., X. Diao, and M. McMillan. 2019. "The Recent Growth Boom in Developing Economies: A Structural-Change Perspective." In *The Palgrave*

Handbook of Development Economics, ed. M. Nissanke and A. Ocampo. New York: Palgrave Macmillan.

Syverson, C. 2011. "What Determines Productivity?" *Journal of Economic Literature* 49: 326–65.

Valerio, A., B. Parton, and A. Robb. 2014. *Entrepreneurship Education and Training Programs Around the World: Dimensions for Success.* Washington: World Bank.

World Economic Forum. 2020. *Future of Jobs Report, 2020.* Geneva: World Economic Forum.

TWO

Opportunities for Youth Employment in Sub-Saharan Africa

Progress and Prospects

LOUISE FOX AND DHRUV GANDHI

Throughout the 21st century, as economies have been buffeted by volatile economic cycles—including the recent COVID-19 pandemic—and increasingly strong technological winds of change, enhancing employment opportunities has taken an even stronger position on center stage in development policy discussions. The reasons are obvious—billions of people in the developing world are trying to exit poverty through better jobs, providing higher incomes for themselves and their families. The quality of employment opportunities is important for the employed, for those who wish to work but cannot find work or lack access to opportunities, and for others who depend upon the income employment provides. Improvements in job opportunities are strong signals of the quality and strength of economic transformation and development.

As the world's youngest region, improving employment opportunities is especially important in Sub-Saharan Africa (SSA), for several reasons.[1] First, the 43 percent of the population under the age of 15 years mostly depends on the incomes that their parents earn for their own survival, growth, and personal development. At the same time, 41 percent of the population lives in poverty, and the children who grow up in these households risk permanent physical and social damage and even death owing to malnutrition and childhood illness, and lack of quality education and other opportunities to build human capital (Beegle and Christiaensen 2019). Second, owing to past high fertility, SSA has the fastest-growing labor force in the world, and every year many young people struggle to enter employment and find a livelihood. Third, sustained economic growth, needed to finance the investments to build more resilient economies and societies, requires steady increases in output per person working (labor productivity). This outcome means producing and selling more, in part by employing more people more productively and taking advantage of new opportunities emerging in a globalizing world, without succumbing to the risks to sustained growth that such a strategy involves. For all these reasons, SSA leaders and policymakers have set enhancing employment opportunities as one main objective of their development strategies.

Owing to the high share of youth in the working-age population compared with other regions, much of the employment discussion in SSA has centered on youth's opportunities and challenges, and how to address these. Youth is a time of transition from dependent childhood to independent adulthood, and economic independence—often achieved through employment—is an important aspect of this transition. However, youth opportunities depend on the overall opportunities in the economy, which depend on the extent of economic transformation and development. Richer countries offer better jobs, and countries get rich by developing productive employment opportunities—the two processes are inextricably linked. For this reason, an analysis of youth employment opportunities and challenges is connected to overall employment challenges stemming from the pace and structure of economic transformation.

Better jobs are generally found in modern, productive enterprises, and one characteristic of developing countries is a lack of these modern enterprises relative to the supply of labor coming from the population. For this reason, a focus of employment policies in developing countries needs to be on encouraging more firms to be created and to grow, expanding private sector wage employment, especially in more productive sectors. This happens fastest when new and existing firms create the goods and services they sell using a lot of labor (labor-intensive production processes). But employment policies cannot stop there. A stylized fact of development today is that until countries reach at least upper-middle-income status, the majority of jobs will be found in small-scale household farms and firms. SSA is no exception, so a key employment challenge for policymakers is how to raise incomes in the informal sector, even as they work to create the conditions in the formal economy that allow the share of employment in the informal sector to decline.

Africa was making progress on these issues, and many countries were achieving better employment outcomes before the onset of the global COVID-19 pandemic with the ensuing economic, social, and health consequences for the population. While only the richer and more developed countries have suffered an increase in unemployment (for reasons elaborated in the fourth section below), most countries have seen a fall in labor incomes—the average for SSA as a whole in 2020 was estimated at about 10 percent. This was a large hit for households already at or below the poverty line to absorb.

While SSA began to recover in 2021, the global economic turmoil stemming from the war in Ukraine, economic sanctions, and tightening monetary policy constitute another set of difficulties for the region. The impact of these external shocks on household incomes will make employment policy an even more salient issue in the years ahead. Developing solutions requires knowing the shape of the problem, and the mechanisms and external forces that cause changes over time. Until recently, getting a clear picture of the employment opportunities and challenges in SSA has not been easy, as the data simply were not available. Over the past decade, countries have produced and published more data on who is working and what they are doing more frequently, and data quality has improved. Yet creating aggregate estimates across the subcontinent and analyzing how patterns have changed over time remains a challenge, owing to frequent changes in questionnaires and variable definitions leading to a lack of comparability over time within one country, as well as a lack of cross-country comparability.

The purpose of this chapter is to illuminate the opportunities and challenges for employment policy in SSA by analyzing recent trends in the labor supply, labor demand, and labor market and employment outcomes, and by identifying what is known about the drivers of these outcomes, and their consequences for Africa's youth. This is achieved by (1) carefully aggregating labor market and employment data across SSA countries to provide an updated snapshot of the youth employment challenge today (pre-pandemic); (2) highlighting where the region has made progress in addressing employment challenges, and benchmarking this progress against the progress of other developing regions; (3) summarizing recent literature as well as using new data to drill down on key dimensions of the employment challenge, exploring questions such as how youth make the transition into employment, why informality persists, and which types of countries are best positioned to improve employment opportunities; and (4) based on this analysis, offering a menu of policy options to help countries develop better opportunities for youth in the labor force now and those expected in the future.

Themes explored include:

- Labor supply: the demographics of today's working-age population, who is and is not working, and why;
- Labor demand and employment outcomes: the complex structure of employment and livelihoods and how it changes with country income growth;
- The relationship between mineral resources and employment structure;
- Why labor markets do not clear—who is unemployed, who is underemployed, and what are the skills-mismatch problems;
- What do youth want out of the labor market, and how do they go about getting it; and
- Employment and development policy implications of the findings given above.

This review finds that youth entering labor market, seeking employment, face a set of constrained choices. The constraints include the level of economic development and transformation—which creates better employment opportunities for all, and the rate of labor force growth—which limits the share of youth that can get those opportunities.

The good news is that, as incomes and levels of economic development and transformation improve in SSA, youth and adult employment outcomes improve. In other words, when countries achieve balanced economic growth and transformation, better employment opportunities follow. SSA outcomes are similar to those found in developing countries in other regions, after controlling for income level; SSA countries are mostly not behind the rest of the world. Lower-middle-income countries (LMICs) in SSA show better employment outcomes, as they have more wage employment, less underemployment, and less employment in agriculture (a sector characterized by underemployment, low earnings, and income risk). Youth unemployment is an exception, as it is higher in SSA's LMICs than in low-income countries (LICs). But, once again, this SSA result is consistent with international experience, as youth unemployment tends to rise with a country's income level until countries reach upper-income status. Employment outcomes tend to be worse in LMI resource-rich countries because income improvements do not correlate well with development outcomes—either in the labor market or outside it.

The SSA labor force continues to grow rapidly—about 3 percent per annum, which poses economic development and labor absorption challenges that may not be fully appreciated by stakeholders. But the share of youth in the total labor force in SSA is falling, although there is significant heterogeneity across the continent. Participation of youth falls as income rises because youth spend more time in school—one reason why the share of youth in the labor force is falling in countries such as Kenya and Ghana. Nevertheless, SSA has the highest percentage of children under age 15 working, as well of youth under age 19, an outcome that compromises the skill development of the future labor force.

Africa has both an underskilling and overskilling problem. The poor quality of education systems along with mismatches between education curriculums and skills required in the labor market means that years of education do not translate well into better employment outcomes, even in urban areas where the more educated labor force, especially youth, live and work. Unemployment is highest among those with the highest levels of education, and, once they enter the labor force, the well-educated are highly likely to report that their skills are not being used. This trend suggests that African countries, especially the LMICs, have created more skills than opportunities. This economic disequilibrium will not automatically be corrected by economic growth; new firms that use a combination of high-skill and low-skill labor need to be created. From this perspective, policies encouraging an expansion of sectors for industries without smokestacks (IWSS)—such as export agriculture and agro-processing, construction, and tourism—combined with programs and reforms to improve the quality of education and increase the range of skills covered, could benefit the youth expected to enter the labor force in decades to come.

Young women in SSA face a number of gender-specific obstacles to better employment outcomes. Too many young women are married and have children before the age of 18, limiting educational attainment and the development of socioemotional skills, as well as leading to worse health outcomes during pregnancy. Moreover, at the macroeconomic level, early pregnancy contributes to higher fertility. Once they enter the labor force, a range of social factors impede women's ability to earn income, including lack of secure access to land and other assets and credit, as well as occupational segregation and workplace harassment norms that impede equal pay.

African youth are optimistic about their future, despite the struggles they face today in entering the labor force—which for youth entering in 2020–22 were compounded by the COVID-19-induced recession. Finding and developing a livelihood could be made easier through preemployment preparation of youth, either inside school or in parallel in the community, which would include developing key socioemotional employability skills, as well as providing information about opportunities and their expected job content and income.

Our results show that the employment policy agenda in SSA is first and foremost an economic transformation agenda, including raising within-sector productivity in lower-productivity sectors such as agriculture and expanding output and employment in higher-productivity sectors. Supporting firm entry and growth—both of which are low at present—should be a priority. The case studies in this volume indicate that if the IWSS-related policy agenda is pursued, economic opportunity for youth would widen considerably.

Even with the best economic policies, owing to high labor force growth, an informal economy will be normal for the next several decades in SSA. The SSA employment agenda in LIC and LMICs needs to tackle productivity issues in this sector, both on and off the farm and in urban areas. Improving access to digital services has demonstrated its value and should be a high priority, for the most part through investments and policies to lower information and communication technology service costs. Policies to encourage growth in IWSS sectors such as tourism should try to also encourage linkages between larger, formal firms and the informal sector by building out and lengthening local supply chains.

The employment policy agenda should also tackle medium- and long-term challenges, including SSA's LICs' and LMICs' poor learning outcomes, which limit the contribution of education to incomes and economic transformation. Another challenge is SSA's stubbornly high fertility. The two challenges are related. A projected slow fertility decline will cause labor force growth to continue at a high level, which tends to reduce employment transformation. But it will also limit the capacity for improved educational outcomes, given the need for constant growth in service units to serve a growing population of children.

COVID-19 has posed immediate challenges for SSA countries and governments. However, it does not appear to be changing the direction of past outcome trends in SSA, only halting progress. SSA's medium-term challenges remain.

Data and Classifications

The data for the analysis in this chapter are from SSA country household surveys (for a list of countries, the country classification, and surveys used, see appendix 2-1, which comes from Fox and Gandhi 2018).[2] These surveys are supplemented by data from the International Labor Organization (ILO), including modeled estimates to analyze trends because many SSA countries have not regularly conducted surveys in the past. Data for over 40 countries are aggregated, weighted, and presented by income group:[3]

- Low-income countries (LICs);
- Lower-middle-income countries not dependent on mineral resource export earnings (LMICs);
- Lower-middle-income-countries dependent on mineral resource income (resource-rich, RR);[4]
- Upper-middle-income countries (UMICs).

Presenting data by income groups shows how employment behavior and outcomes change as countries get richer. However, how a country gets rich matters a lot for the development of employment opportunities. In particular, an abundance of mineral wealth, especially in a less-developed country, is associated with a larger state, a less developed and less diversified domestic private sector, and overall worse development outcomes compared with countries at a similar level of income (Frankel 2012). In terms of employment outcomes, in low-income countries, the patterns are quite similar, as the overall poverty and low level of economic development are about the same; the mineral wealth has not produced enough domestic income to matter, so we do not show them as a separate group. But the data for LMIC countries does show different patterns for the RR group compared with the others. SSA has few countries in the UMIC group, and several are RR, including South Africa, which, because of its larger population essentially determines the outcomes in this group.

While everyone's employment outcomes depend on the opportunities presented in the economy, youth face particular challenges in finding and seizing economic opportunities. One challenge is the continuing need for skill acquisition. Neurological evidence shows that youths' brains are still developing in areas related to emotional regulation and self-control (Heckman and Kautz 2013). Employment search skills and the socio-emotional "employability" skills valued by employers are usually learned through experience (tacit learning), not through formal skill development (although certain types of pedagogy are more effective at forming these skills than others; see the discussion by the World Bank 2018). It is widely accepted that experience on the job is valued and rewarded, both as a signal that these employability skills have been acquired as well as reflecting real skill gains acquired through work. But youth who have acquired socio-emotional skills may have trouble signaling this result (Carranza et al. 2020), despite the value of these skills to employers.

A second challenge is the need for many youth to create their own employment, owing to the lack of wage jobs on offer in the less-developed private sectors of low- and lower-middle-income countries. In the agricultural sector, this may mean acquiring land, inputs, and tools. In the non-agricultural sector, it may mean acquiring inventory to sell, tools to provide services such as hairdressing or repair, or raw materials needed to produce home-made goods such as food or craft furniture. In all cases, savings are needed, either from one's family and network, or from earnings acquired by working for someone else as a wage worker or dependent contractor, or a combination. The need to meet this challenge may cause youth to experience spells of unemployment or underemployment combined with shorter periods of employment than adults (Bridges et al. 2016).

To highlight these differences, outcomes for youth are presented separately from those for adults where possible. In this chapter, youth are

defined as individuals age 15–24 years, which is the United Nations definition. "Youth" is both a social and demographic construct, however, and
"youth" as a target age group is defined differently in different countries.
The meaning of youth also differs by gender, as poor young women may
already be independent from their birth families, married, and having
children in the youngest age range of youth (15–18), even while males of
the same age still live with their parents (Filmer and Fox 2014). Males as
well as females from more fortunate backgrounds and in richer countries
may still be in school in their early 20s and dependent on their parents.

Recognizing that these challenges do not magically end when youth
reach the age of 25, survey data nonetheless suggest that most youth in SSA
are economically independent by age 25 (Mason et al. 2017; Filmer and Fox
2014), and some are even supporting younger siblings who are still living
with their parents. Thus, for the most part, the age cutoff of 25 serves the
purposes of this chapter.

Demographics of Labor Supply and Employment

Africa's demographics determine the potential labor supply today and for at
least the next 20 years. Behavioral responses of Africa's working-age population to their economic opportunities (e.g., demand for labor given education), needs (e.g., household consumption requirements vs. household chores
and care), and social circumstances (e.g., behavioral norms for women's
employment)—determine who actually works and why. Although a growing
(and employed) labor force contributes to economic growth as each worker
adds value in the economy, rapid labor force growth puts downward pressure
on wages as the economy struggles to absorb the inflow. For this reason,
the analysis here starts with Africa's demographic trends.

The SSA working-age population (15–64) numbered 587 million in 2018,
accounting for 54 percent of total regional population and about 14 percent
of the world's total working-age population. Over the next two decades, the
working age population will increase by about 20 million per year. Owing to
population aging in all other parts of the world, SSA's share of the working-
age population is projected to rise over the next decades. While it is true that
SSA is the world's youngest region, the working-age share of the population
passed its lowest point in 1987 (at about 50 percent) and has been rising ever
since, while the dependency ratio reached peak at the same time (figure 2-1).

FIGURE 2-1. **Dependency Ratio, Actual and Projected, by Region**

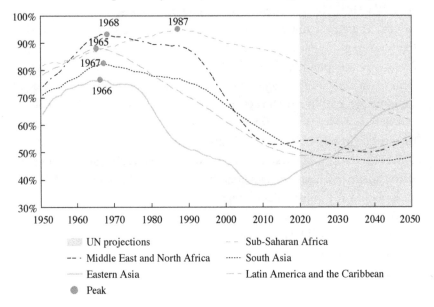

Source: United Nations World Population Prospects, 2019 (medium variant).

Note: The working-age population is estimated at age 15–64 years; the dependency ratio is the population out of working age over the working-age population.

Importantly, this change has been slower than in other parts of the world, owing to slower fertility decline (Mason et al. 2017), and the peak came significantly later than other regions, all of which are now aging rapidly, except South Asia and the Middle East. A falling dependency ratio helps bring a potential demographic dividend; however, the size of the dividend depends in part on the rate of change in the dependency ratio.[5] SSA's ratio peaked at a very high point, and is falling slowly (similar to that of the Middle East), so prospects for an Africa-wide dividend appear limited. However, some countries in SSA that have been able to reduce dependency more rapidly may be able to reap a small dividend.

Not surprisingly, Africa's labor force is also the youngest in the world, but the labor force is gradually aging as well. Youth's share of the working-age population peaked at 38 percent in 2001 and has been declining ever since. Now, owing to the fact that youth participate less than before because they are more likely to be in school, or, if female, may be already out of the labor force caring for young children, in addition to longer life expectancy enabling people over age 50 to still work, the youth share of the employed population is even lower, at 24 percent, and this share will continue to decline. If Africa's slow decline in fertility relative to improvements in life expectancy persists, the youth share of the labor force is expected to decline more slowly in SSA than in other regions of the world, so most countries will continue to see many young people entering the labor force during the coming decades.

The behavior of SSA's households suggests that current trends will persist. For example, child marriage and pregnancy rates in SSA are the highest of any region in the world; 10 percent of young women in Africa today have a child before the age of 18; in South Asia, that share is 2.5 percent (UNICEF 2020). Having a child before the age of 18 has multiple negative consequences: It puts a woman at increased risk for complications and even death; pregnant females are often forced to drop out of school; it raises overall fertility, which can put the development of all children in the house at risk; and it raises total national fertility, which can have negative macro-level consequences. Controlling for the factors that normally reduce fertility (household income, women's education, and urbanization), Bongaarts (2017) found a unique and positive African fertility effect compared with countries in other regions of the world, which explains the slow decline projected in figures 2-1 and 2-2.

The subcontinental trends shown in figures 2-1 and 2-2 hide substantial regional variation, reflecting heterogeneity in the demographic transition among SSA countries. Most African countries have raised life expectancy substantially over the last 30 years, such that Africa-wide life expectancy at birth is 60 years. Some countries—such as Rwanda, Ghana, Kenya, and Zimbabwe—have lowered total fertility substantially (to below four children per woman if she survives through her reproductive child-bearing years), through a combination of higher girls' educational attainment and increased availability of contraception. In other countries, such as Niger, the fertility rate has barely moved in the last 20 years, and is stuck at seven. In Nigeria, life expectancy is only 54 while fertility is 5.4. As a result, the youth share of the working-age population has not peaked in Niger, the Democratic Republic of the Congo (DRC), and Nigeria, while it is headed steadily down in Ethiopia, Ghana, and Kenya (figure 2-3). As a result, the region-wide average sits between the growing youth population in Nigeria (with 200 million people) and the DRC (with 86 million), and the falling youth population of Ethiopia (112 million) and Kenya (47 million). But only South Africa has a youth share of the labor force near the level of South Asia or Latin America.

FIGURE 2-2. **Youth Share of Working-Age Population,
Actual and Projected, by Region**

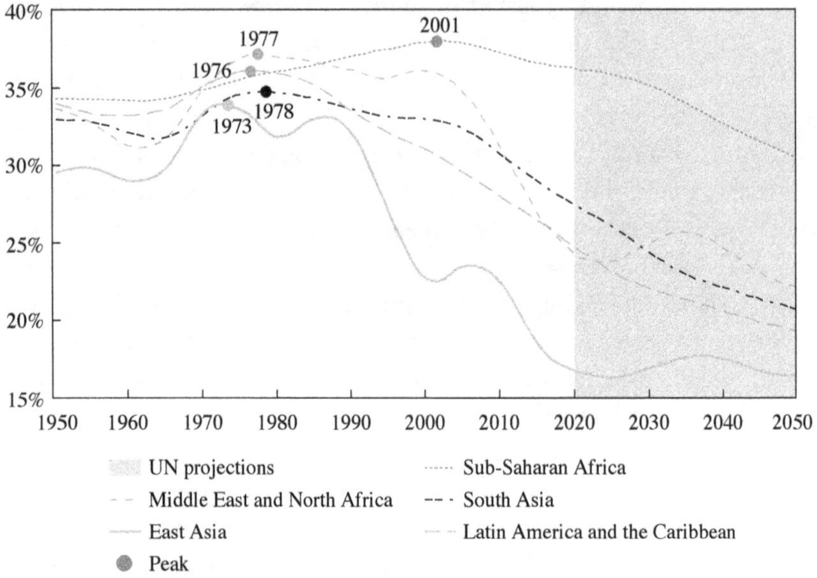

Source: United Nations World Population Prospects, 2019 (medium variant).

Note: Youth are the estimated population age 15–24 years. The working-age population is estimated at age 15–64.

Labor force participation—the difference between the working-age population and those who are out of the labor force—is high in Africa, but is consistent with trends observed in other regions, the rates decline with household income (figures 2-4 and 2-5; Klasen et al. 2019). Most of the decline is in female labor force participation, for several reasons: (1) in low-income countries, women with young children are able to combine work with childcare; but, as home-based activities such as farming and informal household businesses decline as a share of employment, women are more likely to withdraw from the labor force to care for children; and (2) richer households can afford to have women participate less in peak child-bearing and -caring years (age 20–45) (figure 2-6). A strong negative effect of fertility on female labor force participation has been found in several studies, most recently by Bloom and others (2009) for a large group of developing countries. This study found an 8-percentage-point effect starting at age 20–24, with a cumulative 15-percentage-point effect at age 35–39. Nigeria, which dominates the resource-rich LMIC group, has higher fertility,

FIGURE 2-3. **Youth Share of the Working-Age Population, Selected Countries**

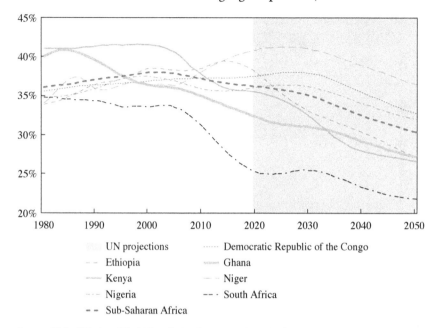

Source: United Nations World Population Prospects, 2019 (medium variant).

Note: Youth are the estimated population age 15–24 years. The working-age population is the estimated population age 15–64.

controlling for income, which maybe one reason that the youth labor force participation rates are lower in the RR group than other LMICs (see figure 2-7, showing a higher proportion of young women not employed and not in school); another reason could be inconsistent data.[6]

Labor force participation also declines with income among youth, as secondary schooling becomes widely available, and households can afford to keep their children in school. By the time countries reach UMIC status, over 80 percent of youth age 15–19 are in school and not working, whereas in LICs, only about 40 percent are able to achieve this status, while another 14–20 percent are able to stay in school by working. Compared with other regions, African LICs and LMICs have a high percentage of youth in the 15–17 age range working during some part of the year, as estimated by Dolislager and others (2020), at 57 percent (63 percent of males); compared with 30 percent in LAC and 20 percent in Asia.[7]

Fully one-third of youth age 15–19 in African LICs have already dropped out of school and are working, although, in a few cases, youth may be

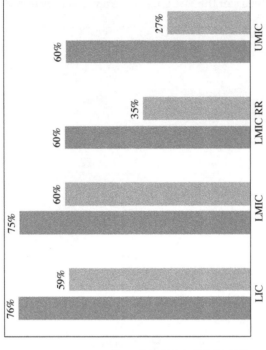

FIGURE 2-4. Labor Force Participation Rate, by Region 2019

Labor force participation rate

Source: Estimates of the labor force participation rate—ILO modeled—were accessed via World Development Indicators.

Note: Excludes high-income countries; labor force weighted.

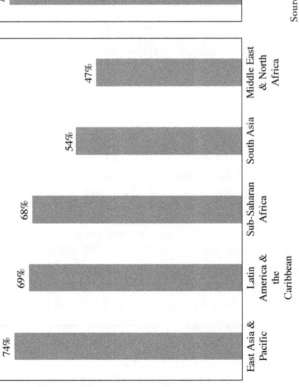

FIGURE 2-5. Labor Force Participation Rate, Sub-Saharan Africa

Labor force participation rate

Source: Fox and Gandhi 2018.

Note: LIC = low-income countries; LMIC = lower-middle-income countries; RR = resource-rich; UMIC = upper-middle-income countries. Labor force weighted.

FIGURE 2-6. Female Labor Force Participation Rate, by Age Group, Sub-Saharan Africa, 2019

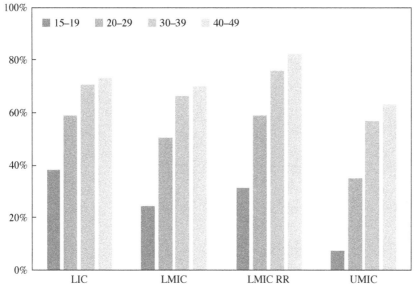

Source: US Agency for International Development, DHS Statcompiler.

Note: LIC = low-income countries; LMIC = lower-middle-income countries; RR = resource-rich; UMIC = upper-middle-income countries. Unweighted averages.

working in order to get the money to go back to school. In all countries, as youth get older, they are more likely to work, although the share of women working lags that of men, especially in the higher-income group. In middle-income countries, about one-third of women age 20–24 are neither in school nor working (i.e., neither working nor in education or training). Although a recent Gallup poll found overwhelming support among men and women in SSA for women to have a paid job, the extent to which the large share of young women who are neither working nor in education represents a choice to care for children or a lack of support systems for women who wish to combine working with caring for children and household chores is unclear (Ray and Esipova 2017).

Working children under the age of 15 are both a serious economic and social problem and, at the same time, make important contributions to the livelihoods of many households in SSA. Child labor is not considered in the estimates given above or elsewhere in the chapter, as the analysis only

FIGURE 2-7. **Education and Employment Status of Youth, Sub-Saharan Africa**

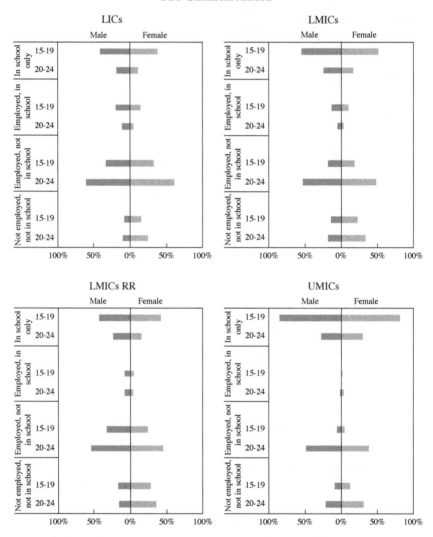

Source: Youth labor force participation rate by sex, age, and school attendance status—ILOSTAT database.

Note: LIC = low-income countries; LMIC = lower-middle-income countries; RR = resource-rich; UMIC = upper-middle-income countries. Population weighted average.

covers the working-age population. Yet SSA has the highest share of children engaged in some kind of economic activity. Dolislager and others (2020) estimated that labor hours contributed by people outside the working-age population (age 65+ and under 15) accounted for about 10 percent of total labor hours recorded in low- and lower-middle-income SSA countries; the majority of this estimate was from child labor. In other regions, only 2.3 percent of total reported hours over the year were attributed to children under age 15. Most children work part time in a household activity (farming or business). While not intrinsically harmful—indeed, this type of activity can help transfer valuable skills—studies have nonetheless found that child labor in SSA is also associated with lower school attendance and achievements (Filmer and Fox 2014). Excessive child labor thus exacerbates poor labor market outcomes for youth.

In sum, while the labor force in Africa is young compared with those of other regions, in most SSA countries, the immediate employment pressure of the youth bulge is lessening, owing to a combination of fertility declines that started in the last years of the 20th century and increased school enrollment in the 15- to 24-year-old demographic. As a result, the youth cohort entering the labor force today is much smaller than what is often projected based simply on population growth—only about 7–9 million a year in a labor force of about 440 million, a far cry from the 20 million projected (Abdychev et al. 2018). Any increased time that youth spend in education, a positive development, contributes to this result. One potentially negative factor slowing labor force growth is the declining female labor force participation rate as countries get richer. While the trend in Africa is like what is observed in other regions, African LMICs could arrest this decline through investments and programs that make it easier to combine employment and child-rearing, raising overall returns to public investments in the education of girls, for example. To improve human development outcomes, African countries should introduce programs and policies to reduce child labor and limit marriage and pregnancy before age 18.

Where Is Africa Employed Today?
The Growth of Employment Opportunities

Youth entering the labor force today are more educated than their parents, and they want better jobs than their parents have. Better jobs require economic transformation—an improvement in productivity in the low-labor-productivity sectors and an increase in employment opportunities in high-labor-productivity sectors paying higher wages, and usually offering more employment security through the creation of formal wage jobs. Sustained economic transformation in other regions catalyzed the growth of higher-paying wage jobs, and, through this process, created improvements in material welfare. To what extent is the process of economic transformation creating new employment opportunities, and how do these trends compare with those in other regions? To address this question, we now turn to employment patterns by sector and type.

African employment profiles by sector are not very different from those of other regions of the developing world when countries are sorted by income. In LICs, the agricultural sector (including fishing and forestry), usually a low-productivity sector, is where most people work (figure 2-8), and Africa is no exception, although African LICs report an especially high share of employment in agriculture, reflecting high levels of poverty and low levels of transformation in SSA's LICs. As countries get richer, employment opportunities in other sectors increase and the labor force, especially new entrants, are less likely to report agricultural employment (figure 2-9). In both Africa and other regions, the second-most important sector group for LICs and LMICs, and the most important sector group for UMICs, is public and private services—including trade, transportation, finance, and communications, as well services dominated by public employment including education, health, and public administration. The service employment share in Africa is higher in LMICs and UMICs than in other regions, especially in the UMICs, owing to the very low share of the labor force working in agriculture in South Africa. Service sector employment has been growing as a share of total employment as the share of employment in agriculture has declined (figure 2-9).

Africa's employment profile does differ with other regions with respect to the share of employment in industry, including mining, manufacturing, and construction. This sector does not account for a large share of employment around the world owing to high capital intensity, but the share reported by Africans, especially in lower middle-income countries, is lower than in other developing regions. Within industry, the SSA employment share in both manufacturing and construction is lower than in other regions, while the share in other industry (mostly mining, but also utilities) is larger, reflecting the importance of mineral extraction in many African economies. The small share of employment in manufacturing in Africa has been noted by many (e.g., Newfarmer, Page, and Tarp 2019; Rodrik 2015;

FIGURE 2-8. **Employment by Sector and Income Group, Sub-Saharan Africa and Rest of the World, 2018**

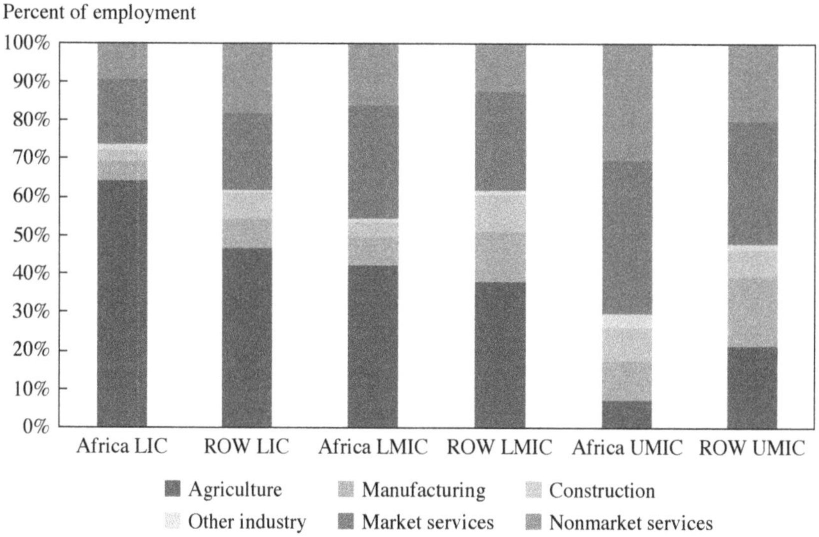

Percent of employment

Source: Employment distribution by economic activity—ILO-modeled estimates, ILOSTAT database.

Note: LIC = low-income countries; LMIC = lower-middle-income countries; RR = resource-rich; UMIC = upper-middle-income countries; ROW = rest of the world. Employment weighted average. Market services include trade, transportation, hospitality, ICT, and finance, real estate, and professional and administrative services. Nonmarket services include public administration, health, education and social work, arts, entertainment and recreation, and domestic services.

African Development Bank 2019). This volume argues that owing in part to Africa's late start in developing a manufacturing sector, the development of a high-value service sector offers an additional employment creation strategy, which should be explored.

This simple picture of employment by sector is one of the most-reported employment statistics in the world, but it hides important nuances in how people work in low- and lower-middle-income countries. Employment in smallholder farming alone is usually not enough to sustain a household above the poverty line (Beegle and Christiaensen 2019), so many people, especially in rural areas, work in more than one sector. One reason is the seasonality of employment: Rain-fed agriculture usually leads to months of inactivity, so people seek opportunities in other sectors in the offseason. A second reason is that, as the agriculture sector develops, household incomes rise,

FIGURE 2-9. **Employment Trends in Sub-Saharan Africa, 2000 and 2018**

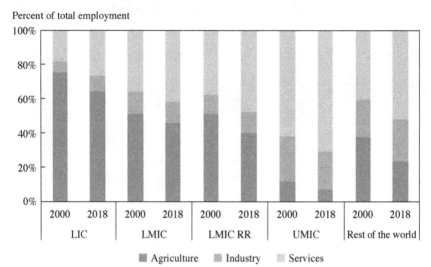

Source: Employment distribution by economic activity—ILO-modeled estimates, ILOSTAT database.

Note: LIC = low-income countries; LMIC = lower-middle-income countries; RR = resource-rich; UMIC = upper-middle-income countries. Employment-weighted average.

bringing increased demand for nonfarm goods and services, encouraging rural households to start and maintain nonfarm businesses. In addition, as medium-sized farms with more capital become more prominent and profitable, smallholder farmers tend to reduce their activities on their own farms to seek out opportunities elsewhere, usually off the farm. These opportunities may be farm-related (e.g., input supply or transportation of product) or nonfarm, such as miscellaneous retail trade. In rural Tanzania, survey data collected in 2005 showed that over half those employed worked in more than one sector, usually agriculture and nonfarm self-employment (Filmer and Fox 2014); similar results were found in 2018 by Yeboah and others (2020) for rural Ghana, Tanzania, and Zimbabwe. This phenomenon, known as "mixed livelihoods," is common across rural areas and small towns in SSA but is less common in cities, where people are more likely to specialize in one activity or sector.

Comparing the data shown in table 2-1 with those shown in figure 2-9 gives an indication of the extent to which figure 2-9 *overstates the importance of the agricultural sector in employment, and probably also overstates the*

Table 2-1. **Share of Hours Worked by Type of Employment and Area (%)**

Type of employment	Urban			Rural			Total		
	Male	**Female**	**Total**	**Male**	**Female**	**Total**	**Male**	**Female**	**Total**
Own-farm	10	13	11	42	45	44	32	35	34
Farm wage	6	3	5	9	5	8	8	5	7
Off-farm wage	54	34	46	20	11	16	30	18	25
Nonfarm household enterprise	30	50	38	29	39	33	29	42	34
Total	100	100	100	100	100	100	100	100	100

Source: Michael Dolislager, private communication.

Note: Numbers reported are simple averages. Countries included are Ethiopia, Malawi, Niger, Nigeria, Tanzania, and Uganda.

decline in employment in this sector. Table 2-1 reports detailed data on hours worked *over the year* for the working population in six SSA low- and lower-middle-income countries. In contrast to the data shown in figure 2-9, these data show that *only 37 percent of total reported hours worked were in agriculture.*[8] Reported hours worked in agriculture were higher in rural areas, but still not over 50 percent. Notably, the share of hours worked in agriculture were about the same for men and women, but men were more likely to be employed off their farm in agricultural wage work. Only in the rural hinterland (where the population density is particularly low) were more than half of total hours worked reported to be in the agricultural sector (Dolislager et al. 2020).

Until countries reach the upper-middle-income level, informal sector employment is the norm. A shortage of wage employment opportunities relative to labor supply results in the majority of employment opportunities found in household farms and businesses—the informal sector. Nonagricultural informal sector employment accounts for 33 percent of total hours worked in rural Africa, and 38 percent of total hours worked in urban Africa (table 2-1) (Dolislager et al. 2020). Unlike in agriculture, in both rural and urban areas, women are much more likely to find work in this sector. Most of these businesses are self-employers and involve retail trade (kiosks or market stalls selling household consumables or farm inputs). Other popular sectors are informal agro-processing (milling grains, pressing oilseeds, making soap or candles, harvesting, and selling honey) or other types of craft manufacturing (making and selling furniture, baked or other cooked foods, or charcoal), and service sector providers such as hairdressing, running a bar, and or doing small repairs. Many service providers are also agents for mobile money. The craft manufacturers or retail traders sell their goods and services almost exclusively to other households and are popular in rural and urban areas as they are willing to sell small amounts (one or two cigarettes; one bread roll; a small amount of cooking oil), which is helpful for lower- and middle-income households that may not have a steady income or any credit, and so would not be able to purchase their daily needs from larger, more established businesses (Fox and Sohnesen 2016). Importantly, this sector depends on household incomes from agriculture or wage employment, as well as income earned within the sector for demand, so any type of local economic crisis such as a natural disaster or trade or transportation shock hits this sector very quickly (Filmer and Fox 2014).

Wage employment outside the agricultural sector—working for someone who is not a member of one's own family, and who is paid in cash or in kind—is generally considered more desirable employment, as the income risk is lower and the conditions of work tend to be better, including the possibility of paid overtime and benefits such as paid leave and social insurance.[9] By hours worked, it is the most common type of employment in urban areas, reflecting the tendency of both public sector entities and private firms to locate there, and it is relatively unimportant in rural areas. Wage employment in enterprises offers opportunities for specialization, including use of skills gained through education or training, and tends to be both more productive (monetary value of output per worker) and better paid. This is less true of casual day labor or temporary jobs, which account for about half of wage employment in low- and lower-middle-income SSA countries (Filmer and Fox 2014).

Wage employment has grown more rapidly in non-RR LMICs (figure 2-10), reflecting the entrance of new firms responding to a better investment climate.[10] In all LICs and LMICs, the share of wage employment in total employment is larger for men. In the LIC countries, the share of wage employment in men's employment went from 15 to 20 percent, but in women's employment it only went from 7 to 10 percent. Women seem to be catching up in non-RR LMICs, but this may be attributable to women without wage employment dropping out of the labor force (a selectivity issue).[11]

In RR LMIC countries, the expansion of wage employment has mostly been in the public sector (table 2-2). Only 18 percent of the wage employment shown in figure 2-10 is in the public sector in non-RR LMICs, but 43 percent of the wage employment in RR countries is in the public sector. The pattern of high public sector wage employment and low private sector wage employment in RR economies is not unique to Sub-Saharan Africa, as it is common and often worse in the Middle East and North Africa (Assaad 2019). For example, in 2000, over 50 percent of educated new entrants to the labor force in Algeria and Tunisia took public sector jobs. In 2014, in Egypt, over 25 percent of *total* employment was found in the public sector; the share was even higher in Jordan and Algeria (Assaad 2019). Wage employment in African UMICs is high, but outcomes in this category are dominated by South Africa, which has exceptionally low agricultural sector employment given its income level (see figure 2-9); this is why African UMICs seem to be doing better than the rest of the world on this dimension.

FIGURE 2-10. Wage Employment, Sub-Saharan Africa, by Gender and for the Rest of the World

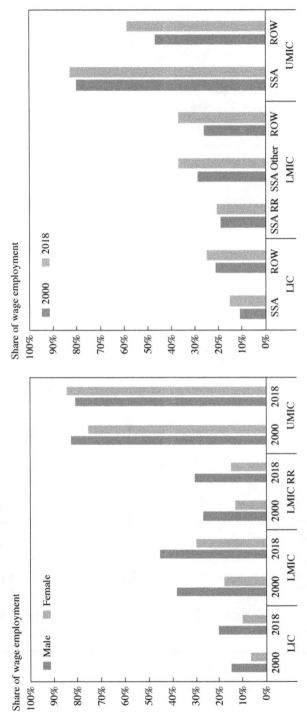

Source: Employment distribution by status in employment—ILO-modeled estimates, ILOSTAT database.

Note: LIC = low-income countries; LMIC = lower-middle-income countries; RR = resource-rich; UMIC = upper-middle-income countries; SSA = Sub-Sharan Africa; ROW = rest of the world. Employment-weighted averages.

Table 2-2. Wage Employment as a Share of Total Employment in SSA LMICs and RR LMICs

	Wage employment percentage
LMICs	34
Of which, public sector	6
RR LMICs	23
Of which, public sector	10

Source: Fox and Gandhi 2018.

Note: SSA = Sub-Saharan Africa; LMIC = lower-middle-income countries; RR = resource-rich. Employment-weighted averages.

In sum, African employment patterns—reflecting the intersection of labor supply and demand—are showing signs of transformation in the LICs and LMICs. Notwithstanding the dearth of industrial employment and overall lower incomes in African LMIC countries, the share of wage employment in non-RR LMIC countries is near the average in LMICs in other regions, despite rapid labor force growth, reflecting significant progress toward transformation in the face of demographic headwinds, spurred by expansion of output in the service sector. In LICs, wage employment shares are behind the other regions, reflecting lower average income levels in this category compared with the rest of the world; wage employment levels are also behind in the RR countries. Most of the employment in Africa is in the private sector (including self- and family employment).

Unemployment, Underemployment, and Skills Mismatch

Youth enter the labor force hoping to be able to earn a living. Sometimes there are opportunities, but they cannot find them (a matching problem). This means that youth need to keep searching. Sometimes youth do not have enough skills for the opportunities available, so they need to return to school or find another way to gain the skills they need. Often, however, youth have skills, but there are few opportunities compared with the number entering the labor force. In this case, they need to look for or create new opportunities—by starting a self-employed business, for example—even though in these new opportunities, at least initially, they may not be working to their full potential. All these situations, be they unemployment (not working at all but searching) or underemployment (working below potential),

FIGURE 2-11. **Unemployment and Underemployment
in Sub-Saharan Africa**

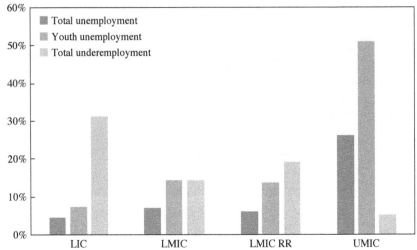

Source: Fox and Gandhi 2018.

Note: LIC = low-income countries; LMIC = lower-middle-income countries; RR = resource-rich; UMIC = upper-middle-income countries. Weighted averages. Underemployment is defined as working less than 40 hours per week in all activities and being willing to work more hours but not able to find work.

reflect disequilibria in the matching of labor supply and demand in the labor market. While they can never be completely eliminated, one objective of labor market policy is to reduce the amount of time youth and other labor force participants spend in this situation.

Unemployment, widely viewed as a leading and reliable indicator of distress in the labor market, is not widespread in SSA until countries reach upper-middle-income status (figure 2-11). The pattern in SSA is like the pattern in other parts of the world, which is that the unemployment rate tends to be highest in middle-income countries (figure 2-12). Open unemployment is usually low in low-income countries because it is both futile and unaffordable. Most households have limited savings to finance a job search, and there are few wage jobs to be found. To be employed in these countries means creating your own job or joining with household members in a farming or nonfarm activity. Although youth unemployment is typically

FIGURE 2-12. **GDP per Capita and the Youth Unemployment Rate**

Youth unemployment rate

GDP per capita (log scale)

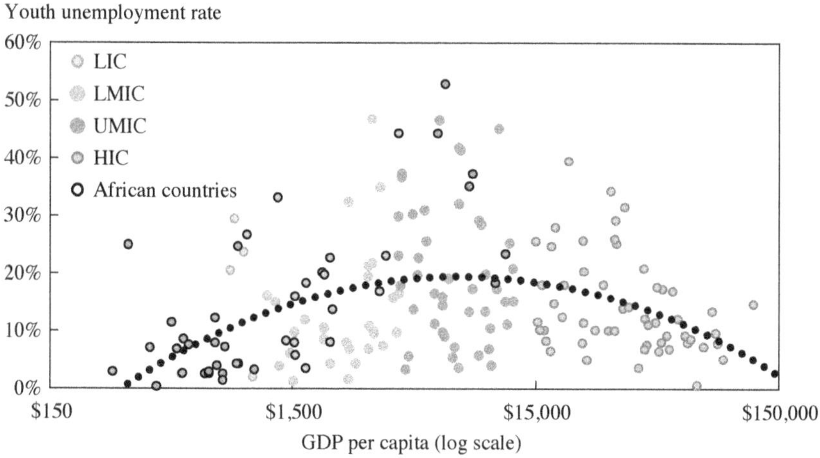

Source: ILO-modeled estimates of youth unemployment accessed via World Development Indicators.

Note: LIC = low-income countries; LMIC = lower-middle-income countries; UMIC = upper-middle-income countries; HIC = high-income countries.

higher than the country-wide average (figure 2-11), the difference is very slight in the poorest countries.

As countries get richer, they produce more wage job opportunities relative to the supply of labor, and households have more resources to finance a job search. Education levels and job aspirations also rise, however. This creates the situation of higher unemployment among educated youth, especially those with secondary school but no further education, as is regularly found in SSA's urban areas (figure 2-13). South Africa is a particularly bad example of this problem, but middle-income countries in the Middle East, North Africa, and Latin America also show a similar pattern (Palmer 2017). One reason for the pattern of higher unemployment among more educated youth is that the demand for labor with intermediate skills (e.g., completed secondary education) has not grown as fast as the supply of this labor—educational attainment has risen faster than labor demand. Related to this trend is the increased capital intensity of manufacturing, which has meant that the types of jobs that people with this level of education used to take are now less common all over the world (Rodrik 2015). Once countries reach the high-income stage, the average unemployment

FIGURE 2-13. **Youth Unemployment by Education Level in Sub-Saharan Africa**

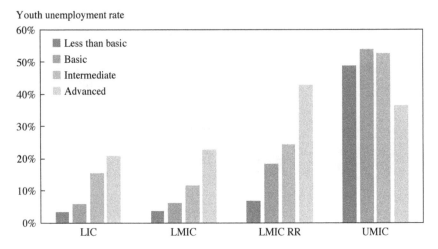

Source: Youth unemployment by sex and education, ILOSTAT database.

Note: LIC = low-income countries; LMIC = lower-middle-income countries; RR = resource-rich; UMIC = upper-middle-income countries. In the education classifications, "less than basic" is pre–primary school or lower; "basic" is completed primary school; "intermediate" is completed secondary or postsecondary technical or vocation school/training; and "advanced" is attended any type or level of tertiary education. For further information on education classifications, see http://uis.unesco.org/en/topic/international-standard-classification-education-isced.

rate drops substantially as the quality of education improves, the supply of job opportunities (labor demand) relative to the labor supply comes back into alignment, and education and postschool training and job assistance systems do a better job of helping match employers and job seekers.

Underemployment is more common than unemployment in low- and lower-middle-income countries. Underemployment refers to underutilized labor. The definition most commonly measured is *hours-related underemployment*, which happens because the working person is willing to put in more hours but they cannot get more hours of work, either because of seasonality, or because the job they are doing is inherently part-time—in U.S. parlance, a person is involuntarily part time. Hours-related underemployment is associated with a high share of employment in agriculture or casual labor, so this is more common in poor countries (see figure 2-11).

A second definition, often referred to as a skills mismatch, is *not being able to find a job that utilizes the training or skills that a person has acquired*; for

FIGURE 2-14. **Skills Mismatch in Sub-Saharan Africa**

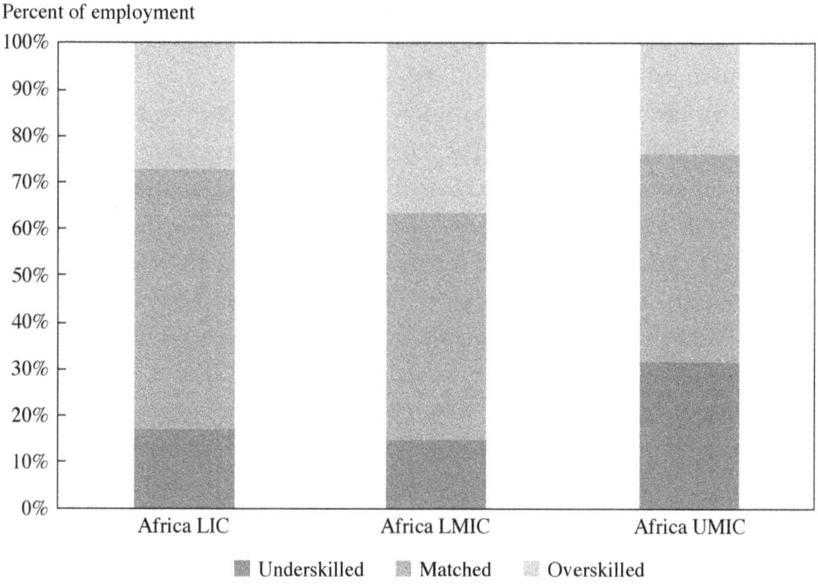

Percent of employment

Source: Employment by educational mismatch, statistical approach; ILOSTAT database.

Note: LIC = low-income countries; LMIC = lower-middle-income countries; UMIC = upper-middle-income countries. Employment-weighted average; includes data for 21 African countries.

example, a taxi driver or waiter with a postgraduate degree, or a laid-off middle manager working as a retail clerk. As African countries grow their economies and expand education, skills mismatch underemployment seems to be becoming more important (figure 2-14). In urban areas, World Bank STEP surveys found that 40 percent of the labor force in Ghana and 25 percent of the labor force in Kenya reported that their own education exceeds the education required for their current job (Handel, Valerio, and Sánchez Puerta 2016). Interestingly, the most underutilized skills reported in this study were digital ones. The ILO skills mismatch measure compares the employed person's education with median years of education found by all employed people in that occupational group. Its results (as seen in figure 2-14) show that, while those who seem to be well matched, statistically, with their occupation are the largest single group, the rate of over-skilling (skill underutilization) is highest in LMI countries. The African Development Bank (2019) found that reported overskilling increases with education level completed. Notably, the African Development Bank also finds that education is poorly correlated with labor productivity, which may be one reason why employers are less likely to hire well-educated job entrants. These results are consistent with the high rate of unemployment among more educated people in LMICs.[12]

The problems with the absorption of educated youth in SSA's economies have been attributed in part to SSA's education systems. Although African countries spend a high share of public and private expenditures on education, the efficiency of their expenditures is low. The overall quality of SSA education is poor, and learning outcomes (as measured by standardized tests) for SSA's children are worse compared with those of their peers in other regions, even controlling for income level (Filmer and Fox 2014; World Bank 2018; Arias, Evans, and Santos 2019). The pattern is most extreme in RR countries, which have some of the worst human development outcomes across the board, controlling for income (de la Brière et al. 2017). The curriculum and teaching methods are also not oriented toward developing noncognitive skills and employability knowledge that is helpful for navigating the labor market, especially in secondary and postsecondary education systems.

As a result, graduating youth do not know how to interact with potential employers to find a job, or to interact with self-employed mentors to find out how they could do better. Employers cite a lack of socioeconomic skills as the main reason they do not like to hire youth who are recent graduates (Filmer and Fox 2014; Fox 2019). Postsecondary formal technical and vocational training programs have been a massive and expensive failure (Filmer and Fox 2014; Arias, Evans, and Santos 2019) in part because they do not focus on these skills, although internships within these programs seem to help build them.

Difficulty navigating the labor market is not only an urban issue; research on Nigeria and Tanzania cited by Fox (2019) and on Ghana, Tanzania, and Zimbabwe cited by Yeboah and others (2020) shows that secondary and postsecondary school graduates in small cities and rural towns do not have an easy time either. Rural education is of even worse quality than in urban areas and is still costly. Yeboah and others (2020) report that many rural youth express disappointment with the career outcomes available once they complete junior or senior secondary school, and cite a lack of funds and/or poor exam scores as the main reason they were unable to continue their education. In African school-to-work transition surveys, the aspirations of rural youth for the type of occupation they wanted were high and were not consistent with their education—which was too low and did not provide the skills they needed—or the opportunities in their area (OECD 2018).

In sum, SSA does not have worse youth unemployment than other regions, after controlling for income level and the presence of mineral exports. Indeed, unemployment in most SSA low- and lower-income countries is below the estimated regression line shown in figure 2-12. But outcomes could be better, especially for educated youth, as figure 2-11 shows. Several microeconomic studies have shown that African youth often have no idea where employment opportunities are expanding, or what specific jobs or occupations pay as an entry-level wage (Filmer and Fox 2014; Fox 2019). As a result, educated urban youth in Africa spend years after leaving school searching for formal wage employment, hoping for a higher wage or better job than they are likely to receive, and ultimately the majority do not succeed (Bridges et al. 2016). It is possible that, as wage employment opportunities increase in urban and peri-urban areas, these search costs could diminish.[13] However, a stronger focus within the education system on both necessary cognitive skills as well as overall preparation for entering the labor market either as a wage employee or in self-employment could reduce these employment frictions for youth.

Evaluating SSA Youth Employment Outcomes and Challenges

The analysis in the previous sections shows that, controlling for income group today—an indicator of economic transformation and development—SSA's employment outcomes are in many ways similar to those of the rest of the world. This finding suggests that as SSA's countries travel on their economic development journey, *they are not following a divergent path with respect to employment outcomes.* The major exception is the structure of employment by sector. LMIC SSA countries have not been able to generate the share of employment in industry that other LMIC countries outside SSA have achieved. As the share of employment in agriculture has declined, the share of employment in services has grown. Much of this service employment is informal. As a result, while wage employment as a share of total employment has grown as non-RR SSA countries move into the LMIC status, it often does not come with the benefits expected (income security and protection), while in RR countries wage employment is well behind the averages for LMIC countries outside SSA. This different pattern of employment transformation has been a source of policy concern for some time (Rodrik 2015) and motivates the case studies in the IWSS research project.

Most discussion of SSA youth employment issues refer to the large youth bulge within SSA demography—a labor supply problem. However, all other regions of the world have also been through this demographic phase (figure 2-2), and most countries have managed to employ their youth productively. A young labor force does not by itself constitute an employ-ment problem. In absolute numbers, the size of SSA's youth population is not large compared with those of Asian countries at their peak youth share of the working-age population. Rather, what sets SSA apart as a region is the slow rate of change. Of the 25 highest-fertility countries in the world, all are in SSA. The first country outside Africa on the list is Afghanistan, which ranks 27th.[14] The rate of labor force growth and the dependency ratio are dropping much more slowly in SSA than in other regions, and this creates employment challenges.

The employment consequences of high fertility appear to be under-appreciated in SSA compared with other regions. Fewer children are asso-ciated with higher public and private expenditures per capita on human capital (Mason et al. 2017), indicating that lower fertility could improve future employment outcomes. Lower fertility also slows future labor force growth, which could improve future employment opportunities. La Porta and Shleifer (2014) find that slower labor force growth is a necessary condition for reducing the share of informal self-employment or family employment in total employment while increasing the share of formal wage jobs. Africa is already behind the rest of the world in the share of wage employment in total employment. La Porta and Schleifer's results suggest that Africa will not be able to climb out of this deficit soon, meaning that Africa's high fertility will have long-lasting effects on future employment outcomes.

Africa has both an overskilling and an underskilling problem. Highly educated youth in LMICs are more likely to be unemployed, and, when employed, more likely to report that their skills are not being used, sug-gesting a skills surplus. Unemployment among educated youth is both frustrating for youth and a waste of human capital. Yet African educational attainment is low compared with income peers, whether measured by years of education or test scores. Most analysts predict that SSA will need a more skilled and better suited labor force than exists today in order to absorb the new technologies being used now or about to be deployed in other parts of the developing world (Arias, Evans, and Santos 2019; African Development Bank 2020); the IWSS case studies that are analyzed in this volume predict this as well. Education is a long-term investment, and youth entering the labor force today may work for another 40 years or more. The question is not whether to continue to expand access to quality education but how to do so efficiently and affordably, building all the skills African youth need, while at the same time growing an economy that can use these skills.

In opinion surveys and focus groups, especially those conducted in more urbanized settings, African youth are as optimistic as youth in other regions (Ichikowitz Family Foundation 2020). However, youth have differing views on their desired employment outcomes. Urban youth participating in the Kenya Youth Empowerment Program reported a strong preference for a formal wage job of any kind, valuing the job security and social insurance provisions, and expressed a willingness to take lower earnings for job security (Assy et al. 2018). However, these youth did not have experience working in a factory or other private business. After engaging in this type of work in Ethiopia, youth with secondary school degrees quit their wage job, preferring to start their own business (Blattman and Dercon 2015). The African youth survey, conducted in the first half of 2019, found that about three-quarters of the mostly urban and educated youth interviewed valued technology and wanted to start their own business in the next five years, and two-thirds said that they already had a business idea (Ichikowitz Family Foundation 2020). However, these youth may underestimate the challenges they will face: An OECD (2018) study concluded that only a small fraction of youth entrepreneurs in SSA are successful, and very few end up employing others. In SSA, as in other regions, the median age of growth-oriented entrepreneurs who employ other people is 30 or above, and the average age is even higher, indicating a long tail of older entrepreneurs (Mabiso and Benfica 2019). Researchers have found that most successful entrepreneurs first work for someone else, learning business skills.

Qualitative surveys of rural African youth reveal that they struggle to make a living but remain optimistic. These surveys highlight the opportunities a growing and commercializing rural area offer youth, including the promise of using new technology to increase productivity both on and off the farm. Contrary to some narratives, SSA's youth do stay in rural areas, search for, and find productive employment opportunities (Mabiso and

Benfica 2019). A survey in rural Ghana and Uganda depicts a youth population struggling to get land for farming or capital to start a business, and not benefiting from public investments of donor projects, despite a plethora of government and donor initiatives (Williams 2017). Other evidence suggests that in countries with land still available, both farm and nonfarm sectors provide opportunities for income generation, which youth are seizing (Sumberg et al. 2020). Yeboah and others (2019) find that, while youth are getting access to land later in life than their parents owing to land scarcity and longer lifespans of their elders, in countries that have enabled land rental markets, youth are seizing this opportunity. Youth report that the most valuable livelihood skills they gained were from parents, relatives, or mentors; family and friends were also the main source of capital to start a farm or nonfarm business, in addition to youth's savings (Yeboah et al. 2020).

All over the world, women face specific difficulties in accessing productive employment (World Bank 2012), and Africa is no exception. Early marriage and childbirth interrupt human capital development and reduce income earning prospects later; they also exacerbate Africa's world-high maternal mortality. Once they enter the labor force, African women have less access to wage employment, and women's farms and businesses are on average less productive than men's, reflecting disparities in access to land, capital, and financing, along with earlier gender gaps in educational attainment (Beegle and Christiaensen 2019). Women face harassment at their place of work if it is outside the home. Women also face discrimination due to social norms around acceptable activities for women as well as underestimation of their potential. In some countries, women do not have the necessary legal rights to operate an independent business (e.g., the right to own land and assets in their own name; the right to take out a loan independent of their husband) (Beegle and Christiaensen 2019; World Bank 2019). On the World Bank's composite score of women's economic legal rights, SSA scores well above the regions of the Middle East and North Africa and South Asia (World Bank 2019). The variance is much higher than other regions, however, showing wide heterogeneity among African countries.[15] As in other regions, females of all ages spend significant time on unpaid household chores. Evidence on Africa is sketchy owing to lack of time-use data, but Beegle and Christiaensen (2019) estimate that adult women spend 2.5 to 7 times as many hours per week on domestic and care work than men.

Policy Options to Improve Employment Prospects
for Africa's Youth

Africa faces employment challenges on both the supply and demand sides, which have a negative impact on youth prospects. On the supply side, longer life expectancy combined with a slow decline in fertility has raised labor force growth to 3 percent a year in the last decade. Youth are entering the labor market with more education but fewer skills than their years of education would indicate. They are also missing some key skills (notably soft skills) owing to weaknesses in educational systems. Meanwhile, slow growth in labor demand has hindered the creation of the formal wage jobs Africa's youth desire, and what they expect their education to prepare them for. Demand for labor in formal private firms and the public sector below the fast-growing labor supply is causing informality to persist. These factors, combined with an "aspirations gap" between youth's expectations and the employment opportunities available, have led to unemployment and underemployment. Opportunities and outcomes are best in the non-RR LMICs, which provides a base for some optimism: If African countries can keep growing and transforming, opportunities will continue to improve.

As discussed above, the only way to improve youth's income-earning prospects significantly and sustainably is to improve all employment and earnings opportunities through economic transformation. Economic growth without transformation—as in resource-rich economies—is much less effective, as the outcomes in Africa's RR LMIC countries show. Transformation, through the creation of modern, higher-productivity firms, can gradually replace informal employment with formal employment in Africa. This then, is a key direction for policy to support IWSS sectors in creating more productive jobs.

The best way to increase good jobs (formal sector wage jobs) is to encourage the entrance and growth of large firms (Ciani et al. 2020). Large firms play an outsized role in economic transformation and employment creation since they tend to use newer technology, pay higher wages, and are more likely to export. They push transformation forward and support resiliency because they are better able to weather economic storms. They often structure the market for medium-sized and smaller firms operating in related sectors that will be their suppliers and retailers, thus helping to ensure their survival as well (e.g., the large automakers in the United States, Europe, Japan, and South Korea structure the auto parts supply market).

Most large firms (those employing over 100) start off large, although a few start as medium-sized firms (20–50 employees) and grow (Ciani et al. 2020). Small firms do not grow large; a firm that starts with fewer than 20 employees has a less than 1 percent chance of growing to over 100 employees, even if it survives its first five years (which they mostly do not; see Quak and Flynn 2019).

Large firms can be created through foreign direct investment or through domestic investment. But for firm creation, domestic business regulation must encourage entry. Too often, this does not happen in Africa, mostly because existing large firms exercise political power to obtain regulatory hurdles that reduce competition from new entrants. For example, in Kenya, an economy with a shortage of wage employment opportunities that should have significant firm entry, only 21 percent of firms are under five years old (World Bank 2016). Meanwhile, the correlation between productivity and employment growth is negative in Africa (Diao et al. 2021; World Bank 2016).

Firms also face other constraints in Africa, which raise costs relative to imports and increase risk for investors, reducing the creation of new formal sector wage jobs. The financial system is not performing its intermediation role effectively, as Africa has the lowest net credit to the private sector as a share of gross domestic product of any region in the world (World Bank 2020). It is expensive to operate in Africa's urban areas; as a result, they are not fulfilling their agglomeration potential (Page et al. 2020). One issue is high land prices and land transaction costs, owing to poorly functioning land tenure systems. Transportation and other logistics services prices are high in both time and money. Energy prices are among the highest in the world. While this partly reflects a major infrastructure deficit in Africa that can be traced back to colonial times, it also reflects poor management of publicly owned service providers (Bond 2016), an issue that could be addressed more quickly than building more infrastructure. The importance of constraints varies by country and sector, but the range argues for a comprehensive and long-term private sector development strategy if youth employment goals are to be achieved (Quak and Flynn 2019).

Raising productivity in the informal sector, both on the farm and off the farm, should be a priority for employment policy. Informal employment will be normal for decades, even under the best transformation scenarios, given the expected growth of the labor force relative to available and expected future wage-earning opportunities. African agriculture is characterized by low labor and land productivity but also wide variance, showing that there is widespread scope for improvements through public investment in research (to develop more resilient and productive crop and livestock varieties), and in infrastructure construction and maintenance (to reduce the cost of the long supply chains that get crops to urban and overseas markets and reduce postharvest wastage; Beegle and Christiaensen 2019). Investment in reforms and institutions that make it easier for youth to get access to land (through land sales or rentals) would also help raise productivity, as youth, with more education, can more easily adopt new technology (Mabiso and Benfica 2019). These investments should be an employment priority. Enhancing rural-urban infrastructure will also increase productivity and earnings of non-farm household businesses in rural areas and small cities or towns.

In urban areas, policies supportive of informal business could increase incomes; but urban planning in SSA rarely includes supporting this activity (Filmer and Fox 2014). Supportive policies would include, for example, providing access to convenient workspaces (including but not limited to market stalls) with adequate infrastructure (water, electricity), where customers can easily reach vendors (e.g., night markets and market spaces at bus stops) (Filmer and Fox 2014). Policies should support informal cross-border traders as well.

Improving access to digital services and increasing e-commerce opportunities—by, for example, developing efficient e-commerce payment systems—would also support informal businesses through access to banking services (mobile money), customers (gig platforms), and suppliers (placing orders). Businesses started by youth could easily adopt this technology if it is affordable, as could women, who have been shown to benefit more proportionately from such technological adoption (Ahmad et al. 2020). However, this adoption has not been widespread, in part because SSA has some of the highest costs in the world for mobile cellular and broadband service. As a percentage of gross national income (GNI) per capita, the world average monthly mobile cellular services cost is 5.7, but the African-wide average is 13 (Mabiso and Benfica 2019). In part, this reflects a lower GNI per capita, but it also reflects some of the highest prices in the world, especially for countries in West and Central Africa. Conversely, other African countries—such as Kenya, Nigeria, Guinea, and the Southern Africa Customs Union countries—have demonstrated the path to lower-cost services.

Youth-targeted interventions are tempting for donors and governments alike—after all, if youth are not getting the outcomes they want and need, why not help them? For the most part, this logic is faulty, as it ignores the source of the problem: the economy and the pace of economic transformation. By attempting to help youth, it in effect blames the victim for the difficulties (Fox et al. 2020). As a result, youth-targeted interventions, especially those focused on posteducation technical skill building, do not have a good track record in developing countries, and are rarely cost effective (Fox and Kaul 2018). African labor markets, especially in LMICs, have displayed limited absorptive capacity for skilled labor—more jobs are needed. Education and training programs do not create jobs. If a training program does manage to place youth in a wage job in an enterprise, most likely this outcome is because someone else was displaced from that job (Fox and Kaul 2018).

Few current employers cite a lack of education as a major constraint on expanding employment, but they do complain about youth lacking the employability skills (i.e., noncognitive skills and information) employers want.[16] And youth who will not be able to get a wage job and need to run a farm or a nonfarm business as their livelihood need noncognitive skills such as negotiation, a business mind-set, and the like as well. Several programs in SSA have been successful at teaching these skills and are now starting to be scaled up (Fox and Kaul 2018). The programs are supplementary for formal education systems, held either in the community after school or at schools, after normal classroom instruction ceases for the day, and seem to be cost-effective models for remedying the socioeconomic skill-building deficits in general education programs. Programs are aimed at helping youth start a business (a microenterprise) have achieved these outcomes, but there is no medium-term evidence on the success of these ventures. That these programs have been structured separately from formal educational curricula is a testament to the difficulty of achieving major change in public education systems.

Evidence suggests that women in particular benefit from developing socioemotional skills (Fox 2019). Socioemotional skills help women overcome barriers to improved employment, and to broader economic and social outcomes. Employment-related outcomes from socioemotional skill development programs include higher self-employment earnings through better negotiations with supplies and customers, and better access to wage jobs, perhaps through an increase in confidence as well as knowledge of opportunities. Other outcomes include later marriage and childbirth, and more economic empowerment within the household and community (Fox 2019; Mabiso and Benfica 2019). These results suggest a productive avenue for closing the gap between women's employment outcomes and men's.

Over the medium to long term, Africa's employment challenges could diminish if a more rapid fertility decline reduces the growth of the labor force. Although steps taken today will not pay off immediately (most of the labor force entrants for the next 20 years have already been born), countries should still make investments as they can have social benefits earlier. Many countries in SSA have a high, unmet demand for contraception, indicating a fruitful area for government expenditures. Another important policy goal should be to reduce child marriage and births to mothers under the age of 18. Achieving this goal would have payoffs in less than 20 years by reducing maternal mortality and reducing the dropout rate among teenage girls.

Conclusion

African countries, especially those that have been able to transition to LMIC status and avoid the "mineral curse," have improved their employment outcomes significantly. The long period of economic growth between 2000 and 2018 no doubt contributed considerably. The main factor that holds back progress is the lack of large-scale job creation. The main argument of this book is that IWSS sectors have the potential to generate productive jobs at scale. In addition, some factors, such as underdeveloped factor markets (land and finance), inhibit the growth of formal firms along with the informal sector; and social norms and a lack of legal rights hold women back. As David McKenzie noted in his review of active labor market programs in developing countries, urban labor markets work pretty well at matching youth (and adults) with the jobs available (McKenzie 2017).

Nonetheless, youth entering the labor market to seek employment face a system of constrained choices. These constraints include the level of economic development and transformation—which determines the growth of better employment opportunities for all, and the rate of labor force growth, which limits the share of youth who can seize those opportunities when they are created.

Africa has both an underskilling and overskilling problem. The poor quality of education systems means that years of education do not translate well into better employment outcomes, even in urban areas where the more educated labor force, especially youth, live and work. At the same time, unemployment is highest among those with the highest levels of education, and, once they enter the labor force, the well-educated are highly likely to report that their skills are not being used.

These trends suggest that African countries, especially the LMICs, have created more skills than opportunities for youth. This economic disequilibrium will not automatically be corrected by economic growth. The solution is not to reduce access to education, as youth entering the labor force today will likely have another 40 to 50 years of work. As technology changes, they will need the foundational skills that should be attained during primary and secondary education to continue to be productive. What SSA's countries need is more new firms that use a combination of high-skill and low-skill labor. Usually these are large firms with over 100 employees. Both foreign direct investment and domestic investment can create these firms, given the right incentives.

Owing to high labor force growth, the informal sector will be normal. The SSA employment agenda in LICs and LMICs needs to tackle productivity issues in this sector, both on and off the farm and in urban areas. Improving access to digital services has demonstrated its value, and should be a high priority. For the most part, this means investments and policies to lower service costs.

Other factors that will continue to hold back employment outcomes for SSA's youth, now and in the medium term, include:

- fragility and conflict—which lower economic growth, reduce public investment, and inhibit human capital development;
- poor economic governance in resource-rich economies;
- high fertility, which inhibits human capital development, crowds youth and adults into the informal sector, and, through early childbirth, negatively affects women's economic prospects; and
- laws and norms that permit or encourage early marriage and reduce economic opportunities for women.

These are medium to long-term challenges—as are the education and skills development ones—but if progress can start now, as part of a post-COVID-19-pandemic "build back better" agenda, constraints can be eased and future opportunities for youth can improve.

African youth are optimistic about their future, despite the struggles they face today in entering the labor force—which, for youth entering in 2020–22, was compounded by the COVID-19-induced recession. This optimism can be a positive force for change.

Africa still needs better data on labor market outcomes, and they need to be collected more frequently. Reliable data on earnings, especially in the agriculture and nonfarm informal sectors, are difficult to find. Recent changes in the international definition of employment are making cross-country comparisons, as well as comparisons over time, more difficult. This issue needs to be addressed flexibly.

Finally, several African countries are entering or have recently entered the resource-rich club (wherein 50 percent of their exports are minerals). Some of these RR countries now have a vibrant private sector offering opportunities in commercial agriculture and private enterprises, as well as in informal businesses, and are developing an African digital economy based on a more educated labor force (e.g., Ghana, Kenya, and Senegal). These countries should take care to avoid the mineral curse, with its negative effects on economic growth and nonmineral tradable sectors, because the subsequent negative effects on youth employment outcomes could be serious, as the data in this chapter show.

Acknowledgments

This chapter was prepared as part of the Africa Growth Initiative's Industries without Smokestacks project. The authors are grateful to Haroon Bhorat, John Page, Landry Signé, and Abebe Shimeles for helpful comments.

Appendix

Appendix 2-1. Countries Included and Surveys Used

Country	Resource/income classification	Year of survey
Angola	Lower-middle-income resource rich	2011
Benin	Low income	2011
Botswana	Upper-middle-income	2016
Burkina Faso	Low income	2014

(continued)

Appendix 2-1. (continued)

Country	Resource/income classification	Year of survey
Burundi	Low income	2013
Cameroon	Lower-middle-income resource rich	2014
Cape Verde	Lower-middle-income	2018
Central African Republic	Low income	2008
Chad	Low income	2011
Comoros	Lower-middle-income	2013
Congo, Dem. Rep.	Low income	2012
Congo, Rep.	Lower-middle-income resource rich	2011
Côte d'Ivoire	Lower-middle-income	2015
Eswatini	Lower-middle-income	2016
Ethiopia	Low income	2015
Gambia, The	Low income	2015
Ghana	Lower-middle-income	2015
Guinea	Low income	2012
Guinea-Bissau	Low income	2010
Kenya	Lower-middle-income	2016
Lesotho	Lower-middle-income	2010
Liberia	Low income	2014
Madagascar	Low income	2015
Malawi	Low income	2016
Mali	Low income	2018
Mauritania	Lower-middle-income resource rich	2014
Mauritius	Upper-middle-income	2018
Mozambique	Low income	2015
Namibia	Upper-middle-income	2018
Niger	Low income	2014
Nigeria	Lower-middle-income resource rich	2013
Rwanda	Low income	2018
Senegal	Lower-middle-income	2017
Seychelles	Upper-middle-income	2017
Sierra Leone	Low income	2014
South Africa	Upper-middle-income	2018
Sudan	Lower-middle-income resource rich	2011
Tanzania	Low income	2014
Togo	Low income	2015
Uganda	Low income	2016
Zambia	Lower-middle-income resource rich	2014
Zimbabwe	Lower-middle-income	2014

Source: Fox and Gandhi 2018.

NOTES

1. Throughout this chapter, "SSA" and Africa are used synonymously.

2. In some countries, older surveys have been used instead of recent ones to ensure that employment is measured consistently. For more details, see Fox and Gandhi (2021, appendix B).

3. World Bank 2019 data are used for income group classification. GNI per capita is below $1,026 in low-income countries, between $1,026 and $3,995 in lower-middle-income countries, and between $3,996 and $12,375 in upper-middle-income countries.

4. LMIC countries are considered resource rich if minerals accounted for at least 50 percent of goods exports from 2006 to 2010. Export data come from the Atlas of Economic Complexity initiative at Harvard University. Natural resource export share (nonrenewable resources such as oil, gas, coal, and other minerals but not agricultural commodities) was used because these data are more widely available than resource rents as a share of public expenditures or as a share of gross domestic product. Following Lashitew, Ross, and Werker 2020, the cut-off for resource rich is 50 percent; countries with a mineral export share below this level exhibit less tendency toward the "resource curse" syndromes—lower gross domestic product growth, Dutch disease, poor business environment, and less developed economic institutions, and lower human capital. The period 2006–10 was used so that the resource rich syndrome had time to unfold and infect employment outcomes.

5. In addition to a falling dependency ratio, productive jobs to boost national saving and investment are essential to fully harness the demographic dividend.

6. When measured using the standard 7-day recall, Nigerian youth labor force participation is quite low. When measured using a longer recall, as in LSMS-ISA surveys, participation rates are about 50 percent. For more details see Fox and Gandhi (2021, appendix B).

7. In the other regions, most of the surveys analyzed in the study were from middle income countries (LMICs and UMICS).

8. The countries included are Ethiopia, Malawi, Niger, Nigeria, Tanzania, and Uganda.

9. For a discussion of types of wage work and nonwage work, including risks and opportunities, see https://ilostat.ilo.org/resources/methods/classification-status-at-work/.

10. Measured by the World Bank's Doing Business Index, the highest SSA LMIC ranking is that of Kenya, at 56; the next four are Côte d'Ivoire, at 110; Ghana, at 118; Lesotho, at 122; and Senegal, at 123. Among the LMIC RRs, the highest is Zambia, at 85; the next four are Nigeria, at 131; Mauritania, at 152; Cameroon, at 167, and Sudan, at 171. See http://documents.worldbank.org/curated/en/688761571934946384/pdf/Doing-Business-2020-Comparing-Business-Regulation-in-190-Economies.pdf.

11. On average, wage jobs are better paying than nonwage jobs. Women in LMICs who are below age 30—an age where they would be more likely to have young children at home—are less likely to participate in the labor force than women in LICs (figure 2-6). One would expect that lower-earning women would be more likely to be out of the labor force when taking care of children if they can, as the opportunity cost of being out of the labor force would be lower.

12. High reservation wages among well-educated youth may be another reason for higher unemployment, as discussed above and by Filmer and Fox 2014.

13. Globally, the majority of nonfarm wage employment in developing countries is found in urban areas, and the majority of hours worked in wage employment take place there (Dolislager et al. 2020).

14. See https://worldpopulationreview.com/countries/total-fertility-rate/.

15. Sudan is the lowest-ranking country in SSA, with a score only slightly above that of Saudi Arabia, while Mauritius is the highest-ranking country—it has the same score as Germany, and a higher score than the United States.

16. This finding emerged in all the IWSS case studies.

REFERENCES

Abdychev, A., C. Alonso, M. E. Alper, M. D. Desruelle, S. Kothari, Y. Liu, M. Perinet, S. Rehman, and M. A. Schimmelpfennig. 2018. *The Future of Work in Sub-Saharan Africa*. Washington: International Monetary Fund.

African Development Bank. 2019. *African Economic Outlook 2019*. Abidjan: African Development Bank. https://www.afdb.org/en/documents/document/african-economic-outlook-aeo-2019-107319.

———. 2020. *African Economic Outlook 2020*. Abidjan: African Development Bank.

Ahmad, H. A., C. Green, F. Jiang. 2020. "Mobile Money, Financial Inclusion and Development: A Review with Reference to African Experience." *Journal of Economic Surveys* 34: 753–792.

Altenburg, T., S. Bilal, G. Maci, and W. te Velde. 2018. *A Rapier Not a Blunderbuss: Why the EU Must Do Better in Supporting African Job Creation*. Brussels: European Think Tanks Group. https://ecdpm.org//wp-content/uploads/ETTG-A-rapier-not-a-blunderbuss-Why-the-EU-must-do-better-in-supporting-African-job-creation-february-2018-.pdf.

Arias, O., D. K. Evans, and I. Santos. 2019. *The Skills Balancing Act in Sub-Saharan Africa: Investing in Skills for Productivity, Inclusivity, and Adaptability*. Washington: World Bank.

Assaad, R. B. 2019. "Public Employment in the Middle East and North Africa." IZA World of Labor.

Assy, A. E., T. Ribeiro, D. Robalino, F. Rosati, M. L. S., Puerta, and M. Weber. 2018. *The Jobs That Youth Want and the Support They Need to Get Them:*

Evidence from a Discrete Choice Experiment in Kenya. Bonn: IZA Institute of Labor Economics.

Beegle, K., and L. Christiaensen. 2019. *Accelerating Poverty Reduction in Africa*. Washington: World Bank.

Blattman, C., and S. Dercon. 2015. "More Sweatshops for Africa? A Randomized Trial of Industrial Jobs and Self-Employment." Unpublished paper.

Bloom, D. E., D. Canning, G. Fink, and J. E. Finlay. 2009. "Fertility, Female Labor Force Participation, and the Demographic Dividend." *Journal of Economic Growth* 14: 79–101.

Bond, J. 2016. "Infrastructure in Africa." *Global Journal of Emerging Market Economies* 8: 309–33.

Bongaarts, J. 2017. "Africa's Unique Fertility Transition." *Population and Development Review* 43: 39–58. https://doi.org/10.1111/j.1728-4457.2016.00164.x.

Bridges, S., L. Fox, A. Gaggero, and T. Owens. 2016. "Youth Unemployment and Earnings in Africa: Evidence from Tanzanian Retrospective Data." *Journal of African Economies* 26: 119–39. https://doi.org/10.1093/jae/ejw020.

Carranza, E., R. Garlick, K. Orkin, and N. Rankin. 2020. *Job Search and Hiring with Two-Sided Limited Information about Workseekers' Skills*. Policy Research Working Paper 9345. Washington: World Bank.

Ciani, A., M. C. Hyland, N. Karalashvili, J. L. Keller, A. Ragoussis, and T. Tran. 2020. *Making It Big : Why Developing Countries Need More Large Firms*. Washington: World Bank. https://openknowledge.worldbank.org/handle/10986/34430.

de la Brière, B., B. Filmer, D. Ringold, D. Rohner, K. Samuda, and A. Denisova. 2017. *Human Capital in Resource-Rich Countries*. Washington: World Bank.

Diao, X., M. Ellis, M. McMillan, and D. Rodrik. 2021. *Africa's Manufacturing Puzzle: Evidence from Tanzanian and Ethiopian Firms*. NBER Working Paper 28344. Cambridge. MA: National Bureau of Economic Research.

Dolislager, M., T. Reardon, A. Arslan, L. Fox, S. Liverpool-Tasie, C. Sauer, and D. L. Tschirley. 2020. "Youth and Adult Agrifood System Employment in Developing Regions: Rural (Peri-urban to Hinterland) vs. Urban." *Journal of Development Studies* 0: 1–23. https://doi.org/10.1080/00220388.2020.1808198.

Filmer, D., and L. Fox. 2014. *Youth Employment in Sub-Saharan Africa*. Washington: World Bank. http://elibrary.worldbank.org/doi/book/10.1596/978-1-4648-0107-5.

Fox, L. 2019. *Economic Participation of Rural Youth: What Matters?* SSRN 3521170.

Fox, L., and D. Gandhi. 2018. "Youth Employment in Sub-Saharan Africa: Progress and Prospects." Africa Growth Initiative Working Paper 26, Brookings. www.brookings.edu/articles/youth-employment-in-sub-saharan-africa-progress-and-prospects/.

Fox, L, and U. Kaul. 2018. *The Evidence Is In: How Should Youth Employment Programs in Low-Income Countries Be Designed?* World Bank Policy Research Working Paper 8500. https://doi.org/10.1596/1813-9450-8500.

Fox, L., and T. P. Sohnesen. 2016. "Household Enterprises and Poverty Reduction in Sub-Saharan Africa." *Development Policy Review* 34: 197–221. https://doi.org/10.1111/dpr.12152.

Frankel, J. A. 2012. "The Natural Resource Curse: A Survey of Diagnoses and Some Prescriptions." HKS Faculty Research Working Paper Series.

Handel, M. J., A. Valerio, and M. L. Sánchez Puerta. 2016. *Accounting for Mismatch in Low-and Middle-Income Countries: Measurement, Magnitudes, and Explanations.* Washington: World Bank.

Hartrich, Steve. 2018. *Can We Create Better Jobs in Africa's Booming Construction Sector? Looking to Market Systems Analysis to Point Us in the Right Direction.* Geneva: International Labor Organization. http://www.ilo.org/empent/areas/value-chain-development-vcd/briefs-and-guides/WCMS_652333/lang--en/index.htm.

Heckman, J., and T. Kautz. 2013. *Fostering and Measuring Skills: Interventions That Improve Character and Cognition.* NBER Working Paper 19656. Cambridge. MA: National Bureau of Economic Research. http://www.nber.org/papers/w19656.

Ichikowitz Family Foundation. 2020. *The Rise of Afro-optimism: African Youth Survey 2020.* https://ichikowitzfoundation.com/wp-content/uploads/2020/02/African-Youth-Survey-2020.pdf.

ILO (International Labor Organization). 2013. *Resolution I—Resolution Concerning Statistics of Work, Employment and Labour Underutilization.*

IMF (International Monetary Fund). 2022. *World Economic Outlook Update.* https://www.imf.org/en/Publications/WEO/Issues/2022/01/25/world-economic-outlook-update-january-2022.

Klasen, S., J. Pieters, M. Santos Silva, N. Tu, and L. Thi. 2019. "What Drives Female Labor Force Participation? Comparable Micro-Level Evidence from Eight Developing and Emerging Economies." IZA Insitute of Labor Economics. https://docs.iza.org/dp12067.pdf.

La Porta, R., and A. Shleifer. 2014. "Informality and Development." *Journal of Economic Perspectives* 28. https://www.aeaweb.org/articles?id=10.1257/jep.28.3.109.

Lashitew, A. A., M. L. Ross, and E. Werker. 2020. "What Drives Successful Economic Diversification in Resource-Rich Countries?" *World Bank Research Observer.*

Mabiso, A., and R. Benfica. 2019. "The Narrative on Rural Youth and Economic Opportunities in Africa: Facts, Myths and Gaps." IFAD Research Series 61.

Mason, A., R. Lee, M. Abrigo, and S. H. Lee. 2017. "Support Ratios and Demographic Dividends: Estimates for the World." Population Division, United Nations, New York.

McKenzie, D. 2017. "How Effective Are Active Labor Market Policies in Developing Countries? A Critical Review of Recent Evidence." *World Bank Research Observer* 32: 127–54.

Newfarmer, R., J. Page, and F. Tarp. 2019. *Industries without Smokestacks: Industrialization in Africa Reconsidered.* Oxford University Press.

OECD (Organization for Economic Cooperation and Development). 2018. *The Future of Rural Youth in Developing Countries.* Paris: OECD Publishing. https://www.oecd.org/en/publications/the-future-of-rural-youth-in-developing-countries_9789264298521-en.html.

Page, J., J. Gutman, P. Madden, and D. Gandhi. 2020. "Urban Economic Growth in Africa: A Framework for Analyzing Constraints to Agglomeration." Brookings. www.brookings.edu/research/urban-economic-growth-in-africa-a-framework-for-analyzing-constraints-to-agglomeration/.

Palmer, R. 2017. "Jobs and Skills Mismatch in the Informal Economy." http://www.ilo.org/skills/pubs/WCMS_629018/lang--en/index.htm.

Quak, E., and J. Flynn. 2019. *Private Sector Development Interventions and Better-Quality Job Creation for Youth in Africa.* https://opendocs.ids.ac.uk/opendocs/handle/20.500.12413/14907.

Ray, J., and N. Espiova. 2017. *Millions of Women Worldwide Would Like to Join the Workforce.* https://news.gallup.com/poll/205439/millions-women-worldwide-join-workforce.aspx.

Rodrik, D. 2015. *Premature Deindustrialization.* NBER Working Paper 20935. Cambridge. MA: National Bureau of Economic Research. http://www.nber.org/papers/w20935.

Sumberg, J., J. Chamberlin, J. Flynn, D. Glover, and V. Johnson. 2020. "Landscapes of Rural Youth Opportunity." IFAD Research Series 47, http://dx.doi.org/10.2139/ssrn.3521380.

UNICEF. 2020. *Online Dataset: Child Marriage.* Data set. https://data.unicef.org/topic/child-protection/child-marriage.

Williams, T. 2017. *Invisible Lives: Five Takekways from New Research.* New York: MasterCard Foundation. https://mastercardfdn.org/research/invisible-lives-five-takeaways-from-new-research/.

World Bank. 2012. *World Development Report 2013: Jobs.* Washington: World Bank.

———. 2016. *Kenya: Jobs for Youth.* Social Protection and Labor Global Practice. Washington: World Bank.

———. 2018. *World Development Report 2018: Learning to Realize Education's Promise.* Washington: World Bank.

———. 2019. *Women, Business and the Law 2019 : A Decade of Reform*. Washington: World Bank. https://openknowledge.worldbank.org/handle/10986/31.

———. 2020. "World Development Indicators 2020." https://datacatalog. worldbank.org/dataset/world-development-indicators.

Yeboah, T., E. Chigumira, I. John, N. A. Anyidoho, V. Manyong, J. Flynn, and J. Sumberg. 2020. "Hard Work and Hazard: Young People and Agricultural Commercialisation in Africa." *Journal of Rural Studies*.

Yeboah, F. K., T. S. Jayne, M. Muyanga, and J. Chamberlin. 2019. "Youth Access to Land, Migration and Employment Opportunities: Evidence from Sub-Saharan Africa." IFAD Research Series 53.

THREE

Rwanda

Harnessing the Power of the Next Generation

RICHARD NEWFARMER AND ANNA TWUM

Structural Transformation and Job Creation:
The Past as Prelude to the Future

Young workers hold the promise of future growth in Rwanda. High, if declining, fertility rates, together with sharp reductions in child mortality, have propelled rapid increases in population and a young labor force. In the last half-decade, the labor force has grown at just under 3 percent annually. Fully half the population is younger than 19 years. With 70 percent of the labor force located in rural areas, the epicenter of high fertility rates, and already with one of the highest rural density on the continent, pressures on land are enormous. The economy must therefore grow rapidly—*and for decades*—to create the number of jobs necessary to pull youth, women, and other new labor market entrants into productive activities that will raise living standards.

In the last two decades, the Rwandan economy has indeed grown rapidly; with growth in output at close to 8 percent annually since 2000, Rwanda has generally been featured among the most rapidly growing economies on the continent. A distinctive feature of Rwanda's post-1994 economic growth is the peculiar form of structural transformation; workers have progressively moved out of agriculture, but not into manufacturing—the pattern of growth in East Asia and today's high-income countries—but rather into services (Ggombe and Newfarmer 2017).

This "services-first" pattern of industrial transformation prompts several questions: Can Rwanda generate sufficient productivity growth without relying on a surge in manufacturing to drive overall economic growth? Can it produce exports necessary to power growth, the ultimate determinant of rising average wages? And finally, can it produce a sufficient number of high-productivity jobs to raise incomes, especially of young, women, and unskilled workers?

Indeed, the strongest growth opportunities exist in commodity-based agro-processing and services trade—what we have called "industries without smokestacks" (IWSS) (Newfarmer, Page, and Tarp 2018). *A central premise for this study is that these activities can lead the structural transformation process in tandem with manufacturing growth.* Much as with smokestack industries, agribusiness and food processing, two examples of IWSS, employ both unskilled and semiskilled workers, require less physical capital per unit of output, are tradable, and exhibit high returns from the application of new technology. Moreover, many of these sectors' products are traded regionally (e.g., food products and, beverages) because they are responsive to local tastes, are bulky to transport or require proximity to raw materials. Services exports, another IWSS sector, already amounting to half Rwanda's export earnings, are central to its future, and include tourism and higher-skill services such as business process outsourcing, health care, and higher education.

Overview: The Rwandan Labor Market

According to the National Institute of Statistics of Rwanda (NISR) Household Survey, of the 11.8 million Rwandans in 2017, some 6.8 million were of working age—that is, between the age of 16 and 65 years.[1] Of these, 5.9 million were economically active and 5.8 million were employed. Women outnumbered men in the employed labor force by about 7 percentage points, a probable legacy of the 1994 genocide, when men were disproportionately killed. Some three-quarters of the labor force participated actively, and unemployed workers numbered about 100,000, amounting to an unemployment rate of about 5.3 percent, according to the government's narrow definition. Youth unemployment was higher, but not dramatically so, at 7.9 percent.[2]

The largest share of the labor force is in agriculture: about 40 percent (excluding subsistence agriculture) and 70 percent (including subsistence agriculture). The NISR does not include subsistence farmers in in its labor force surveys, conducted after 2016. In this study, we capture the population of subsistence farmers since we rely mostly on household surveys that not only have a more comprehensive coverage but also date back to 2000, with three benchmark years: 2000, 2010, and 2017.

Nonetheless, some of the descriptive statistics from the narrower labor force surveys are worth noting. Based on the most recent survey report for 2019, unemployment affects 15.2 percent of the labor force, while 26.8 percent of employed workers deal with time-related underemployment. Women, the rural population, youth, and mature middle-aged people are more likely to be out of the labor force. Women are close to 17 percentage points more likely to be unemployed than men (45 percent vs. 62 percent labor force participation), as they more frequently engage in unreported subsistence agriculture and unpaid domestic labor. The rural population is more likely to be out of the labor force than the urban population (49 percent vs. 67 percent labor participation rate), due to a higher likelihood of participation in subsistence agriculture and more limited access to job opportunities. Finally, youth and mature middle age persons, having received only a limited education, are also less likely to be integrated into the labor force (although a significant share of youth who are out of labor force will be in education full time). Underemployment is more prevalent in rural areas, compared with urban ones. Rural workers experience similar unemployment to urbanites (15.2 percent vs. 15.3 percent). However, they are almost three times more likely to be underemployed (31.9 percent vs. 12 percent), due to high temporality and the seasonality of agricultural employment and scarcity of opportunities in rural areas (RLFS 2019).

The Future Challenge: Creating Jobs for an Expanding Population

With a current population of nearly 13 million and a population growth rate of 2.1 percent annually, Rwanda has to create jobs at a rapid rate to absorb new workers coming into the labor force. The NISR estimates that

Table 3-1. Workers Will Be Looking for Jobs in Cities in the Coming Decade: Working Age and Youth Employment, 2020–32 (thousands)

	2020	2032	No. of additional jobs	% increase	Annual growth
Working age (15–64)	7,171	9,824	2,653	37.0	2.7
Urban	1,750	3,218	1,468	83.9	5.2
Rural	5,421	6,605	1,184	21.8	1.7
Youth (15–24)	2,576	3,059	483	18.8	1.4
Urban	653	1,057	404	61.9	4.1
Rural	1,922	2,001	79	4.1	0.3
Memo:					
Total	12,663	16,332	3,669	29.0	2.1
Urban	2,773	4,900	2,127	76.7	4.9
Rural	9,890	11,433	1,543	15.6	1.2

Source: NISR Populations Projections (2018).

the working-age population will be one-third of total population, and the urban workforce will increase by more than 80 percent in the next 12 years. This means of the 2.7 million jobs that will be needed, and some 1.5 million will have to be in cities (table 3-1).

The challenge will be not in creating jobs but in creating *good* jobs— that is, ones with progressively higher productivity. In poor countries, nearly everyone who can work does. As in other low-income countries, in Rwanda, citizens cannot rely on social insurance or transfers, as they can in rich countries. In slow-growing countries with an expanding labor force, new entrants typically find work in low-productivity jobs. The answer to whether this is likely to happen in Rwanda depends in large measure on the recent pattern of growth.

Growth, Productivity, and Employment:
Two Decades of Structural Transformation

Fortunately, Rwanda's process of structural transformation has involved the movement of workers and capital into progressively higher-productivity activities; a pattern that has not followed the conventional path of agriculture to industry to services. Instead, structural transformation has involved growing employment in a host of activities that have manufacturing-like characteristics. These IWSS sectors tend to create jobs at a rate faster than subsistence agriculture, have a higher productivity, be tradable, and exhibit rapid technological change.

A look at Rwanda's employment dynamics shows that employment in IWSS sectors has grown more rapidly than the rest of the economy. Table 3-2 shows the relative growth of IWSS, manufacturing, and non-IWSS sectors using the benchmarks of household surveys conducted in 2000 and 2016. The share of labor in subsistence agriculture has progressively declined since 2000—from 87 to 67 percent. The high-employment growth sectors were agro-processing, horticulture, and export agriculture; business and financial services; tourism; and construction. These sectors, which employed only 5 percent of the population in 2000, nearly more than tripled in size, to 16 percent, by 2017.

These trends accelerated in the 2010–17 period. The IWSS activities accounted for about a third of new jobs created, compared with a much smaller share in the first half of the period.[3] Rwanda is only now beginning to develop its manufacturing sector, so the sector's contribution to employment—while growing at more than twice the rate of overall employment—still amounted to only 1 percent of total employment in 2016 (table 3-2).

Out of Agriculture into Activities with a Higher Labor Productivity

Shifts out of agriculture have transformed the structure of the Rwandan economy. Labor productivity in agriculture—outside horticulture and export crops, such as coffee, tea, and pyrethrum—has remained low, so workers have migrated to other activities where they could find better jobs. In 2017, labor productivity in subsistence agriculture was RWF 0.42 million per worker, only one-fifth of the levels in the IWSS and manufacturing sectors.

IWSS sectors are about twice as productive as the economy as a whole (figure 3-1). In 2017, labor productivity, defined as value added per worker, in the IWSS sectors was relatively close to that of manufacturing and was more than five times more productive than other non-IWSS sectors. The reduction in employment share for the non-IWSS sectors is mostly from the reduction in the share of workers in agriculture. However, subsistence agriculture continues to be a major employer, followed by informal trade and the domestic services sector—a largely informal sector employing about the same number of workers as the construction sector (table 3-2).

Table 3-2. IWSS Have Grown More Rapidly Than Manufacturing and Other Activities

	Employment (thousands)			Employment share		Annual % growth
	2000/2001	2016/2017	Change	2000/2001	2016/2017	2000–2017
Total employment	3,796	5,825	2,030	100%	100%	3%
Total IWSS	201	922	721	5%	16%	9%
Export crops and horticulture	92	140	48	2%	2%	3%
Agro-processing	5	35	30	0%	1%	12%
Construction	26	255	229	1%	4%	14%
Tourism	17	157	141	0%	3%	14%
ICT	—	12	12	—	0%	—
Transportation	25	151	126	1%	3%	11%
Maintenance and repairs	11	35	24	0%	1%	7%
Financial and business services	15	49	34	0%	1%	7%
Trade (excl. tourism): formal	10	86	76	0%	1%	13%

Manufacturing (excl. agro-processing)	25	85	60	1%	1%	7%
Other Non-IWSS	3,569	4,818	1,249	94%	83%	2%
Agriculture	3,296	3,926	630	87%	67%	1%
Mining	6	51	45	0%	1%	13%
Utilities	4	11	6	0%	0%	5%
Trade (excl. tourism): informal	82	296	215	2%	5%	8%
Domestic services	82	239	157	2%	4%	7%
Government	71	202	130	2%	3%	6%
Other	28	94	66	1%	2%	7%

Source: Authors' calculations using National Institute of Statistics of Rwanda Integrated Household Survey: EICV1, EICV3, EICV4.

Note: Numbers might not match published reports. Details of adjustments are not available for replication. Working age population is defined as 16 years and over by the NISR. Employment for "export crops and horticulture" and "tourism" are estimated using Aragie and others (2017). Employment for ICT is not reported in 2000. Agriculture includes subsistence agriculture. Employment in trade (formal and informal) is estimated using ratios of employment from the Rwanda Establishment Census.

FIGURE 3-1. **Labor Productivity for IWSS, Like Manufacturing, Is Higher Than for Non-IWSS**

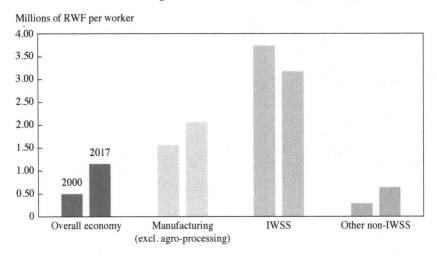

Source: Authors' calculations using EICV1, EICV3, EICV5, and Rwanda National Accounts.

Note: IWSS = industries without smokestacks.

The IWSS sectors have labor productivity levels comparable to manufacturing, RWF 3.4 million per worker, as compared with RWF 2.1 million. Within the IWSS grouping, the highest productivity levels are found in financial and business services, information and communications technology (ICT), and agro-processing. Horticulture and formal trade are not as high, but even these sectors have labor productivity levels that surpass those in noncommercial agriculture. The IWSS activities are not the only high-productivity areas of employment with higher productivity. Mining, utilities, government, and other categories all present higher labor productivity than noncommercial agriculture.[4]

Structural Change Has Been Growth-Enhancing

As workers have moved out of noncommercial agriculture into higher-productivity activities, the economy has grown at rates of about 8 percent annually. However, Rwanda has experienced some volatility in growth rates, mainly because of weather-induced fluctuations in agricultural production in the 2000–2016 period. Nonetheless, the extent of structural transformation has been impressive (figure 3-2).

The size of the bubbles in figure 3-2 corresponds to the size of sectoral employment in 2017, and the quadrants show low-productivity sectors

FIGURE 3-2. Labor Is Moving into Higher-Productivity Activities, Led by IWSS

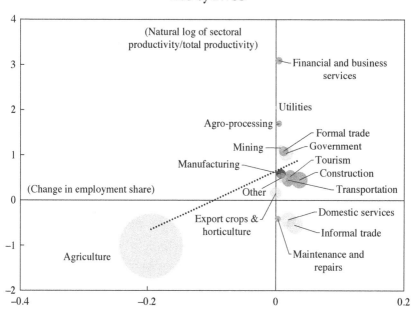

Source: Authors' calculations using National Household Surveys 3 and 5, and Rwanda's National Accounts. The sizes of the bubbles equal the employment share in 2017.

with declining employment in the left lower quadrant contrasted with high-productivity, increasing employment sectors in the top right quadrant. The upward-sloping regression line demonstrates that structural transformation has been sharply positive. The light gray bubbles indicate the IWSS sectors, the dark gray bubbles are manufacturing, and the medium gray bubbles are the other non-IWSS activities. While workers in manufacturing have relatively high productivity compared with those in traditional agriculture, the IWSS sectors collectively employ many more people. In effect, to date, they have played a far more important role in the growth process of Rwanda than has manufacturing.

As workers have moved from subsistence agriculture into other activities, labor productivity in agriculture has risen somewhat, with fewer workers associated with the same or rising production. Correspondingly, labor productivity rates fell slightly in the 2010–16 period with the entry of additional workers, as is evident in trends for agro-processing, tourism, transportation, and formal trade. Still, the sectors that are gaining workers have a higher productivity than subsistence agriculture.

Growth Creates Jobs

Between 2000 and 2017, growth in value added of the IWSS sectors resulted in more jobs than value-added growth in non-IWSS sectors, including manufacturing. Sectoral employment elasticity measures—a measure of the responsiveness of employment to value-added growth—provide another way to measure job creation and labor intensity. Using value-added and employment estimates from 2000 and 2017, we estimate an economy-wide employment elasticity of 0.21.[5] The lowest elasticity is observed in the non-IWSS sectors excluding manufacturing, estimated to be about 0.17 (table 3-3). The IWSS sectors show employment elasticities close to double those of the manufacturing sector, indicating that the growth in IWSS sectors has translated into stronger employment growth relative to other sectors (table 3-3). Said differently, IWSS has increased its value added by 278 percent but increased its share of employment by 358 percent.

Not only have IWSS sectors been strong drivers of growth, but they have also intensely created jobs for women and young people in particular. Compared with non-IWSS and manufacturing, IWSS sectors have an elasticity of 1.26, significantly higher than the elasticity for the overall economy of 0.04 and about double that of manufacturing, which is about 0.56. We observe a similar trend for youth employment. Once again, IWSS emerges as a strong generator of jobs for youth, followed by non-IWSS sectors and the manufacturing sector. These findings position IWSS sectors as an important tool for government policy to boost employment for women and the youth.

Growth in IWSS sector exports have outpaced growth in non-IWSS sectors, with the strongest growth coming from tourism, horticulture, and agro-processing. Table 3-4 breaks down export revenues in 2011 and 2017, revealing a reliance of the economy on exports from IWSS sectors: 60 and 61 percent of total formal exports, respectively; the majority of these exports are concentrated in services, coffee, and tea. Non-IWSS sectors—mainly manufacturing (excluding agro-processing), government services, and mining—made up about 38 and 42 percent of formal exports in 2011 and 2017 but grew more slowly or at about the same pace as IWSS sectors.

IWSS Sectors Demand Greater Skills

Although IWSS sectors are relatively more skill intensive than non-IWSS sectors, they also emerge as significant employers of low-skilled labor, employing nearly 13 percent of the 4.8 million low-skilled workers in 2017

Table 3-3. Growth and Jobs: A Sectoral Perspective

| Sector | 2000–2017 | | | 2010–2017 |
	Change in GDP	Change in employment	Employment elasticity	Women employment elasticity	Youth employment elasticity
Overall economy	256%	53%	0.21	0.04	0.08
Total IWSS	278%	358%	1.10	1.26	0.28
Export crops and horticulture	118%	52%	0.44	5.87	0.28
					0.15
Agro-processing	181%	618%	3.41	3.92	1.95
Construction	494%	879%	1.78	0.42	0.24
Tourism	707%	839%	1.19	0.81	0.18
ICT	—	—		—	—
Transportation	642%	501%	0.78	-0.08	0.05
Maintenance and repairs	335%	217%	0.65	-0.03	0.54
Financial and business services	181%	220%	1.22	0.32	0.24
Trade (excl. tourism): formal	387%	755%	1.95	1.95	0.14

(continued)

Table 3-3. (continued)

Sector	2000–2017				2010–2017
	Change in GDP	Change in employment	Employment elasticity	Women employment elasticity	Youth employment elasticity
Manufacturing (excl. agro-processing)	350%	240%	0.69	0.56	−0.13
Other Non-IWSS	206%	35%	0.18	0.01	0.07
Agriculture	145%	19%	0.13	−0.03	0.06
Mining	541%	752%	1.39	0.09	−0.01
Utilities	24%	143%	5.85	−3.85	0.33
Trade (excl. tourism): informal	387%	262%	0.68	0.68	0.21
Domestic services	644%	193%	0.30	0.21	0.06
Government	311%	182%	0.59	0.30	−0.15
Other	644%	231%	0.36	0.15	−0.08

Source: Authors' calculations using EICV1, EICV3, EICV5 and Rwanda National Accounts.

Note: Employment elasticity is defined by measures the growth of employment relative to the growth of the economy. Value added is approximated for sectors not directly reported in the national accounts. For export crops and horticulture, value added is estimated using Aragie and others (2017). Employment numbers for ICT are not reported in 2000. Employment elasticity for 2010–2017 is 0.93. Youth employment elasticities are calculated for 2010–2017 because of issues verifying the youth employment number for 2000.

Table 3-4. IWSS Exports Have Powered Rwandan Growth in the Last Decade

	2011		2017		2011–2017
	USD million	Share	USD million	Share	Annual % growth
Industries without smokestacks (IWSS)	552	60%	1255	61%	15%
IWSS services exports	392	43%	943	46%	16%
Transportation	51	6%	194	9%	25%
Tourism	252	27%	438	21%	10%
Telecommunication	53	6%	19	1%	−16%
Reexports	37	4%	292	14%	41%
IWSS goods exports	160	17%	311	15%	12%
Horticulture	3	0%	16	1%	32%
Coffee and tea	130	14%	154	8%	3%
Other agricultural products	6	1%	8	0%	4%
Agro-processing	21	2%	60	3%	19%
Manufacturing	46	5%	58	3%	4%
Light manufacturing	6	1%	14	1%	17%
Textiles	13	1%	14	1%	1%
Other manufacturing	27	3%	30	1%	2%
Non-IWSS	323	35%	740	36%	15%
Mining	165	18%	392	19%	16%
Government and other services	158	17%	348	17%	14%
Total exports (goods and services)	922	100%	2053	100%	14%

Source: Authors' calculations using data from National Bank of Rwanda (2017) and ASYCUDA.

Note: Authors' calculations from ASCYUDA data do not include adjustments from export surveys.

(table 3-5), compared with the 1.3 percent employed by the manufacturing sector.[6] About 26 percent of workers in IWSS are either high-skilled (5 percent) or medium-skilled workers (21 percent), with the financial, business services, and ICT sectors emerging as the most skill intensive of the IWSS sectors. IWSS sectors with the highest share of low-skilled workers are formal trade, export crops, horticulture, maintenance, and repairs (table 3-5). The skill breakdown of IWSS sectors more or less parallels the skill distribution in the manufacturing sectors. Conversely, non-IWSS sectors are more low-skill-intensive, with only 16 percent of

Table 3-5. Jobs in IWSS, Like Manufacturing, Tend to Require Higher Skills: Breakdown of Sectoral Employment by Skill Level, 2017

	Absolute			Share		
	High skilled	Skilled	Low skilled	High skilled	Skilled	Low skilled
	('000)					
Total employment	157	760	4,827	3%	13%	84%
Total IWSS	37	177	628	4%	21%	75%
Export crops and horticulture	1	16	141	0%	10%	90%
Agro-processing	2	8	26	5%	21%	74%
Construction	9	59	187	3%	23%	73%
Tourism	6	25	29	9%	42%	48%
ICT	4	5	3	33%	43%	24%
Transportation	4	37	111	3%	24%	73%
Maintenance and repairs	1	7	28	2%	19%	80%
Financial and business services	11	18	20	23%	36%	41%
Trade (excl. tourism): formal	1	3	82	1%	4%	95%
Manufacturing (excl. agro-processing)	2	19	63	3%	23%	74%
Other non-IWSS	117	563	4,137	2%	12%	86%
Agriculture	13	389	3,523	0%	10%	90%
Mining	0	5	46	0%	9%	91%
Utilities	2	5	4	14%	51%	35%
Trade (excl. tourism): informal	0	13	284	0%	4%	96%
Domestic services	2	38	199	1%	16%	83%
Government	79	84	38	39%	42%	19%
Other	21	30	43	23%	32%	45%

Source: Authors' calculations using EICV1, EICV3, EICV5.

Note: Totals of sectors by skill level do not match totals presented in table 3-1 because of missing information on education. High skilled = post-secondary education; skilled = secondary education; low skilled = lower than secondary education.

workers falling in the high-skilled and skilled categories; government and utilities sectors are exceptions, with most workers considered skilled and high skilled (around 80 and 65 percent), respectively.

Scenarios for the Future: Emerging Demand for Skilled Workers

What does the future hold? This section presents a "business-as-usual" scenario to estimate the labor demand and skill distribution of the Rwandan labor force in 2035, if the economy maintains an average annual growth rate of 8 percent, similar to its past performance. The government, working with the World Bank, put together an aspirational growth scenario, calibrated so that Rwanda could become an upper-middle-income country by 2035. It is indeed aspirational, in that the scenario entails historically high growth rates roughly equivalent to those China experienced after its 1978 reforms—between a 10 and 12 percent annual growth rate in gross domestic product (GDP). Under the scenario, we look at how employment trends evolve for the IWSS, manufacturing, and non-IWSS sectors along with changes to the sectoral skill distribution.

GDP estimates for IWSS and non-IWSS sectors are projected by decomposing an overall economic growth rate of 8 percent to growth rates at the sectoral level based on past performance and projection from the Ministry of Finance. Using the employment shares and elasticities emerging from the two recent household surveys (2010–11 to 2016–17) as parameters for the aggregates, we project employment growth to 2035 based on the projected growth of IWSS and other sectors to construct a sectoral distribution of employment in 2035 based on labor force projections from the government (table 3-6).[7]

In this illustrative scenario, with an overall annual GDP growth of 8 percent, employment is projected to grow at an annual rate of 3 percent (the elasticity for the whole economy between 2017 and 2035 is 0.37). The IWSS sectors are projected to grow at a rate slightly higher than that of the economy (10 percent), and non-IWSS sectors other than manufacturing would grow at a slower pace of 6 percent, primarily because of the much lower growth rate needed in subsistence agriculture due to structural transformation. Based on projections, agro-processing, tourism, ICT, and transportation—all priority sectors under the government's development agenda—will lead growth in IWSS value added in 2035.

Table 3-6. A Growth Scenario to 2035: Projected GDP at 8 Percent and Labor Demand in 2035

	GDP			Employment				Share of total employment	
	2017	2035 (proj)	Annual growth	2017	2035 (proj)	Add. jobs	Annual growth	2017	2035 (proj)
	billions RWF	billions RWF		('000)	('000)	('000)			
Overall economy	6,692	26,642	8%	5,825	9,825	3,999	3%	100%	100%
Total IWSS	3,139	16,099	10%	922	3,463	2,541	8%	16%	35%
Export crops and horticulture	188	754	8%	140	500	360	7%	2%	5%
Agro-processing	222	1,443	11%	35	240	204	11%	1%	2%
Construction: formal and informal	460	2,160	9%	255	901	646	7%	4%	9%
Tourism	306	2,001	11%	157	685	527	9%	3%	7%
ICT	115	1,037	13%	12	100	88	12%	0%	1%
Transportation	272	1,282	9%	151	486	335	7%	3%	5%
Maintenance and repairs	27	65	5%	35	63	27	3%	1%	1%
Financial and business services	1,254	5,955	9%	49	209	160	8%	1%	2%
Trade (excl. tourism): formal	295	1,401	9%	86	280	194	7%	1%	3%

Manufacturing (excl. agro-processing)	175	1,118	11%	85	442	358	10%	1%	5%
Other Non-IWSS	3,125	9,426	6%	4,818	5,919	1,100	1%	83%	60%
Agriculture	1,639	3,713	5%	3,926	4,391	465	1%	67%	45%
Mining	186	1,036	10%	51	139	88	6%	1%	1%
Utilities	95	529	10%	11	16	5	2%	0%	0%
Trade (excl. tourism): informal	196	648	7%	296	478	181	3%	5%	5%
Domestic services	178	990	10%	239	408	169	3%	4%	4%
Government	653	1,570	5%	202	332	130	3%	3%	3%
Other	178	938	10%	94	156	62	3%	2%	2%

Source: Authors' calculations using EICV1, EICV3, EICV5 and Rwanda National accounts.

Note: Employment projections are based on projected employment elasticities and GDP in 2035.

These growth dynamics carry over to employment projections between 2017 and 2035: 8 percent annual growth for IWSS; 10 percent for manufacturing, and 1 percent for non-IWSS (table 3-6). These parameters imply that IWSS would move from 16 percent of employment to about 35 percent by 2035, while the share of manufacturing would increase by 4 percentage points, to about 5 percent of total employment. Non-IWSS sectors in this scenario make up 60 percent of total employment; 45 percent coming from subsistence agriculture and more than half the remaining share coming from domestic services and government.

This pattern of growth would most certainly create a strong demand for labor—and especially skilled labor (table 3-7). The demand for high-skilled workers would outpace the growth of even moderately skilled workers as well as the demand for low-skilled workers. The IWSS sectors, together with manufacturing, are main drivers of this process. We rely on the trend of skill change for different sectors between the 2010 and 2017 Household Surveys to project the sectoral skill demand in 2035. Since these estimates are not bounded by the size of the labor force, we take the skill distribution of the extra jobs created between 2017 and 2035 (based on 2000–2017 trends) and apply those distributions to our bounded estimates of additional labor demanded in 2035.[8]

This methodology is sensitive to the fact that future employment (which equals labor demand in our scenario) is a combination of a stock of existing workers whose skills distribution will not change on average and a flow of new workers who will add to the skill pool. Table 3-7 summarizes our estimated skill distribution for 2035. Similar to our previous tables, the definition of skill is defined based on education level: high-skilled workers are those with a postsecondary education; skilled workers have either completed secondary school or at least have some years of secondary education; and unskilled workers have less than a secondary education or no formal education whatsoever.

In 2017, workers were predominantly low-skilled, and IWSS sectors were relatively more skill intensive than manufacturing and other non-IWSS sectors. In 2035, we estimate a shift not only in the overall skill distribution of workers in the overall economy but also within the IWSS and non-IWSS sectors. Across the board, there is an upskilling of the labor pool, with the number of skilled jobs highest in IWSS sectors.[9]

Can Rwanda satisfy this demand for high-skilled and moderately skilled workers? Based on an academic study, the "Future Drivers of Growth"

Table 3-7. The Jobs of the Future Will Require Greater Skills: Projected Labor Demand by Skill

	2017			2035 (projected)						Annual % growth 2017–2035		
	High skilled	Skilled	Low skilled	High skilled	Skilled	Low skilled	High skilled	Skilled	Low skilled	High skilled	Skilled	Low skilled
				('000)								
Total employment	3%	13%	84%	507	3,709	5,609	5%	38%	57%	7%	9%	1%
Total IWSS	4%	21%	75%	229	2,205	1,030	7%	64%	30%	11%	15%	3%
Export crops and horticulture	0%	10%	90%	7	296	197	1%	59%	39%	15%	18%	2%
Agro-processing	10%	69%	21%	3	122	115	1%	51%	48%	4%	17%	9%
Construction	3%	23%	73%	26	683	192	3%	76%	21%	6%	15%	0%
Tourism	9%	42%	48%	68	546	71	10%	80%	10%	9%	12%	0%
ICT	33%	43%	24%	18	80	3	17%	80%	3%	8%	16%	–1%
Transportation	3%	24%	73%	61	301	124	12%	62%	25%	17%	12%	1%
Maintenance and repairs	2%	19%	80%	1	24	38	1%	38%	61%	0%	7%	2%
Financial and business services	23%	36%	41%	43	135	31	21%	65%	15%	8%	12%	2%
Trade (excl. tourism): formal	1%	4%	95%	3	17	260	1%	6%	93%	7%	9%	7%

(continued)

Table 3-7. (continued)

	2017			2035 (projected)						Annual % growth 2017–2035		
	High skilled	Skilled	Low skilled	('000)						High skilled	Skilled	Low skilled
				High skilled	Skilled	Low skilled	High skilled	Skilled	Low skilled			
Manufacturing (excl. agro-processing)	3%	23%	74%	20	145	278	5%	33%	63%	13%	12%	9%
Other Non-IWSS	2%	12%	86%	258	1,359	4,301	4%	23%	73%	4%	5%	0%
Agriculture	0%	10%	90%	13	854	3,524	0%	19%	80%	0%	4%	0%
Mining	0%	9%	91%	0	93	45	0%	67%	33%	0%	18%	0%
Utilities	14%	51%	35%	2	11	4	11%	66%	22%	1%	4%	0%
Trade (excl. tourism): informal	0%	4%	96%	0	21	457	0%	4%	96%	—	−1%	3%
Domestic services	1%	16%	83%	2	205	201	0%	50%	49%	1%	10%	0%
Government	39%	42%	19%	175	128	29	53%	39%	9%	4%	2%	−2%
Other	23%	32%	45%	66	47	43	42%	30%	28%	6%	3%	0%

Source: Authors' calculations using EICV1, EICV3, EICV5, and Rwanda National accounts. 2035 estimates are projected.

Note: Skill breakdown for 2035 is based on skill distribution in 2017 from EICV5. Adjusted estimates for tourism are distributed using skill distribution in EICV5. Informal trade is assumed to be fully skilled and low skilled in 2035.

Table 3-8. Projected Skill Deficit, 2035

	High skilled	Skilled	Low skilled
		('000)	
Projected labor supply (World Bank)	491	3,340	5,993
High growth scenario: 8% annual growth rate			
Projected labor demand:	507	3,709	5,609
Skill gap	16	368	−384

Source: Authors' calculations using EICV1, EICV3, EICV5, and Rwanda National accounts. 2035 estimates are projected.

Note: Skill breakdown for 2035 is based on skill distribution in 2017 from EICV5. Adjusted estimates for tourism and trade are distributed using skill distribution in EICV5. Labor supply by skill in 2035 is projected using World Bank (2020, figure 0.19), 5% tertiary, 35% some secondary, 60% less than secondary.

study by the Rwandan Government and World Bank put together a business-as-usual scenario for the labor supply in 2035: 6 percent of the supply will consist of high-skilled workers, 34 percent of skilled workers, and 60 percent of low-skilled workers.[10] Juxtaposing the anticipated supply with the anticipated demand shown in table 3-7 reveals a looming gap in skills that might well develop over the next decade and a half. The shortage could well exceed 3 percent of the demand if the government does not make a jump in its workers' skill development (table 3-8).

Before exploring ways the government could remedy this deficit, the subject of the final section, it is helpful to drill down into specific value chains to understand constraints on IWSS development.

Value Chains for IWSS Subsectors: Potential, Problems, and Policy

To drill down on ways growth in the IWSS sectors will have ramifications throughout the economy, it is helpful to focus on several important value chains.[11] As with manufacturing, the IWSS sectors have a large direct and indirect effect on employment creation. High-productivity export crops and horticulture, agro-industry, tourism, and ICT are particularly dynamic.

In 2017, these activities accounted for about 345,000 workers, a number that is four times the employment in manufacturing. As labor is released from agriculture in coming years, these subsectors, along with IWSS

FIGURE 3-3. **Coffee and Tea Are Still the Most Important Export Crops (thousands of dollars)**

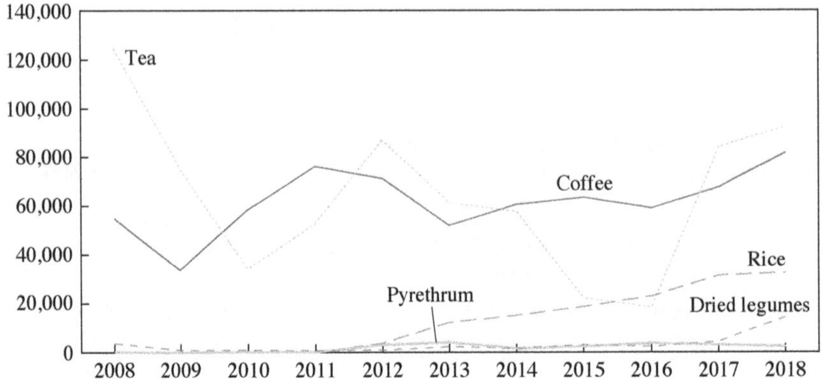

Source: International Trade Centre, trade statistics.

activities in general, will become more important sources of jobs for young people and women entering the labor market. Using an employment elasticity approach, together with realistic assumptions for GDP growth, it is likely that these four IWSS subsectors will employ more than five times the number of manufacturing workers in 2035. This section elaborates on value chains associated with these subsectors to explore some of the obstacles to their growth that require policy attention.

Export Crops and Horticulture

Export agriculture and horticulture in 2017 employed about 140,000 workers and is likely to employ many new workers over the next decade, perhaps growing threefold by 2035. Between 2013 and 2018, export revenues from agricultural crops more than doubled, from about $225 million to $516 million (NAEB 2019). Within the export sector, tea and coffee still dominate, though other traditional exports—pyrethrum, wheat, and maize (corn) flour— and newer export products—including stevia, essential oils, and hides— are increasing as a share of export revenues (figure 3-3). Regional markets account for a large share of export crops and low-value horticulture, while the EU and Asia market has been a growing market for high-value horticultural products like flowers and chillies. Each of these commercial products—and their respective value chains—have been the subject of extensive analyses; and for each, the government has developed sophisticated policy approaches.[12]

The National Export Strategy (2010–15) highlighted the importance of export diversification as a key priority, focusing on several nontraditional subsectors, including horticulture. Horticultural products have increased in importance, nearly doubling in tonnage between 2008 and 2012 with further increases between 2012 and 2020.

By 2024, the government aims to double revenue from regional and international exports of agricultural crops—both traditional and nontraditional. To do this will require improvements in the promotion of export crops in key markets; sustained increases in private sector investments; continuous commitment to high-quality production and productivity; and cost-competitive air and sea freight, and ground logistics for exports in strategic value chains (NAEB 2019). Together with broad policy objectives for the sector, the government has also identified priority value chains to drive future growth; horticultural products (primarily French beans, macadamia nuts, pyrethrum, and cut flowers), essential oils, stevia, and the traditional crops—tea, coffee, cereals.

Horticulture is prime for exponential growth. Indeed, the annual six months of rainfall are ideal for horticulture farming; the wet and cool climate in the high-altitude North and West are convenient for temperate fruits, big-headed roses, and herbs, while avocadoes, beans, chillies, and Asian vegetables thrive well in the sunny and warm South and East.[13] Over the past decade, there has been a steady increase in the number of horticulture exporters in the country, owing to improvements in productivity, market access, and standards; export revenues from horticulture have doubled, from about $10 million in 2013–14 to $23 million in 2017–18 (NAEB 2019). However, limited land for expansion and inadequate knowledge of proper crop cultivation, fertilizer use, pest management, postharvest handling, and export procedures continue to plague the horticulture sector. One potential growth area for horticulture is organic farming; organic produce attracts a higher price in export markets, driven by evolving customer preferences for healthy and environmentally safe produce. However, the high cost of obtaining an organic license implies that the majority of horticulture farmers are not licensed organic farmers.

Other challenges to the sector include low productivity, augmented by a gap in the knowledge and skills required to cultivate high-yield varieties, and low access to and high costs of inputs in the sector, as well as nonexistent or inadequate quality management and low market access. The government has stepped up efforts to train farmers on agricultural and agronomic practices through various government and private initiatives. Farmer schools and extension services have been effective in upskilling farmers. In addition to this, the supply of inputs has been improved through the One Acre Fund, a private initiative to provide financing to farmers for timely access to inputs. It is also worth noting the role of private sector investment in increasing capacity and support for greater market access. There is also potential for Rwanda to maximize revenues from horticulture by reducing the costs of airfreight between Kigali and international markets, which are among the highest in the region. With airfreight costs substantially reduced, Rwanda will be in a position to serve the increasing demand for fresh fruits and vegetables in the East African Community (EAC) region and the Democratic Republic of Congo (DRC).[14]

Agro-Processing: The Case of Dairy

Agro-processing is an industry where Rwanda has a natural comparative advantage. Agro-processing uses perishable produce to convert to processed foods, such as corn and wheat flour, bread, biscuits, dairy, and beverages, such as milk and juices. Some of these products, such as biscuits, are differentiated consumer goods. Moreover, Rwandan producers enjoy unique access to the large (if low-income) populace in the DRC. In 2017, this sector employed about 35,000 workers, and if it is to absorb the 2035 projected labor force for the sector, it needs to be able to grow by about 8 percent annually. Under this scenario, its employment level is projected to increase a little over threefold in the next decade and a half (table 3-6).

While each of the sector's several products have different value chains, the case of one product, dairy, can illuminate some of the main issues in the sector. The dairy sector is unique, in that a small number of large processing firms heavily dominate. These firms are located in Kigali and source their raw materials directly from farmers and from milk-collecting firms. Large firms primarily purchase from the import sector as inputs into the production process, but also from other large firms. Value-added-tax data allow an analysis of production chain relationships but exclude the common practice of processing milk within the household for auto-consumption or micro-low-profit sale. Figure 3-4 shows medium-sized dairy intermediaries who purchase from the farmer and then resell to the dominant firm in the industry.

One firm, Inyange Industries, dominates milk production in the sector. This firm knits virtually the entire market together. Also attached to this firm are smaller dairy companies that either process dairy products themselves and share some of the same supplier firms, or work as suppliers to

FIGURE 3-4. One Firm Is at the Center of the Dairy Industry

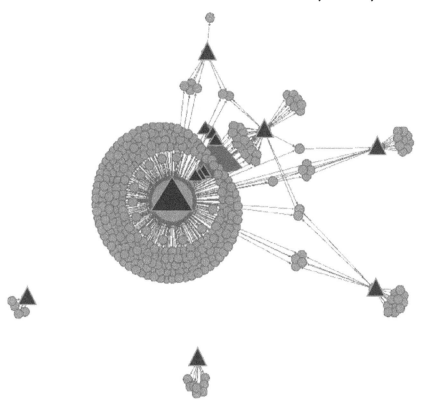

Source: Spray and Argawal (2016). Figure has been adapted for black and white print.
Figure originally in color with firms represented by different colored circle.

Note: In this figure, each circle indicates a firm and each edge is a transaction within the fiscal
year 2013/14. Larger circles indicate the firm has more connections to other firms in the sector.
Triangles indicate the firm is in the dairy sector; a circle indicates the firm is either a customer
or supplier of the sector.

the main dairy producer. Finally, there are other dairy producers that do
not share any linkages to the other firms in the sector. The market power
of the dominant firm is circumscribed by a competitive fringe of local
informal producers and import competition, primarily from ultra-high-
temperature producers in Uganda.

Critical imported inputs into the production process include machinery,
cartons and packages, and flavorings. Most of these inputs are too techni-
cally challenging for local producers to manufacture, though eventually it
is likely that further simple packaging will begin to appear in Rwanda and/or
the EAC. Imports to the sector include animal products from the DRC,

chemical products from Kenya and Uganda, and plastics, paper cartons, and rubber from Kenya and Uganda as well as electrical and other machinery from other countries.

Most sales of the industry go to the domestic market. However, exports of concentrated and nonconcentrated milk, butter, and yogurt have become important share of exports going to the East African regional market. Historically, the DRC alone has accounted for over 70 percent of dairy exports. However, in 2018, about 50 percent of milk exports went to Uganda, with similar exports values going to the DRC.

In the dairy sector, the government has fostered growth through its indirect support of the dominant firm, a company that belonged to the Rwandan Patriotic Front's Crystal Ventures conglomerate.[15] The state has also fostered the sector's growth through the One Cow Per Poor Family Program, launched in 2006 with the aim to improve nutrition and the incomes of low-income families. So far, the program has distributed close to 350,000 cows. Alongside this initiative, a school milk program was piloted in 2011 to provide milk to grade-schoolers and a ready market for milk producers. Infrastructure investments were also made to set up a national network of milk collection centers, together with support for husbandry services and disease control.

As a result of these initiatives, Rwanda has achieved close to 70 percent of its targeted milk production under its medium-term development strategy; milk production increased from about 50,000 metric tons in 2000 to almost 850,000 metric tons in 2018. The national cattle herd has been transformed from one dominated by low-productivity local cow breeds to a national herd of 1.35 million, with close to 55 percent of the herd made up of improved dairy breeds. Per-capita milk consumption has also steadily increased, from below 20 liters per year in the 1990s to 64 liters per year in 2015.

Despite improvements in the sector, the government is still addressing two major constraints in the sector: low productivity and low milk quality. To provide incentives to invest in more high-performing farms and postharvest operations, pricing plans that reward quality are essential to both issues. Increasing the prevalence of quality-based pricing requires government leadership and continuing technical assistance to small producers. Improving value added and product differentiation are concomitant goals necessary to promote intra-industry trade.[16] In 2016, the government passed a ministerial order to regulate the collection, transporting, and sale of milk. Inspections were ramped up and training programs were designed and implemented to upskill producers, distributors, and sellers on approved safety standards.

FIGURE 3-5. **Tourism Revenues (millions of dollars)**

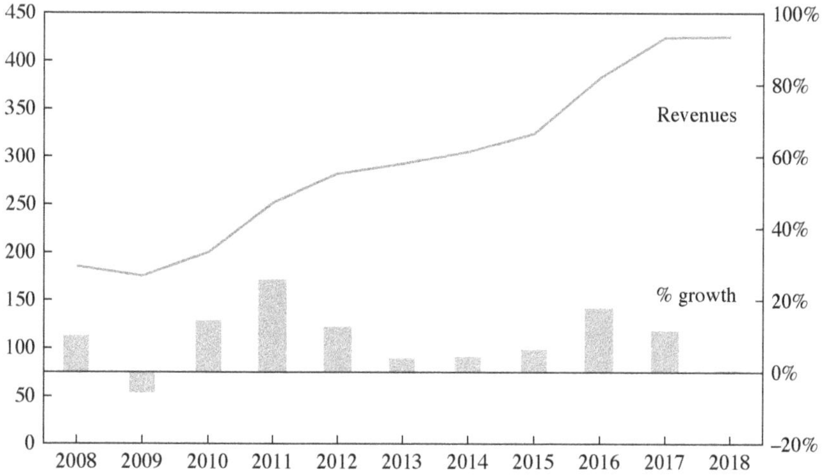

Source: Authors' calculations using National Bank of Rwanda data.

Regional cooperation is also imperative. At the moment, all the countries in the region are expanding their capacities to produce similar value-added products such as ultra-high-temperature milk, yogurt, butter, ghee, and cheese, thus creating excessive price competition that has led to the imposition of nontariff barriers throughout the EAC. Greater regional cooperation considering the comparative advantage of each country could lead to more competition in processed, differentiated products. Regional interventions could bring additional support to innovative production and marketing models being developed, such as dairy hubs, cooperatives, and dairy self-help groups (see Bingi and Tondell 2015). All these measures would have to be coupled with a reduction in nontariff barriers in the sector.[17] The numerous permits and regulatory signoffs to engage in trade create obstacles to effective trade.

Tourism: More Than Just Gorillas

Tourism has been the single most important source of foreign inflows since 1999, surpassing the combined traditional exports—coffee, tea, and unprocessed minerals (Daly and Gereffi 2017). In 2018, tourism generated over $400 million in revenue (figure 3-5) and consists of four main industries: accommodation services, food and beverages, passenger transportation services, and travel agencies (figure 3-6). Today, tourism employs

FIGURE 3-6. **Hotels Are at the Center of the Tourist Sector**

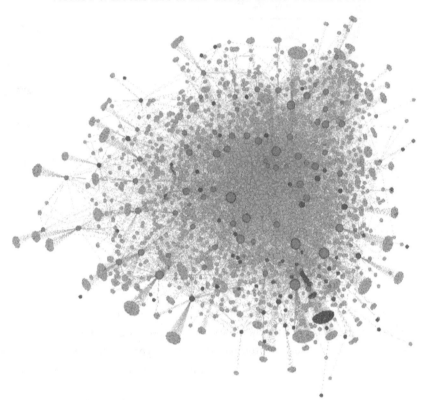

Source: Spray and Agrawal (2016).

Note: In this figure, each circle indicates a firm and each edge is a transaction within the fiscal year 2013/14. Larger circles indicate the firm has more connections to other firms in the sector. Dark circles indicate that the firm is a large hotel, a gray circle with a black border indicates that the firm is a tour company, and light gray circles represent suppliers to these firms.

more than 3 percent of the labor force. Its workforce is relatively skilled, but the industry has created jobs for low-skilled workers, many of which can be improved through targeted training.

The government has placed an emphasis on the sector by supporting improvements in tourism infrastructure to increase annual tourism visits. Construction and renovation of accommodation units, such as hotel rooms, are also on the rise, especially in Kigali, which might bring down the cost of accommodations and increase tourist arrivals in future years.

Consequently, foreign and domestic investment in the sector has been substantial in the last 10 years. In 2016–17, the private sector invested close to

$300 million in the tourism sector (Rwanda TSA 2017; figure 3-5), with a significant share going to accommodations and food and beverages serving services facilities. Complementary investment from the government over that period totalled close to $150 million at the national and district levels. Substantial investments have gone into Bugesera Airport, Kigali International Airport, the Kigali Convention Centre, the Kivu belt, sports centers, and the national carrier, Rwandair. This has led to a diversification away from simply gorilla-based tourism, toward a new strategy of meetings, incentives, conferences, and exhibitions (known as MICE).

Hotels are by far the biggest companies in this sector, and they purchase goods from numerous other smaller companies. Many of these hotels are linked across the whole sector and support a large supply chain (figure 3-6). However, unlike in the agricultural or dairy sector, the importance of any one firm is much smaller, meaning that the market is more robust to firm-level shocks. For example, if one hotel went out of business, it is likely that the bankrupt hotel's suppliers would be absorbed by other hotels in the industry. Similarly, having more firms is likely to reduce the risk of monopoly pricing, as competition prevents any one firm from setting prices above the equilibrium market price.

Tour companies are also crucial to the tourism sector's market structure. Although tour companies are not as large as hotels in their number of customers, many of the tour companies have linkages between hotels essentially linking up the sector. Without these tour companies, it is unlikely that there could be so many hotels operating.

Imports are key to the functioning of the tourism sector, constituting 77 percent of the backward supply chain trade volume. The tourism sector's biggest suppliers are the wholesale and retail sectors, as well as other key service sectors, such as construction, ICT, and food vendors. The sector buys a large volume of materials typically associated with construction: basic metals, cement, furniture, glass, and ceramic products (Spray and Argawal 2016).

The government has used public investment as its main instrument of industrial policy, with substantial investments in a convention center, a new airline, remodelling its existing airport, and beginning construction of a new airport. The government has guaranteed loans of selected hotel construction companies, and hotel capacity has expanded geometrically. It has invested heavily in overseas marketing—including on the shirts of Arsenal soccer players in Britain. It has worked with Kenya and Uganda in setting up a regional tourist visa and has eased entry requirements for most African countries and many high-income countries. It has begun focusing on medical tourism, with the aim of making Rwanda the medical tourism hub of the EAC region. Investment in high-class and specialized hospitals like the Rwanda Military Hospital, where patients from the EAC region and beyond could come for high-quality medical services, is expected to boost medical tourism in particular, and generally increase tourist arrivals and revenue. Notwithstanding numerous challenges in realizing this goal, Rwanda has the potential to attract medical tourists from the DRC, where health services are relatively less efficient.

The main challenges, putting aside the COVID-19 pandemic crisis, are continuing to upgrade services and attractions. If the average length of stay is doubled from its current average of less than 4 days (Rwanda TSA 2017) to a week, it would markedly expand tourism revenues (English and Murray 2016). Working with tour operators and hotel chains to bring in more tourists could well create a new tourist circuit that would link the gorillas, the virgin forests, and the attractions on Lake Kivu to the big game parks in Tanzania and Kenya.

ICT: Driving Innovation

Rwanda, like many other African countries, has benefited from a leap-frog from the twentieth-century fixed-line technology directly into the twenty-first-century mobile technology. By 2017, telephony, mobile money, telecommunication equipment, and computers comprised some 12,000 workers, a small share of the total labor force. These numbers do not include a large section of relatively low-skilled workers acting as vendors to mobile money.

All told, the sector is growing and is likely to become more important in the next decade and a half. The government's high growth and aspirational scenario projects employment in ICT to rise to about 100,000 workers by 2035.

Mobile phone ownership stood at about 67 percent in 2017, and 4G LTE (Long-Term Evolution) was rolled out in November 2015, with an ambitious target of connecting 95 percent of the population to the technology by mid-2017. About 22 percent of Rwandans use the internet, according to 2017 estimates (ITU 2020). In the financial services sector, the digitization agenda has seen tremendous modernization of service delivery and the emergence of pro-poor and augmenting financial innovations.

Mobile money—a financial product that allows users to make financial transactions via mobile phone—was introduced in February 2010, and has since revolutionized financial inclusion and payment efficiency; mobile money users shot up from nearly 200,000 in 2010 to over 4 million in 2019. Partnerships between mobile network operators and commercial banks have taken place to leverage market potential among people formerly without access to the financial system, especially in rural communities. Unexploited opportunities still exist for Rwanda to achieve its goal of being the ICT hub of the EAC, expanding its exporting of ICT services in the region and increasing the competitiveness of its exports.

ICT contributed 1 percent of GDP in 2018 (Rwanda National Accounts 2019), and it has received a policy focus under the multiphase National ICT Strategy and Plan: the first phase (2001–5) focused on institutional, legal, and regulatory reforms, liberalization of the telecom market, and reducing entry barriers. The second phase (2006–10) centered on establishing a world-class communications infrastructure as a backbone for the country's communication needs. The major goal in the third phase (2011–15) was to develop ICT for improved service delivery in both the private and public sectors. In the last phase (NICI 3), the government aimed to use ICT to build a highly skilled and knowledgeable labor force (skills development), stir competition and innovations in the private sector, empower communities through improved access to information (community development), improve efficiency and service delivery in government operations (e-Governance), and secure the country's cyberspace and information assets (cyber security). Many of these objectives remain central under the new ICT Hub Strategic Plan (2019–24), with a particularly strong focus on skills upgrading and job creation.

ICT continues to drive innovations in several sectors, offering great growth potential for the economy. The government is a major consumer of ICT services through its line ministries and authorities. One of the main landmark digitization initiatives was the establishment of electronic and mobile declaration (e-declaration and m-declaration) of tax returns in the Rwanda Revenue Authority in 2011. The success of this initiative was backed by the 2015 introduction of mobile payment for taxes, both initiatives ultimately saving taxpayers time and transportation costs that would be incurred in declaring and paying taxes. The regulatory agency, the Rwanda Development Board, has worked closely with technology solutions companies to earmark the digitization of 100 services, including application for birth certificates, registration, and school examination fee payment, among other key services.

The education sector has also embraced ICT by designing online learning platforms and the creation of a private–public partnership between the government of Rwanda and technology company Postivo BGH, in 2014, to set up a laptop factory in Kigali and sell laptops to schools. The development of mobile apps such as Rapid SMS, and e-Diagnosis in the health sector, have eased knowledge sharing and patient tracking by health service providers. In the agriculture sector, the Fertilizer Voucher Management System helped to smooth the distribution of fertilizers to farmers; farmer uptake rose by 11 percent between 2013 and 2014. Other market platforms like e-Soko help farmers to access real-time price information for agricultural produce.

The government has identified a few major challenges to the sector: expansion of critical ICT infrastructure and investments has been slow; digital literacy and enrollments in ICT related programs remain low; and costs of hard infrastructure ICT projects are high due to additional transportation costs. Addressing these challenges would require government and private sector solutions that are capable of attracting the required investments.

The cost of implementing the 2019–24, strategy is estimated at about 1 percent of total GDP. The government plans to rely on a menu of financing options; grant financing, government financing, and debt and equity financing where possible, as well as private sector financing. To address issues of poor project implementation and management the government has committed to implementing a results-based management system with consistent monitoring and evaluation against strategic objectives. Finally, the government, recognizing the importance of preparing the labor force to support the growth of the ICT sector, has outlined a detailed strategy to tackle barriers that the labor force faces securing ICT-related jobs.

Back to the Big Picture: Commonalities and Constraints

Five common patterns emerge from this review of value chains in the IWSS sectors in Rwanda. First is the centrality of imported inputs and services to the sector's success. Whether horticulture, agro-processing, tourism, or ICT, access to imported inputs at border prices has been key to the international competitiveness of the sector, which is evident in export performance. Similarly, the role of services—notably transportation, finance, and construction services, among others—as inputs in all four sectors has been a keystone in the foundation of these sectors' performance.

A second pattern is the role of public investment and government strategy in launching and nurturing the private sector. Public investment in horticulture has taken the form of irrigation, cold storage facilities, and transportation; in dairy, it has taken the form of a state-controlled company to promote value added and quality upgrading as well as public procurement through school feeding programs. In both sectors, quality grading, improving access to fertilizer and other inputs, and strengthening backward linkages have proved fundamental. Furthermore, in tourism, public investment has been a driving force in hotel development, air transportation, site development in gorilla tourism, and the convention center; and in ICT, public procurement has played an important role.

Third, in all these sectors increasing productivity has required exporting. Global markets are of course central to coffee, tea, cut flowers, and tourism. Regional markets have been particularly important for agro-processing, such as flour from maize, and dairy products, particularly in the form of exports to the DRC.

Fourth, in all these sectors, technology will be crucial for further development, for increasing exports, and for creating high-productivity jobs. This is both a constraint and an opportunity. In all sectors, technology is pivotal for future growth and job creation and access, and adaption to technology requires significant investments. At the same, many aspects of the next stage of sectoral technologies are already known and an aggressive public sector and an innovative private sector can search these out and adapt them to Rwanda's scale and capabilities. Here, too, government programs— such as those under development through the National Industrial Research and Development Agency, the Rwanda Development Bank, and the Rwanda Development Board—will play a leading role.

Fifth and finally, these sectors will all entail substantial increases in employment for young people and other new entrants into the labor force. However, two caveats foreshadow our overall conclusions. First, the emergence of these sectors will require not only new technologies but also more skilled workers to make them grow. The technologies employed will create a skill bias with respect to the growth model. On average, the percentage of low-skilled workers will decline in these IWSS sectors, and the percentage of high- and medium-skilled workers will increase. This underscores the need to upgrade educational quality if the government's aspirational scenario is to be achieved. Second, without offsetting fiscal policies and efforts to improve educational opportunities for youth, particularly from the poor rural sectors, this skill-biased pattern of growth implies a strong tendency for income to become more unequal. These two considerations we take up in more detail in the concluding section.

Policies to Promote Youth Employment

Filling the jobs of tomorrow in Rwanda will require significant investments in children, youth, and adult workers, notably including women. Business surveys already point to the lack of skilled labor as a major constraint on business growth—and this is only likely to intensify. Increasing the human capital of young Rwandan workers has three components: basic skills, creating technical skills, and creating advanced conceptual skills. With an average education attainment of 4.1 years of school, the country has to focus on providing the basic skills essential for the post-2020 economy in Rwanda. Even as it increases time in school, the country needs to improve educational outcomes if it is to achieve its high growth aspirations. Second, it needs to upgrade its secondary schools and vocational and educational training systems. Finally, the country will benefit from further reforms to its tertiary school system and universities.

Basic Education Is Fundamental

Even though the expected years of school of a typical student in Rwanda have doubled, from 5.7 to 11.1 years over the 1990–2017 period, Rwanda's current workforce's average school of 4.1 years remains below the Sub-Saharan mean (5.6 years) and the average for low Human Development Index countries (4.7 years). This shortage of basic education challenges late-stage upskilling initiatives, as certain skills (e.g., languages) are more easily trained at a young age (NSDEPS 2020).

Improving access to basic schooling is a high priority. Even though all children have nominal access to schools, primary education is not completely cost-free to parents. Parents may have to invest in school uniforms, and it is not unusual for parents to contribute to schools. Children are not infrequently turned away from taking exams for failure to pay incidental fees. Making primary education truly cost-free may require increasing the per student benefit paid to schools. Outsourcing primary education to the private sector more broadly is unlikely to reduce costs significantly but offers some gains at the margin.

Improving educational quality must go hand in hand with increasing cost-free access. For example, roughly 85 percent of students who have completed grade 3 were rated "below comprehension" on a recent reading test, while one in six students could not answer a single reading comprehension question (Government of Rwanda and World Bank 2020). Recruiting, training, and monitoring teachers are important components of upgrading basic education. At present, many teachers are not fully equipped to teach their subjects. While teacher salaries are an important determinant of workforce quality, the government, with the help of the International Growth Centre, has been experimenting with nonmonetary rewards, such as pay-for-performance and choice in school assignment for teachers during periodic rotations, to encourage quality. Reducing class size is no less important. In Rwanda, students not performing satisfactorily on end-of-year exams are held back, and classes are large, with varying ages of students in the same grade, especially in the early grades. Another issue is the language of instruction. Providing education during the first three years in Kinyarwanda before transitioning to English would improve basic literacy. Since many teachers themselves lack proficiency in English, leveraging Rwanda's past investment in technology to provide upper-primary and secondary school teachers with regular opportunities to improve their English could improve teaching (Government of Rwanda and World Bank 2020).

Vocational Education Is No Less Important

Technical and vocational education and training (TVET) has a current enrollment of slightly more than 30 percent of Rwandan youth. Unfortunately, TVETs have not been fully effective in preparing students for the workforce; employers rank programs poorly—only 60 percent of employers found TVET graduates to have satisfactory skills. In 2018, the unemployment rate among TVET graduates amounted to 17 percent; roughly half of TVET graduates reported that they were not satisfied with their skills development. This can be attributed to two elements: insufficient private sector involvement in curriculum design and implementation; and nascent performance tracking, especially for TVET institutions with regard to labor market outcomes. Collecting and disseminating information on the quality of skills providers and the returns to different skills would improve quality and encourage participation in high-return programs.

Tertiary Education Will Increase the Supply of High-Skilled Workers

Even though university enrollments have doubled in the last decade, only 8 percent of tertiary-age youth are enrolled in tertiary education, well below the level in middle-income countries. Moreover, relatively few graduates are specializing in key job creation fields, such as science and engineering. Just 6 percent of university students in Rwanda are enrolled in engineering, manufacturing, and construction; and only 9 percent are studying sciences. If Rwanda intends to grow its manufacturing and technology sectors, then the number of students in sciences and engineering clearly also needs to grow (Government of Rwanda and World Bank 2020).

Increasing access to financing (including private) would expand enrollment. Enrollment in high-return fields could be increased through financing incentives and higher-quality science and engineering instruction in earlier grades. Creating incentives for researchers to develop and adapting innovations to benefit industries and getting industries to pay for the research are essential to reap the maximum returns to innovation.

The Policy Response: The National Skills Development
and Employment Promotion Strategy

In late 2019, the Rwanda Development Board, in collaboration with the Ministry of Education and other official agencies, launched the National Skills Development and Employment Promotion Strategy (NSDEPS). This strategy is squarely aimed at addressing shortcomings in the current educational system and provide new direction to labor force development in the future. The program is comprehensive and organized on three pillars, each of which has a subset of actionable programs with defined performance benchmarks:

- *Skill development.* Beyond improvements in the education system highlighted above, three NSDEPS initiatives are worth highlighting. The National Training and Education Excellence Program will create visibility on how effective TVETs, and higher education institutions are, reward best-performing institutions, identify best practices, and solve critical emerging issues. The Market-Led Education Initiative will support a demand-led approach, through elevating the voice of the private sector, reinvigorating the Sector Skills Councils, and ensuring that the sectoral skills gaps are clear. The Capacity Development Program will (1) allow skills development to be responsive to investors and the development priorities of the government (e.g., financial hub, health tourism) and should complement the Rwanda Development Board's investment promotion activities; and (2) support capabilities development within the public sector.

- *Employment promotion.* Focusing on small and medium-sized enterprises, this pillar seeks to provide access to markets, access to finance, and access to business advisory services through four programs. First, the Access to Markets Program will support Rwandan firms by facilitating access to domestic and international markets. Second, the Access to Capital Program will provide appropriate finance to Rwandan businesses, enabling them to grow when they can. Third, the High-Quality Business Advisory Services Program will build businesses capabilities and know-how. And finally, the Labor Market Analysis Program will provide analysis on the impact of government policies on employment, to inform decisionmaking.

- *Matching workers with jobs.* At present, jobseekers and employers struggle to connect effectively with each other. Only about 5 percent of unemployed Rwandans have used employment services or online tools to seek employment. The Evidence Based Workforce Planning and Matching Program will support an ecosystem where employers and workers can find each other, and educators can adapt rapidly as workforce needs change. An integrated data system connecting job-seekers profiles and job opportunities will be the cornerstone to achieve this goal. Furthermore, it will enable an ongoing labor market planning to bring the demand and supply sides more aligned over time. The Strengthening Employment Services and Career Guidance Program will promote active linkages between skills supply and demand, providing incentives for career services and matching providers based on performance. The Graduate Labor Market Transition Program will build market-relevant skills among the youth and help firms and institutions identify and test suitable talent. The Global Talent and Opportunity Program will support the closing of skills gaps through the import of talent (foreign and diaspora), by proactively seeking out these individuals and facilitating their transition into the Rwanda jobs market.

The Challenges Ahead

Rwanda's effort has made great strides in using structural transformation to drive its growth and job creation. Its policies have generated a diverse and increasingly complex economy in which jobs have been created at a rapid pace in higher productivity activities. This process has pulled workers out of subsistence agriculture into IWSS—including high-productivity agriculture and services—as well as incipiently manufacturing. These sectors have led the growth process. Manufacturing, though still small, is becoming a dynamic complement to this process.

The growth process creates a demand for ever-higher-skilled labor. While producers complain even today that the lack of availability of skilled workers inhibits their growth, the aggregate numbers in the government's aspirational scenario and value chain analysis show that this is likely to be the case in the decades ahead.

This means that the government must rapidly invest in its workers and innovation to sustain its growth momentum, lest the lack of skill workers and professionals become a brake on growth. Moreover, the skill bias inherent in the growth process—driven by IWSS and manufacturing—will likely drive an undesirable increase in inequality. Thus, there are two reasons to invest heavily in workers' skills: namely, to avoid letting skill shortages weigh down growth rates, and to ensure that the rising incomes are more equitably shared.

This review of policies and programs offers a source of optimism. The government has developed a sophisticated set of policies to use skill development, business creation, and job matching to alleviate any skill deficit and constraint on growth. The challenge ahead will be to realize the potential of these programs.

NOTES

1. NISR projections; see https://www.statistics.gov.rw/publication/rphc4-population-projections.

2. As of 2016, the NISR rolled out a new Labour Force Survey (LFS) to replace employment reporting through the National Household Survey (EICV). The first pilot of the LFS was held in 2016, with surveys done every year after the conclusion of the pilot. For this chapter, we use the EICV to allow for a trend analysis from the period 2000–2017. Employment definitions have changed under the LFS. Overall, employment dynamics are similar across both surveys except for the definition of subsistence agriculture.

3. Our IWSS classification is based on the International Standard Industrial Classification of All Economic Activities (ISIC), which sets international standards for how to categorize economic activities within an economy. By design, the ISIC structure allows for more detailed categorizations of economic activity. Most of our sectors are directly mapped onto ISIC sections; adjustments are made to more precisely estimate agro processing, exports and horticulture, repairs, domestic services and trade. Agro-processing mainly consists of food and beverage production using ISIC group level under divisions 10–33. Similarly, the classification for repairs and domestic services is established at the ISIC group level under divisions 45–47, 94–96, and 97–98.

4. "Other" is a mishmash of activities, ranging from "domestic services" (roughly half the employment) to "repairs and maintenance," and "personal services" such as hair dressing.

5. Formula used to calculate employment elasticity: $emp\_elasticity_{s(t)} = \dfrac{\%\Delta\ labor_{s(t,t-1)}}{\%\Delta\ GDP_{s(t,t-1)}}$ $emp\_elasticity_{s(t)}$ = Estimates employment elasticity for sector s in period t; $labor_{s(t)}$ = Labor force of sector s in period t; $GDP_{s(t)}$ = GDP of sector s in period t; s = *sector (agro-processing, tourism, utilities . . .)*; t = *period*.

6. This chapter defines skill using educational attainment as a proxy. High-skilled are workers that have at least some tertiary education; medium-skilled workers are those that have complete primary and have some secondary education; and low-skilled have some primary or no formal education.

7. First, instead of linearly projecting GDP from historical GDP, we project GDP in line with existing economic growth targets from the government and labor force projections by the national statistics agency. Second, we project labor demand using adjusted employment elasticities and bound demand by the projected size of the working age population in 2035. Third, we project skill distribution by sector using the trend in changes in skill distribution between 2010 and 2017.

8. To project the skill breakdown of labor supply in 2035, we use skill projections from a joint country study by the Government of Rwanda—the Future Drivers of Growth Report (2020)—and the World Bank. Under a "business as usual scenario", 5 percent of the labor supply in 2035 will be high-skilled, 35 percent will be skilled, and the remaining 60 percent will be low-skilled. The numbers are estimated on the current growth rate of school enrollment.

9. We estimate the breakdown of projected labor force for each sector by high-skilled, skilled, and low-skilled using this estimation:

$$labor_{sv(2035)} = labor_{sv(2017)} + \left(\left(labor_{s(2035)} - labor_{s(2017)} \right) \right) * shr\_labor_{sv(2017)}$$
$$s = \text{sector} \left(\text{agro-processing, tourism, utilities} \ldots \right)$$
$$v = \text{high-skilled, skilled, low-skilled}$$

$labor_{sv(2035)}$ = Projected labor force of sector s in 2035 by skill level v; $labor_{sv(2017)}$ = Projected labor force of sector s in 2017 by skill level v; $shr\_labor_{sv(2017)}$ = Share of difference between sector s labor force in 2017 and 2010 by skill level v.

10. Based on Lutz, Butz, and KC (2014).

11. This section draws on Ggombe and Newfarmer (2018), Spray and Agarwal (2016), and Murray and Wolf (2017).

12. On coffee, see, for example, Morjaria (2017).

13. This section is adapted from Ggombe and Newfarmer (2018).

14. Beyond this, the government has committed to horticultural development through: earmarking sites for horticultural cultivation; investing in agricultural land information systems and irrigation facilities; developing a cold chain system, including Kigali pack house; setting up a modern cold storage facilities at Kigali International Airport; improving feeder roads, electricity supply, and reliability and air connectivity to horticulture production areas; and providing prospective exporters with access to subsidized finance through an export growth facility. There are also initiatives to improve access to finance, notably through the export growth facility managed by the Rwanda Development Bank. Tax incentives and investment aftercare services are also key investment facilitation strategies for the sector.

15. *The Economist* reported that Brookside Dairies, owned by the family of Kenyan President Uhuru Kenyatta, acquired a majority holding in Inyange Industries from Crystal Ventures; see *Economist* (2017).

16. This section benefits from Bingi and Tondell (2015).

17. See Jensen and Keyer (2012).

REFERENCES

Abdulsamad, A., G. Gereffi, and A. Guinn. 2017. "Dairy Value Chains in East Africa." International Growth Centre, London.

Aragie E., X. Diao, and J. Thurlow. 2021. "A 2017 Social Accounting Matrix (SAM) for Rwanda." International Food Policy Research Institute. Washington, DC.

Bingi, S. and F. Tondell. 2015. *Recent Developments in the Dairy Sector in Eastern Africa: Towards a Regional Policy Framework for Value Chain Development.* Maastricht: European Centre for Development Policy Management.

Cadot, O., and M. Malouche. 2012. *Non-tariff Measures: A Fresh Look at Trade Policy's New Frontier.* Washington, DC: World Bank.

Daly, J., and G. Gereffi. 2017. "Tourism global value chains and Africa." WIDER Working Paper 2017/17, United Nations University, World Institute for Development Economics Research, Helsinki.

Daly, J., G. Gereffi, and A. Guinn. 2017. "Maize Value Chains in East Africa." International Growth Centre, London.

Economist. 2017. "Party of Business: The Rwandan Patriotic Front's Business Empire."https://www.economist.com/business/2017/03/02/the-rwandan-patriotic-fronts-business-empire.

Ggombe, K., and R. Newfarmer. 2017. "Rwanda: From Devastation to Services—First Transformation." WIDER Working Paper 2017/84, United Nations University, World Institute for Development Economics Research, Helsinki.

Government of Rwanda. 2017. "Tourism Satellite Account, 2017." Government of Rwanda, Kigali.

———. 2019a. "National Agricultural Export Development Board Strategic Plan 2019–2024." Government of Rwanda, Kigali.

———. 2019b. "National Skills Development and Employment Strategy: 2019–2024." Government of Rwanda, Kigali.

International Trade Center. No date. "Trade Statistics, Export and Import Statistics." Data set.

International Telecommunication Union. 2020. "Mobile Phone Subscriptions, 2020." Data set.

Jensen, M., and J. C. Keyer 2012. "Standards Harmonization and Trade: The Case of the East African Dairy Industry." In *Non-tariff Measures: A Fresh Look at Trade Policy's New Frontier*, edited by O. Cadot and M. Malouche. Washington: World Bank.

Lutz, W., W. P. Butz, and S. KC. 2014. *World Population and Human Capital in the Twenty-First Century.* Oxford University Press.

Ministry of Finance and Economic Planning. 2020. "Rwanda Updated Macroeconomic Framework (2020)."

Morjaria, A., and R. Macchiavello. 2016. "Fully Washed Coffee Exports in Rwanda: Market Structure and Policy Implications." International Growth Centre, London.

Murray, S., and S. Wolf. 2017. "Tourism Value Chains in East Africa." International Growth Centre, London.

National Bank of Rwanda. 2017. "Balance of Payments." Government of Rwanda, Kigali.

National Institute of Statistics Rwanda. 2017. "Rwanda Integrated Household Living Conditions Survey 5 (2016/2017)." Data set. Government of Rwanda, Kigali.

————. 2018. "Rwanda Labor Force Survey (2018)." Data set. Government of Rwanda, Kigali.

————. 2019. "Rwanda Labor Force Survey (2019)." Data set. Government of Rwanda, Kigali.

Newfarmer, R., J. Page, and F. Tarp, eds. 2018. *Industries without Smokestacks: African Industrialization Revisited*. Oxford: Oxford University Press.

Spray, J., and V., Agrawal. 2016. "Enterprise Map of Rwandan Maize, Tourism and Dairy Value Chains." International Growth Centre, London.

World Bank and Government of Rwanda. 2020. "Future Drivers of Growth in Rwanda: Innovation, Integration, Agglomeration, and Competition." Washington: World Bank. https://openknowledge.worldbank.org/handle/10986/30732.

FOUR

Uganda

Leaving Agriculture in Search of Progress on Transformation

MADINA GULOBA, MEDARD KAKURU, JAKOB RAUSCHENDORFER, AND SARAH N. SSEWANYANA

D espite its impressive economic growth of more than 6 percent on average over the last two decades, Uganda's unemployment rate remains high. Additionally, about a third of all Ugandans still source their livelihoods from low-productivity subsistence farming, and another third are either employed in informal trading activities or as low-wage workers on farms. Manufacturing, which has recently been the key driver of decent jobs and economic transformation in East Asia, has lost momentum. This chapter considers the role of industries without smokestacks (IWSS) in Uganda. It documents that IWSS provide about a fifth of jobs in the country, make up the majority of its export basket, have higher output per worker, and demand higher skills from their employees. However, evidence of employment shifting toward these more productive sectors is limited thus far. In an illustrative scenario of 7 percent annual growth, we project a slight shift of employment toward more productive IWSS sectors of the economy by 2030. However, to unlock employment growth in the relatively more productive IWSS sectors identified by the government as priorities—horticulture, agro-processing, and tourism—the country will need to remove a number of cross-cutting and sector-specific constraints and ensure that the workforce is adequately equipped with respect to soft skills and problem-solving, as well as digital skills.

Introduction

Uganda has one of the youngest populations in the world.[1] Driven by rapid population growth exceeding an average 3 percent a year since 2000, today about 75 percent of Ugandans are below the age of 30 years (UBOS 2018, 12). In addition, while aggregate economic growth has been strong—averaging above 6 percent over the last two decades—job creation has been dragging behind. Unemployment is high, and is estimated at 7.6 percent for Uganda's working-age population and 13.9 percent for its youth, among the highest in Sub-Saharan Africa.[2] Additionally, most employed citizens find jobs in low-productivity activities like informal trading or traditional agriculture. About a third of the working-age population continues to source their livelihoods exclusively from subsistence farming.[3]

Manufacturing—the key driver of structural transformation, productivity growth, and decent jobs in East Asia between 1950 and about 1990—seems less and less likely to become an engine of growth and welfare in the country. For example, according to the data presented in this chapter, the relative contribution of the manufacturing sector to employment in Uganda has been declining over the course of the last two decades, and anecdotal examples for the failure of different manufacturing activities abound.

At the same time, other, more skill-intensive activities have emerged as nonnegligible contributors to growth, employment, and export earnings in the country. These activities are distinct from manufacturing but share many of the desirable features of traditional industry. They are tradable, allowing firms to overcome the small size of the domestic market, realize economies of scale, and tap into the global value chains that today make up most of world trade. They are also more skill-intensive and have a higher output per worker than traditional agriculture. Additionally, firms in these sectors can grow rapidly after the adoption of new technologies and can benefit from agglomeration effects. In Uganda, these sectors include commercialized and often export-oriented horticulture and floriculture, agro-processing (e.g., juices, beverages, and baked goods), telecommunication services, tourism, and transportation. Given that these industries are both remarkably different and at the same time very similar in their characteristics to traditional manufacturing, Newfarmer, Page, and Tarp (2018) call them industries without smokestacks (IWSS).[4] In this chapter, we analyze the role of the IWSS sectors in Uganda. Specifically, we characterize their contribution to the economy to date and ask whether they could play the same role as manufacturing once did in driving structural transformation in the country and pulling workers out of subsistence farming and into better and more productive employment.

To this end, the chapter is organized as follows. In the second section, we give a brief background of Uganda's labor market. In the third section, we analyze the role of the IWSS sectors in Uganda's economy and identify their role in employment, output, and exports and also provide a comparison with non-IWSS sectors regarding the productivity and skill intensity of activities. In the fourth section, we explore future scenarios, with a focus on identifying the country's distribution of jobs under its aspirational ambition of 7 percent economic growth. Focusing on the three sectors identified by the government as priorities—agro-processing, horticulture, and tourism—the fifth section is concerned with identifying constraints on growth in the IWSS sectors. We conclude with policy recommendations in the sixth section.

Uganda's Labor Market: A Problem Statement

Between 2012/13 and 2016/17, Uganda's population increased from 34.1 million to 37.7 million (UBOS 2017) and is estimated to reach a total of at 74 million by 2040. Since 2000, the population growth rate has averaged more than 3 percent a year (World Bank 2020, 42). This rapid expansion of the population has resulted in the country having one of the youngest populations in the world, with more than 75 percent below the age of 30.

In table 4-1, we employ two waves of the Uganda National Household Survey (UNHS) conducted in 2012/13 and 2016/17 to present key

Table 4-1. Key Characteristics of Uganda's Labor Market

Characteristic	2012/13			2016/17			Absolute Growth	Annualized % Growth
	Female	Male	Total	Female	Male	Total		
All (15–65 years)								
Working-age population	8,354	7,569	15,922.0%	10,100	8,814	18,914	2,991	4.2%
Labor force, narrow	3,966	4,712	8,973	4,630	5,392	10,021	1,048	2.7%
Employed (%)	92.5%	94.4%	90.4%	89.0%	95.4%	92.4%	1,145	3.2%
Narrow unemployment rate (%)	7.5%	5.6%	9.6%	11.0%	4.6%	7.6%	–97	–5.6%
Subsistence farmer only	3,251	2,250	5,501	3,738	2,307	6,045	544	2.3%
Youth (15–24 years)								
Working-age population	3,079	2,904	5,982	3,635	3,245	6,879	897	3.4%
Labor force, narrow	1,298	1,422	2,719	1,295	1,399	2,694	–25	–0.2%
Employed (%)	76.9%	81.6%	79.4%	81.5%	90.4%	86.1%	162	1.8%
Narrow unemployment rate (%)	23.1%	18.4%	20.6%	18.5%	9.6%	13.9%	–187	–9.7%
Subsistence farmer only	1,279	1,118	2,396	1,269	999	2,268	–129	–1.3%

Sources: UBOS UNHS surveys, 2012/13 and 2016/17.

Note: All numbers are in thousands, unless specified differently. The categories "absolute growth" and "annualized % growth" refer to growth over the period 2012/13–2016/17. Employment calculations exclude Ugandans active exclusively in subsistence farming.

characteristics of Uganda's labor market.[5] The table shows that in 2016/17, Uganda's working age population (15 to 65 years) was about 18.9 million, split between about 8.8 million men and 10.1 million women. Reflecting Uganda's rapid population growth, between the two surveys the working-age population increased by a staggering 4.2 percent. In 2016/17, there were almost 6.9 million youth (15 to 24 years), corresponding to about 37 percent of Uganda's total working-age population.

Considering broad employment indicators, the total size of the labor force age between 15 and 65 years was about 10 million in 2016/17, while the total youth labor force stood at 2.7 million Ugandans. Expressing these numbers as shares of the respective working-age populations results in a labor force participation rate of about 53 percent for all Ugandans and 39 percent for the country's youth. Unemployment among youth was considerably higher than among those of working age and stood at 13.9 percent, compared with 7.6 percent for all Ugandans. Additionally, for both age groups, the number in wage employment grew at a pace slower than that of the working-age population but outpaced the growth of the labor force.

Wage employment opportunities aside, for both age groups, subsistence farming is still the only source of livelihoods for a large share of the working-age population: About 32 percent of all persons in either age group relied on subsistence farming as their sole source of livelihood in 2016/17.[6] Finally, regarding gender, table 4-1 reveals that labor force participation is lower among females. Additionally, unemployment among female workers is higher, and drastically so. For both age groups, the unemployment rate is about twice as high for females as for males, standing at 11 percent for the working-age population (vis-à-vis 4.6 percent for male workers) and 18.5 percent for the country's youth (compared with 9.6 percent for male youth).

In many ways, the messages emerging from table 4-1 clearly define the country's labor market challenge and reemphasize the importance of the study at hand. Unemployment in Uganda—especially among youth—is substantial, and about a third of the working population continues to rely on low-productivity subsistence farming for their livelihoods.[7] The key question for policymakers is which types of economic activity are likely to solve the country's unemployment problems in the future and have the capacity to provide productive jobs that contribute to aggregate economic growth and prosperity. The next sections of this chapter are concerned with this question and assess the role and characteristics of IWSS in the country.

The Role of Industries without Smokestacks in Uganda's Economy

In this section, we analyze the contribution of IWSS to the Ugandan economy. What is the role of IWSS in providing livelihoods and employment in the country? How does labor productivity in these sectors compare with labor productivity in non-IWSS sectors, and is there evidence for workers moving into more productive activities? What is the contribution of IWSS to the country's overall economic output as well as exports? And what skill requirements do IWSS sectors have in comparison with non-IWSS activities?

Industries without Smokestacks Provide a Fifth of Ugandan Jobs

Table 4-2 considers the significance of IWSS from a jobs perspective and shows employment in different IWSS and non-IWSS sectors, as well as in manufacturing, for Uganda's working-age population (15 to 65 years), relying on data from the Uganda National Household Survey's 2012/13 and 2016/17 waves, augmented with employment in formal firms registered as taxpayers with the government.[8] Limitations of having only two periods of survey data aside, a number of important patterns emerge from this illustration.

First, table 4-2 shows that in 2016/17, IWSS sectors provided employment for only about 20 percent of all Ugandans working either exclusively in subsistence farming or in any of the IWSS or non-IWSS sectors. Manufacturing absorbed roughly 3 percent of workers, and non-IWSS sectors accounted for a combined 78 percent of all employment, with agriculture as well as low-productivity informal trading activities (e.g., street vending) together absorbing about 70 percent of all workers. Crucially, in this illustration, non-IWSS agriculture includes subsistence farming, which in 2016/17 occupied some 6 million Ugandans, or about a third of the country's working-age population. Among IWSS sectors, information and communications technology (ICT), as well as maintenance and repairs, are still somewhat negligible from a jobs perspective, while the remaining IWSS sectors all contribute to employment in similar shares (each between 2 and 3 percent).

Changes in the employment distribution between the two periods suggest that the importance of IWSS increased, while the relevance of both manufacturing and non-IWSS declined.[9] The data also suggest that employment in IWSS sectors with an annualized growth rate of 6.8 percent grew faster than both the economy wide average (2.9 percent annualized growth,

Table 4-2. IWSS Sectors Provide About a Fifth of Ugandan Jobs, 2016/17

	Employment			Employment share		Annual % Growth,
	2012/13	2016/17	Change	2012/13	2016/17	2012/13–2016/17
Overall Total (15–65 years)	13,568	15,297	1,729	100%	100%	2.9
Total IWSS	2,292	3,026	734	17%	20%	6.8
Agro-food processing	535	300	–235	4%	2%	–14.2
Horticulture and export crops	285	350	65	2%	2%	5.0
Tourism	260	355	95	2%	2%	7.6
ICT	36	39	3	0%	0%	2.0
Transportation	306	500	194	2%	3%	12.0
Construction	356	417	61	3%	3%	3.9
Maintenance and repairs	113	113	0	1%	1%	0.0
Finance & business services	121	435	314	1%	3%	31.3
Trade formal (excl. Tourism)	280	517	237	2%	3%	15.0

(*continued*)

Table 4-2. (continued)

| | Employment | | | Employment share | | Annual % Growth, 2012/13–2016/17 |
	2012/13	2016/17	Change	2012/13	2016/17	
Manufacturing	586	387	–199	4%	3%	–10.2
Total Non-IWSS	10,690	11,885	1,194	79%	78%	2.6
Agriculture	8,205	9,121	916	60%	60%	2.6
Mining	66	86	20	0%	1%	6.5
Utilities	13	30	17	0%	0%	20.5
Trade informal (excl. Tourism)	1,420	1,472	52	10%	10%	0.9
Domestic services and household	98	185	87	1%	1%	15.6
Government	546	600	54	4%	4%	2.3
Other services	342	390	48	3%	3%	3.2

Sources: UBOS UNHS surveys, 2012/13 and 2016/17; URA-PAYE data.

Note: All numbers are in thousands, unless specified differently. Growth figures are relative to the UNHS 2012/13 survey. Differences between total employment in tables 4-1 and 4-2 are due to missing data on sectoral affiliation in the household surveys and because we add Ugandans active exclusively in subsistence farming to the overall total. "Agriculture" includes Ugandans employed in agriculture (e.g., as farm workers in the production of food crops) as well as individuals sourcing their livelihoods exclusively from subsistence farming. Consequently, subtracting the number of subsistence farmers from total employment in this table results in the total number of Ugandans in waged employment (15,297 – 6,045 = 9,252, for 2016/17). To identify employment in "trade formal (excl. tourism)" and "trade informal (excl. tourism)," we proceed as follows. First, we calculate the number of workers who report being engaged in trading activities in the UNHS 2012/13 and 2016/17, providing us with totals not distinguished by formal and informal. Next, we employ data on firms from the Pay-As-You-Earn (PAYE) data collected by the URA and calculate the number of workers employed by taxpaying, formal trading firms (e.g., supermarkets and car retailers). Finally, we subtract the number of formal employees from the totals inherent in the UNHS data to identify workers engaged in informal trading activities (e.g., street vending).

including employment in subsistence farming) as well as employment in non-IWSS (2.6 percent). Employment in non-IWSS agriculture, including subsistence farming, grew at a rate slower than the economy-wide average. With respect to the role of IWSS as a source of employment among youth, patterns closely match the ones for the working-age population. For example, and referring to the 2016/17 data, IWSS contributed about 20 percent of all employment opportunities for the youth.[10]

In sum, the figures provided in this section suggest that IWSS do not yet play a crucial role in Uganda's labor market, with more than two-thirds of the labor force generating livelihoods in non-IWSS agriculture, subsistence farming, and informal trade. Notably, employment growth in IWSS is higher than in non-IWSS activities, suggesting that these sectors could play a more important role in the future.

Labor in IWSS Is More Productive Than the Country-wide Average

While still relatively small in its contribution to Ugandan employment, a key insight from our data is that labor in IWSS sectors is much more productive than in non-IWSS and manufacturing and consequently than Uganda's economy-wide average. In figure 4-1, we present aggregates of average output per worker (in millions of Uganda shillings) for the economy as a whole, for aggregate IWSS and non-IWSS sectors, and for manufacturing as a benchmark. Economy-wide labor productivity maintained relatively stagnant over the four-year period captured by our data, remained high in IWSS, increased in manufacturing, and increased slightly in non-IWSS.[11] High labor productivity in IWSS is driven by agro-food processing, ICT, finance, and business services, as well as formal trade. Notably, labor productivity in agriculture (inclusive of subsistence farming)—the backbone of Uganda's economy, and a direct source of income for about 60 percent of Ugandans—has remained the country's least productive sector, with an output of about 1.2 million Uganda shillings per worker per year in 2016/17 (about $340). In comparison, labor productivity in more commercialized and export-oriented horticulture and export crops is about three times as high.[12]

Evidence for Ugandans Moving into Higher-Productivity Activities Is Limited

While IWSS sectors are more productive, we find mixed evidence for labor moving out of agriculture and into these sectors. In figure 4-2, we employ more aggregated data than are available in the Ugandan household

FIGURE 4-1. **IWSS Are the Most Productive Sectors
in the Ugandan Economy**

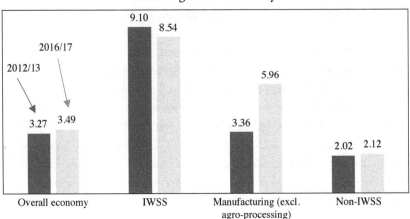

Source: Authors' calculations.

Note: Constructed from UBOS statistical abstracts, UNHS 2012/13 and 2016/17 data sets, as well
as URA PAYE data. Figures show output per worker in million UGX (constant 2009/10 values).
IWSS includes "construction (formal and informal)," and non-IWSS includes agriculture,
inclusive of subsistence farming. The considerable rise in the productivity of the manufacturing
sector is due to the data suggesting a decline of the labor force but an increase in GDP of the
sector. To identify employment in formal and informal trade (excl. tourism), we proceed as follows.
First, we calculate the number of workers who report being engaged in trading activities in the
UNHS 2012/13 and 2016/17, providing us with totals not distinguished by formal and informal.
Next, we employ data on firms from the Pay-As-You-Earn (PAYE) data collected by the URA and
calculate the number of workers employed by taxpaying, formal trading firms (e.g., supermarkets
and car retailers). Finally, we subtract the number of formal employees from the totals inherent in
the UNHS data to identify workers engaged in informal trading activities (e.g., street vending).

surveys and analyze the movement of workers across activities with different levels of productivity over a longer time horizon (2000–2017). The size
of a bubble is proportional to a sector's employment share in 2017. The
y axis orders sectors by relative productivity in 2017 (output per worker),
while the x axis shows the percentage-point change in the share a sector
holds in total employment between 2000 and 2017.

While no disaggregated data at the IWSS level were available for a long
enough period,[13] a number of important messages regarding structural
change in the country emerge from this illustration. First and foremost, the
share of employment held by Uganda's agriculture sector has remained very
sizeable and even increased slightly over a period spanning almost 20 years.[14]
Second, while some workers seem to have moved into higher-productivity

FIGURE 4-2. **Evidence of Ugandan Workers Moving
into Higher-Productivity Activities Is Limited**

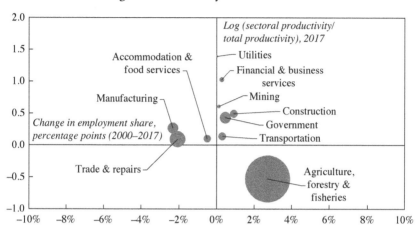

Source: Authors' calculations.

Note: Sectoral employment estimates are taken from the International Labor Organization (ILO) (https://ilostat.ilo.org/data) and sectoral output (GDP) is taken from the Uganda Bureau of Statistics (https://www.ubos.org/explore-statistics/9/). "Quarterly GDP at constant prices, Oct. 2018"). Agriculture, forestry, and fisheries is inclusive of subsistence farming as well as of commercial IWSS activities. Individual sectors are aggregated at the levels available in both sources of data. For example, the ILO provides employment data for "utilities," while UBOS provides data for "water" and "electricity," which we group together to construct the GDP for "utilities."

sectors—including IWSS activities such as construction, transportation, and financial and business services—the employment share held by the manufacturing sector has decreased by about 2 percentage points.[15] In sum, this illustration suggests that structural change has been somewhat stagnant over the last two decades: Most workers have remained in low-productivity activities.

IWSS Sectors Grow Faster Than Non-IWSS and Manufacturing

Between the two periods captured by the Uganda National Household Survey—2012/13 and 2016/17—gross domestic product (GDP) in IWSS sectors grew faster than both non-IWSS and manufacturing (table 4-3). Especially, tourism, ICT, and construction grew rapidly, driven by an inflow of foreign visitors and strong economic growth overall, which fueled demand for the construction sector. From a jobs perspective, we find at least tentative evidence that growth in IWSS sectors leads to more jobs than growth in

Table 4-3. IWSS Sectors Grow Faster and Have a Higher Employment Elasticity

	GDP at constant market price 2009/10 (billion UGX)		Change in GDP %	Change in employment,%	Employment elasticity
	2012/13	2016/17	2012/13–2016/17	2012/13–2016/17	2012/13–2016/17
Overall Total	44,386	53,327	20%	13%	0.63
Total IWSS	20,845	25,845	24%	32%	1.33
Agro-food processing	1,789	2,097	17%	-44%	-2.55
Horticulture and export crops	1,255	1,378	10%	23%	2.33
Tourism	1,283	1,552	21%	37%	1.74
ICT	3,836	5,657	47%	8%	0.18
Transportation	1,323	1,674	27%	63%	2.39
Construction	2,936	3,834	31%	17%	0.56
Maintenance and repairs	322	344	7%	0%	0.00
Finance & business services	5,108	6,110	20%	260%	13.23
Trade formal (excl. Tourism)	2,993	3,199	7%	85%	12.30

Manufacturing	1,970	2,308	17%	−34%	−1.98
Total Non-IWSS	21,571	25,174	17%	11%	0.67
Agriculture	10,098	11,091	10%	11%	1.14
Mining	631	802	27%	30%	1.12
Utilities	1,373	1,727	26%	131%	5.07
Trade informal (excl. Tourism)	2,691	2,876	7%	4%	0.53
Domestic services and household	235	266	13%	89%	6.73
Government	2,062	2,659	29%	10%	0.34
Other services	4,481	5,753	28%	14%	0.49

Sources: UBOS Statistical abstracts, UNHS 2012/13 and 2016/17 data sets, as well as URA PAYE data.

Note: Where we could not group GDP at IWSS and non-IWSS levels, we used shares of broader activities to proxy missing sectors. Specifically, we proxy sectoral GDP for "maintenance and repairs," "trade formal (excl. tourism)," and "trade informal (excl. tourism)" with "trade and repairs." Manufacturing was generated from the category "agro-processing and manufacturing." For the categories "agriculture" and "horticulture" and "export crops," we use the category "horticulture and agriculture." GDP figures for non-IWSS agriculture are inclusive of subsistence farming. The changes in employment used in this table are adopted directly from table 4-2. Differences between subsectoral grouping in the GDP and the employment data may therefore exist. The overall GDP excludes taxes on products. "Employment in non-IWSS agriculture" includes Ugandans employed in agriculture (e.g., as farm workers in the production of food crops), as well as individuals sourcing their livelihoods exclusively from subsistence farming. To identify employment in "trade formal (excl. tourism)" and "trade informal (excl. tourism)," we proceed as follows. First, we calculate the number of workers who report being engaged in trading activities in UNHS 2012/13 and 2016/17, providing us with totals not distinguished by formal and informal. Next, we employ data on firms from the Pay-As-You-Earn (PAYE) data collected by the URA and calculate the number of workers employed by taxpaying, formal trading firms (e.g., supermarkets and car retailers). Finally, we subtract the number of formal employees from the totals inherent in the UNHS data to identify workers engaged in informal trading activities (e.g., street vending).

non-IWSS sectors. Sectoral employment elasticities—measuring the increase in employment as a result of output increases at the sector level—are higher for IWSS than for non-IWSS and manufacturing, and therefore are higher than the nationwide average, which we estimate as 0.63. We cautiously interpret this as a finding that growth in IWSS sectors generates more jobs than growth in other sectors.[16]

IWSS Sectors Account for About 70 Percent of Uganda's Export Earnings

Uganda exports too little: Formal exports of goods and services amounted to about 17 percent of GDP in 2017, compared with 24 percent for the Sub-Saharan African average (World Bank 2021). Against this background, an important observation is that growth in IWSS sectors seems to also have been driven by external demand for these goods and services. IWSS exports (both goods and services) make up almost 70 percent of Uganda's total exports and—resembling their contribution to domestic output—have outpaced manufacturing (table 4-4). As for non-IWSS exports, close to all mining exports are gold, which is widely known not to be mined in the country itself but smuggled in from neighboring countries. Within the IWSS sectors, tourism is by far the most important sector, while agro-processing and coffee and tea (the country's traditional export crops) account for the bulk of IWSS goods exports. A final observation— mirroring the declining importance of manufacturing from an employment perspective in the country—is that manufacturing exports have declined over the course of the last decade.[17]

IWSS Are More Skill Intensive Than Non-IWSS and Manufacturing

IWSS sectors are more skill intensive than non-IWSS sectors and manufacturing, while also providing a large number of jobs for unskilled persons (table 4-5). Among all workers active in IWSS, about 34 percent are either high skilled or skilled. For manufacturing, the same figure is 10 percent, while for non-IWSS only about 9 percent of all workers are skilled or high skilled, a figure largely driven by a sizable number of government employees, who usually have high levels of educational attainment. Unsurprisingly, high-wage sectors such as ICT, as well as finance and business services, emerge as those sectors with a disproportionally large share of highly skilled and skilled workers. Additionally, tourism—a sector dependent on workers who are capable of engaging with demanding international customers—employs a large number of skilled Ugandans.

Table 4-4. IWSS Contribute About 70 Percent to Uganda's Export Basket

Sector	2011		2017		2011–2017
	USD (million)	Share of total goods and services exports, %	USD (million)	Share of total goods and services exports, %	Annualized % growth
Total IWSS	2,662	69%	3,133	68%	2.9%
IWSS services exports	1,392	36%	1,431	31%	0.5%
Transportation	150	4%	156	3%	0.7%
Tourism	960	25%	941	20%	−0.3%
Telecommunications	75	2%	39	1%	−8.0%
Government and other services	164	4%	260	6%	9.8%
Financial and business services	43	1%	35	1%	−3.1%
IWSS goods exports	1,270	33%	1,702	37%	5.7%
Horticulture	2	0%	8	0%	50.0%
Coffee and tea	548	14%	652	14%	3.2%
Other agricultural products	247	6%	373	8%	8.5%
Agro-processing	473	12%	669	15%	6.9%

(continued)

Table 4-4. (continued)

Sector	2011		2017		2011–2017
	USD (million)	Share of total goods and services exports, %	USD (million)	Share of total goods and services exports, %	Annualized % growth
Manufacturing total	390	10%	334	7%	–2.4%
Textiles	107	3%	73	2%	–5.3%
Other manufacturing	283	7%	261	6%	–1.3%
Total non-IWSS	785	20%	1,124	24%	7.2%
Mining	429	11%	575	13%	5.7%
Informal cross-border exports	356	9%	549	12%	9.0%
Total exports (goods and services)	3,837		4,591		3.3%

Sources: UNComtrade (2020); Atlas of Economic Complexity (2020); Bank of Uganda (2021).

Note: Goods exports are identified through the codes of the World Customs Organizations Harmonized System nomenclature, and services are classified in line with the United Nation's Extended Balance of Payments Services Classification. Tourism includes personal and business travel. Service exports may include additional categories for which data are not available (e.g., construction). "Informal cross border exports" are collected by the Bank of Uganda and consist of informal exports to Uganda's immediate neighbors. "Other agricultural exports" are included under IWSS goods exports, due to being exported by formal firms.

Table 4-5. IWSS Are More Skill Intensive Than Non-IWSS or Manufacturing (2016/17 Data)

	Absolute ('000)			Share		
	High skilled	Skilled	Low skilled	High skilled	Skilled	Low skilled
Overall Total	782	1,404	13,113	5%	9%	86%
Total IWSS	315	730	1,980	10%	24%	65%
Agro-food processing	5	79	216	2%	26%	72%
Horticulture and export crops	0	2	347	0%	1%	99%
Tourism	20	262	73	6%	74%	21%
ICT	11	25	3	29%	63%	9%
Transportation	2	90	409	0%	18%	82%
Construction	11	14	392	3%	3%	94%
Maintenance and repairs	1	28	84	1%	25%	74%
Finance & business services	184	192	58	42%	44%	13%
Trade formal (excl. Tourism)	80	40	397	15%	8%	77%

(continued)

Table 4-5. (continued)

	Absolute ('000)			Share		
	High skilled	Skilled	Low skilled	High skilled	Skilled	Low skilled
Manufacturing	6	37	345	1%	9%	89%
Total Non-IWSS	461	637	10,788	4%	5%	91%
Agriculture	18	73	9,030	0%	1%	99%
Mining	0	4	82	1%	5%	95%
Utilities	3	13	15	9%	42%	49%
Trade informal (excl. Tourism)	0	147	1,325	0%	10%	90%
Domestic services and household	0	24	161	0%	13%	87%
Government	428	142	31	71%	24%	5%
Other services	12	234	145	3%	60%	37%

Source: Authors' own calculations using UBOS UNHS survey (2016/17) and URA-PAYE data.

Note: In the UNHS 2016/17 data, some individuals do not report their sectoral affiliations but not their occupations. To maintain consistency with employment figures reported in previous tables of this chapter, we obtain the distribution of low-skilled / skilled / highly skilled workers per subsector from the UNHS 2016/17 and apply the resulting shares to total employment per sector reported in table 4-2. Skill definitions are as follows. Highly skilled occupations include managers and professionals. Skilled occupations include technicians and associate professionals; clerical support workers; and service and sales workers. Low-skilled occupations include skilled agricultural, forestry and fishery workers; craft and related trades workers; plant and machine operators and assemblers; and elementary occupations. We manually adjust the skill distribution in one category "trade informal (excl.) tourism" since the skill definitions used would suggest that informal traders are skilled "sales workers." To adjust for the resulting high share of skilled workers in this category, we keep the total employment number for this sector and apply the skill distribution from a similar country (Rwanda) to the resulting total. The original distribution in the Ugandan data for "trade informal (excl. tourism)" is 1 percent highly skilled workers, 95 percent skilled workers, and 4 percent low-skilled workers (figures rounded). "Agriculture" includes Ugandans employed in agriculture (e.g., as farm workers in the production of food crops) as well as individuals sourcing their livelihoods exclusively from subsistence farming. Since no data on the skill profile of subsistence farmers were available, we adopt the one for other non-IWSS agriculture for this activity. To identify employment in "trade formal (excl. tourism)" and "trade informal (excl. tourism)," we proceed as follows. First, we calculate the number of workers who report being engaged in trading activities in UNHS 2012/13 and 2016/17, providing us with totals not distinguished by formal and informal. Next, we employ data on firms from the Pay-As-You-Earn (PAYE) data collected by the URA and calculate the number of workers employed by tax paying, formal trading firms (e.g., supermarkets and car retailers). Finally, we subtract the number of formal employees from the totals inherent in the UNHS data to identify workers engaged in informal trading activities (e.g., street vending).

Uganda's Future Labor Market:
An Illustrative Scenario of 7 Percent Annual Growth

The recent National Development Plan III formulates the Government of Uganda's highly ambitious goal of reaching a GDP per capita of just below $1,200 by fiscal year 2024/25, propelling the country to middle-income status.[18] To achieve this goal, the government expects the economy to grow by 7 percent a year over this period (NPA 2020, xxi). In this section, we adopt this economic growth ambition to provide an illustrative scenario with a view on the likely sectoral distribution in the labor market in 2030. To compute the potential future distribution of jobs in Uganda, we rely on observed historical patterns and a number of assumptions about employment elasticities as well as the distributions of jobs across various skill levels within any given activity. The goal of this exercise is to make tentative statements regarding the future distribution of jobs per each economic activity as well as the skills required by these positions.

We provide projections for aggregate and sectoral GDP in 2030 by combining observed sectoral growth rates with Uganda's 7 percent aspiration and forecast from our baseline year (2016/17) to 2030.[19] To convert projected economic growth at the sectoral level into labor market outcomes, we combine forecasted growth rates with sectoral employment elasticities, taking into account our previous observation that IWSS sectors reveal greater employment elasticities than non-IWSS activities.[20] The results of this exercise are presented in table 4-6; also see table 4-7.

In this scenario, IWSS sectors—with 8 percent annual GDP growth— expand somewhat faster than non-IWSS (6 percent) and twice as fast as manufacturing (4 percent). Economy wide employment grows at close to 3.7 percent, slower than employment growth in the IWSS sectors (5.8 percent). Employment in non-IWSS (especially agriculture) is growing at a much slower pace (3.1 percent), while manufacturing grows at 4.3 percent. In the aggregate, this projection suggests that the Ugandan economy would shift slightly toward the more productive IWSS sectors, with the contribution of IWSS to employment increasing by a 6 percentage points, in contrast to the declining importance of non-IWSS, especially non-IWSS agriculture, and a close-to-stagnant contribution of manufacturing.[21] Among the IWSS sectors, activities that demand higher skills of their workers—such as tourism, finance and business services, ICT, and agro-processing—grow at a faster pace than the country-wide average.

Table 4-6. The Sectoral Distribution of GDP and Jobs in 2030: An Illustrative 7 Percent Growth Scenario

	GDP			Employment				Share of total employment	
	2016/17 Billion UGX (2009/10 const. prices)	2030 (proj.) Billion UGX (2009/10 const. prices)	Annual growth	2016/17 ('000)	2030 (proj.) ('000)	Add. Jobs ('000)	Annual growth	2016/17	2030 (proj.)
Overall Total	53,328	128,225	7%	15,297	24,647	9,350	3.7%	100%	100%
Total IWSS	25,845	72,562	8%	3,026	6,325	3,300	5.8%	20%	26%
Agro-food processing	2,097	4,107	5%	300	693	393	7%	2%	3%
Horticulture and export crops	1,378	2,049	3%	350	559	209	4%	2%	2%
Tourism	1,552	3,470	6%	355	712	357	5%	2%	3%
ICT	5,657	28,879	13%	39	162	123	12%	0%	1%
Transportation	1,674	4,519	8%	500	1,177	677	7%	3%	5%
Construction	3,834	11,807	9%	417	1,194	777	8%	3%	5%
Maintenance and repairs	344	455	2%	113	149	36	2%	1%	1%
Finance & business services	6,110	13,031	6%	435	997	562	7%	3%	4%
Trade formal (excl. Tourism)	3,199	4,244	2%	517	682	166	2%	3%	3%

Manufacturing	2,308	3,861	4%	387	668	281	4.3%	3%	3%
Total Non-IWSS	25,174	51,802	6%	11,885	17,654	5,769	3.1%	78%	72%
Agriculture	11,091	16,511	3%	9,121	13,396	4,275	3%	60%	54%
Mining	802	2,206	8%	86	165	79	5%	1%	1%
Utilities	1,727	4,548	8%	30	61	31	6%	0%	0%
Trade informal (excl. Tourism)	2,876	3,814	2%	1,472	1,840	368	2%	10%	7%
Domestic services and household	266	450	4%	185	226	41	2%	1%	1%
Government	2,659	7,770	9%	600	1,388	788	7%	4%	6%
Other services	5,753	16,504	8%	390	576	186	3%	3%	2%

Source: Authors' calculations.

Note: Baseline figures (2016/17) constructed from UBOS Statistical Abstracts and UNHS 2016/17 as well as URA-PAYE data. To project GDP in 2030, we adopt observed sectoral growth rates and scale them up by a constant factor to meet the government's 7 percent aggregate growth ambition over this period. To project sectoral employment, we begin from the baseline figures in 2016/17 and combine projected GDP growth at the sectoral level with the employment elasticities detailed in the annex, table 4-10. We then apply the resulting distribution profile of jobs in different IWSS and non-IWSS sectors to the projected labor force in 2030, which we calculate by applying the labor force participation rate for 2016/17 (53 percent) to the projected working-age population of 32.4 million (UBOS 2015). We further assume an unemployment rate of 5 percent (down from 9.6 percent in 2012/13 and 7.6 percent in 2016/17). Finally, since non-IWSS agriculture is inclusive of subsistence farming, we add to this figure the expected number of subsistence farmers, applying the observed "employment" growth rate of 2.5 percent for this sector to the period 2017–30. Non-IWSS agriculture includes Ugandans employed in agriculture (e.g., as farm workers in the production of food crops) as well as individuals sourcing their livelihoods exclusively from subsistence farming. To identify employment in "trade formal (excl. tourism)" and "trade informal (excl. tourism)," we proceed as follows. First, we calculate the number of workers who report being engaged in trading activities in UNHS 2012/13 and 2016/17, providing us with totals not distinguished by formal and informal. Next, we employ data on firms from the Pay-As-You-Earn (PAYE) data collected by the URA and calculate the number of workers employed by taxpaying, formal trading firms (e.g., supermarkets and car retailers). Finally, we subtract the number of formal employees from the totals inherent in the UNHS data to identify workers engaged in informal trading activities (e.g., street vending).

Table 4-7. Uganda's 7 Percent Growth Scenario: Projected Jobs by Skill Level

| | 2016/17 | | | 2030 (projected) | | | | | | Annual % growth (2016/17–2030) | | |
| | Share | | | ('000) | | | Share | | | | | |
	High skilled	Skilled	Low skilled	High skilled	Skilled	Low skilled	High skilled	Skilled	Low skilled	High skilled	Skilled	Low skilled
Overall Total	5%	9%	86%	2,082	3,316	19,248	8%	13%	78%	8%	7%	3%
Total IWSS	10%	24%	65%	877	1,942	3,507	14%	31%	55%	8%	8%	4%
Agro-food processing	2%	26%	72%	13	295	385	2%	43%	56%	7%	11%	5%
Horticulture and export crops	0%	1%	99%	0	4	555	0%	1%	99%	0%	3%	4%
Tourism	6%	74%	21%	49	551	111	7%	78%	16%	7%	6%	3%
ICT	28%	63%	9%	31	60	72	19%	37%	44%	8%	7%	26%
Transportation	0%	18%	82%	110	283	784	9%	24%	67%	36%	9%	5%
Construction	3%	3%	94%	135	236	823	11%	20%	69%	21%	24%	6%
Maintenance and repairs	1%	25%	74%	7	38	104	5%	26%	70%	15%	2%	2%
Finance & business services	42%	44%	13%	423	440	134	42%	44%	13%	7%	7%	7%
Trade formal (excl. Tourism)	15%	8%	77%	108	35	539	16%	5%	79%	2%	-1%	2%

Manufacturing	1%	9%	89%	11	191	466	2%	29%	70%	6%	14%	2%
Total Non-IWSS	4%	5%	91%	1,195	1,183	15,276	7%	7%	87%	8%	5%	3%
Agriculture	0%	1%	99%	3	272	13,121	0%	2%	98%	-13%	11%	3%
Mining	0%	4%	95%	0	7	158	0%	4%	96%	0%	4%	5%
Utilities	9%	42%	49%	6	26	30	9%	42%	49%	6%	6%	6%
Trade informal (excl. Tourism)	0%	10%	90%	37	214	1,589	2%	12%	86%	—	3%	1%
Domestic services and household	0%	13%	87%	0	24	202	0%	11%	89%	—	0%	2%
Government	71%	24%	5%	1,137	221	31	82%	16%	2%	8%	3%	0%
Other services	3%	60%	37%	12	419	145	2%	73%	25%	0%	5%	0%

Source: Authors' calculations.

Note: Baseline figures (2016/17) constructed from UBOS Statistical Abstracts and UNHS 2016/17 as well as URA-PAYE data. To compute the number of jobs per each skill-level and sector in 2030, we proceed as follows. First, we take the number of employed workers in 2016/17 per each sector and each of the three skill levels. To compute the distribution of additional/new jobs within a sector across different skill levels, we obtain sector- and skill-level-specific employment growth rates from the two UNHS survey waves (2012/13 and 2016/17), which provide us with projected employment demand at this level in 2030. Since the resulting aggregate figures per sector are slightly larger than our sector-level projections for labor demand, we apply the resulting distribution of new jobs across the three skill levels to the previously calculated sectoral totals of new/additional job per subsector. Due to data-related inadequacies, we have to rely on IWSS/non-IWSS aggregates in some cases. We detail these assumptions in table 4-11. "Agriculture" includes Ugandans employed in agriculture (e.g., as farm workers in the production of food crops) as well as individuals sourcing their livelihoods exclusively from subsistence farming. To identify employment in "trade formal (excl. tourism)" and "trade informal (excl. tourism)," we proceed as follows. First, we calculate the number of workers who report being engaged in trading activities in UNHS 2012/13 and 2016/17, providing us with totals not distinguished by formal and informal. Next, we employ data on firms from the Pay-As-You-Earn (PAYE) data collected by the URA and calculate the number of workers employed by tax paying, formal trading firms (e.g., supermarkets and car retailers). Finally, we subtract the number of formal employees from the totals inherent in the UNHS data to identify workers engaged in informal trading activities (e.g., street vending).

Next, we ask what type of workers will be required in Uganda's labor market under this 7 percent high-growth scenario. In line with our result of stronger growth in the more skill-intensive IWSS sectors, we find a shift toward skilled and high-skilled workers (table 4-7).[22] In our scenario, the aggregate skill profile of the labor force would shift moderately to skilled and highly skilled workers: While in 2016/17 only about 14 percent of Ugandan workers were skilled *or* highly skilled, by 2030 our scenario suggests that the same figure would increase to 21 percent. In IWSS, the shift would imply an increase of skilled or highly skilled workers from 34 percent to 45 percent, while in non-IWSS the same shift would be from 9 percent to 14 percent.[23] One crucial observation emerging from this exercise is that while IWSS continue to be more skill-intensive than non-IWSS, there is a distinct shift within most sectors toward more skilled workers.

The key question is whether Uganda will be able to adequately train and educate its workforce. While recent labor market surveys seem to suggest that job-education mismatches are not yet a severe issue for Ugandan employers,[24] future developments such as increasing automation in many agricultural activities or an emerging demand for digital skills (e.g., marketing, online payments and booking activities) may well create future obstacles in the labor market.[25]

Unlocking Transformative Growth:
The Case of Agro-processing, Horticulture, and Tourism

In the previous sections, we have documented the growing potential of IWSS for the Ugandan economy. We present evidence that IWSS sectors are already nonnegligible contributors to economic growth in the country, account for about 70 percent of the country's export earnings, and display higher productivity than non-IWSS sectors (and even manufacturing in the case of activities like ICT or financial services). At the same time, the preceding analysis also demonstrates that a large share of the population is still employed in low-productivity agriculture, with about a third of the working-age population deriving livelihoods from subsistence farming. Given the potential of IWSS to provide decent jobs for Ugandans in the future, a key question from the vantage point of policy is what obstacles prevent further growth and job creation in these sectors.

In this section, we employ both secondary information as well as insights from a small firm-level survey conducted for this study to identify constraints to growth in IWSS. To make the analysis tractable, we concentrate on three types of economic activities that have been identified as priorities by the government: agro-processing, horticulture, and export crops, as well as tourism. In 2017, these three IWSS sectors alone accounted for more than half Uganda's export earnings, contributed 10 percent to national output, and provided employment for about 1 million Ugandans, compared with just below 400,000 jobs available in manufacturing.

Agro-processing

In its National Development Plan III (NDP III), the Ugandan Government identifies "agro-industrialization" as one of its' key development programs to be pursued over the next five years.[26] Agro-processing includes agro-based manufactures like flour from graining rice, maize or cassava, but also of more sophisticated and high-value products like juices, dairy products, sauces, confectionary, beverages, and baked goods. Driven by rising domestic and regional demand, agro-processing has become the dominant activity in the country's manufacturing sector.[27] According to the index of industrial production published by the Ugandan Bureau of Statistics, food processing and beverage production alone account for about 60 percent of the country's manufacturing output (UBOS 2019). Agro-based manufactures have also played a key role in helping the country grow exports and diversify its export basket, which is now less dominated by primary products like maize, raw cotton, or unprocessed coffee (figure 4-3). Given that agriculture dominates the Ugandan economy, economic activities targeted at adding value to raw produce domestically are a key opportunity to drive growth and employment in the country.

Among the key challenges and constraints to further growth in Uganda's agro-processing sector are the following. First and foremost, the growth of Uganda's agro-processing sector is a direct function of productivity in the country's agricultural sector as a whole, which provides agro-processing units with the raw inputs required to produce final products. Fowler and Rauschendorfer (2019) find that the limited supply of raw materials is one central reason for the stark underutilization of installed agro-processing facilities in the country.[28] Raising productivity in the country's agricultural base (e.g., through better extension services or the adoption of modern seeds and fertilizers) therefore bears the greatest promise for increasing the country's growth of agro-based manufacturing activities.

On the external side, Uganda has duty-free and quota-free access to the members of the East African Community (EAC) customs union.[29]

FIGURE 4-3. **Composition of Uganda's Export Basket Over Time: Agro-Based Manufactures Have Become Increasingly More Important and Have Driven Export Growth and Diversification**

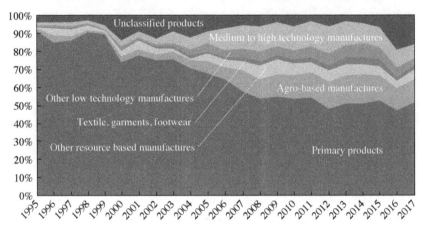

Sources: Fowler and Rauschendorfer (2019); data from the 2019 UNCTADStat database.
The "Lall classification" used to identify different product categories is provided by Lall (2000).

Benefiting from a high degree of external protection in the EAC's tariff program for agro-based manufacturers,[30] physical proximity as well as similar standards for products intended for human consumption, members of the EAC absorbed about 40 percent of Ugandan exports in 2018, including the vast majority of the country's exports of agro-based manufactures. In light of the importance of regional markets as drivers of demand for Uganda's agro-based manufactures, an obstacle and threat to further growth is that EAC members frequently undermine mutual market access through non-tariff barriers and that the region is riddled by trade impeding conflict.[31] Such obstacles do not only have an impact on trade itself but also deter foreign direct investment, which, for example, played a crucial role in transforming Uganda's dairy sector over the past decade by incentivizing quality upgrading throughout the value chain to cater to the high demands of internationally oriented milk exporters (cf. Van Campenhout et al. 2019).

With respect to employment and skills specifically, the figures presented in the previous sections show that just below three-quarters of workers employed in agro-processing are low-skilled, with the remaining quarter mostly consisting of skilled workers and a few highly skilled managers. When surveying a small number of Ugandan agro-processing firms with a focus on identifying skill requirements for employment, we find that about

80 percent of employees in these firms work in occupations that can be classified as "plant and machine operators," as well as "skilled agricultural, forestry and fishery workers."[32] About a quarter of workers had only some or completed primary education, while another quarter had also some secondary education. About half the workers had completed secondary education or higher. Regarding likely future jobs, agro-processing firms reported a demand for personnel working with producers of raw inputs to improve quality (e.g., a milk-processing firm reported a demand for trainers to support milk farmers in adopting to best milk handling practices). The enterprises also stated that increasing automation as well as opportunities such as online marketing, will require digital skills in the future—for example, for using mobile applications and for efficiently coordinating work.

Horticulture

Uganda's horticultural sector can be subdivided into two product categories, both of which are highly export oriented: coffee and tea—the country's traditional cash crops—as well as floriculture and fresh fruits and vegetables (FFV). Coffee is still Uganda's most important export product and accounts for about a fifth of its total exports (excluding gold) in any given year. While still comparatively small in economic significance, cut flowers and FFV have shown impressive growth over the past two decades (cf. figure 4-4), and in 2018 accounted for about 3.6 percent of total exports excluding gold. Crucial for constraints on growth—and in stark contrast to agro-based manufactures, which are mostly consumed domestically or sold to regional partners—horticultural products (especially coffee and flowers) are almost exclusively produced to be exported to the high-value markets in the north.

The strong orientation of coffee, tea, floriculture, and FFV toward high-value markets in the north is helpful in identifying key constraints (and threats) on growth in these sectors. Given that access to these markets is crucial for the sector's success, it should be a priority to reduce the time and cost associated with trading, as well as making sure that Ugandan producers have the possibility to showcase that their products are safe for human consumption through standards and accreditation.

With respect to coffee, the country has an opportunity to significantly increase the value of its exports by upgrading quality domestically. Morjaria (2020) suggests that the structure of Uganda's coffee market— a large number of small-holder farmers that only reach international

FIGURE 4-4. **Exports of Flowers and Fruits and Vegetables Have Shown Substantial Growth**

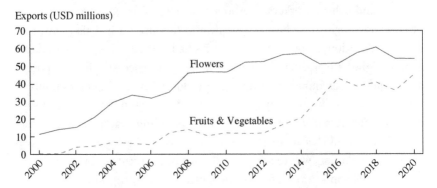

Source: Data from the Bank of Uganda (2021). Fresh fruits and vegetables include crops like citrus, pawpaw, mangoes, pineapple, tomatoes, bananas, and peppers.

markets through a small number of exporters—provides an opportunity to realize quality upgrading (e.g., only harvesting ripe cherries) by encouraging mandatory export standards.

As for employment and skills, as evident from the figures presented in the preceding sections based on the Uganda National Household Survey 2016/17, almost all workers (99 percent) in the sector are low-skilled, reflecting the low educational requirements for farm work in activities like the cultivation of flowers or crops like coffee. When surveying four firms in this sector,[33] we find this aggregate statistic confirmed: More than 90 percent of all young workers employed by these enterprises can be classified as "skilled agricultural, forestry and fishery workers," of which more than 60 percent have not completed primary education and only about 10 percent have completed secondary education. Crucially, however, this status quo in employment does not seem to reflect the requirements of the sector: Firms report a skill gap with respect to problem solving, resource management, and soft skills—abilities associated with completed primary and/or secondary education.

Tourism

Tourism has become one of Uganda's most important sectors and has superseded coffee (the country's traditional export crop) as the country's leading earner of foreign exchange (figure 4-5).[34] In 2016/17 the sector provided

FIGURE 4-5. **Tourism Has Become More Important Than Coffee**
for Uganda's Export Performance

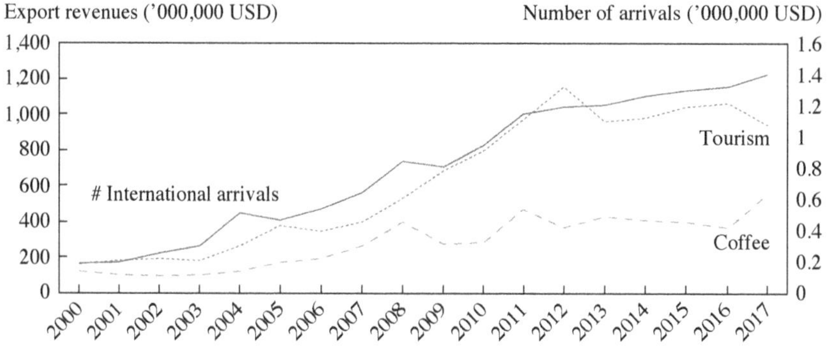

Export revenues ('000,000 USD)   Number of arrivals ('000,000 USD)

Sources: World Bank, World Development Indicators, 2020; UNComtrade (2020).

about 360,000 jobs for Ugandans, almost as many as the country's manufacturing sector (excluding agro-processing). Between 2000 and 2017, both the
number of international arrivals as well as receipts from tourism increased
more than fivefold (figure 4-5). The Government of Uganda recognizes the
potential of tourism as a sector capable to provide jobs and stimulate growth,
both directly and indirectly through linkages with domestic suppliers: the
NDP III declares that "tourism is important for increasing forex earnings,
creating jobs and alleviating poverty" (NPA 2020, 95).

Its potential aside, several constraints prevent the country from fully
reaping the potential of tourism as a driver for (environmentally friendly)
growth and job creation.[35] First, managing Uganda's wildlife and especially
its gorillas—the country's key attraction compared with other potential
destinations in Africa—is pivotal from the vantage point of ensuring that
tourism continues to be a driver of growth in Uganda. To prevent practices like poaching, the government has adopted a policy of providing local
communities near national parks with 20 percent of revenues generated
from park entrance fees (Ahebwa and English 2018, 8). Second, access to
key attractions—especially Bwindi National Park, home to the country's
gorillas—needs to be improved. The long ride from the international airport in Entebbe to Bwindi is one of the key disadvantages that Uganda has
relative to its main competitor in gorilla tracking, neighboring Rwanda.
Third, the country still suffers from a negative and conflict-associated
international image and seems mostly to be associated by potential visitors

FIGURE 4-6. Movement of Labor across Sectors, at the IWSS Level

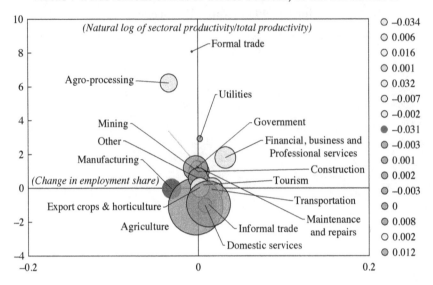

Source: Authors' own illustration using the 2016/17 UNHS data set.

Note: Light gray bubbles represent IWSS sectors, dark gray bubbles are manufacturing, and medium gray bubbles are non-IWSS sectors. The sizes of the bubbles are proportional to the employment share of a sector in 2016/17.

with its former dictator, Idi Amin. Active marketing in key source markets through overseas agents has shown to produce first results in the form of a higher number of international arrivals from these origins.

Finally—and most crucial, from the vantage point of driving employment growth in the sector—the sector is highly dependent on a skilled workforce. According to UNHS 2016/17, about three-fourths of workers employed in Uganda's tourism sector are classified as "skilled," rendering the industry the country's largest employer for skilled workers (cf. table 4-6). A sizable share of workers is highly skilled (6 percent), and the sector does not employ many workers that can be classified as low-skilled. This distribution is reflective of the reliance of the sector on a workforce capable of catering to the demands of international customers. In a small survey of eight Ugandan hospitality firms (mainly hotels), we find these assertions confirmed. Especially among the hotels with confirmed star rating levels, we find that the vast majority of employed youth are employed as "services and sells workers" and have completed secondary education (high school).

Interviewed managers reported an increasing need for digital skills (using mobile applications or online booking systems), as well as a need for problem-solving skills (i.e., solving novel, ill-defined problems in a real-world setting).[36] In their review of the country's tourism sector, Ahebwa and English (2018, 11) conclude that "the quality of personnel available to work in the tourism sector is generally considered to be low."

Cross-Sectoral Constraints on Growth

Beyond the sector-specific issues presented in the previous sections, several cross-sectoral constraints prevent higher growth in both IWSS as well as non-IWSS sectors and manufacturing. The next subsections outline key obstacles that appear to affect growth in a multitude of Ugandan sectors at once.

Miscoordination between Government Entities Is Rife and Hampers Effective Policy Action

Especially in industrial policy and agro-industrialization, a number of government institutions with overlapping responsibilities do not seem to coordinate well, which prevents a concerted push for commercializing agriculture through, for example, targeted public investments.[37] This issue seems less prevalent in the tourism sector, where the Ministry of Tourism, Wildlife, and Antiquities is the institution responsible for setting policy objectives, supported by topic-specific (and often private sector led) organizations like the Association of Ugandan Tour Operators, the Uganda Hotel Owner's Association, and the Uganda Wildlife Authority.

Access to Imported Inputs Is Insufficient and Undermines Globally Competitive Production

All three IWSS sectors discussed in the preceding sections either already realize close to all their earnings in international markets (horticulture and tourism) or benefit substantially from regional markets that provide them with the opportunity to overcome a small domestic market (agro-processing). To compete internationally, it is pivotal that these firms have access to imports that matter for competitive production. Such imports include equipment (e.g., milk processing machinery in agro-processing), direct inputs (e.g., fertilizer and packaging materials for flower exporters), but also consumer items that meet international standards (e.g., towels, mattresses, and tableware for hotels in the tourism sector). While many enterprises benefit from firm-level plans exempting them from duty and value-added-tax payments on imported inputs (cf. Rauschendorfer and Twum 2021), the statutory tariff rates on many factors of production are 10 percent or 25 percent in the country's main tariff schedule, rendering imports costly for firms without preferential access.

Infrastructure Like Roads and Access to Electricity Is Insufficient

A lack of transportation infrastructure is prevalent in the country and disrupts many value chain activities. As of May 2019, Uganda had a road network of about 146,000 kilometers (MoFPED 2019), which translates to a road density of 60.6 kilometers / 100 square kilometers. Although Uganda's road density is among the highest in Sub-Saharan Africa, the quality of the roads is low—only 22.2 percent of the national road network is paved (MoFPED 2019). Similarly, insufficient access to electricity curbs growth. In the 2013, in the World Bank's enterprise survey, about 35 percent of companies reported access to electricity to be a major obstacle.

Barriers to Exporting Are Often Homemade and Prevent Firms from Exploiting Available Opportunities

Ugandan firms enjoy duty-free and quota-free access to almost all viable destination markets;[38] however, "red tape"—burdensome procedures associated with exporting and importing—prevent firms from entering trading activities. It should be noted that in recent years, Uganda has made considerable strides in bringing down the time and cost of trading through trade facilitation interventions like the adoption of the National Electronic Single Window. Since IWSS activities are tradable and exhibit scale economies, further removing these barriers will be important to foster growth.

Policy Recommendations

Uganda is plagued with unemployment challenges. The jobs being created (especially for the youth) are not enough to absorb the rapidly growing labor force. The analysis presented in this chapter also indicates that structural transformation has been stagnant and the importance of the manufacturing sector as an employer has been declining considerably in recent years. IWSS sectors—which could be a substitute driver for job creation and structural transformation due to being tradable, having high productivity, and since they reveal economies of scale—are currently not growing fast enough to replace the role of non-IWSS sectors like low-productivity agriculture in providing livelihoods or to make up for the role of manufacturing in driving the structural transformation process in the country, although employment in these sectors is growing faster than in non-IWSS sectors.[39]

As described in the previous sections, insufficient growth of IWSS sectors can be attributed to a host of challenges, most of which relate to the business climate. IWSS sectors are largely formal and export-oriented enterprises and hence feel challenges in the business environment more keenly, particularly those that relate to trade and the regulatory environment. Nonetheless, Uganda finds itself on a growth trajectory that is increasingly seeing IWSS sectors driving the process of structural transformation. For example, from our findings, it is evident that there has been a shift of employment away from manufacturing and to highly productive service activities, such as finance and business services, transportation, ICT, and tourism. These IWSS activities are found to offer jobs that require a high degree of skills, while non-IWSS activities mainly provide employment for low-skilled workers. To date, non-IWSS sectors—most importantly, informal trade and noncommercial agriculture—still employ the majority of the country's workers.

Regarding the three IWSS sectors considered in more detail in this chapter—horticulture, agro-processing, and tourism—the available data from the Uganda National Household Surveys as well as a small firm-level survey suggest that all three sectors (tourism in particular, and horticulture to a lesser degree) will require skilled workers in the future. Drawing from firm survey results, with respect to soft skills there is a noticeable gap in problem-solving skills. Regarding future skill requirements, digital skills in the areas of marketing, online booking systems, and the use of phone applications will be paramount. Consequently, the government should ensure that both learning and training curricula incorporate these requirements, which would significantly reduce the possibility of a future skills mismatch.

Having noted that the importance of manufacturing in Uganda is declining in many ways (GDP, employment, and exports), while IWSS sectors are gaining ground, there is a need to channel support to these three sectors to increase their pace of growth and realize their job creation potential. The next subsections consider each of these sectors focused on in this chapter and provide policy recommendations for achieving the goal of higher sectoral growth by overcoming the constraints on growth presented earlier in the chapter.

Horticulture

As a first priority, the government needs to intensify training for extension workers with a specialization in horticulture. Extension workers will also need to be equipped with irrigation technology, which is necessary for most horticultural production.

Since the majority of the sector's produce (e.g., cut flowers, fresh fruits and vegetables, and coffee and tea) is exported to high-value markets in the EU or the United States, it is paramount for the government to address barriers to continuously accessing these markets. These should be priorities:

- address nontariff barriers—such as delays, high transportation costs, and burdensome procedures—when trading;
- increase testing capacities in the country, allowing producers to verify that products are safe for human consumption;
- in the same way as for agro-processing, many firms in the sector rely on imported materials to produce their final output (e.g., Kraft paper for packaging cut flowers). The government should ensure that access to these inputs is possible at affordable costs through a sensible tariff program.

Agro-processing

The current government focus of offering fiscal incentives (e.g., tax holidays) does not appear to be effective in stimulating investment in the agro-processing sector and also comes at considerable fiscal costs to the public in the form of revenue forgone that could be used to invest in infrastructure or education.[40] Additionally, there is evidence that the investment floor for local investors is too high (currently at $10 million) and should be lowered so that more willing investors qualify for these incentives. Given these concerns, the government should instead concentrate on solving the rampant supply side constraints (most crucially, in special economic zones and industrial parks) and ensure continued access to key markets for firms active in the sector. This would allow firms to develop economies of scale and employ more workers in the future. Specifically, the government should concentrate on these key issues:

- provide avenues for more affordable access to credit (e.g., through reform of the banking sector, or financing plans like the Agricultural Credit Facility under the Bank of Uganda);

- provide cheap and stable supplies of water and electricity and reduce the cost of internet usage;
- improve physical infrastructure (e.g., roads and border crossings);
- ensure that access to key growth markets in the region is maintained and expanded by working with the East African Community and toward the implementation of the African Continental Free Trade Area;
- reducing the cost of trading by investing in physical and digital trade infrastructure (e.g., One Stop Border Posts with neighboring countries, and an expansion of digital initiatives like the National Electronic Single Window); and
- ensure that agro-processors have access to imported inputs through an adequate tariff policy.

In addition, agro-processing is heavily reliant on the performance of Uganda's agricultural sector as a whole. Low productivity in agriculture ultimately implies reduced raw materials for agro-processing firms to operate sustainably and exploit installed capacity. This implies a need to raise farm-level productivity through the adoption of modern inputs and better extension services.

Tourism

To boost growth in the tourism sector, interventions in the area of skilling the workforce are most important to ensure that the high demands of international clients are met with an adequately skilled workforce. The government needs to invest in education to enhance skills of youth so they are suitable for the available jobs. Among others, government should incorporate problem-solving and digital skills in the training curriculum, starting already at the lower levels of education. This is particularly important because even the sectors that employ low-skilled workers require these skills. By implication, education has an impact on the competitiveness of the tourism industry, and hence is worthy of government investment efforts. Regarding digital skills in particular, these are needed for marketing efforts, dealing with online booking systems, and similar tasks. Beyond this focus on training the labor force, there is scope for the government to boost growth in the tourism sectors through the following (cf. Ahebwa and English 2018):

- managing and preserving the country's wildlife by preventing poaching and enabling local villages to benefit from tourism;

- improving access roads to key attractions like Bwindi National Park; and
- strengthening the brand of Uganda as a tourism destination through targeted marketing actions.

Across all sectors, in an effort to avoid future skills mismatches, it is prudent that policymakers know where future jobs are. This will enable the government to decide where to devote resources that are intended to improve training.

Annex: Additional Tables and Figures

Table 4-8. Sectoral GDP and Employment Data at Higher Levels of Aggregation (2017)

	Employment ('000)	GDP (billion UGX)*	Productivity (million UGX/ worker)
Total	15,012	59,918	4.0
Agriculture, forestry, and fisheries	10,910	12,868	1.2
Mining & quarrying	58	943	16.1
Manufacturing	599	4,451	7.4
Utilities	18	1,786	98.7
Construction	313	3,882	12.4
Trade & repairs	1,317	6,527	5.0
Transportation & storage	312	1,714	5.5
Accommodation & food services	284	1,435	5.1
Finanical & business services	118	5,018	42.5
Government	671	7,233	10.8

Sources: Sectoral employment estimates are taken from the International Labor Organization (https://ilostat.ilo.org/data) and sectoral output (GDP) is taken from the Uganda Bureau of Statistics (https://www.ubos.org/explore-statistics/9/, "Quarterly GDP at Constant Prices, Oct. 2018").

* GDP is in constant prices (2009/10 values).

Note: Sectoral definitions: Individual sectors are aggregated at the levels available in both sources of data. For example, the International Labor Organization provides employment data for "utilities," while UBOS provides data for "water" and "electricity," which we group together to derive GDP for "utilities." With respect to cross-checking aggregate employment elasticities for the Ugandan economy, Kapsos (2005, 41) estimates values between 0.23 and 0.40, while more recent estimates from the International Monetary Fund (2019) suggest an economy-wide elasticity of 0.6 for the period 2000–2017.

Table 4-9. Employment Elasticities at Higher Sectoral Aggregation and Over a Longer Time Horizon

Sector	GDP (billion UGX, const. 2009/10 prices)		Employment ('000)		Employment elasticity, 2009–17
	2009	2017	2009	2017	
Total	39,937	59,918	10,895	15,012	0.76
Agriculture, forestry, and fisheries	10,699	12,868	7,306	10,910	2.43
Mining & quarrying	433	943	34	58	0.63
Manufacturing	3,410	4,451	574	599	0.14
Utilities	1,076	1,786	10	18	1.16
Construction	2,283	3,882	231	313	0.50
Trade & repairs	5,255	6,527	1,274	1,317	0.14
Transportation & storage	1,011	1,714	256	312	0.31
Accommodation & food services	853	1,435	263	284	0.12
Financial & business services	3,075	5,018	86	118	0.59
Government	4,320	7,233	526	671	0.41

Sources: Sectoral employment is taken from the International Labor Organization (https://ilostat.ilo.org/data), and sectoral output (GDP) is taken from the Uganda Bureau of Statistics (https://www.ubos.org/explore-statistics/9/, "Quarterly GDP at Constant Prices, Oct. 2018").

* GDP is in constant prices (2009/10 values).

Note: Sectoral definitions: Individual sectors are aggregated at the levels available in both sources of data. For example, the International Labor Organization provides employment data for "utilities," while UBOS provides data for "water" and "electricity," which we group together to derive GDP for "utilities." With respect to cross-checking aggregate employment elasticities for the Ugandan economy, Kapsos (2005, 41) estimates values between 0.23 and 0.40, while more recent estimates from the International Monetary Fund (2019) suggest an economy-wide elasticity of 0.6 for the period 2000–2017.

Table 4-10. Employment Elasticities Observed and Elasticities Used for Projections

Sector	Observed employment elasticities: 2012/13–2016/17	Sub-sectoral employment elasticities used for projections: 2016/17–2030
Overall Total	0.63	
Total IWSS	1.33	
Agro-food processing	–2.55	1.20
Horticulture and export crops	2.33	1.00
Tourism	1.74	0.70
ICT	0.18	0.70
Transportation	2.39	0.70
Construction	0.56	0.80
Maintenance and repairs	0.00	0.70
Finance & business services	13.23	1.00
Trade formal (excl. tourism)	12.30	0.70
Manufacturing	–1.98	0.90
Total Non-IWSS	0.67	
Agriculture	1.14	0.75
Mining	1.12	0.45
Utilities	5.07	0.55
Trade informal (excl. Tourism)	0.53	0.50
Domestic services and household	6.73	0.20
Government	0.34	0.60
Other services	0.49	0.20

Source: Authors' calculations.

Note: Aggregate employment elasticities at higher levels of aggregation can be found in table 4-9. As for cross-checking aggregate employment elasticities for the Ugandan economy, Kapsos (2005, 41) estimates values between 0.23 and 0.40, while more recent estimates from the International Monetary Fund (2019) suggest an economy-wide elasticity of 0.6 for the period 2000–2017.

Table 4-11. Distribution of Additional Jobs in 2030 per Sector across Different Skill Levels

Sector	Additional jobs in 2030	Distribution of new jobs across skills			Documented edits to original computations
		High skill	Skilled	Low skill	
Overall Total	9,350	13%	24%	63%	None.
Total IWSS	3,300	16%	29%	55%	None.
Agro-food processing	393	2%	55%	43%	None.
Horticulture and export crops	209	0%	1%	99%	None.
Tourism	357	8%	81%	10%	None.
ICT	123	16%	29%	55%	Edited: Took IWSS Aggregate.
Transportation	677	16%	29%	55%	Edited: Took IWSS Aggregate.
Construction	777	16%	29%	55%	Edited: Took IWSS Aggregate.
Maintenance and repairs	36	16%	29%	55%	Edited: Took IWSS Aggregate.
Finance & business services	562	42%	44%	13%	None.
Trade formal (excl. Tourism)	166	17%	-3%	85%	None.

(continued)

Table 4-11. (continued)

Sector	Additional jobs in 2030	Distribution of new jobs across skills			Documented edits to original computations
		High skill	Skilled	Low skill	
Manufacturing	281	2%	55%	43%	Edited: Took values of "agro-food processing" due to similar technologies.
Total Non-IWSS	5,769	10%	18%	72%	
Agriculture	4,275	0%	5%	96%	None.
Mining	79	0%	3%	97%	None.
Utilities	31	9%	42%	49%	None.
Trade informal (excl. Tourism)	368	10%	18%	72%	No. Took non-IWSS Aggregate.
Domestic services and household	41	0%	-1%	101%	None.
Government	788	90%	10%	0%	Edited: Mostly highly educated individuals.
Other services	186	0%	100%	0%	Edited: Smoothed out negative values.

Source: Authors'calculations.

Note: To compute the distribution of additional jobs within a sector across different skill levels, we obtain sector- and skill-level-specific employment growth rates from the two UNHS survey waves (2012/13 and 2016/17), which provide us with projected employment demand at this level in 2030. Since the resulting aggregate figures per sector are slightly larger than our sector-level projections for labor demand, we apply the resulting distribution of new jobs across the three skill levels to the previously calculated sectoral totals of new/additional job per sub-sector (the first column in the table above). Non-IWSS agriculture is inclusive of subsistence farming.

NOTES

1. This chapter is a shortened version of "Employment Creation Potential, Labor Skill Requirements, and Skill Gaps for Young People: A Uganda Case Study," by M. Guloba, M. Kakuru, S. N. Ssewanyana, and J. Rauschendorfer, AGI Working Paper 37, 2021. The reader should note that to facilitate comparability of the different case studies included in this volume, modifications with respect to the calculation of employment figures for different sectors and sectoral definitions were made. Consequently, the employment figures presented in this chapter do not necessarily correspond to those presented in the longer working paper. Details with respect to the calculation of employment figures for specific sectors are provided below each of the relevant tables.

2. Throughout this chapter, the age definition of "working age" is 15 to 65 years. Figures that pertain to "youth" refer to persons age 15 to 24 years.

3. See table 4-1 for key characteristics of the labor market.

4. For the purposes of this chapter, we include these sectors as industries without smokestacks (IWSS): horticulture and export crops (e.g., coffee, tea, and cut flowers), agro-food processing (e.g., juices), tourism, ICT, construction, maintenance and repairs, and finance and business services as well as formal trading activities (e.g., formal distribution services, such as retailers and wholesalers). Throughout the chapter, "manufacturing" excludes agro-food processing (e.g., juices, beverages, and grain milling), unless specified differently.

5. Throughout the chapter, it is important to note that while the availability of two waves of household survey data allows for calculating growth rates, these are based on surveys conducted only about four years apart from each other. Differences between the two periods should therefore be interpreted with caution once the analysis is taken to the sectoral level, because they could be nonsystematic and instead driven by factors like year-specific effects. For example, in 2016/17 the country was affected by droughts, which had an impact on agricultural activities and poverty.

6. This is a decrease from the 34.96 percent reported in UNHS 2012/13.

7. However, note that this age group in Uganda's education system is mostly in school and that working below 18 years is also considered child labor by law.

8. For the purposes of this table and the remainder of this chapter, we include Ugandans working in subsistence farming in the category non-IWSS *agriculture*. This addition explains differences between the economy-wide growth of employment presented in table 4-2 in comparison with table 4-1. While the Ugandan government has decided to not count subsistence farming as a "job" or "employment," this is done to facilitate comparability of the different country case studies presented in this book.

9. It is worth noting that a large share of Uganda's manufacturing sector consists of agro-processing (e.g., grain milling, juices, and beverages), so the

low and declining numbers for manufacturing may be misleading and should not be interpreted as Uganda "deindustrializing." However, when employing longer time series in figure 4-2, we find the declining role of manufacturing in Ugandan employment confirmed.

10. Please refer to the longer working paper of this chapter for more detail on the youth and gender dimension of IWSS in Uganda: Guloba et al. 2021.

11. The increased output per worker in the manufacturing sector is a result of the declining employment in the sector as found in our data. The resulting figures for the 2016/17 period should therefore be treated with caution, but the qualitative results remain unchanged.

12. While the stark difference between output per worker in IWSS and non-IWSS reported in this section is in part attributable to outliers in the underlying household survey data, it should be noted that the qualitative differences between more service oriented and commercialized sectors hold at higher levels of aggregation. Employing sectoral employment data from the International Labor Organization and GDP data at the same level of sectoral aggregation from the Uganda Bureau of Statistics, we find an average output per worker of 1.2 million UGX for Ugandan agriculture in 2017, compared with 12.4 million UGX in construction, 5.0 million UGX in trade and repairs, 5.1 million in accommodation and food services (as a proxy for tourism) or 5.5 million UGX in transportation. Output per worker in manufacturing (including IWSS activities like agro-food processing, which make up the bulk of manufacturing activities in Uganda) stands at 7.4 million UGX (see table 4-8 in the annex of this chapter).

13. Figure 4-6 provides an illustration at the IWSS level using the UNHS 2012/13 and 2016/17, only capturing four years.

14. While we are not able to distinguish between commercial IWSS agriculture (horticulture, tea, coffee, etc.) and subsistence farming with respect to employment, available output data suggest that IWSS commercial agricultural activities has grown faster over the course of the last decade. According to the sectoral GDP data available from UBOS, "cash crops" grew at an average of 3.2 percent a year, while "food crops" grew at 1.9 percent a year between 2009 and 2017. Our findings with respect to agriculture are therefore inconclusive since we are not able to track the movement of labor between different activities within the sector.

15. In the same way as agriculture, "trade and repairs" include both informal and formal trading activities.

16. Given the short time periods between the two surveys as well as issues associated with grouping employment and GDP at IWSS level, estimated employment elasticities at the sectoral level should be treated with caution. When we use longer time series (2009–17) and more aggregate sectoral GDP and employment figures from UBOS and the International Labor Organization, we estimate an economy-wide employment elasticity of 0.76, which is

largely aligned with the aggregate presented in table 4-4 (see table 4-9 in the annex for elasticities at higher aggregation). Using data ranging from 2000 to 2017, the IMF (2019) estimates an economy-wide employment elasticity of 0.6.

17. Again, it should be noted that Uganda's manufacturing sector largely consists of agro-processing activities like grain milling, beverages, baked goods, and similar agro-based products, which we single out in table 4-4 as "agro-processing."

18. For context, in 2019 Uganda's GDP per capita was $794 (World Bank 2021).

19. Specifically, since Uganda did not grow at the envisioned 7 percent rate between the two survey periods 2012/13 and 2016/17, we scale up sectoral growth rates with a constant that results in 7 percent aggregate growth over the period 2016/17 to 2030.

20. As evident from table 4-4, for many sectors the elasticities obtained from using two waves of household survey data that are only four years apart from each other suggest unrealistic employment elasticities—e.g., due to declining sectoral employment combined with positive GDP growth at the same level of aggregation (e.g., in manufacturing). Employment elasticities used for the projection part of this paper are shown in table 4-10 in the annex alongside observed elasticities.

21. While manufacturing is exclusive of agro-processing, which contributes a large number of jobs in the sector, an even marginal increase in the share of manufacturing in Ugandan employment is actually contrary to observed long-term patterns in the past. See also figure 4-2.

22. To compute the number of jobs per each skill-level and sector in 2030, we proceed as follows. First, we take the number of employed workers in 2016/17 per each sector and each of the three skill levels. To compute the distribution of additional/new jobs within a sector across different skill levels, we obtain sector- and skill-level-specific employment growth rates from the two UNHS survey waves (2012/13 and 2016/17), which provide us with projected employment demand at this level in 2030. Since the resulting aggregate figures per sector are slightly larger than our sector-level projections for labor demand, we apply the resulting distribution of new jobs across the three skill levels to the previously calculated sectoral totals of new/additional job per subsector. Due to data-related inadequacies, we have to rely on IWSS/non-IWSS aggregates in some cases. We detail these assumptions in table 4-11 in the annex.

23. The sizable share of highly skilled workers in non-IWSS is almost exclusively driven by workers employed by the government, which generally has high demands regarding formal educational attainment.

24. E.g., Khamis (2019, 19) employs the recent Manpower Survey Uganda 2016/17, which reports that when asked the question "How many permanent/

temporary/elementary employees do not have required qualification?" 96 percent of interviewed employers report to have zero employees in this category.

25. See also the reports from a small survey of firms in Uganda in the next section.

26. Specifically, the NDP III states that "agro-industrialization will be pursued to transform the subsistence agriculture sector to a commercial and competitive sector. This is required to increase household incomes of the majority (over 70 percent) of Ugandans directly and indirectly dependent on agriculture. This will be achieved by increasing export value of selected agricultural commodities, increasing the agricultural sector growth rate, increasing labour productivity in the agro-industrial value chain, creating jobs in agro-industry, and increasing the proportion of households that are food secure" (NPA 2020, 1). It should be noted that the NDP III understands agro-industrialization to entail both agro-processing (e.g., manufacturing of juices) as well as the development of horticulture, fresh fruits and vegetables and export-oriented cash crops like coffee and tea.

27. Domestically, dietary shifts have driven demand for agro-based manufactures. E.g., van Campenhout et al. (2019, 7) report that domestic consumption of milk per year and person had increased from 10 liters in 2002 to about 33 liters in 2012.

28. The World Bank (2012) reports that "most agro-processing industries (cotton ginning, coffee processing, dairy processing, grain milling, oilseeds processing, and animal feed milling) are operating at less than 50 percent capacity." See also EPRC (2018), which asserts that agro-manufacturing industries remain "stunted and operating below installed capacities."

29. The EAC comprises Kenya, Tanzania, Rwanda, Burundi, South Sudan and Uganda.

30. E.g., the tariff charged on dairy imports from countries outside the EAC is 60 percent ad valorem, providing a considerable price advantage for Ugandan exporters of milk to the region.

31. E.g., over the course of 2019 and 2020, Kenya banned imports of dairy products from Uganda, asserting the products had not been manufactured whole in the region but were produced from imported milk powder (cf. East African 2020). Similar directives had been made for poultry and eggs. Similarly, over 2019, Rwanda and Uganda closed the main border used for bilateral trade between the two countries (Katuna), greatly affecting bilateral trade, while the ongoing South Sudanese civil war continues to undermine exports to South Sudan.

32. Please see the longer version of this chapter for detailed survey results. The survey covered seven Ugandan agro-processing firms mostly involved in food-processing activities like juice manufacturing, baking, milling as well as the distribution of finished goods. Given the small size of the survey, results should not be taken as representative for the sector.

33. These are two flower exporters and two producers of FFV.

34. In 2017, exports of coffee and tea combined generated $652 million, while tourism provided the country with $941 million in foreign exchange.

35. This section draws on priorities identified by Ahebwa and English (2018).

36. See the longer working paper version of this chapter for additional details.

37. An illustrative example of this is the selection of value chains that are to be prioritized for increased support and commercialization. Rauschendorfer and Fowler (2019) compare value chains selected by different institutions like the Ministry of Agriculture, Animal Industry, and Fisheries; the Ministry of Finance, Planning, and Economic Development; or the National Planning Authority and show that there is little consensus as to which value chains are to be prioritized.

38. Under the East African Community customs union, Ugandan firms access markets like Kenya, Rwanda, and Tanzania duty and quota free and close to free trade exists with the countries of the COMESA Free Trade Area. Ugandan exporters also export duty free and quota free to the EU under the unilateral Everything But Arms Agreement and to the United States under the African Growth and Opportunity Act.

39. This totals 5.3 percent annualized employment growth in IWSS, compared with 4.4 percent annualized growth in non-IWSS (cf. table 4-2).

40. Eissa et al. (2021) estimate that the fiscal costs of tax incentives in Uganda are just below 1 percent of the country's GDP.

REFERENCES

Ahebwa, W., and P. English. 2018. "How Can Tourism Become a Driver of Economic Growth in Uganda?" IGC Final Report S-43437-UGA-1.

Bank of Uganda. 2021. "External Sector Statistics." https://www.bou.or.ug/bou/bouwebsite/Statistics/Statistics.html.

EPRC (Economic Policy Research Centre). 2018. "Fostering a Sustainable Agro-industrialisation Agenda in Uganda."

Eissa, N., P. Manwaring, N. Ntungire, and J. Rauschendorfer. 2021. "What Is the Fiscal Cost of Tax Incentives in Uganda?" IGC Final Report.

Fowler, M., and J. Rauschendorfer. 2019. "Agro-industrialisation in Uganda: Current Status, Future Prospects and Possible Solutions to Pressing Challenges." IGC Working Paper F-IH-UGA-006-2.

Guloba, M., M. Kakuru, S. N. Ssewanyana, and J. Rauschendorfer. 2021. "Employment Creation Potential, Labor Skill Requirements, and Skill Gaps for Young People: A Uganda Case Study." AGI Working Paper 37.

International Monetary Fund. 2019. "IMF Country Report No. 19/126 – Uganda."

Kapsos, S. 2005. "The Employment Intensity of Growth: Trends and Macroeconomic Determinants." International Labor Organization, Employment Strategy Paper.

Khamis, M. 2019. "Uganda Skills and Job Analysis." World Bank.

Lall, S. 2000. "The Technological Structure and Performance of Developing Country Manufactured Exports 1985–1998. QEH Working Paper QEHWPS44. University of Oxford.

NPA (National Planning Authority). 2020. "Third National Development Plan (NDP III) 2020/21–2024/25." https://library.health.go.ug/monitoring-and-evaluation/work-plans/third-national-development-plan-ndpiii-202021-202425.

Newfarmer, R., J. Page, and F. Tarp. 2018. *Industries without Smokestacks: Industrialisation in Africa Reconsidered.* Oxford University Press.

MoFPED (Ministry of Finance, Planning, and Economic Development). "Maintenance of National Roads: What Are the Key Challenges?" Budget Monitoring and Accountability Unit Briefing Paper (21/19). Minister of Finance, Planning, and Economic Development, Uganda.

Morjaria, A. 2020. "Uganda's Coffee Sector: Raising Quality for Exports and Growth." PowerPoint presentation at webinar on "agriculture and agro-industrialization," with Private Sector Development Unit of Ministry of Finance, Planning, and Economic Development. October 21.

Rauschendorfer, J., and A. Twum. 2021. "Unmaking of a Customs Union: Regional (Dis)integration in the East African Community." *World Trade Review*, 1–12.

UBOS (Uganda Bureau of Statistics). 2013. "Uganda National Household Survey 2016/13."

———. 2017. "Uganda National Household Survey 2016/17."

———. 2018. "Statistical Abstracts 2018." https://www.ubos.org/wpcontent/uploads/publications/05_2019STATISTICAL_ABSTRACT_2018.pdf.

Uganda Revenue Authority. 2018. "Pay-As-You-Earn Data on Firm Staffing."

Van Campenhout, B., B. Minten, and J. Swinnen. 2019. "Domestic versus Export-Led Agricultural Transformation: Evidence from Uganda's Dairy Value Chain." International Food Policy Research Institute.

World Bank. 2012. "Uganda Promoting Inclusive Growth Transforming Farms, Human Capital and Economic Geography: Synthesis Report." Report 67377-UG.

———. 2020. "Uganda Economic Update, 16th Edition: Investing in Uganda's Youth."

———. 2021. "World Development Indicators: GDP Growth."

FIVE

Ethiopia

Building on Manufacturing Momentum to Create New Jobs in Other Sectors

TSEGAY G. TEKLESELASSIE

Introduction and Country Context

In the past decade and half, Ethiopia has registered notable economic growth. Its average growth since 2004 has hovered around 10 percent. This growth has largely been driven by substantial public investment in infrastructure, coupled with solid performance of the service and construction sectors, which have benefited from modest mobility of labor from the agricultural sector. For example, out of the 9.27 percent average real gross domestic product (GDP) growth registered between 2010 and 2019, the agricultural sector contributed 2.32 percentage points, construction 2.5 percentage points, manufacturing 0.65 percentage points, and service 3.8 percentage points. Hence, in particular, the service sector has contributed to about 41 percent of the GDP growth in the last decade.

Extreme poverty (the percentage of the population living below the international poverty line) fell from 55 percent in 2000 to 23.5 percent in 2015/16 (e.g., NPC 2017) The achievement in terms of reducing poverty largely came from a modest growth in agriculture rather than structural transformation (World Bank 2015).

Between 2003 and 2006, the unemployment rate for the urban labor force in general, and for youth in particular, showed a marked decline. However, since 2006, the unemployment rate has been slightly increasing. In 2018, the unemployment rate for the general urban labor force stood at 19 percent, while for youth it was 25 percent. It should be noted that women face higher unemployment rates than men. For example, in 2018, the unemployment rate for women in urban Ethiopia was close to 27 percent, while men faced an unemployment rate of 13 percent.[1] Low earnings, underemployment, and vulnerable employment characterize rural Ethiopia, which again is an indicator of people living in a state of working poverty (e.g., Hino and Ranis 2014).

This is despite a policy focus on labor-intensive light manufacturing. Performance in value added, exports, and employment generation in the strategic sectors—such as textiles and garments, leather, cement, pharmaceuticals, construction, and agro-processing (food and beverages, honey, meat, and dairy)—has been below par.

Some sectors, such as textiles and garments, have gained special attention from the government, as shown by the construction of industrial parks focusing on these industries. While some industrial parks have been constructed and are owned by the private sector, the majority of them currently are public. Sheds in the public industrial parks are rented out to enterprises at highly subsidized rates. Currently, 13 industrial parks are in operation in different parts of the country. The agro-processing industry has also been among the priority sectors. Concrete interventions to support the sector will likely surface after the implementation of the four integrated agro-processing industrial parks that are under construction. The integrated agro-industrial parks are also public, but are financed mainly by the regional states. Establishment of the integrated agro-processing industrial parks can help address such issues as improved provision of infrastructure such as electricity, access to land, and enhanced services such as customs. The three-year homegrown economic reform agenda prepared in September 2019 has added sectors such as tourism, logistics, and mining to its priority sectors, in addition to manufacturing and agriculture.

The main objective of the current study is to investigate the potential of industries without smokestacks (IWSS) to create decent and sustainable jobs, particularly for youth. The focus here is on the agro-processing (particularly food and beverages), horticulture, tourism, and transportation sectors.

Since the preparation of its 2002 industrial development strategy (FDRE/MoI 2002), Ethiopia has emphasized the promotion of labor-intensive industries that aim to create decent jobs, enhance linkages with the agricultural sector, and bolster export competitiveness. An active industrial policy that aimed at transforming the structure of the economy, particularly from agriculture to industry and higher-value services, however, came with the Growth and Transformation Policy I (2010–15) (MoFED 2020) and the Growth and Transformation Policy II (2015–20) (NPC 2016) (hereafter, GTP I and GTP II).

The Government of Ethiopia developed various policies and strategies of active interventions to pave the way for the private sector to play a leading role. Support has been directed toward selected export-oriented and import-substituting sectors, such as textiles, leather, cement, and pharmaceuticals. Interventions have included direct capacity-building support and fiscal incentives such as tax holidays, a reduction of indirect taxes on capital goods, and preferential credit for selected sectors. Heavy government investment in infrastructure is envisaged to enhance the competitiveness of the private sector (e.g., Gebreeyesus 2013).

The construction of industrial parks since 2015 has constituted the apex of active industrial policy in Ethiopia. A key objective of constructing industrial parks has been increasing the share of the manufacturing sector in GDP. Through these policies, the government hopes to achieve several economic goals: boosting exports, attracting foreign direct investment, alleviating foreign exchange shortages, and reducing reliance on government borrowing and investments by state-owned enterprises (Zhang et al. 2018).

The big-push approach to develop industrial parks aims to pave the way for the private sector to be the economy's engine of growth. Industrial parks can be built by either the federal or regional government, the private sector, or through public and private partnerships. Eleven industrial parks have been built to date at the federal level, all of which are operational. Some of these industrial parks are specialized (e.g., Hawassa specializes in textiles and garments), while others can accommodate firms from various sectors. The industrial parks are designed to boost linkages, improve services through one-stop shops (e.g., customs clearance within the parks) and provide uninterrupted power supply and effluent treatment plants.

Aggregate Trends

With a population of about 109 million in 2018, Ethiopia is the second-most-populous country in Africa, after Nigeria. While it has had one of the fastest-growing economies in the past decade and a half in the world, it remains one of the poorest.

In recent years, the service sector has overtaken the agricultural sector in having the largest share of valued added, with close to 47 percent in 2017, followed by the agricultural sector, contributing 36 percent. The industrial sector has the lowest share, of about 17 percent of GDP in the same period, even though it has registered significant growth since 2013, after stagnating in the decade before 2013.

The share of the manufacturing sector (i.e., the industrial sector excluding construction) remained less than 5 percent of GDP until 2017, which is very low even by Sub-Saharan Africa standards, where it stands at 10 percent. In 2018/19, the share of the manufacturing sector rose to close to 6.8 percent as some of the industrial parks started to be populated by enterprises. The corresponding sectoral shares in 2000 were agriculture (55.3 percent), services (37 percent), and industry (9.7 percent).[2] Hence, in recent decades, the service sectors and the construction subsector have shown the fastest growth.

The pace of structural transformation is even slower when it comes to employment. Although the share of employment in agriculture has recently declined, most of the workforce is concentrated in the agricultural sector, with limited job opportunities available outside. Construction and "other services" have absorbed most of this change. The service sector employs 22 percent of the labor force, while the industrial sector employs less than 10 percent. The remaining 70 percent of the workforce is absorbed in agriculture. In 2000, agriculture employed close to 86 percent of the labor force, followed by services, with about 10 percent, while the industrial sector employed about 4 percent. Hence, structural transformation in terms of employment in the past two decades has been low. The changes in value added show that the modest labor mobility from agriculture to the service sector has resulted in higher output per worker.

Key supply-side problems—such as power outages, logistics, and short-ages of foreign exchange—are more likely to affect the manufacturing sector compared with the service sector. Moreover, the manufacturing sector has to compete with imports from the international market. On the other hand, competition in the service sector is largely from other domestic firms, and hence less fierce.

The service and construction sectors are protected from international competition through government policy (e.g., Gebreeyesus 2019). For example, some key services—such as wholesale, finance, logistics, and real estate—are allowed only for domestic firms, and there is a strong incentive to engage in those sectors. Another key factor for the growth of the con-struction sector is pubic investment on infrastructure as a policy focus by the government to enhance private sector competitiveness.

In terms of exports, the agriculture sector continues to be the major export source for the country. Based on data from the National Bank of Ethiopia, in 2017, the shares of the leading exports were coffee (31 percent), oilseeds (12.4 percent), khat (*Catha edulis*; 9.6 percent), and gold (7.4 percent). With shares of about 6 percent, 4 percent, and 3 percent, respectively, animals and animal products, leather and leather products, and textiles and apparel trailed. Manufacturing exports, typically leather and textiles, fell behind the agricultural items in export shares, indicating that structural transformation in terms of export remains low.

Labor Market Outcomes

The pace of urbanization in Ethiopia has been fast in recent years. For example, between 2003 and 2018, the urban population grew annually, on average, by 5.7 percent. Similarly, the youth population (age 15–29) grew annually, on average, by 5.3 percent. The labor force, measured by the eco-nomically active population (those aged 10 and above), exhibited an annual growth rate of 6.2 percent. Hence, the labor force in urban areas has increased even faster than the population growth rate of urban areas. The provision of decent jobs to the ever-growing labor force is a key challenge for the Ethiopian government.

In 2018, the unemployment rate for the general urban labor force was 19 percent, while for youth it was 25 percent. The unemployment rate for women in the same year was 27 percent. More than a third of young women remain unemployed. Even those employed face high underemployment (50 percent), low earnings, and job insecurity in both rural and urban areas.

Another crucial indicator of the outcome of the labor market is the duration of unemployment. More than a third of unemployed persons (35 percent) have been unemployed for more than 8 years. More than 60 percent of unemployed persons were unemployed for a year or more. This indicates a severe lack of job opportunities. The long duration of unemployment has had an adverse psychological impact on the well-being of the labor force. Moreover, a long spell of unemployment results in skill obsolescence.

Similarly, underemployment results in a large proportion of workers being classified as working poor. About half of the employed workforce is willing to take additional jobs, which are a result of either low pay or too few working hours.

The rate of unemployment by education level is one of the indicators of the effectiveness of the education system. In 2018, unemployment among secondary school graduates was about 28 percent, followed by those with technical and vocational education and training (TVET), and then diploma graduates at above 23 percent. In the same year, those with a university degree and above faced an unemployment rate of 16 percent, while those with an elementary education had an unemployment rate of about 14 percent. The group with the lowest unemployment rate is made up of those with no formal education, which may show that this group has no choice but to engage in any type of job that is available. In 2003, those with a university degree and above had a lower unemployment rate (9 percent) than the rate in 2018 (16 percent). The rise in the unemployment rate of the highly educated group in recent years has been a source of concern, as it can indicate the ineffectiveness of the education system or the existence of a skills mismatch (e.g., Beyene and Tekleselassie 2018).

Patterns of Growth: The Role of the IWSS Sectors

The IWSS sectors include agro-industry and horticulture, tourism, business services, including services based on information and communications technology (ICT), and transportation and logistics (Newfarmer, Page, and Tarp 2018). The key characteristics of enterprises in the IWSS sectors include being tradable, having the ability to absorb large numbers of moderately skilled labor, having higher-than-the average value

Table 5-1. Labor Productivity by Sector

Sector	Labor productivity (thousands of local currency)		
	2000	2010	2017
Total	13.72	21.41	33.17
Total IWSS	24.84	65.07	91.73
Agro-processing	23.90	22.56	60.80
Horticulture		614.96	299.93
Tourism	3.14	19.91	61.30
Transportation	74.78	99.94	136.59
Financial and business services	261.74	228.13	157.03
Trade	22.98	45.38	68.26
Manufacturing	11.44	20.17	37.53
Other Non-IWSS	12.12	15.53	24.48
Agriculture	9.66	11.95	16.25
Mining	75.55	29.95	15.68
Utilities	77.77	47.00	44.73
Construction	55.94	73.70	176.83
Government	54.43	72.83	80.69
Other	9.89	5.38	4.04

Source: Author's compilation using data from the Planning and Development Commission for 2015/16 and 2020.

Note: Coefficients for 2011 and 2015/6 were used to estimate the ratio of horticulture in agricultural value added for 2010 and 2017.

added per worker, exhibiting a capacity for technological change and productivity growth, and displaying evidence of agglomeration economies.

Sectoral Productivity Levels and Trends

Table 5-1 reports labor productivity measured as value added per worker. In 2017, labor productivity for the IWSS sectors was birr 91,730, which was close to three times that of overall labor productivity, close to 2.44 times that of manufacturing, and 3.75 times that of non-IWSS industries. Between 2000 and 2017, overall labor productivity grew annually, on average, at 8.34 percent, while the IWSS industries grew by about 16 percent. Manufacturing and non-IWSS industries grew at 13.4 percent and 6 percent, respectively, in the same period.

Following McMillan and Rodrik (2011) and McMillan, Rodrik, and Sepulveda (2016), we decompose the sources of aggregate labor productivity into *within productivity* (own sector productivity changes due to technological change and capital accumulation) and structural *transformation* due to movement of labor from low-productivity to higher-productivity sectors. This specification helps to decompose theses effects:

$$\Delta P_t = \sum_{i=n} \beta_{i,t-k} \Delta P_t + \sum_{i=n} p_{i,t} \Delta \beta_{i,t}$$

where P_t and $p_{i,t}$ are economy-wide and sector productivity, respectively, and $\beta_{i,t}$ is employment in sector i. The decomposing was done for 13 sectors composed of IWSS and non-IWSS industries.

The results show that 67 percent of the aggregate labor productivity change between 2010 and 2017 came from *within-sector* productivity change, while the remainder came from structural change. The disaggregated result by sector is provided in figure 5-1. IWSS industries such as trade, agroprocessing, and hotels and restaurants exhibited high within-sector productivity. Financial services and horticulture gained more from labor mobility toward them. Among non-IWSS industries, the construction sector benefited both from within-sector and structural transformation.

This dominance of within-sector productivity is not surprising at an early stage of industrialization, as most sectors start from low productivity and hence have a potential for within-sector productivity before structural transformation can kick off. Substantial public investment on social infrastructure, such as education and investment, and on agriculture, such as agricultural extension programs, may have contributed to the within-sector productivity gain in the country (e.g., Ferede and Kebede 2015; De Vries, Timmer, and De Vries 2015). While there are differences among countries in Africa in their paths to structural transformation, in the majority of them, the role of structural change has been low. Specifically, in countries such as Ethiopia, Kenya, Nigeria, and Tanzania, acceleration in aggregate productivity has mainly come from gains in within-sector productivity growth (e.g., De Vries, Timmer, and De Vries 2015).

Figure 5-2 provides a bubble chart of sectoral employment share, sectoral productivity, and growth in employment. The sizes of the bubbles indicate employment share, while sectoral productivity and employment growth are shown on the y axis and x axis, respectively. Agriculture remains by far the major employer in Ethiopia, followed by trade (IWSS) and manufacturing (non-IWSS). Looking at employment growth between 2000 and 2017, mining (non-IWSS), finance (IWSS), utilities (non-IWSS),

FIGURE 5-1. Sector Productivity and Structural Transformation

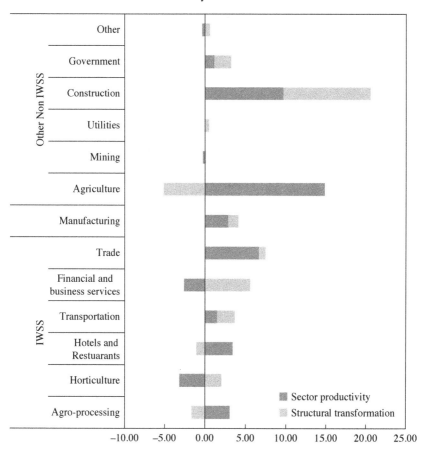

Sources: Author's compilation using data from the Planning and Development Commission and Mengistu et al. (2019).

construction (non-IWSS), and transportation (IWSS) registered the fastest growth. Finance (IWSS) and transportation (IWSS) were the most productive sectors in 2017.

The Growth of Selected IWSS Industries

The IWSS sectors play a crucial role in Ethiopia's economic development by diversifying its industrial base beyond traditional manufacturing. This section examines the growth and significance of the agro-processing,

FIGURE 5-2. **Employment Share, Employment Growth,
and Productivity, 2000–2017**

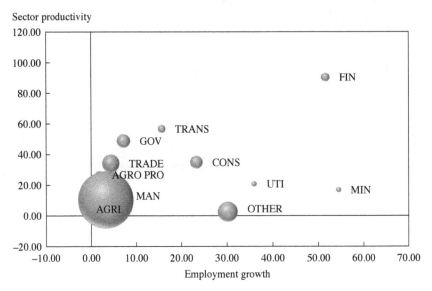

Source: Author's compilation using data from the Planning and Development Commission.

horticulture, tourism, and transportation subsectors. These subsectors have been identified as priority areas in the government's development plans for their roles in job creation, value addition, and export diversification.

Agro-processing: The Food and Beverage Industry

Agro-industry comprises several categories, including food and beverages, paper and wood products, textiles and apparel, leather and leather products, rubber products, and tobacco products. In this study, we focus on the food and beverage industry.

The agro-processing industry has been one of the key priority sectors identified by the Government of Ethiopia in its five-year development plans, such as PASDEP (2005–10), GTP-I (2010–15), and GTP-II (2015–20). The presence of abundant agricultural endowments, such as arable cropland and suitable climate conditions, give the sector a great potential for growth. Growth of agro-processing products will potentially help the country to upgrade its export from low-valued primary commodities that face volatility in international prices to higher-value exports, creating not only more jobs but also decent ones.

FIGURE 5-3. **Trend of Gross Value of Production in the Food and Beverage Industries**

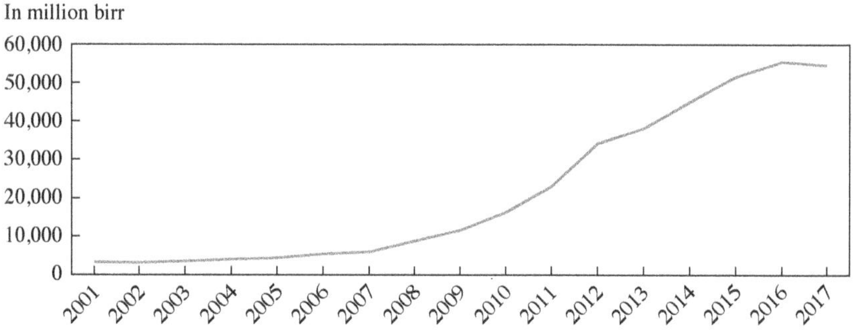

In million birr

Source: Author's compilation using large and medium-sized manufacturing survey by the Central Statistical Agency.

As shown in figure 5-3, the gross value of production of the food and beverage industry of medium-sized and large enterprises rose from birr 3.3 billion in 2001 to birr 54.6 billion in 2017. This is equivalent to an average compounded growth rate of 18 percent.

The food and beverage industry is the leading sector in terms of value creation and employment within the manufacturing sector. The manufacturing sector mainly comprises the food and beverage, textile and garment, leather and leather producers, rubber and plastic, paper and paper products, metallic and engineering products, non-metallic mineral products, tobacco products, and chemicals. Among these, the food and beverage sectors accounted for a third of the value added of the manufacturing sector in 2017, making it the largest contributor even though it is down from 47 percent in 2003 (computed from the Central Statistical Agency's, CSA's, Large and Medium Manufacturing Survey). This is mainly due to a simultaneous increase in the share of other sectors such as nonmetallic mineral products, metallic and engineering products, textiles and garments, and paper and paper products.

According to the medium and large manufacturing firms survey of the CSA, among the large and medium enterprises in food and beverages, the beverage industry accounts for more than half the value addition in its sector. Specifically, malt liquors and soft drinks lead the beverage subsector in value added. Among subsectors within the food category, sugar, grain mill products, and oil lead in contribution to value added.

Labor productivity in the food and beverage industry has shown an upward trajectory, as shown in figure 5-4. In the period 2002/3–2016/17,

FIGURE 5-4. The Labor Productivity of the Food and Beverage Industry

In thousand birr

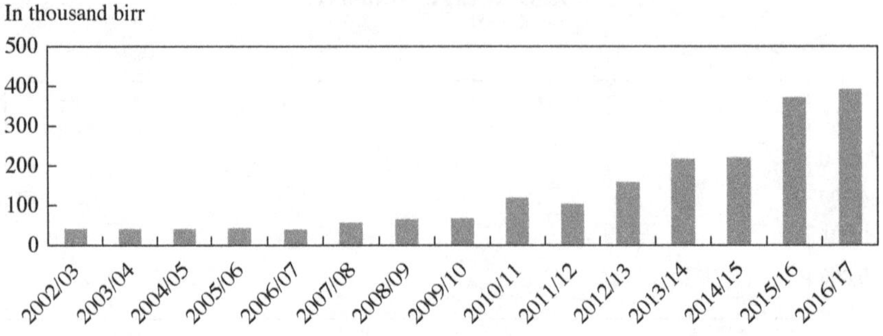

Source: Author's compilation using Large and Medium Manufacturing survey by the Central Statistical Agency.

labor productivity (computed by dividing the gross value of production at a constant price by the number of employees) grew, on average, by 16.5 percent annually.

The food and beverage industry is the largest employer in the manufacturing sector. As shown in figure 5-5, among the large and medium manufacturing industries, the food and beverage sector created the highest number of jobs relative to other manufacturing industries. For example, in 2016/17 the food and beverage industry accounted for about 21 percent of total employed persons in large and medium scale manufacturing.

Ethiopia's export sector is dominated by unprocessed agricultural products such as coffee. The role of the manufacturing sector remains limited. Export earnings from the food and beverage industry are insignificant, but have been increasing, as shown in figure 5-6. According to export data obtained from the Food, Beverage and Pharmaceutical Industry Development Institute (FBPIDI, various years), export earnings from food and beverage products increased from about $21.5 million in 2014/15 to about $63.5 million in 2018/19.

A survey in 2016 by the Ethiopian Development Research Institute showed that about a fifth of manufacturing micro and small enterprises are engaged in the production of food and beverages (Gebreeyesus et al. 2018). In summary, the food and beverage industry has been the main source of value creation and employment. Export earnings from the sector remain limited (but have been increasing in recent years).

In summary, the agro-processing sector has been the largest employer and contributor to GDP among manufacturing industries in Ethiopia. It has

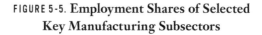

FIGURE 5-5. Employment Shares of Selected Key Manufacturing Subsectors

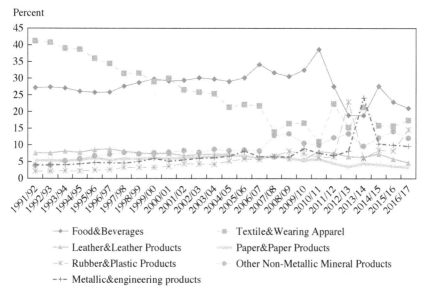

Source: Author's compilation based on Large and Medium Manufacturing survey by the Central Statistical Agency.

FIGURE 5-6. Export Revenue Generated by Food and Beverage Products

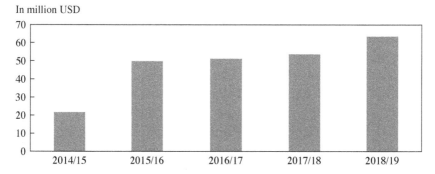

Source: Author's compilation based on data from the Food, Beverage, and Pharmaceutical Industry Development Institute.

also been among the priority sectors in recent years, as the country has been building four integrated agro-industrial parks. However, as discussed in other sections of this chapter, several challenges—such the quality of raw materials, skilled labor power, and poor rural infrastructure—have limited the realization of its full potential. Its labor-intensive nature and potential for linkages with the agricultural sector makes it an ideal sector for propelling structural transformation in Ethiopia. If successful, the thrust of the agro-processing industrial parks lies in the plan to support and link smallholder farmers with agro-processing firms by providing training as well as the provision of accessible warehouses to farmers through rural transformation centers.[3]

Horticulture

In its recent development plans, the Ethiopian government has envisaged promoting the development of agricultural investment, mainly through the promotion of commercialization of the agricultural sector to increase agricultural production and create rural employment opportunities. Horticulture is one of the sectors that has received a great deal of attention in various development plans, mainly in GTPs I and II. In particular, the cut flower industry is one of the highly prioritized agricultural investment vehicles in the country. According to GTP II, the development of horticulture sector plays an important role in ensuring sustainable economic development, mainly through foreign exchange earnings and employment creation (NPC 2016). Further, the sector can play a considerable role in the transformation of smallholders into wage laborers as well as the diversification of the export sector, moving from traditional agricultural to nontraditional agricultural exports.

Horticulture (mainly cut flower farms) is one of the labor-intensive, export-oriented industries in Ethiopia. Despite an effort made by the state farms to produce and export cut flowers to Europe in the early 1980s, the sector thrived in the early 2000s (Gebreeyesus and Iizuka 2012). Since the mid-2000s, the flower industry has registered significant growth.

One of the typical features of the horticulture sector is its potential to create job opportunities for the skilled and unskilled population. Figure 5-7 presents the trend of jobs created in the horticulture sector between 2008 and 2017. Job growth in the industry has been significant. The sector created close to 200,000 job opportunities in 2018. More interestingly, the sector created more jobs for women. For instance, in 2013 about 90 percent

FIGURE 5-7. **Level of Employment in the Horticulture Industry**

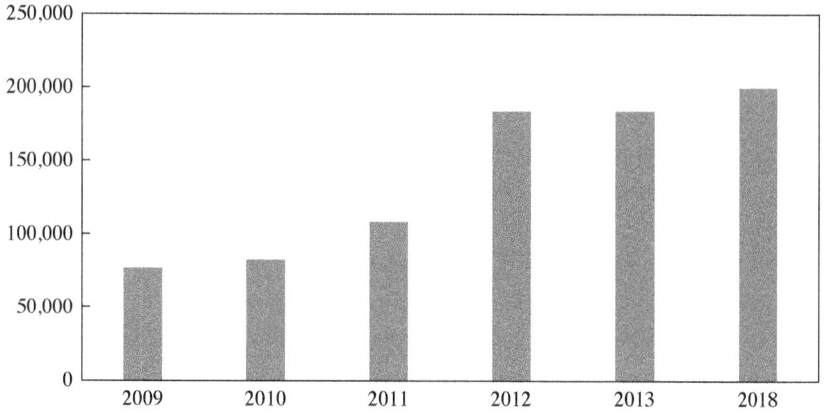

Source: Author's calculation using data from the Ethiopian Horticulture Producer Exporters Association.

FIGURE 5-8. **Foreign Exchange Earnings from the Horticulture Industry by Subsector (Share of Total Exports)**

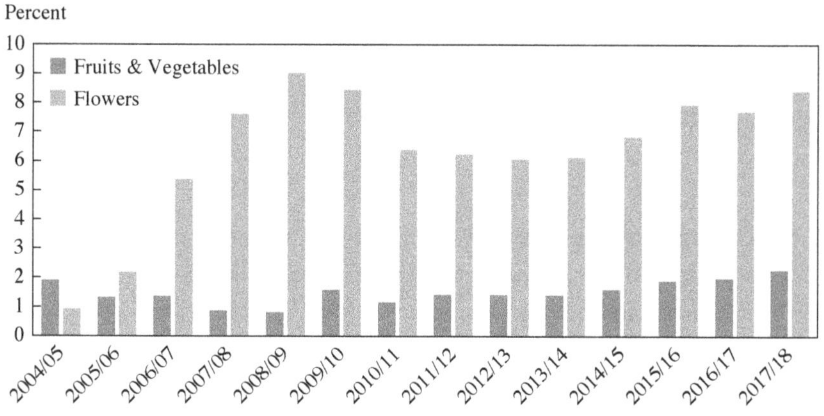

Source: Author's compilation based on the National Bank of Ethiopia's data sets.

of the workforce were females according to data obtained from the Ethiopian Horticulture Producer Exporters Association.

In the 2016/17 fiscal year, agricultural investment created about 285,440 job opportunities for citizens, of which about 140,000 jobs were created in the horticulture industry (NPC 2018). Despite being a new sector, horticulture—typically floriculture—showed impressive growth. Figure 5-8 depicts foreign exchange earnings from horticulture compared with other commodities. Export revenue from the horticulture industry increased from about $24 million in 2004/5 to $203 million in 2009/10, and further increased to $290 million in 2017/18.

Currently, horticulture is the fourth-largest contributor of export revenue to Ethiopia, next to coffee, oilseeds, and manufacturing. In 2017/18, the sector accounted for 10.6 percent of total merchandise exports, of which cut flowers contribute much of the share (about 79 percent). The recent surge of export revenue from the floriculture industry ranked the country second among African countries, after Kenya.

Ethiopia's diverse and suitable climate for horticulture, as well as its large irrigation potential, provide ideal conditions for horticulture.[4] While the focus by the government has been on large and export-oriented types of horticulture, smallholders' horticulture also has immense potential in the country, with its large domestic market and climatic and irrigation potential. Due to its perishable nature, improved market linkage will be crucial in ensuring smallholder farmers' ability to get fair prices for their products. With the high urbanization rate in Ethiopia, demand for horticultural products is expected to increase significantly. Hence, in addition to the support being given to large export-oriented firms, there is a need to design a support system for smallholder horticulture to boost production and hence create decent jobs.

Tourism

Tourism has immense potential in Ethiopia. The country is vast and rich in diverse natural resources, including a wide range of ecological and biodiversity assets, and it boasts numerous cultural and historical sites. Eight cultural sites and one natural site have been registered by UNESCO as World Heritages Sites. Seven other sites are being considered as World Heritages Sites.

The tourism industry is not new to Ethiopia. To promote tourism, the Ethiopian Tourism Organization was established in 1961. However, due to civil wars and the closing of the economy during the socialist government of the 1970s and 80s, tourism largely stagnated for many decades.

After the fall of the socialist government in 1991, the tourism sector started to revive, and it has been on an upward trajectory since the mid-1990s—except in 1998, which showed a dip due to the Ethio-Eritrean war—in 2016, due to nationwide protests; and in 2018, as the country was

FIGURE 5-9. International Arrivals to Ethiopia between 1995 and 2018

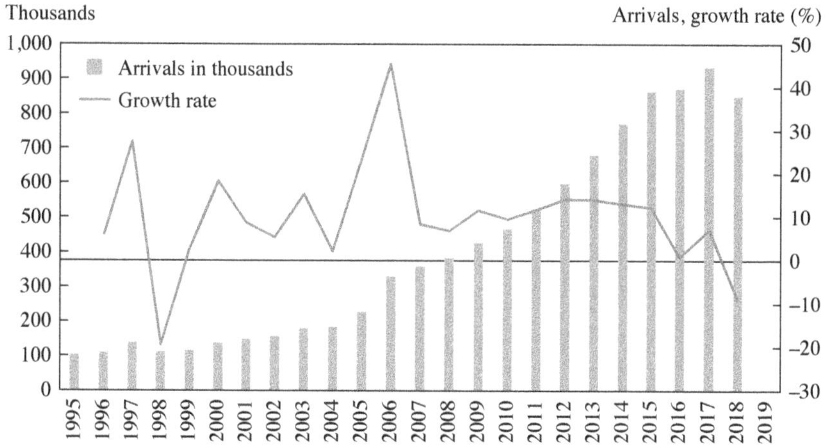

Source: Author's calculations based on World Development Indicators, 2020.

undergoing instability and internal displacement after changes in its admin-istration and the opening of the political space (figure 5-9).

The country registered the highest growth of foreign visitors in 2006 (more than 45 percent growth, compared with 2005). Along with reforms and political and economic stability, the improvement of infrastructure and services has played an important role in advancing the industry. The rising trend in tourism is being driven by the increase in international tourism worldwide, improved air connectivity, and the dynamic economy (e.g., Altes 2018).

Figure 5-10 presents revenue generated from international tourism and its contribution to GDP in Ethiopia. Consistent with the trajectory of arrivals, the amount of revenue generated from the tourism sector has been on a rising trend. Exports have increased from about $117 million in 1995 to more than $3.5 billion in 2018, experiencing rapid growth rates averaging about 14 percent per annum. Since the mid-2000s, revenue from interna-tional tourism has increased rapidly, the figure almost tripled in 2010 and increased sevenfold in 2018.[5]

The increasing role of the tourism sector in the Ethiopian economy can be illustrated by its direct contribution to the country's GDP; it has accounted for more than 3 percent of GDP since 2002. It recorded the highest contribu-tion in 2011 (about 6 percent of GDP).[6] The total contribution of tourism to

FIGURE 5-10. **Receipts from International Tourism
in Ethiopia between 1995 and 2018**

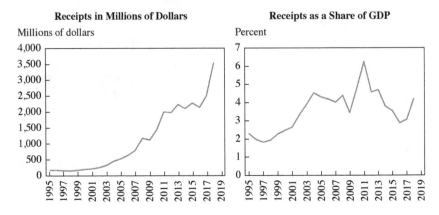

Receipts in Millions of Dollars   **Receipts as a Share of GDP**

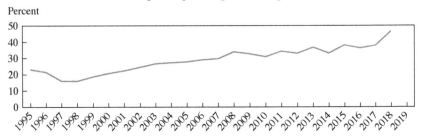

Receipts as a percentage of total exports

Source: Author's calculations based on data from World Development Indicators, 2020.

GDP, however, is much higher than this due, to its indirect and induced effects. The total contribution of travel and tourism to GDP (including wider effects from investment, the supply chain, and induced income effects) was 10.3 percent in 2013.[7] Separate data from the World Travel and Tourism Council's Global Economic Impact report (WTTC 2020b) show that in 2019, the share of travel and tourism in GDP in Ethiopia was 6.7 percent, while the share in total employment was 7 percent, creating close to 2 million jobs.

Figure 5-10 also presents the contribution of the tourist industry to the total exporting of goods and services. Consistent with the number of arrivals and revenue, the export share of the tourism industry has grown remarkably. It increased from 20.6 percent in 2000 to 46.5 percent in 2018, averaging 4.5 percent growth a year.

Especially for youth and women, the tourism industry has substantial employment potential (e.g., Gebreeyesus 2017). Figure 5-11 provides the

FIGURE 5-11. Employment Share of Tourism in Total Employment, 1995–2018

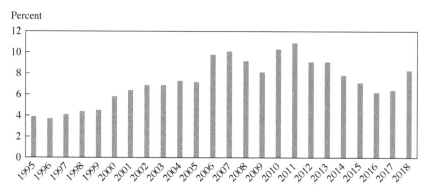

Source: Author's compilation based on data from the World Travel and Tourism Council.

FIGURE 5-12. Foreign Tourists' Arrivals by Region

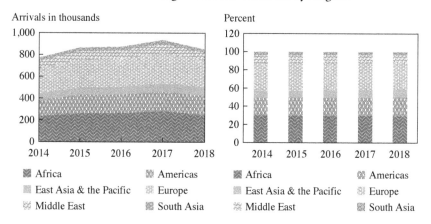

Source: Author's compilation based on data from the UN World Tourism Organization (2019).

share of employment of travel and tourism in total employment. The decline in 2008 and 2009 can be explained by the world economic recession, while the declines in 2016 and 2017 can be ascribed to protests in the country. The average share of employment in travel and tourism in total employment was 5.6 percent, while the average for 2010 to 2018 was 8.4 percent. Overall, the contribution to employment of tourism has increased in recent years.

The top five tourist sources for Ethiopia are the United States (17 percent), the United Kingdom (5 percent), China (5 percent), Germany (4 percent), and Italy (4). Figure 5-12 shows the regions that send tourists to Ethiopia. Among

FIGURE 5-13. **Foreign Visitors: Arrivals by Purpose and Mode of Transportation**

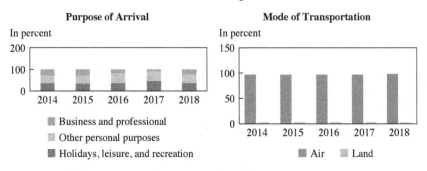

Source: Author's compilation based on data from the UN World Tourism Organization (2019).

countries in Africa, East Africa—mainly Kenya, Sudan, Djibouti, Tanzania, and Uganda—are the largest sources of tourists, followed by West Africa (mainly Nigeria). In the last couple of years, Ethiopia has waived visas before arrival for all member nations of the African Union, which will potentially boost tourism flows (e.g., McKay and Tekleselassie 2018).

The majority of visitors to Ethiopia are for holidays, leisure and recreation, accounting for more than 45 percent in 2016 and 2017. Travel for business and professional purposes accounted for about 23 percent of visitors while the remaining for other personal reasons, as shown in figure 5-13.

Air travel is the major means of transportation for international tourists that visit Ethiopia. About 98 percent of tourists who visited Ethiopia in 2018 arrived by air (second panel of figure 5-11). Ethiopian Airlines is playing a vital role in supporting the tourism sector. According to a 2020 report on the Ethiopian economy (IATA 2020), the air transportation industry and its supply chain support $1.54 billion in GDP in Ethiopia, with a further $2.61 billion of GDP coming from spending by foreign tourists arriving by air.

Transportation

The development of transportation has both direct and indirect consequences. Investment in transportation can play a direct role in reducing traders' logistical costs and time of delivery by minimizing travel times, reducing operating costs, and enhancing access to destinations within the network. Transportation also has an indirect effect on productivity and the spatial pattern of economic development, mainly by stimulating a variety of

FIGURE 5-14. **Value Added for Transportation, Storage,
and Communications (in Constant 2015 Prices)**

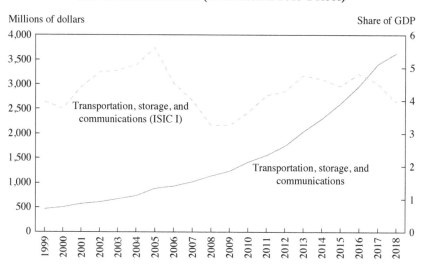

Source: Author's compilation based on United Nations Statistics Division (2020).

interconnected, economy-wide processes. In 2018/19, the service sector recorded 11 percent growth, which was largely ascribed to the expansion of the transportation and communications subsector (21 percent) (NBE 2019).

Figure 5-14 depicts the contribution of the transportation, storage, and communication sectors to Ethiopia's GDP over last two decades. The value added generated by the industry has shown steady growth, increasing from $509 million to more than $3.6 billion in 2018 (an average growth rate of 10 percent). In addition, the sector accounted for about 4 percent of GDP. Further, transportation and communications accounted for 14 percent of the total service output, the second-largest contributor next to wholesale and retail trade (35.9 percent) (NBE 2019).

Air transportation is a key export service sector in Ethiopia. Figure 5-15 shows the export revenue generated from nonfactor service sectors over time. Total service exports have registered significant growth, climbing from about $1.6 billion in 2007/8 to almost triple, to $4.2 billion, in 2017/18.

The success of Ethiopian Airlines, with its remarkable growth over the years, has not only been an important source of foreign exchange but also essential enabling factor for other sectors such as tourism and floriculture exports. Ethiopia being a large, mountainous, landlocked country, the value of air transportation is significant.

FIGURE 5-15. **Export Revenue from Nonfactor Service Sectors**

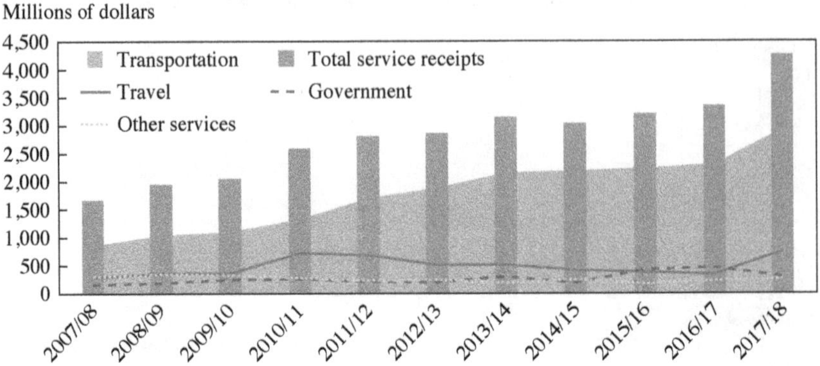

Millions of dollars

Source: Author's compilation based on the National Bank of Ethiopia's data sets.

In addition to air transportation, road and rail infrastructure are key for Ethiopia's economic transformation in supporting the rest of the economics sectors. The logistics and transportation system in Ethiopia remains poor. According to the World Bank's Aggregate Logistics Performance Index (LPI),[8] which combines the four most recent LPI editions (for 2012, 2014, 2016, and 2018), Ethiopia ranks 131 out of 167 countries. Among the components of the LPI, Ethiopia particularly ranks very poorly in infrastructure (140th), tracking and tracing (140th), and timeliness (158th) out of 167 countries. Hence, addressing these constraints will be crucial for unleashing Ethiopia's potential in the transportation sector.

Sectoral Decomposition: IWSS in Comparative Perspective with Manufacturing and Non-IWSS

This section provides a comparative perspective of the IWSS industries vis-à-vis the manufacturing sectors and other non-IWSS industries, particularly focusing on productivity, employment, and exporting. Table 5-2 reports employment growth and share by sector. Non-IWSS industries, particularly agriculture, remain the major employers in the Ethiopian economy. About 87 percent and 85 percent of employment, respectively, comes from non-IWSS industries in 2000 and 2017. Agriculture's share of employment remains high, at 68 percent in 2017, slightly lower than the 80 percent in 2000.

Table 5-2. Comparison of Employment Trends

| Sector | Employment (thousands) | | | Employment share | | Annual percent growth |
	2000	2017	Change	2000	2017	2000–2017
Total employment	26,449.31	47,894.01	21,444.70	100.00	100.00	4.77
Total IWSS	2,479.27	5045.07	2,565.80	9.37	10.53	6.09
Agro-processing	427.05	550.80	123.75	1.61	1.15	1.70
Transportation	162.115	593.715	431.60	0.61	1.24	15.66
Financial and business services	76.35	745.49	669.14	0.29	1.56	51.55
Trade	1,813.751	3,155.061	1,341.31	6.86	6.59	4.35
Manufacturing	1,006.00	2,072.07	1,066.07	3.66	4.25	6.23
Other non-IWSS	22,964.038	40,776.868	17,812.83	86.82	85.14	4.56
Agriculture	21,075.677	32,655.053	11,579.38	79.68	68.18	3.23
Mining	26.74	274.093	247.35	0.10	0.57	54.41
Utilities	38.929	276.762	237.83	0.15	0.58	35.94
Construction	327.01	1,621.588	1,294.58	1.24	3.39	23.29
Government	822.89	1,827.91	1,005.01	3.11	3.82	7.18
Other	672.789	4,121.466	3,448.68	2.54	8.61	30.15

Sources: Author's calculations using data from the Planning and Development Commission and the International Labor Organization.

Note: These data exclude employment in hotels and restaurants due to poor quality. Agro-processing only gives information for medium and large enterprises due to a lack of data; hence, its value is underestimated.

In 2000, the total employment of the IWSS industries was about 9 percent of total employment. The share of IWSS employment increased to 11 percent in 2017. The share of manufacturing in total employment remained about 4 percent in 2000 and 2017. Total employment grew, on average, by close to 5 percent between 2000 and 2017. Employment by IWSS industries grew, on average, annually by 6 percent between 2000 and 2017.

Transportation and financial services particularly showed remarkable growth in the period. Among the non-IWSS industries, mining, utilities, and construction showed employment growth. However, the share of employment in mining and utilities remained very low. The employment data on agro-processing only includes those of medium and large enterprises due to lack of data on smaller enterprises. Hence, the data on the employment of agro-processing has been underestimated. Similarly, employment data in agriculture has been slightly overestimated as it includes horticulture which is normally categorized under IWSS. Therefore, the employment data given in table 5-2 slightly exaggerate the share of agriculture as a non-IWSS sector and underestimate the share of the IWSS industries.

Table 5-3 reports changes in GDP, employment, and employment elasticity. Overall employment elasticity for the period 2000–2017 was 0.28. The employment elasticity of the IWSS industries is 0.24, while that of manufacturing stands at a lower level of 0.18. The other non-IWSS category—which comprises the agriculture, utilities, construction, and government sectors—had an employment elasticity of 0.24 for 2000–2017. Hence, IWSS industries had one of the highest employment elasticities in the period 2000–2017, despite the underestimation due to the exclusion of the booming horticulture sector.[9]

The share of exports by IWSS industries increased from 15.58 percent in 2011 to 19.17 percent in 2017 (table 5-4). The share of IWSS industries can be considered large among those that involve processing. Coffee, the largest export item for Ethiopia, accounting for 30 percent of total exports alone, is categorized under non-IWSS because it is exported predominantly unprocessed. Manufacturing exports remained low, at 6.84 percent in 2017. Export revenue in the last decade has remained stagnant due to a number of supply-side constraints, including power outages, foreign exchange shortages, logistics problems, and skill shortages.

Table 5-3. Changes in GDP (Value Added) and Employment

Sector	% Change in GDP, 2000–2017	% Change in employment, 2000–2017	Employment elasticity, 2000–2017
Overall economy	319.17	89.31	0.28
Total IWSS	432.16	103.49	0.24
Agro-processing	228.12	28.98	0.13
Transportation	568.97	266.23	0.47
Financial and business services	485.78	876.36	1.80
Trade	416.61	73.95	0.18
Manufacturing	575.72	105.97	0.18
Other non-IWSS	265.45	63.40	0.24
Agriculture	160.60	54.94	0.34
Utilities	308.89	610.94	1.98
Construction	1467.65	395.88	0.27
Government	149.91	122.13	0.81

Sources: Author's calculations using data from the Planning and Development Commission and the International Labor Organization.

Table 5-4. Export Shares and Growth

Sector	2011		2017		2011–17
	Millions of dollars	Share	Millions of dollars	Share	Annual % growth
IWSS total	430.44	15.58	544.66	19.17	4.42
IWSS services exports					
Various services	158.49	5.74	195.18	6.87	3.86
IWSS goods exports					
Horticulture	208.37	7.54	250.67	8.82	3.38
Agro-processing	63.58	2.30	98.81	3.48	9.24
Manufacturing total					
Leather and textiles	166.92	6.04	194.29	6.84	2.73
Mining	467.84	16.94	208.98	7.35	–9.22
Total exports (goods and services)	2,762.51		2,841.38		0.48

Source: Author's calculations using data from the National Bank of Ethiopia, various years.

Constraints on IWSS Growth

The IWSS sectors face multiple, multifaceted challenges that hinder their growth and effectiveness across various subcategories. Here, we discuss the constraints on the agro-industrial, horticulture, tourism, and transportation subsectors.

Constraints on Agro-industry

Agro-processing, particularly the food and beverage industry, contributes the highest value added to GDP and employment among manufacturing industries. However, the contribution of the manufacturing industry in general to GDP and employment remains very low. Moreover, export earnings from manufacturing, in general, and agro-industry, in particular, remain insignificant. Ethiopia is lagging in realizing its potential in agro-processing. Some of the key binding constraints for the development of the agro-processing industry are these (Abebe, Tekleselassie, and Haji 2019):

- *A lack of quantity and quality of raw material.* The country currently imports a large amount of wheat, despite large potential arable land to produce domestically. Moreover, the varieties required for agro-processing and the actual varieties being produced by farmers are different. There is also a low productivity of grains. There is also a weak linkage between farmers and agro-processing enterprises.
- *Inadequate skilled manpower.* There is a mismatch between demand and supply of labor. Currently, there are no TVET-level courses specifically in agro-processing except two TVET colleges (Holeta and Wukro Poly Technic colleges), which are providing training in agro-processing at a pilot level. There is a plan to expand courses in agro-processing in other colleges. The skill shortage is not only on the side of production workers, but limited quality and safety standard practices in the agro-processing industry. Admassie et al. (2016) find attracting and retaining skilled labor to be a challenge in agro-processing.
- *Inadequate rural infrastructure.* Poor rural connectivity to link farmers with agro-processing enterprise, limited irrigation practice, and power interruptions pose challenges to the agro-processing industry. Despite substantial improvement in road infrastructure in the country, most of rural Ethiopia remains poorly connected with roads.

Constraints on Horticulture

Despite the presence of many opportunities for doing business in the floriculture industry, many factors hinder further development of the sector. Despite significant improvement in recent years, performance has been below par and lags behind its potential level, as well as major competitors. The following are key bottlenecks of doing business in the cut flower industry.

COOL CHAIN MANAGEMENT (CCM) is the process of planning, implementing, and controlling the efficient, effective flow and storage of perishable goods. CCM is very important to keep the quality of the product; it consists of a farm-level packing house, a cold truck, and airport storage. Cut flowers are one of the easily perishable products. Hence, CMM is important to maintain the quality of cut flower exports. Lack of cold chain management is one of key bottlenecks for cut flower firms in Ethiopia. In particular, there are few refrigerated trucks to transport packed cut flower from farms to airport cold storage. The lack of such service providers raises the investment requirements for exporting firms. For instance, farm cold storage, a packing shed, and investment in trucks and vehicles accounted for about 16 percent of total start-up costs (Gebreeyesus and Sonobe 2012). Further, lacks of handling and forwarding service providers are other key challenges for the floriculture industry. Thus, improving the availability and quality of packaging and handling materials and service providers, cooling facilities, and coordination among key stakeholders are very important to maintain timely and high-quality cut flower exports.

SHORTAGE OF A SKILLED WORKFORCE. The availability of a skilled labor force is very important to produce and deliver high-quality horticulture products. Skilled labor is important during harvesting, packaging, handling, and marketing to be competitive on international markets. In this regard, there are shortages of skilled labor specialized in flower production and marketing. This problem was serious for most early-entrant cut flower farms in the country (Gebreeyesus and Sonobe 2012).

POLITICAL INSTABILITY. Many scholars argue that political uncertainty is a serious malaise for economic development. Political unrest could result in frequent policy changes and adversely affect the economic performance of a given country, mainly by lowering productivity growth and physical and human capital accumulation (Aisen and Veiga 2013). The recent political instability, mainly between 2015 and 2018, highly affected the flower farm industry. For instance, in August 2016, protests occurred in the country, resulting in the destruction of machines, vehicles, and greenhouses of various companies, which exacerbated an estimated more than 11,000 people's loss of their jobs in the flower industry.[10] In general, political disruption, associated with social unrest, could negatively affect the growth of the sector through lower foreign and domestic investment. There is emerging evidence that recent and ongoing conflicts in various parts of the country, including the 2020–22 war in the northern region, have had a severely negative impact on the broader economy.

POOR-QUALITY INFRASTRUCTURE AND LOGISTICAL COORDINATION. Despite expansion in recent years, the country's infrastructure system is characterized by a poor quality of services, the low capacity of the existing road network, and a lack of all-weather road networks. Hence, the low quality of the transportation sector and poor transportation policy are constraining effective and efficient service provision and, hence, hindering effective implementation of various development policies designed to stimulate and intensify national development, of which the horticulture sector is one. In addition, the distinct lack of coordination among diverse actors—such as federal and regional governments, financial institutions, investment promotion agencies, and implementing agencies—deters the full operation of licensed investment projects' exploitation of the existing potential for the horticulture sector.

HIGH COMPETITION. Access to global markets is a big challenge for most developing countries, including Ethiopia, mainly due to intense competition. Further, the lack of market diversification is another main challenge for Ethiopian producers and exporters of cut flowers. For instance, over 90 percent of cut flower exports are destined for the EU market, mainly the Netherlands (Gebreeyesus and Sonobe 2012).

HIGH TRANSPORTATION COSTS. According to the Ethiopian Flower Producers and Exporters Association, air transportation is one of the key constraints they face. Specifically, the sector faces increasing air transportation costs, paying the airline $1.75 per kilogram.[11]

Constraints on the Tourism Industry

Notwithstanding the significant improvement in recent years, the tourism industry in Ethiopia lags behind its potential and in comparison with its peers. Here are some of the key bottlenecks of the tourism industry in the country.

Despite the huge potential for the tourism sector as a source of foreign exchange, employment and value additions to the economy, the industry lacks competitiveness compared with peer countries such as Kenya. The key binding constraints on the growth of tourism in the country include the following (e.g., Wondowossen et al. 2014; UNECA 2015; Gebreeyesus 2017).

A LACK OF INFRASTRUCTURE. Despite its expansion over recent periods, infrastructure development is still at its infancy. There is insufficient transportation infrastructure in Ethiopia, in both quality and coverage (e.g., UNECA 2015). Besides, the transportation infrastructure and other supporting infrastructure—such as hotels and restaurants, health services, and banking services near tourist destinations—remain insufficient.

THE LOW LEVEL OF PROMOTION AND MARKETING. Despite slight improvements recently, tourism marketing and promotion remain at a low level in Ethiopia. For instance, there is a lack of signage for tourist attractions, and even in Addis Ababa there are few brochures or maps of the city or its attractions, and access to tourist products is difficult and can be inappropriately expensive. The lack of effective marketing strategies is one of the key challenges for the development of tourism in Ethiopia.

WEAK COORDINATION AMONG STAKEHOLDERS. Even though the institutional framework is in place, there is weak coordination and implementation capacity due to financial constraints and a lack of skilled labor power. Tourism planning remains fragmented at the national and regional levels.

A LACK OF TRAINED LABOR POWER. Poor human resource capacity is another challenge for tourism in Ethiopia. The sector faces a shortage of diversified skilled labor power of the desired quality, such as guides, marketers, frontline hospitality service providers, and event managers. This has resulted in poor service quality.

In addition, other challenges include (e.g., Altes 2018) a lack of basic and information technology infrastructure and poor digital marketing, a narrow product range offered to the market, and a lack of suitable funding options available for tourism, especially for small and medium-sized enterprises.

Constraints on the Transportation Sector

According to the World Bank (2015), Ethiopia has low ranking in-logistics services; it ranks 104th out of 160 economies, behind Kenya (74th) and

Rwanda (80th). In general, the sector fares poorly on infrastructure and international shipments.

Some of the key constraints facing the transportation sector in Ethiopia include (e.g., AUC 2015; World Bank 2015):

- *An inadequate support system for the sector:* The government's key focus areas have remained on manufacturing. While there has been substantial infrastructure development of road and rails, there has not been a support system for enterprises engaged in transportation systems.
- *Excessive regulatory restrictions on investment opportunities:* Except for Ethiopian Airlines, which enjoyed substantial autonomy in management, the transportation sector remains highly regulated, making investment in it less profitable. Moreover, the transportation and logistics sector is aloof to competition, as domestic investment in it is reserved for only locals.
- *Bureaucratic business environment:* Permits and licenses for engaging in the sector require excessive red-tape and are prone to corruption.
- *Instability in the region:* Political instability in the Horn of Africa has negatively affected transportation links in the region.

Trends into the Future: Potential Growth and Labor Demand

As discussed, the IWSS in Ethiopia have an enormous potential for job creation. In this section, we discuss potential future growth of the industries and trends in labor demand.

Potential Growth and Labor Demand for Agro-industry and Horticulture

AGRO-INDUSTRY AND HORTICULTURE GROWTH POTENTIAL. With a growing economy and the development of the integrated agro-processing industrial parks (IAIPs), the food and beverage industry is expected to grow. According to a forecast by the Ministry of Industry (MoI 2015), the share of food and beverage industries in GDP is expected to rise to 6.3 percent by 2025 from 3.1 percent in 2013. Hence, the food and beverage industry is one of the fastest-growing industries in the Ethiopian economy.

The MoI (2015) forecast employment in the food and beverage industries to grow to about 3.8 million by 2015, from about 66,000 in 2025. This

Table 5-5. Ten-Year Plan for Smallholder Horticulture

Aspect of Horticulture	Millions of quintals		Average annual growth
	2020	2030	2020–30
Main rainy season (Meher)	68	112	6.47
Second season (Belg)	47	54	1.49
Irrigation	65	95	4.62
Total smallholder horticulture	180	261	4.50

Source: Author's compilation using data from MoA (2020).

translates to a compound annual growth rate of close to 50 percent. This was based on ambitious GTP II targets and projections. Like most of the GTP II targets, this is likely an overestimate of actual performance. However, it is indicative of the importance of the sector as a key employment creator. About 90 percent of the jobs in the food and beverage industry in 2025 are forecast to be at the IAIPs, which will be constructed at various locations.

Some of the key issues the establishment of the IAIPs can help address include improved provision infrastructure, such as electricity, access to land, and enhanced services such as customs. Moreover, the Rural Transformation Centres (RTCs) that are being set up will facilitate efficient collection of agricultural outputs from farmers to agro-processors. The RTCs are also envisaged to play a crucial role in enhancing productivity of farmers through training and extension services.

The sectoral 10-year plan by the Ministry of Agriculture (MoA) will promote smallholder farmers engaged in horticulture by enabling them to avail themselves of technologies that enhance productivity in the sector, such as nethouses and greenhouses. Between 2020 and 2030, horticulture by smallholder farmers is expected to grow annually at an average rate of 4.5 percent (table 5-5).

Labor Demand and Skill Requirements in Agro-industry and Horticulture

Currently, the agro-processing and horticulture industries face several gaps in the skills of the workforce. For example, MoI (2015) identified the following gaps in skills.

A LACK OF QUALIFICATIONS AND SKILLS OF THE WORKFORCE. The current workforce lacks formal qualifications under the national qualification framework. This is especially true for agro-processing, where the TVET system does not currently provide training programs for the sector. Hence, the majority of the workforce in agro-processing is informally trained through experience. Moreover, there is limited opportunity for skill development in the existing workforce. Specific occupations facing shortages and skill gaps include:

- Workforce for maintenance and repair of food and beverage production machinery;
- Highly skilled technologists, such as edible oil technologists, turbine specialists, powder milk processors, and fish processing technologists;
- Professionals in the standardization of products and processes in the sector; and
- Product development and innovation.

A LACK OF PRACTICAL ORIENTATION IN THE TVET AND HIGHER EDUCATION SYSTEMS. Graduates employed in the sector demonstrate a lack of competence in production processes due to a lack of practical training. One of the key reasons for this is poor work-based training systems, such as apprenticeships and internships.

According to the MoI (2015), up to 72 percent of the workforce in the food and beverage sector is in the skilled production workforce, whereas the remaining 38 percent is distributed between the professional workforce (engineers and technologists), management and administrative staff. The skilled production workforce includes mostly TVET levels, such as basic operations level I, processing/production II, processing/production III, processing/production IV, and processing V.

Meeting the skill demand of the food and beverage industry at the desired quality will be a daunting challenge for the county's higher education institutions (HEIs) and TVET system. The current skill and labor supply in the country is characterized by low quality, skill gaps and mismatches, low productivity, and high labor turnover (e.g., Beyene and Tekleselassie 2018). Since agro-processing requires modest skills, the potential of the TVET system for producing the required skills is high (e.g., World Bank 2015). However, there is a need for improving the quality of the TVET system as well as the relevance of the programs being offered currently, as they rely less on skill anticipation systems and remain far from being demand-driven.

Table 5-6. Ethiopia Tourism Growth Projections for 2030

Indicator	2020	2030	Average annual growth, 2020–30 (%)
Employment opportunities' focus on youth	1,639,856	6,000,335	26.59
Number of inbound tourists	849,122	7,300,000	75.97
Tourism revenue (billion dollars)	3.17	23.15	63.26
Share of tourism in GDP (10 percent)	6.1	10	6.39

Source: Author's compilation using data from MoCT (2020).

*Potential Growth and Labor Demand for Tourism
and the Transportation Industry*

Based on the projection of the 10-year prospective plan of the Ministry of Culture and Tourism (MoCT 2020), the tourism sector is envisaged to create about 6 million jobs by 2030, up from about 1.6. million in 2020, mostly focusing on youth and women (table 5-6). This translates into annual job creation growth of 26.6 percent. Similarly, the MoCT plans to increase the number of tourists to 7.3 million from its current value of 849,122, which implies an annual average growth rate of 76 percent. In addition, the MoCT has set ambitious targets for revenue generation of $23 billion by 2030, up from the current $3 billion. The share of tourism in GDP is projected to grow to 10 percent by 2030 from its current 6.1 percent. The 2015–25 sustainable tourism master plan prepared by the MoCT and the UNECA also sets ambitious plans for the tourism sector (UNECA 2015). However, those projections will be difficult to achieve unless the country's current political instability is tamed.

The high tourism growth projected in table 5-6 will induce significant labor demand. Similarly, a study by the International Air Transport Association indicates that, currently, air transportation and foreign tourists arriving by air contributed 5.7 percent of the nation's GDP, valued at $4.2 billion and about 1.1 million jobs.[12] The report also showed that if current trends continue, Ethiopia's air transportation market will expand by 226 percent over the next 20 years, which translates into an annual average growth rate of 11.3 percent.

Meeting the labor demand with the desired quality of diversified skilled labor power in several fields—such as guides, marketers, frontline hospitality service providers, and event managers—will be a daunting challenge. The county's higher education and TVET systems will need to be equipped with the desired machinery and human resources to supply the induced labor demand.

Policy Implications: Unlocking Growth Potential and Overcoming Skill Gaps

In this section, we provide policy implication to unlock the growth potential of the IWSS sectors in Ethiopia, focusing on agro-industry (food and beverages), horticulture, the tourism industry, and the transportation sector.

Policy Implications for Agro-industry and Horticulture

To unlock the potential of the food and beverage industry in Ethiopia in order to create gainful employment especially for youth, we suggest various points of intervention. These suggestions are categorized as skill-related and other interventions.

Skill-related suggested interventions include expanding TVET training for skills in production in agro-processing and horticulture industries. Currently, TVET courses in agro-processing are not provided by the TVET system, except at a pilot level, in two polytechnic colleges:

- Roll out the TVET training in agro-processing, especially in colleges near the IAIPs and other potential areas.
- Enhance the quality of the TVET system by implementing cooperative training with the industry.

Skill-related suggested interventions also include enhancing training in managerial skills:

- Introduce a mid-level supervisor training program for agro-processing; and
- Strengthen high management training customized for the agro-processing industry.

Skilled-related suggested interventions also include improving core skills training provision. Ethiopia is at the early stage of industrialization; most workers are sourced from rural areas with experience in agriculture but not in the industry. Hence, to adapt to industry culture, special attention is required in developing the core skills of workers to improve communication, reduce absenteeism, and enhance industrial discipline:

- Introduce pre-employment short-term core skills training for workers who aspire to work in agro-industry.
- Develop standard core skills training for all TVET trainees.

Cross-cutting interventions. Occupational standards for agro-processing are being developed. There is a need to regularly update them in collaboration with industry representatives:

- Enhance HEI/TVET-industry linkage to enhance the provision of cooperative training;
- Equip TVET colleges with up-to-date machinery; and
- Introduce a skill-demand anticipation system: currently, there is no functional skill anticipation system for any industry, which has exacerbated a skills-mismatch in the country.

Other interventions:

- Enhance the quality of inputs by training farmers in new ways of production and desired grain varieties.
- Improve rural infrastructure to link them with agro-processing industries.

Policy Implication for Tourism and Transportation

To unlock the potential of the tourism industry in Ethiopia to create gainful employment, especially for youth, we suggest skill-related and other interventions.

Skill-related suggested interventions include:

- Expand diversified training in the desired quality to produce guides, marketers, frontline hospitality service providers, and event managers, especially near tourist hotspots. Universities close to major tourist destinations can take the lead in tourism training and research.

- Introduce preemployment short-term core skills training for workers who aspire to work in tourism.
- Develop standard core skills training for all TVET trainees and university students in tourism and hospitality.
- Regularly update occupational standards for the tourism industry in collaboration with industry representatives.
- Introduce a skill-demand anticipation system: Currently, there is no functional skill-demand anticipation system for any industry in Ethiopia. The lack of a skill-demand anticipation system has exacerbated the skills mismatch in the country.

Other interventions include:

- Invest in infrastructure to access tourism sites, such as airports, roads, and hotels.
- Enhance coordination between stakeholders in the hotels and hospitality industry.
- Invest in tourism marketing and promotion by learning from more experienced peer countries.
- Enhance digital marketing.
- Expand the range of tourism products.
- Improve visitor management at natural and heritage sites.
- Improve tourism statistics to enhance planning and policies related to tourism.

Conclusion

This chapter has investigated the potential of industries without smokestacks to create jobs in Ethiopia, focusing on agro-processing (particularly food and beverages), horticulture, tourism, and transportation sectors. These categories were selected due to their employment potential, productivity, and tradability. It has also explored the key challenges and provided recommendations focusing on skill implications. The chapter has also provided recommendations to address some of the key challenges posed by a lack of skills.

With close to a 68 percent employment share, agriculture remains the major employer in Ethiopia, followed by trade (IWSS) and manufacturing (non-IWSS). Between 2000 and 2017, mining (non-IWSS), finance (IWSS), utilities (non-IWSS), construction (non-IWSS), and transportation (IWSS) registered the fastest growth in employment. Finance (IWSS) and transportation (IWSS) were the most productive sectors in 2017.

The chapter has identified a number of challenges that hinder the growth of the IWSS sectors in Ethiopia. The constraints relate to inadequate skilled labor power, a lack of quantity and good quality of raw materials, poor infrastructure, high costs of transportation, poor cool chain management, and political instability. If the key constraints that the IWSS sectors face in Ethiopia are addressed, these industries promise to become important sources of employment and high-value contributors to the national economy.

NOTES

1. Figures for labor market outcomes were computed by the author using Urban Employment Unemployment surveys of Ethiopian Central Statistical Agency.

2. Data based on the National Bank of Ethiopia.

3. UNIDO (n.d.).

4. See https://allafrica.com/stories/202101130528.html.

5. The 2019 WTTC annual review of travel and tourism economic impact shows that Ethiopia's Travel & Tourism economy grew by 48.6 percent in 2018, the largest of any country in the world (WTTC 2020b).

6. This was the direct effect, mainly consisting of economic activity generated by industries such as hotels, travel agents, airlines, and other passenger transportation services, excluding commuter services (WTTC 2015).

7. See UNECA 2015.

8. See https://lpi.worldbank.org/international/aggregated-ranking.

9. Value-added and employment data for horticulture in Ethiopia are lumped with agriculture. The most common data on horticulture reported officially in Ethiopia are exports by medium-sized and large horticulture enterprises.

10. See allAfrica.com, which was published on October 26, 2016; and see https://www.floraldaily.com/article/7249/Ethiopian-flower-market-less-rosy-in-the-face-of-unrest/.

11. Market Insider, March 28, 2014. And see "Ethiopian Flower Sector: Bloomer or Gloomer?" International Trade Center, https://www.intracen.org/itc/blog/market-insider/Ethiopian-flower-sector-bloomer-or-gloome/.

12. See https://www.iata.org/en/pressroom/pr/2020-03-04-02/.

REFERENCES

Abebe, G., T. G. Tekleselassie, and J. Haji. 2019. "Skills for Trade and Economic Diversification in Ethiopia: A Background Paper for Drafting of a

Sector Skills Strategy for the Agro-processing Sector in Ethiopia." International Labor Organization, Geneva.

Admassie, A., K. Berhanu, and A. Admasie. 2016. "Employment Creation in Agriculture and Agro-industries in the Context of Political Economy and Settlements Analysis." Partnership for African Social and Governance Research Working Paper 016, Nairobi.

Aisena, F., and J. Veiga. 2013. "How Does Political Instability Affect Economic Growth?" *European Journal of Political Economy* 29: 151–67.

Altes, Carmen. 2018. "Analysis of the Tourism Value Chain in Ethiopia." Paper commissioned by World Bank.

AUC (African Union Commission). 2015. "Services Exports for Growth and Development: Case Studies from Africa."

Ayele, S., G. Ayele, T. Nigussie, and J. Thorpe. 2019. "Policy Incentives and Agribusiness Investment in Ethiopia: Benefit or Deadweight?" APRA Brief Issue 20.

Beyene, B. M., and T. G. Tekleselassie. 2018. "The State, Determinants, and Consequences of Skills Mismatch in the Ethiopian Labour Market." Ethiopian Development Research Institute 021.

CAPA (Centre for Aviation). 2019. *African Aviation Outlook Report, 2019*. Sydney: CAPA.

CSA (Central Statistical Agency). Various years. "Large and Medium Manufacturing Surveys." Addis Ababa.

De Vries, G., M. Timmer, and K. De Vries. 2015. "Structural Transformation in Africa: Static Gains, Dynamic Losses." *Journal of Development Studies* 51: 674–88.

EPAU (Economic and Policy Analysis Unit, International Food Policy Research Institute). 2017. "2010/11 Social Accounting Matrix for Ethiopia." https://doi.org/10.7910/DVN/G84XIB.

FBPIDI (Food, Beverage and Pharmaceutical Industry Development Institute). Various years. Food and beverage export data. Addis Ababa.

FDRE/MoI (Federal Democratic Republic of Ethiopia, Ministry of Information). 2002. "Industrial Development Strategy." Addis Ababa.

Ferede, T., and S. Kebede. 2015. "Economic Growth and Employment Patterns, Dominant Sector, and Firm Profiles in Ethiopia: Opportunities, Challenges. and Prospects." Swiss Programme for Research on Global Issues for Development, R4D Working Paper 2.

Gebreeyesus, Mulu. 2013. "Industrial Policy and Development in Ethiopia: Evolution and Present Experimentation." WIDER Working Paper 2013/125.

———. 2017. "Industries without Smokestacks: Implications for Ethiopia's Industrialization." WIDER Working Paper WP-2017-14. World Institute for Development Economic Research (UNU-WIDER). https://ideas.repec.org/p/unu/wpaper/wp-2017-14.html.

———. 2019. "The Private Sector in Ethiopia's Transformation." In *The Oxford Handbook of the Ethiopian Economy*, ed. Fantu Cheru, Christopher Cramer, and Arkebe Oqubay. Oxford University Press.

Gebreeyesus, M., A. A. G. Abebe, T. Getahun, B. Assefa, H. Medihn, and S. Hussien. 2018. *Main Features of Micro and Small Manufacturing Enterprises in Ethiopia*. Addis Ababa: Ethiopian Development Research Institute.

Gebreeyesus, M., and M. Iizuka. 2012. "Discovery of Flower Industry in Ethiopia: Experimentation and Coordination." *Journal of Globalization and Development* 2: 1–27. doi:10.1515/1948-1837.1103.

Gebreeyesus, M., and T. Sonobe. 2012. "Global Value Chains and Market Formation Process in Emerging Export Activity: Evidence from the Ethiopian Flower Industry." *Journal of Development Studies* 48: 335–48. doi:10.1080/00220388.2011.635199.

Hino, H., and G. Ranis, eds. 2014. *Youth and Employment in Sub-Saharan Africa: Working but Poor*. New York: Routledge.

IATA (International Air Transport Association). 2020. "Economic Report on Ethiopia." https://www.iata.org/en/iata-repository/publications/economic-reports/ethiopia--value-of-aviation/.

Khadaroo, J., and B. Seetanah. 2007. "Transport Infrastructure and Tourism Development." *Annals of Tourism Research* 34: 1021–32.

———. 2008. "The role of Transport Infrastructure in International Tourism Development: A Gravity Model Approach." *Tourism Management* 29: 831–40.

McKay, A., and T. G. Tekleselassie. 2018. "Tall Paper Walls: The Political Economy of Visas and Cross-Border Travel." *World Economy* 41: 2914–33.

McMillan, M. S., and D. Rodrik. 2011. *Globalization, Structural Change and Productivity Growth*. NBER Working Paper 17143. National Bureau of Economic Research.

McMillan, M., D. Rodrik, and C. Sepulveda. 2016. "Structural Change, Fundamentals, and Growth: A Framework and Case Studies." Working paper.

Mengistu Andualem, T., W. F. Bekele, D. Ermias, A. Zewdu, Y. Alekaw, A. M. Causape, and J. C. Malet. 2019. "Ethiopia Social Accounting Matrix 2015/16." Report JRC118413, Joint Research Centre, Seville.

MoA (Ministry of Agriculture). 2020. "10-Year Perspective Plan." Addis Ababa.

MoCT (Ministry of Culture and Tourism). 2020. "10-Year Perspective Plan." Addis Ababa.

MoFED (Ministry of Finance and Economic Development). 2020. "Growth and Transformation Plan I 2010/11–2014/15." Addis Ababa.

MoI (Ministry of Industry). 2015. "Human Resource Requirement Plan for Ethiopian Manufacturing Industries (2016–2025)." Addis Ababa.

NBE (National Bank of Ethiopia). Various years. Various reports. Addis Ababa.

———. 2018. *2018/19 Annual Report*. Addis Ababa.

NPC (National Planning Commission). 2016. "Growth and Transformation Plan II (GTP II) (2015/16–2019/20)—Volume I: Main Text." Addis Ababa.

———. 2017. "Ethiopia's Progress: Eradicating Poverty—An Interim Report on the 2015/16 Poverty Analysis Study." Addis Ababa.

———. 2018. "The Second Growth and Transformation Plan (GTP II) Mid-term Review Report." Addis Ababa.

Newfarmer, R. S., J. Page, and F. Tarp. 2018. *Industries without Smokestacks: Industrialization in Africa Reconsidered.* Helsinki: United Nations University World Institute for Development Economics Research (UNU-WIDER).

Reilly, B., and T. G. Tekleselassie. 2018. "The Role of the United States Visa Waiver Program on Cross-Border Travel." *Applied Economics Letters* 25: 61–65.

UNECA (United Nations Economic Commission for Africa). 2015. "The Federal Democratic Republic of Ethiopia's Sustainable Tourism Master Plan, 2015–2025." Ministry of Culture and Tourism and UNECA, Addis Ababa.

UNIDO (UN Industrial Development Organization). No date. "Integrated Agro-Industrial Parks in Ethiopia." https://isid.unido.org/files/Ethiopia/Integrated-AgroIndustrial-Parks-Overview.pdf.

United Nations Statistics Division. 2020. "Gross Value Added by Kind of Economic Activity at Constant (2015) Prices—National Currency."

UN World Tourism Organization. 2019. "Compendium of Tourism Statistics." Data set. Conceptual references and technical notes are available in the Methodological Notes to the Tourism Statistics Database, http://statistics.unwto.org/method_notes_tourism_stat_database_2019ed.

Wondowossen, T., N. Nakagoshi, Y. Yukio, R. Jongman, and A. Dawit. 2014. "Competitiveness as an Indicator of Sustainable Development of Tourism: Applying Destination Competitiveness Indicators to Ethiopia." *Journal of Sustainable Development Studies* 6: 71–95.

World Bank. 2015. "4th Ethiopia Economic Update: Overcoming Constraints in the Manufacturing Sector."

———. 2020. "International Tourism: Number of Arrivals, Ethiopia." World Development Indicators Database. https://data.worldbank.org/indicator/ST.INT.ARVL?locations=ET.

WTTC (World Travel and Tourism Council). 2015. "Data." London.

———. 2020a. "Data." London.

———. 2020b. "Travel & Tourism: Global Economic Impact & Trends 2020."

Wubalem, Gobie. "A Seminar Review on Impact of Floriculture Industries in Ethiopia." *International Journal of Agricultural Economics* 4: 216–24. doi:10.11648/j.ijae.20190405.14.

Zhang, X., D. Tezera, C. Zou, Z. Wang, J. Zhao, E. A. Gebremenfas, and J. Dhavle. 2018. "Industrial Park Development in Ethiopia: Case Study Report." Inclusive and Sustainable Industrial Development Working Paper.

SIX

Senegal

Overcoming Stagnant Industrialization with New Sources of Job Creation

AHMADOU ALY MBAYE, FATOU GUEYE, ASSANE BEYE,

ABDOU KHADIR DIA, AND MASSAER MBAYE

Country Context and Background

Unlike in industrialized and emerging economies, export-led manufacturing is playing a much smaller role in the structural transformation of Africa's economies. Indeed, while the share of manufacturing in Africa's gross domestic product (GDP) has fallen, on average, since 1980, services absorb the bulk of African workers, leaving agriculture and moving to cities. Senegal is no exception to this trend. While agriculture lost more than 10 percentage points of its labor share between 2004 and 2019, manufacturing increased its share by only 1 percentage point, against 7.6 percentage points for trade. The growing working-age population has almost entirely been absorbed into the informal sector—in particular, agriculture and especially informal services in urban areas. Senegal, therefore, displays similar patterns of structural transformation as other African countries, where growth has failed to relocate resources from agriculture to manufacturing.

With "three major peaceful political transitions since its independence in 1960" (World Bank 2019b) and a total population of nearly 16 million, Senegal is one of Africa's most stable countries. In 2014, the Government of Senegal launched the Emerging Senegal Plan (PSE, for Plan Sénégal Emergent), with the aim to increase the well-being and prosperity of the Senegalese populations by 2035. The PSE is divided into three strategic axes: (1) structural transformation of the economy and growth, which aims at the sustainable creation of wealth and the eradication of poverty in all its forms; (2) human capital, social protection, and sustainable development; and (3) governance, institutions, peace, and security. Recent macroeconomic trends reveal that PSE is showing some signs of success, as Senegal's economic growth averaged 6.6 percent over the 2014–19 period, contrasting with only 3 percent in the period 2009–13. Projections estimate that the same high economic growth will be observed in the upcoming years, especially with the newly discovered oil and natural gas reserves (World Bank 2019b). Growth is mainly driven by contributions from consumption (3.5 percent) and private investment (2.1 percent). It has mainly benefited from three main drivers: agriculture, boosted by support programs; robust external demand; and large investments in infrastructure. This growth also remains characterized by a high level of debt, which went from 60.6 percent of GDP in 2017 to 64.5 percent in 2018, taking into account state-owned enterprises and parastatals. However, the issue of inclusion remains critical, as current job creation has been insufficient in absorbing internal migratory flows or the growing working-age population—especially since employment is mainly informal, resulting in low wages, underemployment, and limited social protections.

Figure 6-1 depicts the Senegal's GDP per capita and related growth rate between 1990 and 2019. Overall, the growth rate in the country's GDP per capita was erratic until about 2014. Relatedly, GDP per capita started recovering from its low levels of the 1990s in 2015, before plummeting again in 2018.

The unemployment rate in Senegal decreased considerably, from 11 percent to 6 percent, between 2011 and 2018 (Macrotrends 2019). According to the World Bank, 90 percent of nonagricultural employment in Senegal is in the informal sector. Furthermore, youth unemployment is relatively high in Senegal, even though some progress has been observed in the past decade ("youth" is herein defined as individuals between 15 and 24 years

FIGURE 6-1. Real GDP per Capita Values and Growth Rates

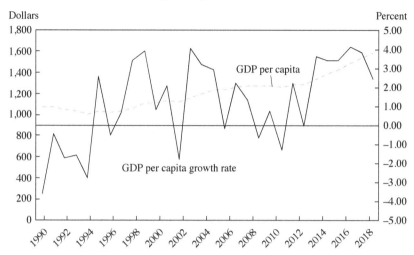

Sources: Authors' calculations using World Bank (2019c), World Development Indicators.

of age). For instance, youth unemployment dropped from 14 percent to 6 percent between 2007 and 2016. Similarly, Senegal has been successful in closing the gender gap in employment; in fact, the difference between the unemployment rates of men and women was about 6 percentage points in 2007 and went down to almost 0 in 2016 (Golub et al. 2019).

Like in many other African countries, the supply of potential workers is high in Senegal, while the number of jobs is often very limited. Between 2001 and 2017, the labor force has grown by close to 2.4 million people in absolute terms, which corresponds to an annual growth rate of 3.41 percent for the narrow labor force (table 6-1). Table 6-1 also shows the breakdown of unemployment by age group, revealing higher unemployment rates among youth. In 2017, youth (15–24 years) unemployment was at 7.82 percent, contrasting with 6.6 percent for older people. While the annual employment growth rate was high (over 4.21 percent of the narrow labor force) between 2001 and 2017, it is worth noting that most of those jobs are low-quality jobs. Official statistics show that total number of employees with social benefits, health coverage, and retirement plans peaked at 435,000 in 2019 (Golub et al. 2019), about 10 percent of existing jobs at that time.

Growth in Senegal, as in many other African countries, has been mainly jobless, as the creation of good jobs has failed to keep pace with the vibrant dynamics of the labor supply. Three main explanations can be given for

Table 6-1. Employment Patterns and Salient Features, 2001–17

Characteristic	2001	2017	Absolute change	Annualized change (%)
Labor market aggregates				
Population 15+	5,567,662	8,752,688	3,185,026	2.87
Employment	3,351,679	5,443,900	2,092,221	3.08
Narrow unemployment	198,828	384,687	185,858	4.21
Narrow labor force	3,550,508	5,828,587	2,278,079	3.15
Discouraged work seekers	250,660	394,052	143,392	2.87
Labor force participation rate (%)				
Narrow labor force participation rate	63.77	66.59	2.82	0.27
Unemployment rate (%)				
Narrow unemployment rate (all)	5.6	6.60	1.00	1.03
Narrow unemployment rate (youth)	8.54	7.82	−0.72	−0.55
Expanded unemployment rate (all)	11.83	12.51	0.69	0.35
Expanded unemployment rate (youth)	14.36	15.39	1.02	0.43

Sources: Authors' calculations using data from ANSD (2019, 2020), ENES (2020), ESAM (2019) and ILOSTAT (2020).

Note: See Bhorat et al. (2019) for definitions of these concepts.

the mediocre job creation performance: Low-productivity agriculture, which saw its value added shrink from 18 percent in 2001 to 17 percent in 2017 (figure 6-2):

- At the same time, mining, which is known to be very capital-intensive, has increased its share of GDP, from close to 0 in 2001 to 3 percent in 2017.
- Finally, manufacturing, which is generally considered an important reservoir of labor, has decreased as a share of GDP, from 23 percent in 2001 to 17 percent in 2017.

When comparing these trends with those observed for employment (table 6-2), important contrasting patterns emerge:

- While, between 2001 and 2017, mining has significantly increased its share of total value added, its share of total employment has remained marginal, at about 1 percent.

FIGURE 6-2. **Contribution to GDP by Sector between 2001 and 2017**

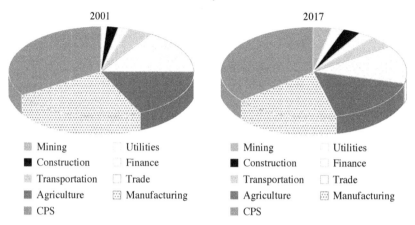

2001   2017

Mining	Utilities		Mining	Utilities
Construction	Finance		Construction	Finance
Transportation	Trade		Transportation	Trade
Agriculture	Manufacturing		Agriculture	Manufacturing
CPS			CPS	

Sources: Authors' calculations using ANSD (2019, 2020).

Note: CPS = community, social, and personal services (public sector).

- Trade, which has a slightly declining share of GDP, increased its share of total employment between 2001 and 2017, when considering both formal and informal trade.
- Manufacturing has lost 0.3 percentage point of its share of total employment, and its share of GDP has slightly decreased, by 5 percent.

Furthermore, both table 6-3 and figure 6-3 show that, between 2001 and 2017, structural transformation was limited. Agriculture is losing employment share to other sectors, while also experiencing slower-than-average growth in labor productivity. For manufacturing, we observe a decrease in its relative productivity growth, while its share in employment is slightly increasing. The trade sector experiences a decrease in relative productivity, contrasting with its increasing share in employment. Mining has one of the highest ratios of sectoral to total productivity, but almost a stagnant share of employment over the sample period.

All these trends suggest a clear absence of any movement of labor from agriculture to manufacturing. By contrast, IWSS sectors, unlike manufacturing, have recorded higher-than-average increases in both productivity and employment share. While this finding lends support to the mainstream literature on a lack of manufacturing-driven structural transformation and premature deindustrialization, it also depicts a clear pattern in

Table 6-2. Changes in Employment and Employment Share in IWSS and Non-IWSS, 2001–17

Sector	Employment 2001	Employment 2017	Change (%)	Employment share 2001	Employment share 2017	Annual avg. emp. growth 2001–17 (%)
	Absolute ('000)					
Total employment	3,351	5,443	62.4	100.0	100.0	3.1
Total IWSS	610	1,234	102.2	18.2	22.7	4.5
Agro-processing	200	367	83.6	6.0	6.7	3.9
Horticulture	63	209	231.7	1.9	3.8	7.8
Tourism	223	446	100.0	6.7	8.2	4.4
ICT	22	33	52.9	0.6	0.6	2.7
Transportation	26	35	32.5	0.8	0.6	1.8
Financial and business services	3	12	289.6	0.1	0.2	8.9
Trade: formal	15	40	160.6	0.5	0.7	6.2
Other IWSS services	58	92	59.1	1.7	1.7	2.9
Manufacturing	189	324	71.1	5.6	5.9	3.4
Other non-IWSS	2,552	3,886	52.3	76.1	71.4	2.7
Agriculture	1,675	2,182	30.3	50.0	40.1	1.7
Mining	32	62	93.8	1.0	1.1	4.2
Utilities	27	38	40.7	0.8	0.7	2.2
Construction	64	134	109.4	1.9	2.5	4.7
Trade: informal	269	701	160.6	8.0	12.9	6.2
Government	39	61	53.7	1.2	1.1	2.7
Other non-IWSS services	445	708	59.1	13.3	13.0	2.9

Sources: Authors' calculations using ANSD (2019, 2020).

Note: Other IWSS services include real estate, specialized scientific and technical activities, and support service activities. Other non-IWSS services include education, human health, social work, art, culture, sports, and recreational activities, services not classified elsewhere, and informal finance.

which IWSS sectors absorb a significant share of the labor leaving agriculture. IWSS are found to be similar to manufacturing in many ways, including that they are tradable, have the capacity for learning and productivity growth, can absorb large numbers of unskilled or moderately skilled labor, and often exhibit scale and agglomeration economies (Newfarmer, Page, and Tarp 2018). Such sectors include: horticulture, agri-business, information-technology-based transportation, formal trade, commercial agriculture, and tourism.

Table 6-3. Ratio of Sectoral Labor Productivity to Average Productivity

Sector	2000	2010	2017
Total IWSS	2.51	2.15	2.17
Agro-processing	1.69	0.93	1.17
Horticulture	2.62	1.61	1.75
Tourism	1.44	1.12	1.02
ICT	2.96	8.05	7.62
Transportation	1.92	2.58	3.50
Financial and business services	12.63	11.20	10.77
Trade: formal	8.08	5.01	4.45
Other IWSS services	7.40	7.42	8.19
Manufacturing	1.58	1.73	1.41
Other non-IWSS	0.57	0.59	0.55
Agriculture	0.33	0.36	0.37
Mining	—	2.82	2.37
Utilities	1.19	2.08	3.09
Construction	0.95	0.47	1.14
Trade: informal	1.30	0.81	0.78
Government	3.61	4.14	4.81
Other non-IWSS services	1.41	1.30	0.81

Sources: Authors' calculations using ANSD (2019, 2020); Direction de l'horticulture.

Note: Other IWSS services include real estate, specialized scientific and technical activities, and support service activities. Other non-IWSS services include education, human health, social work, art, culture, sports, and recreational activities, services not classified elsewhere, and informal finance.

In several parts of the world, tourism plays an important role in stimulating economic growth. At a global level, the tourism sector employs 277 million people and accounts for nearly 10 percent of global GDP (Page 2019). Southern and East African countries have already experienced the sector's huge potential to create jobs and boost economies. Senegal, with its pristine beaches, has a high potential for developing a vibrant tourism sector, which, as of now, is struggling. Horticulture also offers promises for growth. With technological advancements, fresh vegetables and flowers that used to be produced for local consumption can now be transported and sold globally (Page 2019). Information and communications technology services are also significant employment providers, given the globalized nature of economies, which requires connectivity. Finally, the agro-processing sector, which encompasses subsectors like food and beverages, also holds a large potential for growth under the new African Continental Free Trade Area, and thus has a great opportunity for creating jobs and boosting exports.

FIGURE 6-3. **Correlation between Sectoral Productivity and Change in Employment in Senegal, 2010–17**

Natural log of sectoral productivity/average productivity

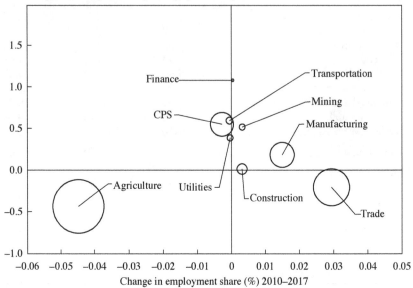

Change in employment share (%) 2010–2017

Sources: Authors' calculations using ANSD (2019, 2020).

Note: CPS = community, social, and personal services (public sector).

Sectoral Decomposition: IWSS in Comparative Perspective with Non-IWSS

In Senegal, industries without smokestacks have the potential, which, if properly leveraged, can dramatically boost good-quality job creation. Already, some industries without smokestacks, namely horticulture and tourism, are doing well in terms of output growth (figures 6-4, 6-5, 6-6, 6-7, and 6-8). Between 1999 and 2019, horticulture increased its value-added more than four times. Manufacturing's increased only 2.7 times, which is also slightly lesser than tourism's 2.8 times. By contrast, agri-business has performed particularly poorly over sample period, with its subsectors (mainly food and beverages) performing worse than manufacturing. This poor growth could be explained by the fact that most of them bear the burden of the same costs associated with manufacturing's inability to grow. For example, while labor regulations are particularly stringent for all industries in Senegal, collective bargaining applicable to manufacturing—and, consequently, agro-processing—has made those regulations even more stringent than in

FIGURE 6-4. **Evolution of Value Added and Employment in the Tourism Sector**

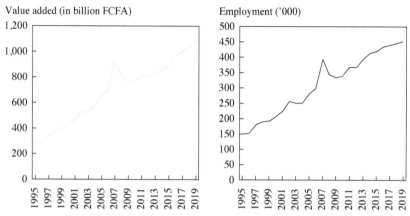

Source: Authors' calculations using data fom World Travel and Tourism Council (2019).

Note: 538 FCFA (franc of Central African States) = $1.

FIGURE 6-5. **Value Added and Employment Growth for Tourism**

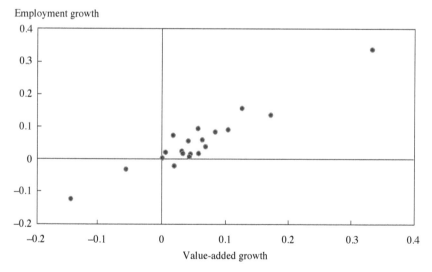

Source: Authors' calculations using data fom World Travel and Tourism Council (2019).

FIGURE 6-6. **Evolution of Value Added and Employment in Agro-processing**

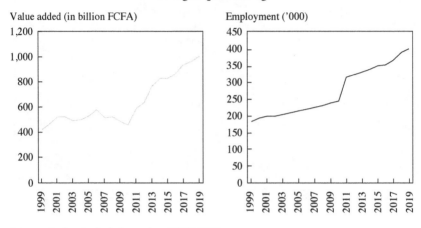

Sources: Authors' calculations using ANSD (2019).

FIGURE 6-7. **Evolution of Value Added and Employment in Horticulture**

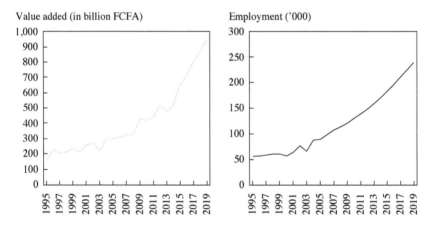

Sources: Authors' calculations using ANSD (2019).

other IWSS sectors. Likewise, costs of financing, which are subsidized for agriculture (and, therefore, horticulture) are far lower than that of manufacturing, where there is no preferential financing.

To compare IWSS job creation with that of non-IWSS, we compare trends in employment increases with those of value added increases for each sector (figures 6-4, 6-6, 6-7, and 6-8). Likewise, table 6-4 compares employment elasticities for IWSS and non-IWSS sectors. While for agro-processing, the point-elasticity is 0.88, it reaches 0.97 for horticulture and 0.96

FIGURE 6-8. **Evolution of Value Added and Employment in Manufacturing**

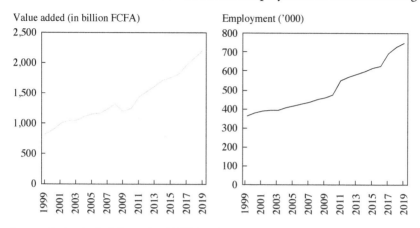

Sources: Authors' calculations using ANSD (2019).

Table 6-4. **Employment-Output Elasticity for Senegal**

Sector	Total	Male	Female
Overall economy	0.55	0.43	0.76
Total IWSS	0.77	0.65	0.97
Agro-processing	0.88	0.73	1.15
Horticulture	0.97	0.9	1.16
Tourism	0.96	0.81	1.14
ICT	0.19	0.13	0.29
Transportation	0.24	0.14	0.41
Financial and business services	0.99	0.9	1.13
Trade: formal	1.17	1.04	1.41
Other IWSS services	0.46	0.35	0.65
Manufacturing	0.54	0.42	0.78
Other non-IWSS	0.48	0.35	0.70
Agriculture	0.3	0.16	0.5
Mining	0.10	0.06	0.13
Utilities	0.19	0.14	0.31
Construction	0.56	0.44	0.68
Trade: informal	1.14	1.0	1.37
Government	0.4	0.29	0.6
Other non-IWSS services	0.52	0.43	0.70

Sources: Authors' calculations; ANSD (2019); Direction de l'horticulture; ILOSTAT (2020).

for tourism. When considering overall IWSS sectors, the employment elasticity, which stands at 0.77 is higher than that of the manufacturing and non-IWSS sectors with respective ratios of 0.54 and 0.48. These results confirm Page's (2019) assertion that, should the bottlenecks on IWSS be removed, they have a much greater potential to foster job creation than other sectors.

These general trends are confirmed by comparing employment elasticities between IWSS and other sectors (table 6-4). Employment elasticity for tourism and agro-processing is at around 0.96 and 0.88, respectively—both higher than manufacturing (0.54). Horticulture's is even higher, at 0.97. Notably, employment elasticities are, in general, much higher for women than for men.

Overall, while IWSS sectors experienced an annual growth rate of employment of 4.5 percent between 2001 and 2017, non-IWSS sectors grew at only 2.7 percent over the same period. Manufacturing's growth rate was even lower, at 3.4 percent (table 6-5). Notably, the comparison of jobs created in IWSS versus non-IWSS reveals that the change in employment in the former tends to affect women, who are traditionally at a disadvantage in the Senegalese labor market, more favorably. Indeed, while, for men, employment in IWSS grew by 3.9 percent a year against 2.4 percent for non-IWSS over the 2001–17 period, women experienced an even higher employment growth rate in IWSS (5.1 percent) over the same period. Notably, however, the employment growth rate for youth (age 15–24) remains much more limited than for older people. Both for IWSS and for non-IWSS, the youth employment growth rate is lower (2.3 percent for IWSS and 0.0 percent for non-IWSS) than that of adults (25+ age bracket), whose employment growth rates are 6.2 percent for IWSS and 4.6 for non-IWSS.

When we consider the skill level of employees (table 6-6), 13.8 percent of IWSS employees are highly skilled, and 33 percent are skilled, compared with 4.9 percent and 33 percent, respectively, for manufacturing, and 13.1 percent and 22.4 percent, respectively, for other non-IWSS sectors. For agriculture, by contrast, 80.3 percent of employees are low-skilled workers.

Thus, there is strong evidence that IWSS can stimulate African economies and provide sustainable employment opportunities for its growing working-age population. However, there are prerequisites for IWSS to deliver the expected results. In Senegal, several constraints relative to the country's political economy, infrastructure, and existing human capital can hinder IWSS's development.

Table 6-5. Demographics of IWSS and Non-IWSS Workers, 2001–17

Category of workers	Absolute change, 2001–17 ('000)			Employment share, 2001 (%)			Employment share, 2017 (%)			Average annual growth (%)			
	IWSS	Non-IWSS	Manuf.	IWSS	Non-IWSS	Manuf.	IWSS	Non-IWSS	Manuf.	IWSS	Non-IWSS	Manuf.	Total
Total	623	1,335	134	100	100	100	100	100	100	4.5	2.7	3.4	3.1
By gender													
Male	264	739	100	51.5	62.4	83.8	52.0	60.0	80.0	3.9	2.4	3.1	2.7
Female	359	596	34	48.5	37.6	16.2	48.0	40.0	20.0	5.1	3.1	4.8	3.6
By age (years)													
15–24	74	47	26	27.8	26.8	38.3	19.8	18.8	30.3	2.3	0.4	1.9	0.8
25–34	90	5	19	26.1	25.5	21.1	20.2	16.9	18.3	2.8	0.0	2.5	0.7
35–65	459	1,282	90	46.2	47.6	40.7	60.1	64.3	51.5	6.2	4.6	4.9	4.9

Source: Authors' calculations using ANSD (2019, 2020), Direction de l'horticulture (2019), and ILOSTAT (2020).

Table 6-6. Breakdown of Sectoral Employment by Skill Level, 2017

Sector	Highly skilled	Skilled	Low-skilled	Highly skilled	Skilled	Low-skilled
	Absolute ('000)			Share (%)		
Total employment	694	1,386	3,363	12.8	25.5	61.8
Total IWSS	171	407	657	13.8	33.0	53.2
Agro-processing	15	110	242	4.0	30.0	66.0
Horticulture	6	42	160	3.0	20.2	76.8
Tourism	56	182	208	12.6	40.8	46.6
ICT	23	7	2	70.0	22.5	7.5
Transportation	2	24	9	4.3	70.1	25.5
Financial and business services	10	1	1	82.0	12.0	6.0
Trade: formal	18	10	12	44.5	24.4	31.1
Other IWSS services	41	29	21	45.0	31.9	23.1
Manufacturing	16	108	200	4.9	33.3	61.8
Other non-IWSS	507	871	2,507	13.1	22.4	64.5
Agriculture	55	375	1,751	2.5	17.2	80.3
Mining	15	27	19	25.0	44.4	30.6
Utilities	17	16	6	43.1	41.2	15.7
Construction	12	36	87	8.8	26.6	64.6
Trade: informal	62	235	404	8.9	33.5	57.6
Government	51	5	4	84.8	8.2	7.0
Other non-IWSS services	295	177	236	41.7	25.0	33.3

Sources: Authors' calculations using ANSD (2019, 2020), Direction de l'horticulture (2019), and ILOSTAT (2020).

Constraints on IWSS Growth

In Senegal, our results show that a vibrant IWSS sector can stimulate the economy and provide sustainable employment opportunities for its growing working-age population. For such growth and job creation to be possible, however, Senegal must address the many constraints affecting its business environment, especially those in its regulatory framework, infrastructure, and skills development.

The Regulatory Environment

Despite recent improvements, the Senegalese regulatory framework still poses big challenges for private enterprises, especially exporting firms. Senegal's rank did improve, from 141th to 123rd between 2019 and 2020,

FIGURE 6-9. Senegal: Ease of Doing Business Score

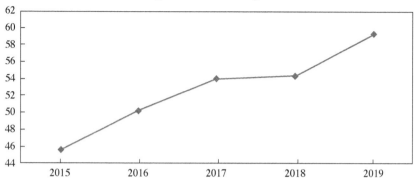

Source: Authors' calculations using World Bank (2019c), World Development Indicators.

Note: 0 = lowest performance to 100 = best performance.

in the World Bank's Ease of Doing Business index (World Bank 2019a), reflecting the country's efforts and progress toward becoming more investment-friendly. Indeed, Senegal's overall score had been steadily improving in recent years (figure 6-9).

More specifically, Senegal has shown significant improvement on indicators like "number of days it takes to administratively start a business," which had shrunk from 91 days in 2015 to 8 days in 2020 (World Bank 2019a). Then again, despite this tremendous progress, the amount of time it takes to establish a business in Senegal is relatively long and tedious compared with that in other countries with similar levels of economic development. Indeed, the process serves as a barrier, as it is not a "one-stop-shop" and is extremely confusing for investors that are not familiar with the Senegalese administrative system, according to the Millennium Challenge Corporation (MCC 2017). Principal restrictions include difficulty in accessing credit, lengthy administrative processes, and a lack of mechanisms for contract enforcement and ownership rights (MCC 2017).

There are several barriers relative to hiring and firing workers. For instance, it costs as much as the equivalent of 38 weeks of wages to part ways with a worker in Senegal (Golub et al. 2015). In terms of overall stability and consistency of labor market legislation, Senegal ranks 187 out of 189 countries (Golub, Mbaye, and Vasilyeva 2019). Indeed, a recent analysis of African export processing zones points to stringent labor market regulations and employment requirements forced on companies to secure space in the Dakar Free Zone (DFZ) as a major cause of the failure of the DFZ (Golub, Mbaye, and Vasilyeva 2019).

FIGURE 6-10. **Most Problematic Factors for Importing in Senegal**

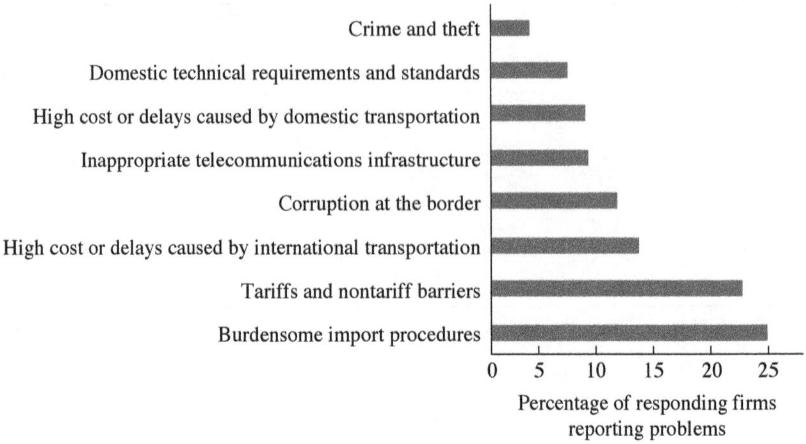

Source: World Economic Forum 2016. Used by permission.

Despite the inception of substantial trade liberalization policies in Senegal since 2000, barriers to importing and exporting persist as another manifestation of Senegal's weak regulatory system (figure 6-10). Indeed, Senegal-based companies are about 33 percent less likely to use foreign materials as production inputs (MCC 2017). Exporting a regular container of products requires up to six documents and up to $1,225 in fees. Importing the same container requires five documents and a $1,740 fee.

Indeed, access to imported inputs at a reasonable cost seems to be a significant obstacle for exports (World Economic Forum 2016). Also, though 66 percent of companies reported facing nontariff barriers to trade, 83 percent of the barriers faced by importers are linked to exceptional or informal payments (MCC 2017).

Contract compliance is another area of weakness in Senegal's business climate, as Senegal ranked 145 out of 189 countries on contract compliance. Furthermore, around 27 percent of businesses characterize contract enforcement as a major constraint to their business (World Bank 2015), primarily due to corruption and a low judicial capacity. Tax administration is also burdensome for Senegalese businesses: The country is ranked 166 out of 190 in terms of tax payments (World Bank 2019a). On average, it takes up to 620 labor hours a year for businesses to register and pay their taxes. Finally, the number of different taxes that a company has to pay can be as high as 58 (MCC 2017).

Infrastructure

Infrastructure plays an important role in shaping a country's business environment. In Africa, in general, and Senegal, in particular, infrastructural services are usually found to be of poor quality in addition to having much higher costs. For example, Senegal's rate of electrification is about 45 percent nationwide (75 percent in urban areas and 17 percent in rural areas) (EnDev 2019), and electricity is more expensive in Senegal than in the average African country (MCC 2017). MCC (2017) also finds that the low electrification of rural areas is detrimental to business competitiveness: Since most horticultural products (as well as other raw materials for agri-business) come from the country's rural areas, the lower electrification of rural areas reduces firms' cost-effectiveness by increasing both costs and uncertainty around production. More specifically, 8 percent of the companies interviewed in the World Bank Enterprise Survey 2014 name electricity as the main constraint to conducting their business activities, whereas 48.2 percent characterize it as a significant constraint on doing business.

Up to 85 percent of Senegal's electricity supply comes from thermal sources, mainly from the heavily subsidized national utility company, SENELEC, which has a monopoly status. Outages—both planned and unplanned—affect all regions of the country. Such transmission losses, along with dependence on older plants, all add to the high electricity costs (MCC 2017). Just connecting to the grid is tough: Electric installations can take firms 75 days and cost as much as 3.42 percent of income per capita (World Bank 2019a). A kilowatt-hour of electricity in Senegal costs about $0.30, while in emerging markets it ranges from $0.04 to $0.08, and $0.13 in Sub-Saharan Africa (MCC 2017).

Ground transportation is also a major constraint on the business environment in Senegal. MCC (2017) estimates that up to 25 percent of paved roads and 53 percent of unpaved roads are in poor condition, and many areas are still enclaved. Cartelization and corruption at checkpoints are further exacerbating the high costs of transportation (MCC 2017). When it comes to the quality of relevant infrastructure, the World Economic Forum (2019) ranked Senegal 106 out of 140 countries. Less than 15 percent of people live near a stretch of at least 5 kilometers of roads. Senegal's telecommunications sector has been liberalized since 1996, and since then has been controlled by a consortium, led by France Télécom, which holds a monopoly status.

Exports

Senegal has the advantage of having a stable national currency and a democratic political system. The country has also made progress in offering a fairly attractive export system, including no export taxes, fast capital and income repatriation, and a decent telecommunications network (MCC 2017). Senegal has also signed several trade agreements providing it with preferential market access, including bilateral deals with many major economies (in particular China and the United States), and it is also a signatory of the Cotonou Agreement, which grants (reciprocal) duty-free access to the African, Caribbean, and Pacific export markets as well as the European Union.

Despite these opportunities, Senegal's exports are still highly concentrated in a limited basket of goods, such as gold (15.5 percent), petroleum oils (14.8 percent), diphosphorus pentaoxide (7.8 percent), frozen fish (6.8 percent), and cement (4.3 percent) (UN Comtrade 2018). Estimates show that 70 percent of nontariff barriers are imposed by foreign regulations, and 30 percent by the Senegalese government itself (International Trade Center 2013). The vast majority of those nontariff barriers relate to import quotas, required special licenses, restrictions on exports, subsidies on exports, phytosanitary and sanitary standards, and rules-of-origin laws (ITC 2013). Most of the foreign direct investment Senegal has received recently has come from emerging nations (China, Brazil, India, and the those in the Middle East), where such standards are much lower. Despite recent reforms in improving the overall functioning of its port, the World Bank still ranks Senegal 141st out of 160 countries—behind other West African countries such as Benin, Côte d'Ivoire, Ghana, and Nigeria—in its Logistics Performance Index (World Bank 2018b).

Agglomeration

Since the mid-1970s, Senegal has begun developing export-processing zones (EPZ), starting in Dakar. The Dakar EPZ provided exemptions from corporate income taxes, customs duties, and equipment taxes, along with unrestricted repatriation of capital and profits. Despite these policies, in 1986, jobs at the Dakar EPZ reached a peak of only 1,200 before declining to 600 in 1990. The project was eventually abandoned in 1999, when it was only housing 14 participating companies with a total of 940 workers. Its inability to ignite job growth reflected significant shortcomings in the overall business climate, in particular labor market rigidities, high energy and transportation costs, and inefficient bureaucratic procedures. The EPZ has struggled to insulate businesses from these problems that are deeply rooted in the Senegalese economy. For example, since its independence, Senegal has suffered from a prolonged period of currency overvaluation, finally ending with a major devaluation of 50 percent in 1994. In addition, Senegal's weak infrastructure, its failure to provide opportunities in a timely manner, and its failure to separate companies from onerous labor market legislation and union agitation, have all played a role in undermining the EPZ (Golub et al. 2019; Farole 2010).

Firm Capabilities

"Firm capabilities" refer to a broad variety of business characteristics, such as expertise, work experience, efficiency, management quality, and the ability to produce new products (Page 2019). Surveys conducted in Senegal have found that most businesses feel they lack the technological and managerial skills to succeed in international markets (Golub et al. 2019). Some of them, for example, are intimidated by the size and price demands of European and U.S. markets. Although they want to sell, they do not trust that they will meet the price and timeliness requirements imposed by demanding international buyers. While one part of the issue is a lack of adequate information, more significantly, they do not believe they have the necessary technical mastery of production (Golub et al. 2019).

One realistic solution might be for African firms to enter into subcontracting agreements with international companies that may help with the transition to more complex and large-scale production. Indeed, according to Golub and others (2019), some of these local firms welcomed the idea of partnerships with foreign firms, particularly if they involve technology transfer but have no idea how to attract foreign buyers to Senegal or how to enter into these partnerships.

A Value Chain Analysis of Industries without Smokestacks in Senegal

In this section, we undertake a value chain analysis of IWSS sectors in Senegal, focusing on horticulture, agri-business, and tourism.

Horticulture

The horticultural industry in Senegal has demonstrated strong dynamism in the last 10 years. National production increased from 860,000 tons in 2011 to 1,320,399 tons in 2017, and exports grew eightfold between 2004 and 2017. The industry's market structure remains fairly concentrated, with about 20 major exporters, 7 of whom account for 75 percent of the total exports, whereas rising domestic demand is supplied by small producers (Golub et al. 2019). Production being mainly concentrated in the Niayes coastal strip and in the Senegal River Valley, Senegal has favorable soil-climatic conditions for horticulture in several areas of the country. The Niayes area occupies the Atlantic fringe of the Senegalese coast north of Dakar and stretches across a length of 180 kilometers of coastline, with widths ranging from 5 to 30 kilometers, with an area of approximately 3,090 square kilometers covering four administrative regions with an estimated 700,000 inhabitants: Dakar, Thiès, Louga, and Saint-Louis. The Niayes area has a sub-Canary style climate with relatively low temperatures for a big part of the year, and thus is favorable to the production of products in high demand in European markets. Other important production areas in Senegal are Saint-Louis and Dagana departments in the Saint-Louis region in northern Senegal.

In 2003, the first foreign horticultural export firm invested in the Senegalese horticultural sector. Since then, the number of major exporters has risen to six, and, simultaneously, the areas being cultivated as well as the variety of products produced continue to grow. All the export companies depend entirely on a vertically integrated production system structured within the organization with primary processing, postharvest handling, and exporting units. About 6,000 jobs have been generated by injecting foreign direct investment into the region, and 80 percent of these jobs are held by women. These jobs entail harvesting, manufacturing, and packaging operations, and the job holders are employed on a permanent, seasonal, or regular basis.

Pest attacks, packaging problems, and a lack of training for producers on new innovative practices and technologies are factors leading to significant postharvest losses, and thus, constraining the growth of the sector. Moreover, the increasing necessity of quality certification and the difficulties of satisfying its demanding quality norms have restricted growth of the sector starting in the early 2000s (Golub, Mbaye, and Vasilyeva 2019; Mbaye and Gueye 2015). A number of other substantial, though not insurmountable, constraints impede expansion of the sector, including relatively high costs of inputs due primarily to scarcities of skilled labor, arable land, water, and credit. These costs are exacerbated by the lack of basic

FIGURE 6-11. Value Chain of the Horticulture Subsector in Senegal

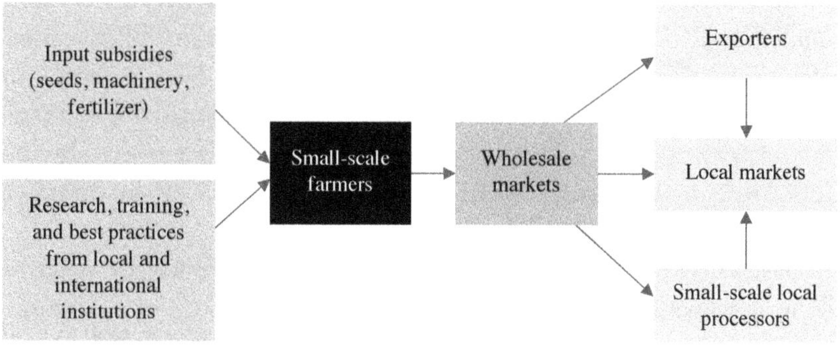

Source: Authors' visualization.

infrastructure, namely good roads. Furthermore, due to the high temperatures in certain areas of the country coupled with the low electrification of those areas, yield losses sometimes reach 40 percent for certain crops such as tomatoes. Furthermore, overproduction during rainy seasons combined with the lack of proper conservation infrastructures leads to loss of income.

The value chain of the horticulture subsector, as shown in figure 6-11, is quite straightforward in Senegal, with a limited number of involved actors. First, farmers, mainly small-scale producers, benefit from input (seeds and fertilizers) subsidies from the government, and many technical inputs from both local and international institutions as a means to bolster their production. After harvest, Senegalese the government create incentives for the local production of horticultural products through protectionist measures by restricting imports and suspending them during periods of peak harvest. Indeed, Senegalese producers have three options: (1) sell in Senegal to intermediaries in local markets; (2) sell to local, small-scale processing firms; and (3) export to foreign markets.

Tourism

In Senegal, the integration of tourism with other sectors like agriculture, fishing, handicrafts, culture, construction, and transportation makes it one of the central sectors of the national economy. La Somone and Saly, the two historic hubs sponsored by tour operators, are now "aging." Recently, new areas are under construction including Pointe Sarène and Nianing. Such projects are also conducted in the context of culture and history promotion around Dakar and the island of Gorée (slavery commemoration), art events

(Dakar Biennale of Contemporary African Art, etc.), historical vestiges and festivals in Saint-Louis, and finally in Touba (the capital of Mourides, which draws 2.5 million people each year on average as part of an annual pilgrimage). Nature and ecotourism, mainly around Sine Saloum and Casamance, are also growing but are currently underexploited due to financial, security, and accessibility issues (e.g., there is only one foreign brand, Club Med, in the region). Other areas of interest such as the desert of Lampoul are potential candidates for site diversification.

Despite these myriad opportunities, the sector currently struggles to live up to its potential. For example, English (2018) underscores the dramatic decline of the tourism sector in Senegal, with the country's Travel and Tourism Competitiveness ranking by the World Economic Forum dwindling from second in Africa, just behind Kenya in the 1980s, to lower than 10th. Likewise, the number of visas issued has fallen in recent years. For example, Sperandio (2015) mentions that the Senegalese consul in Paris issued only 19,738 visas in 2014 and only 3,577 between January and April 2015. He posits that the drops in tourism revenues might be explained by Senegal's decrease as a popular destination and that it "does not sell itself like it used to."

Moreover, a policy mandating visas—under the pretense that it is hard for Senegalese citizens to get visas to Europe and America, therefore, it is only fair to ask tourists to present visas upon entering Senegal—may have backfired (English 2018). Policymakers hoped to generate revenue through visa-processing fees, but, as soon as the biometric visa and associated fees were put in place, tourist visits to Senegal dropped by 30 to 40 percent (Sperandio 2015). Additionally, unrest in the south of the country as well as neighboring countries also deters tourists from visiting Senegal (Sperandio 2015).

A future threat to Senegal's promising tourism sector, however, is climate change and related rising sea levels. Because most of Senegal's tourist attractions are related to some extent to oceanic life, climate change's threat to the country's beaches is already adversely impacting sector.

Information and Communications Technologies

Since the 1997 privatization of Senegal's telecommunication monopoly, SONATEL, with France Télécom as the strategic partner, assessments of the country's level of relevant infrastructure and service quality have been rather favorable. The sector was further liberalized in subsequent years;

now, the country has three companies providing telephone and internet services. Moreover, significant expansion of mobile phone and internet access has led to more than 94 percent of the population having access to a mobile phone and internet. Information-technology-based services are also expanding, and increasingly spanning all sectors of activities. Despite a significant level of investment, including a submarine fiber optic cable, the costs of telecommunications and internet are still rather high in Senegal (English 2018). Moreover, SONATEL still holds a very strong grip on the whole industry, which prevents prices from lowering, and small start-up companies from emerging. Thoughtful reforms in the sector would dramatically contribute to unlocking the huge potential of the sector to thrive and would jump-start both backward and forward linkages within the economy.

Agro-processing

Senegal is an example of the paradox whereby a country has significant agricultural resources but still relies on food imports to feed its population. The irrigable potential of the country is enormous, around 397,100 hectares, but only 106,600 of the areas are managed, including 76,000 hectares in the Senegal River Valley. In addition, while agriculture employs nearly 50 percent of the working-age population, it receives around 11.3 percent of public investment (DGPPE 2018) and contributes only 9.4 percent to the national GDP (ANSD 2020).

Main agri-business value chains include rice, sugar and beverages, flour, and fish and seafood, among other items. The cotton value chain is organized around the national company for textile fibers (SODEFITEX, Société de Développement des Fibres Textiles), which is in charge of cotton ginning. Notably, cotton is characterized by erratic production and exports patterns, as it is subject to the vagaries of rainfall and the volatility of international prices.

Rice production in Senegal has been steadily rising in recent years. Rice cultivation and processing mainly occur around the delta of the Senegal and Casamance rivers. Locally marketed rice is often produced from irrigated rice farms, whereas rain-fed rice is mainly intended for self-consumption. Processing is carried out by the producers themselves or by the service providers. Yields are rather high compared with international levels, and rice growth models predict a potential yield of irrigated rice in the Sahel of 9 to 12 tons per hectare. Other agro-processing value chains include beverages, fish and seafood, food preparation, and salt—all of which have huge exporting potentials that are yet to be realized (Golub et al. 2018).

Sugar in Senegal also has a huge exporting potential, but political-economy-related factors have become an obstacle (Mbaye, Golub, and English 2016), with the government facing pressure from competing interest groups. Sugar is an important part of the local consumption basket of households as well as a rural-based industry. Since 1972, sugar production in Senegal has been controlled by the Compagnie Sucrière Sénégalaise (CSS) in an area of 9,600 hectares near Richard Toll in the Senegal River Valley. Annual production reached about 1 million tons of sugarcane in 2013, or 100,000 tons of refined sugar. The CSS employs about 6,000 workers, with an approximate payroll of CFAF 16 billion (roughly $32 million) in 2013, making it the second-largest employer in Senegal after the government. Many of these workers are part time and are hired for harvesting. Importantly, CSS is also a major importer of sugar. A few large traders, represented by the UNACOIS association (i.e., the Union Nationale des Industriels et commerçants du Sénégal, an association of the most important informal sector actors, operating primarily in commerce and other services such as transportation), are also involved in sugar importing, putting them in open conflict with CSS.

Senegal has historically been one of the world's top producers of groundnut oil and oilcake (Mbaye 2005), which made up 20–30 percent of the country's exports between 1960 and 1980. Starting in the 1990s, unstable market prices, unpredictable weather, and lousy fiscal policies all exacerbated the destabilization of the sector exposing the need to diversify away from peanut oil (Golub and Mbaye 2002; Mbaye 2005). Figure 6-12 shows Senegal's share of the world market in groundnuts and groundnut oil, further highlighting the country's highly variable share of the world market, with a clearly downward trend over time. For example, exports of unprocessed groundnuts have dropped to almost nothing after 1970 from a large global share in the 1960s. Until 2005 the government retained a near monopoly on the production of vegetable oils through the parastatal SONACOS, which was privatized in 2015 and renamed SUNEOR. Several other firms compete with SUNEOR in some product lines, but SUNEOR retains a dominant market share. On the other hand, SUNEOR also faces competition from imported palm oil from Côte d'Ivoire, a member of the West African Economic and Monetary Union, and Southeast Asia. Thus, the main impediments to the sector's competitiveness are the failure

FIGURE 6-12. Senegal's Share of World Exports of
Groundnuts and Groundnut Oil

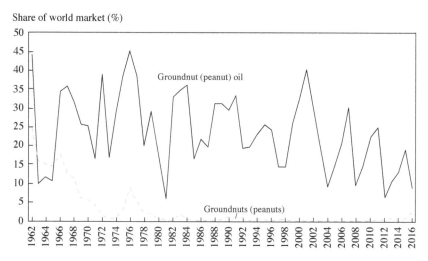

Source: Authors' calculations using World Bank (2019c), World Development Indicators.

to implement bold successful reforms in the groundnut production value chain and permanent fighting among manufacturers and importers/traders.

As the former capital of French West Africa, Senegal experiences unusually strong French influences on its private entrepreneurship. One manifestation of this influence is that French-style baguettes have become a staple consumption item, even though wheat cannot be produced in Senegal. Since flour imports have declined to very small levels since the early 2000s, Senegal imports and processes nearly all the wheat used for its estimated daily consumption of 3 million baguettes. There are four flour producers, with the largest being the Grands Moulins de Dakar, controlled by the same family that owns the sugar monopoly CSS, with about 65 percent market share of the flour market. Thus, like sugar and vegetable oil, flour production is characterized by a dominant figure; but unlike them, it is subject to somewhat more competition. Millers manage their own imports of wheat, from which they produce flour as well as animal feed, with higher profit margins on the latter. Flour is sold to bakeries on credit. Bread is supplied by a competitive market with about 1,000 bakeries around the country. Controlling the price of bread is highly problematic in a situation where flour prices are free to move. For this reason, in late 2012, the new Senegalese government moved to fix the price of flour along with the price of bread. Until now, a very fierce battle involving the different actors along the value chain (millers, wheat and flour importers/traders, as well as bakeries) considerably interferes with policies in the sector.

Senegal is seen as one of the richest fishing grounds in the world, and fish is the main source of protein for the Senegalese population (Golub and Mbaye 2002, 2018; Mbaye 2002). Though its share has been declining since the 1990s, fishing still accounts for around 15 percent of Senegal's exports. The fishing industry is also highly labor-intensive, with direct and indirect employment estimated at about 10 percent of Senegal's working population. Moreover, a large array of activities—including fish processing and distribution—primarily employs women. Over the last 20 years, the fishing industry has encountered many challenges, including overfishing, foreign competition, climate change, and dysfunctional local institutions. All these have resulted in a dramatic drop in fish stocks.

The industry is highly dualistic, with the coexistence of formal industrial and informal "artisanal" fishing, with the latter generating the bulk of employment existing in the industry. These two types of fishing compete to varying degrees for many of these species, with artisanal fishing dominating coastal surface fishing, which consists mainly of smaller fish such as sardines, mostly destined for local consumption or other African countries. On the other hand, industrial fishing dominates the highly lucrative coastal bottom species—such as grouper, yellowfin, mullet, and sole—which are exported, primarily to Europe. Most of the fresh fish exports are caught by artisanal fishermen and are delivered to industrial processing factories located around Dakar. Frozen fish exports mostly originate from the industrial fishing fleet equipped with freezing facilities. Tuna catches are mostly intended for canning. The major impediments limiting the industry's growth include overfishing, inadequate infrastructure (electricity availability), and poor unloading and processing facilities for artisanal fishing.

Future Trends: Potential Growth and Labor Demand

In this section, we look 18 years ahead to estimate the growth of the national economy and how that economic growth will shape IWSS in value-added growth, employment, and skills. We assume that value-added

FIGURE 6-13. **Projection of the Number of Jobs, 2017–35**

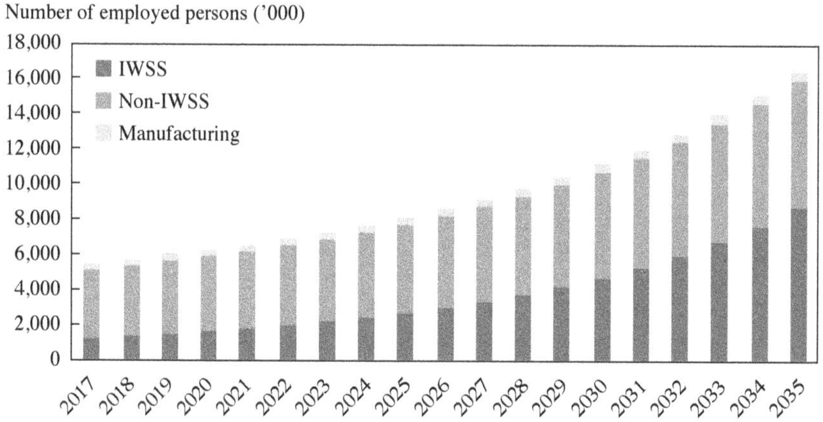

Number of employed persons ('000)

Sources: Authors' calculations using ANSD (2019, 2020) and ENES (2020).

growth for non-IWSS between 2017 and 2035 will be the same as that between 2007 and 2017. For IWSS, we assume the annual growth rate between 2017 and 2035 will be double that of 2007–17. In doing so, we assume that some of the most important hurdles impeding IWSS growth will be removed with relevant policies and investments, as pledged by the government in many recent policy documents. Figure 6-13 depicts the projected evolution of employment for IWSS, non-IWSS, and manufacturing sectors. Unsurprisingly, it shows aggregate IWSS jobs gradually picking up from non-IWSS over time, consistent with previous observations and assumptions.

Table 6-7 shows that, over the 2017–35 period, IWSS jobs will increase more than tenfold to occupy 52.8 percent of the employment share. On the other hand, non-IWSS jobs will increase by more than 329 percent and will occupy 44 percent of the employment share. Among IWSS sectors, horticulture has the highest growth rate, at 19 percent a year over the sample period. The other annual growth rates are 10.1 percent for agro-processing, 7.6 percent for tourism, 12.1 percent for information and communications technology, 13.6 for transportation, and 15.5 for finance.

A breakdown of jobs by skills (table 6-8) shows that, while the share of skilled and highly skilled workers will increase in the overall economy, for IWSS, the increase will be 1.4 percentage points for highly skilled, and

Table 6-7. Projected GDP and Labor Demand

Sector	GDP			Employment				Share of total employment	
	2017	2035 (projection)	Annual growth	2017	2035 (projection)	Add. jobs	Annual growth	2017	2035 (proj)
	(local currency in bn)	(local currency in bn)	%	('000)	('000)	('000)	%	%	%
Overall economy	11,860	77,664	11.0	5,444	16,429	10,985	6.3	100	100
Total IWSS	5,847	58,685	13.7	1,234	8,670	7,435	11.4	22.7	52.8
Agro-processing	934	5,243	10.1	367	1,690	1,323	8.8	6.7	10.3
Horticulture	795	18,205	19.0	209	4,391	4,182	18.4	3.8	26.7
Tourism	996	3,699	7.6	446	1,575	1,129	7.3	8.2	9.6
ICT	550	4,310	12.1	33	50	17	2.3	0.6	0.3
Transportation	265	2,621	13.6	35	62	27	3.3	0.6	0.4
Financial and business services	276	3,710	15.5	12	221	209	17.7	0.2	1.3
Trade: formal	389	2,780	11.5	40	392	352	13.5	0.7	2.4
Others IWSS services	1,641	18,117	14.3	92	289	197	6.6	1.7	1.8
Manufacturing	993	2,444	5.1	324	534	211	2.8	5.9	3.3
Other non-IWSS	5,020	16,535	6.8	3,886	7,225	3,339	3.5	71.4	44.0
Agriculture	1,032	4,183	8.1	2,182	3,359	1,177	2.4	40.1	20.4
Mining	318	1,378	8.5	62	72	10	0.8	1.1	0.4
Utilities	258	2,026	12.1	38	58	19	2.3	0.7	0.4
Construction	335	1,157	7.1	134	272	138	4.0	2.5	1.7
Trade: informal	1,188	3,647	6.4	701	2,504	1,803	7.3	12.9	15.2
Government	636	2,336	7.5	61	103	43	3.0	1.1	0.6
Other non-IWSS services	1,253	1,808	2.1	708	857	149	1.1	13.0	5.2

Sources: Authors' calculations using ANSD (2019, 2020) and Direction de l'horticulture (2019).

Table 6-8. Projected Labor Demand by Skill Level

Sector	2017			2035 (projected)						Annualized growth		
	%			Absolute ('000)			%			%		
	Highly skilled	Skilled	Low skilled	Highly skilled	Skilled	Low skilled	Highly skilled	Skilled	Low skilled	Highly skilled	Skilled	Low skilled
Total employment	12.8	25.5	61.7	2,337	5,238	8,852	14.2	31.9	53.9	7.0	7.7	5.5
Total IWSS	13.8	33.0	53.2	1,242	2,980	4,448	14.3	34.4	51.3	11.6	11.7	11.2
Agro-processing	4.0	30.0	66.0	169	650	871	10.0	38.5	51.5	14.5	10.4	7.4
Horticulture	3.0	20.2	76.8	267	1,247	2,877	6.1	28.4	65.5	23.1	20.7	17.4
Tourism	12.6	40.8	46.6	247	771	557	15.7	48.9	35.4	8.6	8.3	5.6
ICT	70.0	22.5	7.5	36	11	2	73.1	22.0	5.0	2.5	2.2	0.0
Transportation	4.3	70.1	25.5	5	46	11	7.4	74.3	18.3	6.4	3.6	1.4
Financial and business services	82.0	12.0	6.0	186	26	9	84.0	12.0	4.0	17.8	17.7	15.1
Trade: formal	44.5	24.4	31.1	186	128	78	47.5	32.6	19.9	13.9	15.3	10.7
Other IWSS services	45.0	31.9	23.1	145	101	43	50.2	34.9	14.9	7.2	7.1	4.0
Manufacturing	4.9	33.3	61.8	56	195	283	10.5	36.5	53.0	7.2	3.3	2.0
Other non-IWSS	13.1	22.4	64.5	1,040	2,064	4,120	14.4	28.6	57.0	4.1	4.9	2.8
Agriculture	2.5	17.2	80.3	187	717	2,453	5.6	21.4	73.0	7.1	3.7	1.9
Mining	25.0	44.4	30.6	20	35	17	28.1	48.6	23.3	1.5	1.4	-0.7
Utilities	43.1	41.2	15.7	27	26	5	46.2	45.3	8.5	2.7	2.9	-1.2
Construction	8.8	26.6	64.6	32	84	156	11.8	30.8	57.4	5.7	4.8	3.3
Trade: informal	8.9	33.5	57.6	300	942	1,262	12.0	37.6	50.4	9.1	8.0	6.5
Government	84.8	8.2	7.0	90	9	5	86.8	8.2	5.0	3.1	3.0	1.1
Other non-IWSS services	41.7	25.0	33.3	384	250	223	44.8	29.2	26.0	1.5	1.9	-0.3

Sources: Authors' calculations using ANSD (2019, 2020), ENES (2020), and ILOSTAT (2020).

Table 6-9. Sectoral Skill Gap in IWSS

Aspect of gap, 2035	Less than secondary	Secondary	Postsecondary certificate	University
	Absolute ('000)			
Total labor supply	10,937	5,504	1,265	1,073
IWSS labor demand	816	3,963	1,633	1,023
Sectoral skill gap	10,121	1,541	−368	49
Skill availability ratio	13.41	1.39	0.77	1.05

Sources: Authors' calculations using ANSD (2019), Direction de l'horticulture (2019), and O*NET (2019).

Table 6-10. Sectoral Skill Gap in Non-IWSS

Aspect of gap, 2035	Less than secondary	Secondary	Postsecondary certificate	University
	Absolute ('000)			
Total labor supply	10,937	5,504	1,265	1,073
IWSS labor demand	432	1,338	1,085	484
Sectoral skill gap	10,504	4,167	180	588
Skill availability ratio	25.31	4.11	1.17	2.22

Sources: Authors' calculations using ANSD (2019), Direction de l'horticulture (2019), and O*NET (2019).

6.4 percentage points for skilled workers by 2035. In terms of annual growth rate, the number of skilled jobs will increase by 11.6 percent for IWSS, against 4.1 percent for non-IWSS and 7 percent for the overall economy. Tables 6-9 and 6-10 estimate skills gaps for IWSS and non-IWSS by level of education. The tables show that the magnitudes of skills gaps are much larger for non-IWSS than for IWSS when it comes to secondary education or less, and similar magnitudes for post-secondary and university-level education.

Tables 6-11 through 6-13 show occupational skills gaps for some IWSS sectors (horticulture, tourism, and agro-processing). There are serious gaps in critical occupations for these sectors, meaning that IWSS should be expanded to become the leading sector of the economy in the coming years, a significant effort will need to be made to mitigate the skill gap constraint.

Table 6-11. The Occupational Skill Gap for Selected Occupations in Horticulture

Occupation	Years of school		
	Skill supply	Skill requirement	Skill gap
Farmworkers and laborers	6	10	−4
Agricultural equipment operators	6	10	−4
First-line supervisors of agricultural crop and horticultural workers	6	13	−7
Graders and sorters, agricultural products	6	10	−4
Agricultural engineers	6	15	−9
Farm equipment mechanics and service technicians	6	13	−7
Agricultural inspectors	6	13	−7
Food science technicians	6	15	−9

Sources: Authors' calculations using ANSD (2019) and ENES (2020).

Table 6-12. The Occupational Skill Gap for Selected Occupations in Tourism

Occupation	Years of school		
	Skill supply	Skill requirement	Skill gap
Cooks, fast food	6	13	−7
Hosts and hostesses, restaurants, lounges, and coffee shops	6	13	−7
Cooks, restaurants	6	13	−7
Hotel, motel, and resort desk clerks	6	13	−7
Waiters and waitresses	6	13	−7
Dishwashers	6	10	−4
Bartenders	6	13	−7
Lodging managers	6	15	−9
Food preparation workers	6	13	−7
Food service managers	6	13	−7

Sources: Authors' calculations using ANSD (2019) and ENES (2020).

Table 6-13. The Occupational Skill Gap for Selected Occupations in Agro-processing

Occupation	Years of school		
	Skill supply	Skill requirement	Skill gap
Slaughterers and meatpackers	6	13	–7
Cabinetmakers and bench carpenters	6	13	–7
Food batchmakers	6	13	–7
Sawing machine setters, operators, and tenders, wood	6	13	–7
Fabric and apparel patternmakers	6	13	–7
Industrial engineers	6	15	–9
Patternmakers, wood	6	13	–7
Model makers, wood	6	13	–7
Fabric makers, except garment	6	13	–7
Food science technicians	6	13	–7

Sources: Authors' calculations using ANSD (2019) and ENES (2020).

Firm Survey Results

In an effort to better understand youth employment in Senegal's IWSS sectors, a series of 11 interviews were conducted. The 11 interviews were distributed as follows:

- 6 agro-processing
- 3 horticulture
- 2 tourism

Current Youth Employment: The Required Formal Education

In order to better understand youth employment in the IWSS sectors in Senegal, we conducted interviews with 11 companies, including six in the agro-processing sector, three in horticulture, and two in tourism. During these interviews, discussions revolved around these points: the identification of opportunities and constraints to the development of value chains; the three main occupations occupied by young people (15–24 years), as well as the diplomas required to exercise these occupations; skill requirements for the young occupations identified; the importance of digital skills; and medium-term development plans for companies. Interviewees were asked to rate the skill importance levels on a scale of 1 to 5. The skills include:

Table 6-14. Main Occupations for Youth (15–24 Years) in Agro-processing Firms

Profession	Number	Diploma
Accountant	9	BTS/bachelor's/master's degree
Marketer	8	BTS/bachelor's/master's degree
Electrical mechanic	23	BTS
Food technician	20	BTS/bachelor's/master's degree

Sources: Authors' calculations using ANSD (2019) and O*NET (2019).

Table 6-15. Importance of Relevant Skills Required for Main Youth Occupations Identified in the Agro-processing Sector

Type of skills	Accountant	Marketer	Electrical mechanic	Food technician
Basic skills	4.0	3.9	4.0	4.0
Social skills	3.2	4.0	3.2	3.9
Problem solving	4.8	4.6	5.0	5.0
Technical skills	3.5	1.9	4.7	3.9
Systems skills	4.0	3.3	3.4	4.0
Resource management skills	4.0	2.8	3.4	3.7
Mean score	3.9	3.4	3.9	4.1

Sources: Authors' calculations using ANSD (2019) and O*NET (2019).

Table 6-16. Main Occupations for Youth (15–24 years) in the Tourism Sector

Occupation	Number	Diploma
Receptionist	6	BTS/bachelor's degree
Cook	3	High school diploma
Barman	1	High school diploma
Maid	3	Primary school education

Sources: Authors' calculations using ANSD (2019) and O*NET (2019).

basic, systems, social, technical, resource management and problem solving. Tables 6-14 through 6-17 summarize the interview results.

Agro-processing

In Senegal, the agro-processing sector helps solve both issues relative to post-harvest losses and the diversification of products (Diop 2019). The emergence

Table 6-17. Importance of Relevant Skills Required for Main Youth Occupations Identified in the Tourism Sector

Type of skillls	Receptionist	Cook	Waiter	Maid
Basic skills	4.6	4.6	4.2	3.7
Social skills	4.7	4.7	4.3	4.8
Problem solving	4.7	4.7	4.3	4.8
Technical skills	4.4	4.0	4.5	2.3
Systems skills	4.5	3.8	4.0	1.7
Resource management skills	4.8	4.8	4.5	3.9
Mean score	4.6	4.4	4.3	3.5

Sources: Authors' calculations using ANSD (2019) and O*NET (2019).

of small and medium-sized enterprises and industries also helped meet the local high demand in local products such as fruit juices, vegetables, and cereals. The sector is marked by a pronounced duality between a modern structured sector and a multiplicity of formal and informal processing units that limit the development of the value chain.

The conducted interviews allowed for the identification of the four positions most likely to be held by young employees (age 15–24), as summarized in table 6-14. Among those positions, electromechanic was the most frequent. That position requires a professional certification, Brevet de Technicien Supérieur, which is a postsecondary degree. Food technician is the next most frequent position for the youth in the interviewed firms. This position also requires a Brevet de technicien supérieur or a bachelor's degree.

Of these occupations, interviewees identified food technician as the position requiring the most skills (table 6-15). More specifically, respondents noted that basic, systems, and problem-solving skills are necessary for food technicians. Accountants and electromechanics have relatively similar average requirements, and problem-solving skills are the most required for youth occupations in the agro-processing sector. In each of these professions, firm managers deemed computer literacy particularly important as it is needed for sorting and peeling high-quality seeds, prospecting markets, creating invoices, and managing products and human resources.

In the medium term, the interviewed agro-processing firms indicated that they aim to increase their production capacity, acquisition of additional equipment and the recruitment of qualified personnel. The ECOWAS Common External Tariff, which opens up the West African market is also

Table 6-18. Main Occupations for Youth (15–24 Years) in Horticultural Firms

Profession	Number	Diploma
Head of production	2	BTS
Phytosanitary agent	2	BTS
Irrigation agent	16	BTS
Florist	3	BTS
Farm hand	11	Some high school
Driver	1	Primary school education

Sources: Authors' calculations using ANSD (2019), Direction de l'horticulture (2019), and O*NET (2019).

an opportunity these agro-processing firms intend to seize. To do so, it is primordial to bring factories closer to areas of production in an effort to lower production costs and thus increase competitiveness. In the long term, the interviewed firms expressed their intentions to diversify their production lines to better meet market demands.

Tourism

In the tourism sector, table 6-16 shows that the companies interviewed revealed that the profession of receptionist is the most occupied by young people and requires a Higher Technician Certificate or a license. Cooks and maids are also common and require baccalaureate and elementary school degrees, respectively.

In the tourism sector, receptionists and cooks have the highest skill scores among occupations held by the youth (table 6-17). Apart from the systems skills which are less important for cooks, all the other skills appear quite important. Maids require the least amount of skills to perform their job-related duties.

Horticulture

The interviewed firms mainly produce potatoes, peppers, eggplants, onions, sweet potatoes, mangoes, and limes. In the horticultural sector, the positions held by the youth, as shown by table 6-18, are mainly irrigation specialists and agricultural workers, which both require a minimum level of education.

Per the surveys, in the horticultural sector, the phytosanitary agent requires the most skills (table 6-19). Irrigation agents and heads of production

Table 6-19. Importance of Relevant Skills Required for Main Youth Occupations Identified in the Horticultural Sector

Type of skills	Head of production	Phytosanitary agent	Irrigation agent	Florist	Farm hand	Driver
Basic skills	4.2	4.4	4.6	3.8	3.6	2.3
Social skills	3.8	2.8	3.8	3.7	2.8	2.7
Problem solving	4.0	5.0	4.0	3.0	4.0	5.0
Technical skills	3.0	3.5	3.5	2.8	3.4	2.4
Systems skills	3.5	5.0	1.7	2.0	3.0	2.7
Resource management skills	2.9	3.8	4.0	2.8	3.9	5.0
Mean score	3.6	4.1	3.6	3.0	3.5	3.3

Source: Authors' calculations using ANSD (2019), Direction de l'horticulture (2019), and O*NET (2019).

have the same average skill need. However, a head of production seems to require more systems skills compared with an irrigation agent, who requires more technical skills. Farm workers and drivers essentially require skills for problem solving.

According to interviewees, computer literacy seems also necessary for an effective workforce, especially considering the computerization of the drip system that allows for a more efficient management of resources such as water and phytosanitary products. Computerization would also allow for a better simulation of market needs and thus control risks through a good estimate of production quantities. Thus, in the long run, progressive automation of the production and packaging systems could boost growth by limiting post-harvest losses. In the medium term, horticultural firms aim to increase the scale of production in order to profit from the West African market but also the development of advanced technology—and cultivation of relevant digital skills in workers—for better management of post-harvest activities.

Skill Requirements for Youth: Hard, Soft, and Digital Skills

Understanding the skills required for each occupation in day-to-day tasks is essential for identifying the relevant skill capabilities ultimately required for each of the occupations. Thus, in our approach, we asked respondents to classify and rank skills aggregated into six overarching categories that are consistent with classifications provided by O*NET (2019). The importance of a skill, measured on a scale of 1 (not important) to

5 (critically important), can be thought of as how critical it is that an individual has this skill in order to complete their day-to-day tasks.

We also classify these categories according to whether they are a "hard" or "soft" skill:

- Basic skills: skills that facilitate learning or the more rapid acquisition of knowledge (soft skill).
- Social skills: skills that are used to work with people to achieve goals (soft skill).
- Problem-solving skills: skills that are used to solve novel, ill-defined problems in real-world settings (soft skill).
- Resource management skills: skills that are used to allocate resources efficiently (soft skill).
- Technical skills: skills that are used to design, set-up, operate, and correct malfunctions involving application of machines or technological systems (hard skill).
- Systems skills: skills that are used to understand, monitor, and improve socio-technical systems (hard skill).

In addition to these skills, the survey also asks about digital skills, defined as "a range of abilities to use digital devices, communication applications, and networks to access and manage information" (UNESCO 2018). Due to their importance in the current economic climate, these skills are asked about separately in the survey instrument.

Agro-processing

As shown in table 6-20, according to our surveys, food technician is the position held by the youth that requires the most skills, with an average score of 4.1. Respondents noted that, for this profession, basic, systems, and problem-solving skills are most important. Accountants and electrical mechanics have relatively similar requirements in terms of skill scores.

The youth occupations in the agro-industry sector require essentially soft skills (table 6-21). Indeed, according to interviews, soft skills are more important than hard skills for professions such as accountant, marketer, and food technician. However, for the profession of electrical mechanic, hard skills are more important. In each of these professions, digital skills are deemed very important, as tasks include sorting and peeling quality seeds, prospecting markets, creating invoices, and managing products and

Table 6-20. Importance of Skills Required for Main Youth Occupations Identified in the Agro-processing Sector

Type of skills	Accountant	Marketer	Electrical mechanic	Food technician
Basic skills	4.0	3.9	4.0	4.0
Social skills	3.2	4.0	3.2	3.9
Problem solving	4.8	4.6	5.0	5.0
Resource management skills	4.0	2.8	3.4	3.7
Technical skills	3.5	1.9	4.7	3.9
Systems skills	4.0	3.3	3.4	4.0
Mean score	3.9	3.4	3.9	4.1

Source: Authors' calculations.

Table 6-21. Importance of Hard and Soft Skills Required for Youth Occupations in the Agro-processing Sector

Type of skills	Accountant	Marketer	Electrical mechanic	Food technician	Mean score
Soft	4.0	3.8	3.9	4.1	4.0
Hard	3.7	2.6	4.0	4.0	3.6

Source: Authors' calculations.

human resources. In the development plans of the companies surveyed, the digitization of production and packaging equipment occupies a prominent place given potential gains in efficiency. One company director surveyed emphasized the role of digital skills, asserting that "individuals without some level of digital literacy would soon be unable to complete the tasks required in youth in the agro-processing industry occupations."

In the medium term, the interviewed agro-processing firms aim to increase their production capacity as well as the acquirement of additional equipment and the recruitment of qualified personnel. The ECOWAS Common External Tariff, which opens up the West African market, is also an opportunity these agro-processing firms intend to seize by bringing factories closer to areas of production in an effort to lower production costs and thus increase competitiveness.

Table 6-22. Importance of Skills Required for Main Youth Occupations in the Tourism Sector

Type of skills	Receptionist	Cook	Waiter	Maid
Basic skills	4.6	4.6	4.2	3.7
Social skills	4.7	4.7	4.3	4.8
Problem solving	4.7	4.7	4.3	4.8
Technical skills	4.4	4.0	4.5	2.3
Systems skills	4.5	3.8	4.0	1.7
Resource management skills	4.8	4.8	4.5	3.9
Mean score	4.6	4.4	4.3	3.5

Source: Authors' calculations.

Table 6-23. Importance of Hard and Soft Skills Required for Youth Occupations in the Tourism Sector

Type of skills	Receptionist	Cook	Waiter	Maid	Mean score
Soft	4.7	4.7	4.3	4.3	4.5
Hard	4.5	3.9	4.3	2.0	3.7

Source: Authors' calculations.

Tourism

In the tourism sector, receptionists and cooks, among occupations held by the youth, have the highest skill scores. Apart from the systems skills which are less important for cooks, all the other skills appear quite important. Overall, to perform their job-related duties as shown on table 6-22, maids require the fewest skills.

Apart from the profession of waiter, which requires both hard and soft skills, tourism occupations for youth require essentially soft skills (table 6-23). Indeed, the interviews carried out show a predominance of soft skills for professions such as receptionist, cook, and maid. Digital skills are also important in tourism youth occupations, especially for the mastery of management software in hotels.

Horticulture

In the horticultural sector, table 6-24 shows that the phytosanitary agent requires the most skills. Irrigation agents and heads of production have the same average skill need. However, the head of production seems to

Table 6-24. Importance of Skills Required for Main Youth Occupations in the Horticultural Sector

Type of skills	Head of production	Phytosanitary agent	Irrigation agent	Florist	Farm hand	Driver
Basic skills	4.2	4.4	4.6	3.8	3.6	2.3
Social skills	3.8	2.8	3.8	3.7	2.8	2.7
Problem solving	4.0	5.0	4.0	3.0	4.0	5.0
Resource management skills	2.9	3.8	4.0	2.8	3.9	5.0
Technical skills	3.0	3.5	3.5	2.8	3.4	2.4
Systems skills	3.5	5.0	1.7	2.0	3.0	2.7
Mean score	3.6	4.1	3.6	3.0	3.5	3.3

Source: Authors' calculations.

require more systems skills compared with the irrigation agents, who require more technical skills. Skills for problem solving are most important for farm hands and drivers.

Computer literacy seems also necessary given the computerization of the drip system, which allows for a more efficient management of resources such as water and phytosanitary products (table 6-25). Computerization also opens up more information for assessing market needs and thus control risks through a good estimate of production quantities. In the long run, progressive automation of the production and packaging systems could boost growth by limiting post-harvest losses. In the medium term, horticultural firms aim to increase the scale of production in order to profit from the West African market but also the development of advanced technology for better management of post-harvest activities.

An analysis of skills by type shows that, by and large, the horticultural professions occupied by young people require more soft skills than hard skills, with the exception of phytosanitary agent. Moreover, according to the surveys, as modern machinery and equipment are used particularly for irrigation and harvesting systems, digital skills will be increasingly important for horticultural occupations. These digital skills enable the employee to perform a rapid identification of the problems of the irrigation system and, therefore, their resolution.

Table 6-25. Importance of Hard and Soft Skills Required for Youth Occupations in the Horticultural Sector

Type of skills	Head of production	Phytosanitary agent	Irrigation agent	Florist	Farm hand	Driver	Mean score
Soft	3.7	4.0	4.1	3.3	3.6	3.7	3.7
Hard	3.2	4.3	2.6	2.4	3.2	2.5	3.0

Source: Authors' calculations.

Table 6-26. Skill Deficit by Sector

	Skill deficit value			
Skill group	Agro-processing	Tourism	Horticulture	Average IWSS sector
Basic skills	2.0	2.7	2.7	2.4
Social skills	1.8	2.0	1.7	1.8
Problem-solving skills	2.0	3.7	2.0	2.6
Resource management skills	2.0	1.7	3.0	2.2
Technical skills	2.8	1.3	2.7	2.3
Systems skills	2.3	1.3	3.3	2.3
Aggregate	2.2	2.1	2.6	2.3

Source: Authors' calculations.

Skill Gaps of Employed Youth

In the interviews, we also inquired into the skill gap for youth hires in each skill category. Indeed, respondents were asked to consider a category of skills and compare the required level of these skills to the level of the skill exhibited by youth hires in the firm. The skill deficit rating is measured on a 5-point scale, with a rating of 1 indicating that most employees met the skill requirements, and as a result, there is little to no skill gap present. In other words, a rating of 5 indicated that most employees did not meet the skill requirements at all and that there was a critical gap present for the relevant skill.

The results show that the skill deficit is more present in the horticultural sector with a score of 2.6 against 2.2 for the agro-processing sector and 2.1 for the tourism sector (table 6-26). The systems skill deficit for youth jobs in the horticultural sector is particularly striking and might be explained by the workforce consisting mainly of agricultural workers with a very low level of formal education. The lack of technical skills is also worrying in the agro-processing sector since the operation of production and packaging equipment requires a mastery of the operating modes of the machines. In the tourism sector, the lack of problem-solving skills for youth occupations could be explained by the scarcity of continuing training in the hotel and restaurant sector. Indeed, according to the tourism sector respondents, training centers far from tourist areas do not facilitate the continuing training of young professionals.

Policy Implications and Conclusion:
Unlocking Growth Potential and Overcoming Skill Gaps

While certain IWSS sectors in Senegal certainly have the potential for job creation, a number of obstacles stand in the way of the growth of these sectors. Here, we summarize our findings concerning the biggest hindrances to the growth of these IWSS and provide recommendations on how to overcome these hurdles.

Horticulture

Having access to credit in Senegal is a lengthy process and has several limitations relative to obtaining credit from commercial banks. Interest rates are high, and barriers to access to credit are not homogeneous across sexes. More specifically, women have a harder time accessing loans as all the parameters relative to having worthy collateral are, most of the time, linked to the borrower's employment status. Moreover, the horticulture sector lacks qualified and skilled laborers that would enable its operators to be competitive in the international markets by producing high-quality products in the timeframe imposed by international buyers. Finally, the impact of climate change on livelihoods cannot be ignored: The natural resources required to have good yields are getting scarcer and the technological investments necessary to allow producers to adapt to those climatic changes are not made. As result, products are not properly conserved nor transformed thus leading to huge yield losses. To counter these above-mentioned issues, it would be important to make infrastructural investments to minimize yield losses and increase opportunities for conservation and transformation, provide capacity building opportunities, and develop and popularize climate change adaptation measures.

Tourism

The biggest issues in the tourism sector are related to climate change, as Senegal has capitalized on "watercourse tourism," where most tourist activities are centered on water. Therefore, rising sea levels threaten most of those activities. Additionally, most investments around tourism are concentrated in big cities like Dakar. The remote rural areas, which also hold breathtaking tourist attractions, lack adequate infrastructure that would attract private investment. Finally, the tourism sector currently has several policies that are not in line with its policy objectives. Thus, policymakers should make important infrastructural investments in rural areas as a means to attract private investments, and identify and implement climate change mitigation measures that would enable a sustainable exploitation of resources.

Agro-industry

Policymakers must take steps to reduce the barriers to entry to IWSS sectors, especially a lack of adequate infrastructure. For instance, per the World Bank, electric installations can take firms 75 days and cost as much as 3.42 percent of income per capita (World Bank 2019a). Eight percent of the companies interviewed in the World Bank Enterprise Survey 2014 name electricity as the main constraint to conducting their business activities, and 48.2 percent characterize it as a significant constraint. Furthermore, in an effort to increase profit margins, it is crucial to have access to foreign markets with accessible import and export procedures. In Senegal, exporting a regular container of products requires up to six documents and up to $1,225 in fees. Importing the same container requires five documents and a $1,740 fee. Reforms for entry and export of goods are essential for this sector's further growth.

In this chapter, we have analyzed industries without smokestacks and their potential contribution to economic growth and job creation in Senegal. Our main finding is that this potential is huge and can be further leveraged by adopting important policies to improve the business environment. Such policies include removing the many hurdles that exist in Senegal's regulatory framework and deter private enterprise development, including (1) highly rigid labor legislation; (2) a cumbersome and costly tax system; (3) a still-inhibiting importing system; and (4) a weak judicial system and poor contract enforcement environment. Moreover, infrastructure services are also found to be costly and highly unreliable, mainly in the areas of electricity, transportation, and telecommunications. These infrastructural deficiencies are highly detrimental to all IWSS sectors. Removing these hurdles to IWSS growth might considerably change the growth trajectory of Senegal in the near future, by, in our estimates, doubling annual growth rates from their baseline level.

Acknowledgments

The authors would like to thank Richard Newfarmer, Brahima S. Coulibaly, and other participants in two workshops where findings of this study were presented and discussed. We are also grateful to Alle Nar Diop, Adama Seck, Insa Sadio, and Ibrahima Tall for providing useful statistical information to complete the research.

REFERENCES

ANSD. 2019. "Situation Economique et Social."

ANSD. 2020. "Situation Economique et Sociale du Senegal 2017–2018."

Bhorat. H., Allen. C., Asmal. Z., Hill. R. and Rooney. C. 2019. "Addressing Africa's Youth Unemployment Through Industries Without Smokestacks, Framing Paper III: Employment Creation Potential. Labor Skills Requirements and Skills Gaps for Young People—A Methodological Framework." Brookings Africa Growth Initiative.

Caitlin, Allen, Zaakhir Asmal, Haroon Bhorat, Robert Hill, Jabulile Monnakgotla, Morné Oosthuizen, and Christopher Rooney. 2021. "Employment Creation Potential, Labor Skills Requirements and Skill Gaps for Young People, A South African Case Study." AGI Working Paper 26. Brookings Institution.

DGPPE (Direction Générale de la Planification et des Politiques Economiques), Ministère de l'Economie et du Plan, Republique du Senegal. 2018. *Revue Annuelle Conjointe 2018.*

Diop, A. 2019. "Agroalimentaire au Sénégal : enjeux, opportunités et défis." SunuMbay.

Direction de l'horticulture. 2019. "Enquêtes périodiques: 1995–2019." Ministère de de l'agriculture, de la souveraineté alimentaire et de l'élevage.

EnDev (Energising Development). 2019. "Senegal: Energy Situation." https:// endev.info/content/Senegal.

ENES. 2020. "Enquête National sur l'emploi au Sénégal." ANSD.

English, P. 2018. "Senegal: A Service Economy in Need of an Export Boost." In *Industries Without Smokestacks: Industrialization in Africa Reconsidered*, edited by Richard S. Newfarmer, John Page, and Finn Tarp, 254–74. Uni-Wider Studies in Development Economics. Oxford University Press.

ESAM. 2019. "Senegalese Household Survey 1995, 2003 & 2019" ANSD.

Export Senegal. 2017. "La filière cuir et peaux: Une mine d'or sous exploitée." https://www.senegal-export.com/la-filiere-cuir-et-peaux-une-mine.93.html.

Farole, Thomas. 2010. "Second Best? Investment Climate and Performance in Africa's Special Economic Zones." World Bank Poverty Reduction and Economic Management Network, Policy Research Working Paper.

Golub, Stephen, Janet Ceglowski, Aly Mbaye, and Varun Prasad. 2018. "Can Africa Compete with China in Manufacturing?" *The World Economy*, 1–21.

Golub, Stephen, and Aly Mbaye. 2002. "Obstacles and Opportunities for Senegal's International Competitiveness: Case Studies of the Peanut Oil, Fishing and Textile Industries." World Bank Africa Region Working Paper 37.

Golub, S., A. A. Mbaye, L. Chen, F. Gueye, and J. L. T. Garza. 2019. "Constraint to Employment Creation in Africa." In *Creating Decent Jobs: Strategies, Policies and Instruments*, edited by Monga. C., S. Abebe, and A. Woldemichael. Policy Research Document. Abidjan: African Development Bank.

Golub, Stephen, Aly Mbaye, and Hanyu Chwe. 2015. *Labor Market Regulations in Sub-Saharan Africa: With a Focus on Senegal.* Working Paper 201505, University of Cape Town, Development Policy Research Unit.

Golub, S., A. A. Mbaye, and A. Vasilyeva. 2019. "Senegal's International Competitiveness and Employment Creation for Women and Youth: The Product Space Analysis and Fieldwork Findings." Prepared for Development Policy Research Unit of University of Cape Town.

ILOSTAT. 2020. "International Labour Organization, Indicators and Data Tools."

International Trade Center. 2013. "LDC Services Exports: Trends and Success Stories." https://intracen.org/resources/publications/ldc-services-exports-trends-and-success-stories.

Macrotrends. 2019. "Senegal: Unemployment Rate (1990–2020)." https://www.macrotrends.net/countries/SEN/senegal/unemployment-rate.

Mbaye, A. A. 2002. "Capital humain, compétence et productivité du travail au Sénégal: Une analyse empirique." Économies et Sociétés, Série F, numéro 40, *Développement*—IV, nos. 3–4: 567–88.

———. 2015. "Notes on Trade Logistics and Facilitation in Senegal." UNIDO.

Mbaye, A. A., S. Golub, and F. Gueye. 2020. *Formal and Informal Enterprise in Francophone Africa: Analysis and Policies for a Vibrant Private Sector.* University of Cape Town Press.

MCC (Millennium Challenge Corporation). 2017. "Senegal Constraints Analysis Report." https://assets.mcc.gov/content/uploads/2017/05/Senegal_II_CA_withCover.pdf.

Newfarmer, R., J. Page, and F. Tarp. 2018. *Industries without Smokestacks: Industrialization in Africa Reconsidered.* WIDER Studies in Development Economics. Oxford University Press.

O*NET. 2019. "O*NET-SOC 2019 Taxonomy."

Page, J. 2019. "Addressing Africa's Youth Unemployment Through Industries Without Smokestacks, Framing Paper II: Industries Without Smokestacks—Firm Characteristics and Constraints to Growth." Brookings Africa Growth Initiative.

Sperandio, A. 2015. "Senegal: A Sharp Decline in the Touristic Sector." https://www.lejournalinternational.fr/Senegal-a-sharp-decline-in-the-touristicsector_a3204.html.

UN Comtrade. 2018. "UN COMTRADE Database."

UNESCO. 2018. "Digital skills critical for jobs and social inclusion."

UNIDO (UN Industrial Development Organization). 2015. "Rapport Synthétique De L'analyse Des Chaines De Valeur." https://open.unido.org/api/documents/5273324/download/.

Walfadjri. 2014. "Sénégal: Horticulture: Une filière avec ses multiples contraintes. "*Lejecos.* https://www.lejecos.com/Senegal-Horticulture-Une-filiere-avec-ses-multiples-contraintes_a2038.html.

World Bank. 2014. "Senegal: WB Supports Quality Training Programs to Create Jobs for Young People and Skilled Labor in Tourism, Horticulture, and Poultry Farming."

———. 2015. "Senegal: Enterprise Survey Report."

———. 2018a. "Human Capital Index and Components." https://www.worldbank.org/en/data/interactive/2018/10/18/human-capital-index-and-components-2018.

———. 2018b. "Logistics Performance Index." https://lpi.worldbank.org/international/scorecard/radar/254/C/SEN/2018#chartarea.

———. 2019a. *Doing Business 2020.* https://openknowledge.worldbank.org/bitstream/handle/10986/32436/9781464814402.pdf.

———. 2019b. "Senegal: Overview." https://www.worldbank.org/en/country/senegal/overview.

———. 2019c. "World Development Indicators."

World Bank, Enterprise Survey. 2014. https://www.enterprisesurveys.org/en/data/exploreeconomies/2014/senegal.

World Economic Forum. 2016. *The Global Enabling Trade Report 2016.* Geneva: World Economic Forum. https://www.weforum.org/publications/the-global-enabling-trade-report-2016/.

———. 2019. "The Travel and Tourism Competitiveness Report 2019: Travel and Tourism at a Tipping Point."

World Integrated Trade Solutions. 2018. "Senegal Non-Tariff Measure Summary." https://wits.worldbank.org/tariff/non-tariff-measures/en/country/SEN.

World Trade and Tourism Council. 2019. "WTTC Data Gateway."

SEVEN

Ghana

Beyond Jobless Growth to Productive Employment

ERNEST ARYEETEY, PRISCILLA TWUMASI-BAFFOUR,

AND FESTUS EBO TURKSON

Introduction and Country Context

Countries in Sub-Saharan Africa have lately had some of the fastest economic growth rates in the world, second only to East Asia and South Asia.
At the same time, the issues of jobless growth and the poor performance of
manufacturing have become major concerns in the region. It has become
imperative for many African countries to find other ways to boost employment to improve the livelihoods of people, especially given the youthful
nature of the region's population and the over 122 million young people
that are expected to join the continent's labor force by 2022 (ILO 2014).
Notably, a new pattern of growth is emerging in the region, but with higher
growth rates in the services sector, contrary to the manufacturing, export-
led transformation previously observed in East Asia, and with the capacity
to absorb low- to medium-skilled workers.

Ghana is not an exception when it comes to the regional trend of relatively significant growth over a long period not yet reflecting in employment and improvements in employment conditions, especially young people. Ghana has traditionally relied on primary commodities for exports, with gold and cocoa as principal export items, until significant oil finds made Ghana a petroleum exporter in 2010. This resource dependence has, however, exposed the country even more to international commodity price fluctuations, making the need for structural transformation more urgent.

The issue of jobless growth in Ghana has become a major concern against the backdrop of the relatively significant growth observed over time, with a rate of 6.3 percent in 2018, substantially above the Sub-Saharan average of 3 percent. This growth notwithstanding, precarious and vulnerable employment persists in the country, particularly among young people. With an average national unemployment rate of about 6 percent, unemployment among youth is much higher according to estimates from the Ghana Statistical Service. Specifically, about 59.6 percent of youth (persons age 15–35 years) are employed, while 12.1 percent are unemployed, with the remaining 28.3 percent out of the labor force. Also, at least one in three young persons (31.8 percent) are found in self-employment in the non-agriculture sector as own-account workers. Moreover, most employment opportunities for youth are in vulnerable/informal and part-time/temporary jobs (GoG 2014).

Ghana's growth performance since 2014 has been relatively high, except for 2014 to 2016, when real gross domestic product (GDP) growth was about 5 percent. Growth for 2017 was 8.1 percent, for 2018 was 6.3 percent, and has been estimated at 7.0 percent in 2019, significantly exceeding the average Sub-Saharan African growth of 3.5 percent, and among the fastest-growing economies in the world over the last three years.

Ghana's recent growth has been driven mainly by oil production. Nonoil growth has, however, picked up over the last three years, growing faster in 2016 and 2018 than overall growth. Most of this nonoil GDP growth has been driven by the services sector, particularly in information and communication technologies, trade, and health and social work. As shown in table 7-1, the performance of agricultural and industrial sectors starting in 2017 accounts for the growth of GDP in recent times. Consequently, at the end of 2019, Ghana projected higher growth in nonoil sectors over the period 2020–22.

Table 7-1. Real GDP and Sectoral Growth Rates (Percent), 2014–22

Year	2014	2015	2016	2017	2018	2019	2020*	2021*	2022*
Overall	2.9	2.2	3.4	8.1	6.3	7.0	6.8	4.9	4.6
Nonoil	2.7	2.2	4.6	4.6	6.5	5.9	6.7	5.9	5.5
Agriculture	0.9	2.3	2.9	6.1	4.8	6.4	5.1	5.8	5.3
Industry	1.1	1.1	4.3	15.7	10.6	8.8	8.6	3.3	3.3
Services	5.4	3.0	2.8	3.3	2.7	5.4	5.8	6.0	6.9

Sources: Authors' calculations using data from Ghana Statistical Service (2020) and MoF (2020).

*Projected.

FIGURE 7-1. Elasticity of Employment

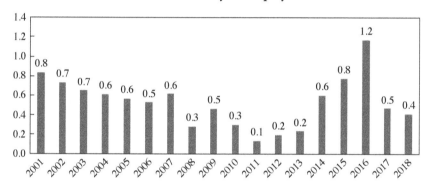

Source: Authors' illustration based on data from World Bank (2020).

The service sector is the largest contributor to GDP. The share of agriculture in GDP has declined steadily, from 30.4 percent in 2006 to 19.7 percent in 2018. The services sector, which has seen a steady rise in its contribution to GDP in the last decade, has become the leading sector in terms of sectoral contribution.

Although this pattern is consistent with trends in other parts of Africa, it is inconsistent with the traditional narrative of structural transformation. As Page (2018) notes, between 1998 and 2015, services exports grew more than six times faster than merchandise exports across Africa, indicating the relevance of the sector in recent times. Notably, economic growth has largely been jobless.

As shown in figure 7-1, the average ratio of employment growth to GDP growth is only 0.5, which indicates a generally weak relationship between

GDP growth and employment. Challenges with job creation in the country are attributable to both demand and supply factors. On the supply side, as in other African countries, a high fertility rate, improved health care, and increased educational attainment have led to a significant expansion in the working-age population. On the demand side, mineral exports, mainly the commencement of commercial oil production in 2010, continue to be the drivers of growth. These activities are not typical of the labor-intensive ones that the country needs in order to absorb the masses of youth seeking employment.

The jobless growth trajectory observed in Ghana and the poor performance of its manufacturing sector have made it necessary for policymakers to direct attention to identifying and supporting sectors with greater employment potential. Ghana needs to chart a course to explore alternative development strategies rather than rely on a structural transformation model based on "traditional" manufacturing activity. Page (2019) has observed that many African economies are turning to "industries without smokestacks" (IWSS) to lead structural change. This trend, to a large extent, is being driven by the dominance of the services sector and the fact that services can be tradable. But notwithstanding this, it is important to note that the sustainability of any employment strategy that is based on IWSS depends on the employment prospects of IWSS, especially the generation of much-needed jobs for youth.

New technologies and the integration of the global economy have revealed the growth potential of some sectors. Such sectors, termed industries without smokestacks, display characteristics of traditional manufacturing: they have tradable output, have higher than average value added per worker, exhibit a capacity for technological change and productivity growth, and display evidence of agglomeration economies. According to Newfarmer, Page, and Tarp (2018), IWSS include agro-industries and horticulture, tourism, business services, and transportation and logistics. This country study identifies agro-processing and tourism as the IWSS sectors with significant potential to lead in the diversification of the Ghanaian economy.

The agro-processing and tourism sectors are already targeted under the government's flagship industrial transformation program. The intention of government is to develop Ghana's industrial landscape for their products to diversify away from cocoa and mineral exports. The government expects that these sectors will be instrumental in addressing the challenges of job creation, promote import substitution, increase revenues from exports, and boost the generation of rural incomes.

An incentive program has been developed to support the growth of these sectors. Both sectors have been found in the literature to have high employment potential and high demand for low to moderate skills, a feature that is consistent with the characteristics of the Ghanaian labor market. The agroprocessing industry is dominated by microenterprises and small firms involved in adding value along the agricultural value chain in horticultural products, vegetables, roots and tubers, and palm oil for both domestic and foreign markets. In tourism, Ghana has several natural, cultural, and heritage resources (historical forts and castles), national parks, a beautiful coastline, unique art, and cultural traditions that can be a source of attraction for the international community.

Employment Patterns and Salient Features

In general, despite the Ghanaian economy's impressive performance of late, employment patterns have not changed much. According to the latest labor force survey (2015), 67.9 percent of the working-age population is actively employed; 71.4 percent of males are employed and 64.7 percent of females. This trend is consistent across all regions of the country.

Table 7-2 presents data on unemployment trends in the country by gender, location, and age cohort based on existing household surveys and the population census. The rate of unemployment has risen marginally over the years. Women have a higher unemployment rate than men, while

Table 7-2. Trends in Unemployment in Ghana, 1992–2017

Unemployment	GLSS 3 1992	GLSS 4 1999	GLSS 5 2006	GLSS 6 2013	GLSS 7 2017	Population census 2000	Population census 2010
Total	2.3	2.7	3.1	5.2	5.1	10.4	5.8
Male	2.2	3.4	3.2	4.8	4.5	10.1	5.4
Female	2.4	2.2	3.0	5.5	5.7	10.7	6.3
Urban	6.7	5.8	6.1	6.5	7.8	12.8	8.0
Rural	0.5	1.2	1.3	3.9	3.5	8.6	3.5
Youth (15–24)	5.2	5.0	6.6	10.9	7.1	16.7	12.9
Adults (25+)	1.4	2.1	1.9	3.4	4.1	8.6	4.0

Sources: Calculations from Ghana Living Standards Survey (GLSS) 3, 4, 5, 6, and 7; Population and Housing Census 2000, 2010.

the unemployment rate among urban dwellers is higher (7.8 percent in 2017) than rural dwellers. The unemployment rate among young people is higher compared with their older counterparts.

Attempts to use industrial policy to enable the manufacturing sector to generate jobs for young people have not been successful. As Ackah, Adjasi, and Turkson (2014) note, Ghana's industrial policy[1] was designed to promote increased competitiveness and enhanced industrial production. It was also designed to provide a broader range of fair-priced, better-quality products for domestic and international markets.

Figure 7-2 shows the pattern of employment by sector between 1990 and 2018. The services sector has been the country's leading employer since 2014, followed by agriculture and industry, respectively. The distribution of employment by specific sectors in Ghana is consistent with the path of structural transformation in most African countries. Employment transitions from agriculture into services over time. Agriculture, as of 2017, employed only 38.6 percent of the total workforce. Over that same period, the contribution of the services sector to employment grew from 25.1 percent of the total workforce to 44 percent. Most jobs in the services sector are low-productivity activities with little or no connection to international markets. In addition, most employment in the services sector is informal and precarious.

Table 7-3 provides a breakdown of employment by sectors across IWSS and non-IWSS sectors between 2013 and 2017. Agro-processing and tourism (both IWSS) are among the sectors that experienced increases in employment and growth rates between 2013 and 2017. Within non-IWSS sectors— that is, other agriculture, forestry and fishing and wholesale and retail—we observe significant changes in employment across the two periods.

Table 7-4 provides a breakdown of labor productivity by sectors across IWSS and non-IWSS between 2013 and 2017. IWSS sectors show higher productivity than manufacturing and non-IWSS sectors. IWSS sectors such as information and communications technology (ICT) and financial and business services have very high productivity. Among the non-IWSS sectors, mining and utilities have the highest productivity, and the lowest productivity is in informal trade.

Figure 7-3 seeks to show the extent of structural transformation that is ideally expected to transition from low-productivity low employment to increasing employment in highly productive IWSS sectors. The slope of the linear regression line indicates whether structural transformation has

FIGURE 7-2. Sectoral Contribution to Employment (Percentage of Total Employment)

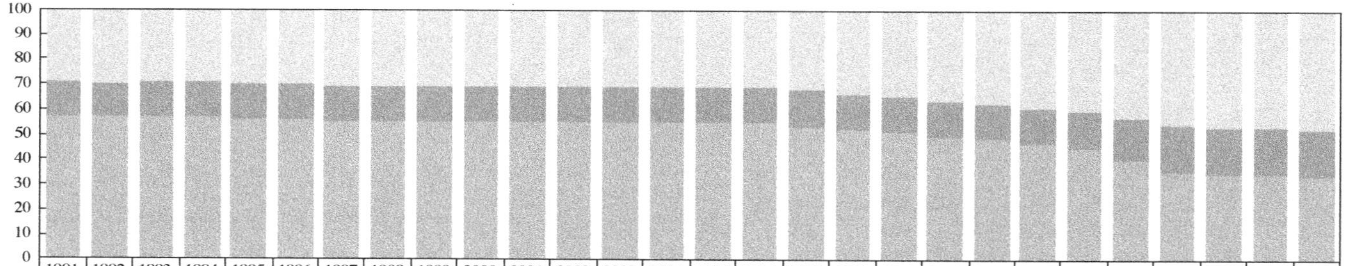

	1991	1992	1993	1994	1995	1996	1997	1998	1999	2000	2001	2002	2003	2004	2005	2006	2007	2008	2009	2010	2011	2012	2013	2014	2015	2016	2017	2018
Services	29.4	29.6	29.0	29.2	29.6	29.7	30.4	30.7	31.1	31.0	31.0	30.9	30.8	30.7	30.7	30.8	32.2	33.3	34.6	36.3	37.7	39.1	40.5	43.4	46.1	46.7	47.1	47.5
Industry	13.8	13.8	14.0	14.1	14.0	14.1	14.0	14.0	14.0	14.0	14.0	14.1	14.1	14.2	14.2	14.2	14.1	14.2	14.0	13.8	13.8	14.1	14.1	16.2	18.7	18.6	18.6	18.6
Agriculture	56.9	56.6	57.0	56.8	56.4	56.2	55.6	55.3	54.9	55.0	55.0	55.0	55.1	55.2	55.1	54.9	53.7	52.5	51.4	49.9	48.4	46.8	45.4	40.4	35.2	34.7	34.3	33.9

Agriculture   Industry   Services

Source: Authors' illustration based on data from World Bank (2020).

Table 7-3. Employment by Sector: IWSS Compared with Non-IWSS

Sector	Employment ('000s)			Employment share (%)		Compound annual growth (%)
	2013	2017	Change	2013	2017	2013–17
Total	8,659	11,082	2,423	100	100	6.4
IWSS Sectors	3,575	4,397	822	41.3	39.7	5.3
Agro-processing	473	721	248	5.5	6.5	11.1
Construction	333	468	135	3.8	4.2	8.9
Export crops and horticulture	1,013	1,048	35	11.7	9.5	0.8
Financial and business services	179	183	4	2.1	1.7	0.6
Information and communications technology	42	47	5	0.5	0.4	2.9
Tourism	419	422	3	4.8	3.8	0.3
Trade (formal)	784	1,196	412	9.1	10.8	11.1
Transportation	378	382	4	4.4	3.4	0.3
Other IWSS services						
Manufacturing	888	1,273	385	10.3	11.5	9.4
Non-IWSS Sectors	4,196	5,412	1,216	48.5	48.8	6.6
Traditional agriculture	2,399	2,480	81	27.7	22.4	0.8
Government	176	69	−107	2.0	0.6	−20.9
Mining	166	164	−2	1.9	1.5	−0.3
Trade (informal)	1,043	1,952	909	12.0	17.6	17.0
Utilities	40	44	4	0.5	0.4	2.4
Other non-IWSS	326	633	307	3.8	5.7	18.0

Sources: Authors' calculations based on GLSS 6 and 7 Surveys from the Ghana Statistical Service.

Table 7-4. Labor Productivity by Sector

Sector	Labor productivity	
	2013	2017
	Ghanaian cedi per worker ('000s)	
Total	24.1	22.6
IWSS	27.9	27.8
Agro-processing	15.6	11.4
Construction	50.0	41.5
Export crops and horticulture	15.6	17.3
Financial and business services	97.5	123.6
Information and communications technology	135.6	196.9
Tourism	20.7	26.3
Trade (formal)	32.6	27.2
Transportation	9.0	7.4
Other IWSS services		
Manufacturing	25.8	21.1
Non-IWSS	20.5	18.8
Agriculture (mainly subsistence)	10.3	11.4
Government	21.6	53.3
Mining	138.1	158.0
Trade (informal)	12.9	8.8
Utilities	108.2	131.9
Other non-IWSS	44.6	29.6

Sources: Authors' calculations based on GLSS 6 and 7 Surveys from the Ghana Statistical Service.

been growth-inducing (positively sloped) or non-growth-inducing (negatively sloped). The sizes of the bubble represent the sector's share of employment in 2016/17. The bubbles with a dotted outline indicate the IWSS sectors, the black bubbles are manufacturing, and the gray bubbles are non-IWSS activities.

As shown in the figure 7-3, labor is moving from traditional agriculture into higher-productivity sectors. Although a negative association is observed between the change in employment and productivity (i.e., a downward-sloping regression line), this association is not significant and does not provide evidence of growth-inducing structural transformation. In addition, while workers in manufacturing have relatively high productivity compared with workers in traditional agriculture, labor resources are still dominated

FIGURE 7-3. **Sectoral Change in Employment Shares and Total Productivity**

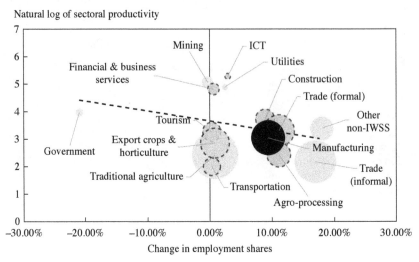

Source: Authors estimations based on GLSS 6 and 7 Surveys from the Ghana Statistical Service.

in relatively low-productivity sectors. More importantly, typical IWSS sectors are more productive than traditional agriculture and absorb a significant share of the change in employment in the 2013–17 period; thus IWSS sectors are playing a major role in employment.

Patterns of Growth: The Role of IWSS

Industries without smokestacks are newly emerging sectors that have similar characteristics to manufacturing and are beginning to play a role similar to manufacturing, especially in employment numbers. Page (2019) provides an important working definition of IWSS as activities that are tradable, have high value added per worker—relative to average, economy-wide productivity—exhibit the capacity for technological change and productivity growth; and show evidence of scale and/or agglomeration economies. Examples of sectors exhibiting these characteristics include horticulture and high-value agri-business, tourism, ICT-based services, business services, and other tradable services (e.g., transportation and logistics). In the case of Ghana, we have identified two IWSS sectors: agro-industry and tourism.

Table 7-5. Distribution of Firms in Agriculture and Manufacturing, 2015

Firm Size (number of employees)	Agriculture[1] (%)	Manufacturing (%)	Total (%)
Microenterprises (1–4)	59.3	89.3	80.7
Small (5–19)	26.1	17.2	17.5
Medium-sized (20–49)	6.9	1.0	1.1
Large (50+)	7.7	0.5	0.7
Total (%)	100.0	100.0	100.0
Total number of firms	2,831	99,437	102,268

Source: Author's calculations using data from the GSS (2017b) Integrated Business Establishment Survey.

[1]Includes forestry and fishing.

Agro-industry

For the purpose of this study, "agro-industry" refers to value added that originates from agriculture, forestry, and fisheries, and that includes simple preservation operations such as drying products to more complex processing, such as upstream processing (processing of agricultural commodities into intermediate products) and downstream processing (processing of intermediate agricultural products to finished products).

The agro-processing industry in Ghana is dominated by microenterprises/ firms involved in value added of horticultural products (cut fruit and fruit juices, vegetables, roots and tubers, nuts, and palm oil) as well as rice and flour milling, fish canning and smoking, cotton ginning, textiles and gar-ments, bakeries, beverages (both alcoholic and nonalcoholic and medicines), dairy products, footwear, and paper. A study of food crop agro-processing firms in Ghana shows that 85 percent of all these firms are microenterprises, 12 percent are small firms, and only 3 percent are medium-sized or large firms (Afful-Koomson and Fonta 2015). The dominance of microenterprises and small firms within the agro-processing industry is confirmed by the Integrated Business Establishments Survey (IBES) done by the Ghana Statistical Service (GSS 2017b).

Table 7-5 shows the distribution of firms within the agriculture and manufacturing subsectors in 2015 (GSS 2017b).[2] Most firms (80.7 percent) within agriculture and manufacturing are microenterprises, while small firms constitute 17.5 percent. Medium-sized to large firms makes up about 2 percent of the 102,268 firms that are in agriculture and manufacturing.

FIGURE 7-4. **Trends in Ghana's Agro-processing Exports, 2001–18**

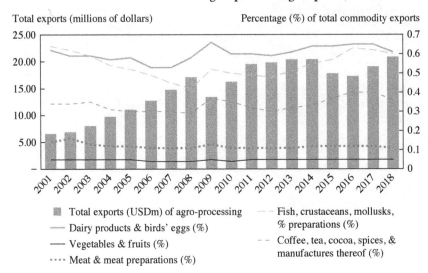

Source: Authors' illustrative calculation based on data from UN Comtrade (2020).

Agro-processing is the most important subsector of the manufacturing sector in output and employment, with food and beverages representing the largest component of processed commodities. Agro-industry is dominated by Ghanaians, who own about 99 percent of all manufacturing firms in the country. Of this number, over half are agro-processing firms. While about 9 percent of large firms in Ghana are owned by foreign entities, less than 2 percent of micro to medium-sized firms are owned by foreigners (GSS 2017a).

Data from the IBES (GSS 2017b) indicate that, in 2015, about 450,000 persons were engaged in agro-processing and related activities. Of these, 24,494 were engaged in the manufacture of beverages, 96,405 in food manufacturing, and over 50,000 in firms operating in crop and animal production, forestry and logging, and fish and aquaculture activities.

Medium-sized to large-scale processors often resort to backward integration for the procurement of inputs and forward integration for the distribution of processed products. Multinational agro-processors are increasingly making use of contract relations in the procurement of agricultural inputs where they can specify their quality and quantity.[3]

Despite the limited value addition in agro-processing, there are some notable value chains. Such chains include palm oil, grains (rice, maize [corn], and sorghum), cassava, fruit, cocoa, cashew nuts, and rubber (MoFA 2015).

Figure 7-4 shows the pattern of export values for five typical agro-processing subsectors: meat and meat preparations; dairy products and birds' eggs; fish, crustaceans, mollusks, and preparations thereof; vegetables and fruit; and coffee, tea, cocoa, spices, and manufactures thereof. Evidence from the figure shows that the value of exports for these products has been increasing steadily, from $6.5 million in 2001 to about $20.9 million in 2018.

Tourism

Tourism has recently seen increased attention due to the view that it can become an effective tool for job creation. The sector's importance in the country's diversification drive is gradually increasing, largely as a result of several policies initiated by the government. The importance of the sector is further demonstrated by the government's intention to renovate and improve various tourist sites. Ghana has several natural, cultural, and heritage resources (historical forts and castles), national parks, a beautiful coastline, unique arts, and cultural traditions that can be a source of attraction for the international community. The country can leverage these sites to address problems of unemployment and poverty.

The tourism sector is labor-intensive, mainly made up of the accommodation and food service subsectors and the arts, entertainment, and recreation subsector. Economic activities within the sector support a diverse and versatile labor market, by providing micro- and small-scale employment opportunities, such as travel and tours, handicrafts, music and dance, and Ghanaian cuisine. The major players in the sector are the Ghana Tourism Authority, hotels and resorts, restaurants and nightclubs, travel agents and tour operators, theater arts operators, music industry players, creative arts producers, and producers of arts, crafts, and handicrafts.

Firms operating within the tourism sector are mainly micro and small firms. Typically, these firms include hotels and other accommodation providers, travel agents, transport owners, and firms providing various forms of arts, culture, and entertainment recreation. As shown in table 7-6, less than 2 percent of firms in tourism are medium-sized, indicating that the sector provides crucial employment opportunities at the micro- and small-scale level.

Over the past decade, employment in the sector has grown over 10 percent annually, mainly in direct employment in accommodation and food services; creative arts and entertainment; libraries, archives, museums, and other cultural activities; gambling and betting (mainly sports betting); as well as sports, amusement, and recreation activities. Between 2005 and 2015, employment in tourism more than doubled, from 172,823 to 393,000, representing an increase of about 127 percent, mainly on

Table 7-6. Distribution of Firms in Tourism, 2015

Firm size (number of employees)	Accommodation and food service (%)	Arts, culture, entertainment, and recreation (%)	Total (%)
Micro (1–4)	85.9	91.9	86.5
Small (5–19)	12.7	5.9	12.1
Medium-sized (20–49)	1.0	1.4	1.0
Large (50+)	0.3	0.8	0.4
Total (%)	100.0	100.0	100.0
Total number of firms	56,352	5,845	62,197

Source: Authors' calculations using data from the GSS (2017b) Integrated Business Establishment Surveys, 2015.

account of an expansion in accommodation and food and beverage service activities.

In 2015, accommodation and food service activities accounted for 92.6 percent of the jobs in the tourism sector. Of every four persons employed within the tourism sector, three are engaged in the food and beverage service activities (table 7-7).

The IBES data given in 2015 show that employment in tourism is mainly concentrated in accommodation and food service activities (over 93 percent). Hotels and tourist shops employed 85 percent of those engaged in accommodation and food service activities, and restaurants accounted for 9 percent, while tour operations and car rentals accounted for 6 percent of jobs under accommodation and food services.

Available statistics from the Ministry of Tourism, Arts and Culture (MoTAC) suggest that the amount of receipts from tourism has increased, although the sector's contribution to both GDP and total export receipts has decreased in recent times. Several possible factors account for the decline, including a slowdown in economic growth between 2014 and 2016, inadequate support from the government, and the Ebola virus outbreak in some West African countries. Domestic tourism increased from 1,353,253 visitors to tourist sites in 2016 to 1,420,915 in 2017, with corresponding receipts from GHS3,210,565 ($583,739.57) in 2016 to GHS3,531,622 ($642,113.09) in 2017 (MoTAC 2020).

Although the tourism sector's contribution to both GDP growth and total export receipts has decreased in recent years, it remains strong. Particularly, starting in 2011, the decrease in the sector's share of GDP could

Table 7-7. Employment Shares of Subsectors in Tourism, 2015

Sector	Number of establishments	Number of persons engaged	Share of employment (%)
Accommodation and food service activities	44,956	229,413	93.3
Accommodation	3,969	44,308	18.0
Food and beverage service activities	40,686	183,280	74.6
Travel agency, tour operators, reservation	301	1,825	0.7
Arts, entertainment, and recreation	4,657	16,385	6.7
Creative, arts, and entertainment activities	351	3,752	1.5
Libraries, archives, museums, and other cultural activities	71	838	0.3
Gambling and betting activities	3,575	8,577	3.5
Sports activities and amusement and recreation activities	661	3,218	1.3
Total tourism	49,612	245,798	100.0

Source: Authors' calculations using data from the GSS (2017b). Integrated Business Establishment Surveys.

be attributed to the significant contribution of the oil and natural gas sectors, due to the discovery of oil in commercial quantities. Also, information from the Ghana Tourism Authority suggests that the number of licensed hotel rooms (including star-rated hotels) and licensed travel agents and tour operators has increased, suggesting the existing opportunities for employment generation within the tourism sector. Total jobs created in both formal and informal tourism enterprises increased from 438,000 in 2016 to 506,967 in 2018.

In the effort to boost tourism and take advantage of the country's historical sites, the government launched the Year of Return campaign in 2019 to commemorate 400 years since the arrival of the first enslaved Africans in Jamestown, Virginia, in the United States. The objective of the campaign was to position Ghana as a key travel destination for African Americans and the members of the African diaspora who were wishing to trace their ancestry—marketing Ghana as a tourism destination. The success of the Year of Return program in boosting tourism—preliminary estimates point to about 200,000 additional international arrivals, with 1.5 million total visitors in 2019—resulted in the development of a follow-up program, named Beyond the Return, which is further expected to boost tourism. Evidently, prospects for tourism are enormous, with important employment implications.

Sectoral Decomposition in Employment and Productivity: IWSS Sectors in Comparative Perspective with Non-IWSS Sectors over the Last Decade

The pattern of employment in Ghana generally reflects the changes that have taken place in the structure of the economy in favor of the services sector. As shown in table 7-3, employment in agro-processing grew at an annual rate of 11.1 percent between 2013 and 2017, outpacing both manufacturing and non-IWSS sectors. Within IWSS, growth was also particularly strong for construction and formal trade activities. Table 7-8 shows the distribution of skills across a selected set of IWSS and non-IWSS sectors.

In the area of skills, the World Bank Enterprise Survey of 2013 showed that the food sector was the most productive, with over 50 percent of its production workforce being skilled. This is, however, low compared with garments, but greater than textiles and close to the average for both IWSS and non-IWSS (table 7-8). The average number of years of experience for a top manager in the food sector is 15 years—a similar value for other sectors that are not IWSS. However, that number is lower for other IWSS sectors that are classified under agro-processing, such as garments, leather, and wood, with 18 years of average experience. This confirms our selection of agro-processing as a typical IWSS sector in Ghana due to the level of productivity observed, proxied by food processing.

Policies to Promote Agro-industry

Recently, the Government of Ghana launched a 10-point agenda as its central policy for industrialization. This agenda prominently features agro-processing.

So far, the National Industrial Revitalization Programme has selected 80 distressed local industries for stimulus packages, which should be used to augment the expansion of these businesses, enabling them to create jobs and compete globally. The "One District One Factory" (1D1F) initiative seeks to

Table 7-8. Distribution of Skilled Workers Across IWSS and Non-IWSS Sectors

Product sector	Proportion of production workforce who are skilled	Ratio of skilled to unskilled	Number of years of experience of top manager
IWSS	53.5	1.7	15.5
Food processing	50.2	1.0	15.3
Textile	31.6	0.5	12.4
Garments	78.6	3.7	18.9
Publishing	54.9	1.2	20.0
Wood	58.7	1.4	20.8
Paper	62.1	1.6	14.0
Leather	65.2	1.9	23.0
Transportation	45.0	0.8	7.5
Non-IWSS	53.3	1.3	15.7
Recycling	26.7	0.4	11.5
Refined petroleum	43.6	0.8	13.3
Chemicals	47.8	0.9	15.5
Basic metal	49.1	1.0	14.2
Nonmetallic	56.5	1.3	13.1
Furniture	58.7	1.4	17.0
Electronics	59.8	1.5	14.8
Fabricated metal	62.2	1.6	15.4
Plastics and rubber	62.7	1.7	19.2

Source: Authors' calculations using data from the World Bank Enterprise Survey (2013).

identify and create business opportunities in local districts and harness the strengths and resources of locals through the use of efficient technology and demand-driven value chain processes. It is designed as a comprehensive program for rural industrialization, driven by the private sector and involving setting up at least one medium-sized or large-scale factory in each of the administrative districts of Ghana—that is, factories in all 265 districts in the medium term. The main objective is to create employment, particularly for youth in rural and peri-urban communities and reducing rural-to-urban migration. The focus is mainly on higher value added in agro-processing for import substitution and exports as well as tourism.

The 1D1F flagship program, based on government estimates, is expected to create 7,000 to 15,000 jobs per district—and 1.5 million to 3.2 million nationwide by the end of 2021. By the end of 2019, 181 factories had been established, and an estimated 14,000 direct jobs and over 100,000 indirect jobs had been created (MOTI 2019). The sectoral distribution of firms already established indicates that 56 percent of the firms are/will be engaged in agro-processing, 22 percent in other manufacturing, and 5 percent in poultry/fish/livestock processing.

Several factors make the agro-processing sector viable in Ghana, including the country's diverse agro-ecological zone, which supports various agricultural products that can be processed; a well-endowed network of water bodies that can support agriculture, especially during the lean seasons; and numerous incentives already in place to promote agro-processing in the country (Owoo and Lambon-Quayefio 2017). Indeed, a technical, financial, and commercial viability analysis was conducted for firms that submitted proposals for the government's flagship 1D1F initiative, and, out of 462 proposals that were received, 191 were found to be viable (MoF 2018), demonstrating the economic viability of the agro-processing.

The Ghana Trade and Investment Gateway Project, with the support of the World Bank, established industrial parks under the Ghana Free Zones Board as export-processing zones (Ackah, Agyire-Tettey, and Turkson 2020). The projects under current development include the Dawa Industrial Zone, the West Park, and the Appolonia Business Park (all of which are located in Southern Ghana). Other feasibility studies are being explored in Central Ghana (Boankra-Ashanti Region) as well as in Northern Ghana.

Policies to Promote Tourism

The overall policy directives for the tourism sector are detailed in the National Tourism Development Plan (2013–27). The Ghana Tourism Development Project is a World Bank–funded project that seeks to improve the performance of tourism in targeted destinations in Ghana. The project is a direct response to a series of critical challenges confronting Ghana's tourism industry.

The National Tourism Development Plan seeks to strengthen the tourism-enabling environment; develop tourism sites and destinations; and provide support to tourism enterprises. This program is supported by projects such as the Marine Drive Tourism Investment Project, which commemorates 400 years of slavery (Year of Return) and the See Ghana, Eat Ghana, Wear Ghana, Feel Ghana campaign.

The Marine Drive Tourism Investment Project is a government initiative aimed at developing sections of the coastline of Ghana's capital city into a state-of-the-art tourism and hospitality enclave. It will cover over 240 acres of land near the Arts Centre in downtown Accra. According to the Ministry of Tourism, when completed, Marine Drive Ghana will attract more investment in trade and improve tourism in addition to generating revenue and employment as well as increasing foreign exchange earnings.

The Year of Return program in 2019 marked 400 years since the first enslaved Africans arrived in Jamestown, Virginia, in the United States. Ghana used this campaign to market the country as a tourism destination with transatlantic trade appeal. The year-long event was designed to incentivize diaspora returnees by waiving some visa requirements and permitting people of African origin the right to apply for an indefinite stay, all in a bid to boost tourism. Preliminary estimates from the Ministry of Tourism, Arts, and Culture show that there were about 200,000 extra international arrivals out of the 1.5 million total number of visitors for 2019, with an additional $1.9 billion in revenue realized—indicating the potential that exists in tourism for the country.

Constraints on IWSS Growth

In spite of the enormous potential of the IWSS sectors to structurally transform the Ghanaian economy, there are constraints that need to be addressed to help unlock the potential of these IWSS sectors in driving the structural transformation needed for sustained and resilient economic growth and development. In Ghana, these include the regulatory environment and requirements, infrastructure, human capital/skills, export capacity, and firm capabilities, along with constraints within production value chains and the potential for future output and employment growth and labor demand.

The Regulatory Environment and Requirements

The regulatory environment within which firms operate in Ghana imposes constraints and invariably increases the costs of operations. It is well documented in various studies on enterprise development in Ghana that the regulatory environment imposes excessive and unnecessary burdens and increased costs on small and medium-sized enterprises (Ackah, Adjasi, and Turkson 2014; Turkson 2010; Abor and Quartey 2010; Baah-Nuakoh et al. 2002).

Ghana has lately made some attempts to reform the regulatory framework to support micro and small firms that were often neglected in earlier reforms. Recently, policymakers have devoted their attention to both the agro-processing and tourism sectors because of the potential that these two sectors have to become significant job creators, in addition to their contribution to output and diversification away from dependence on a few primary commodities and minerals. The major challenge, however, has been with the enforcement of the reforms. The Ghana Tourism Development Plan reported a lack of enforcement of planning control and guidance, leading to inappropriate development to the detriment of tourist resources. Relatedly, there has been a lack of enforcement of rules aimed at ensuring the environmental quality of tourism sites and beaches.

The general regulatory framework has improved marginally, as shown in the country's performance on the World Bank's Doing Business indicators (table 7-A1 in this chapter's appendix), Ghana's overall score increased from 57 percent in 2016 to 60 percent in 2020, propelling the country up the rankings, from 118 to 108. Specific improvements in the regulatory frameworks in access to electricity, trading across borders, and dealing with construction permits were major factors in this change in rank.

Infrastructure

The distribution of Ghana's infrastructure generally reflects the country's spatial distribution of economic activity, with a greater density in the south than in the north. The World Bank reports that Ghana's infrastructure platform is generally advanced, especially when compared with other low-income countries in Africa (World Bank 2010). Institutional reforms targeting ICT, ports, roads, and water utilities have substantially contributed to this success (World Bank 2010). Ghana has succeeded in increasing household access to telephone, power, and water services by developing its national infrastructure. This success has not been confined to urban areas: rural water, electricity, and global systems for mobile communication coverage rates are impressive. However, in 2016, a report by the Ghana Institution of Engineers ranked Ghana's roads and bridges, electric power, and potable water infrastructure systems and networks as generally in a poor to fair condition.

Ghana's National Tourism Development Plan (2013–27) identified poor road infrastructure to reach major tourist sites as a constraint on the sector's growth. More specifically, it notes that road travel along transit corridors is prone to delays, as a result of poor road conditions (potholes, untarred sections, and a lack of general maintenance); frequent, severe speed humps; too many and frequent police checkpoints; toll booths; customs posts; and congestion where the roads pass through towns. Proposals have been made to restore some railway networks through the establishment of a more modern railway network that offers opportunities for tourist movement as well as specific railway-based tourism activities.

The Tourist Sector Development Project (2018) indicated that the cost constraining growth in the sector is the cost of energy. According to the report, energy costs represent about 40 percent of operational cost for hotel accommodations. Energy costs in Ghana are four times the regional average due to poor energy policies, debts downstream of the energy sector, multiple illegal connections, and a failure of the government to pay energy bills.

For agro-processing, constraints relating to poorly developed rural infrastructure (mainly poor roads and the high cost of installing electricity) hamper the ability of actors along the agro-processing value chain to compete effectively. There has been significant improvement in the time and cost it takes to get electricity installed over the last five years, as seen in table 7-A1 in the chapter appendix.

Skills

Ghana's National Tourism Development Plan (2013–27) identified a gap between the quality and quantity of human resources in the tourism sector. Currently, there is no clear national policy framework on training and development of human capital for public, private, and informal firms in the sector. Other challenges include a poor quality of data on human resource development and employment, limited linkage of ICT with tourism human resource development, and low public awareness of tourism employment opportunities.

Most of the agro-processors in Ghana are household or domestic processors that add little value to agricultural commodities. This is mainly because most of these processors have no or low education, lack formal training (skills in agro-processing are acquired mostly through apprenticeship training), and make use of very simple and locally manufactured technology.

Capacity to Export

Tourism is Ghana's fourth-largest foreign currency earner after the major primary export sectors of gold, cocoa, and remittances. Tourism businesses are subject to standards, such as trading standards, import and export rules, consumer protection, and business registration and licensing.

These businesses have not received the incentives that apply to other sectors, such as tax relief. Lengthy, expensive, and complicated visa procedures and policies have limited the development of air travel, and they continue to be obstacles to the continued expansion of travel and the exporting of creative goods.

In agro-processing, entrepreneurs have had a strong desire to export, but several constraints hinder their ability to do so. Ghanaian exporters remain uncompetitive because of higher trade costs and infrastructure constraints. Attempts to increase the proportion of storage facilities as efforts to reduce postharvest losses in the agricultural sector can benefit agro-processing firms. Turkson (2018) has identified burdensome documentation requirements, time-consuming customs procedures, and inefficient port operations that lead to corruption at the ports to be one of the main reasons for very high trade costs in Ghana. In addition, due to the highly perishable nature of most agro-processing products, the lack of cold storage facilities has been a major constraint on exports. Other constraints include the seasonality of agricultural produce as a hindrance to increasing capacity and the inability of exporters to meet strict phytosanitary standards to remain competitive.

Firm Capabilities

The agro-processing industry in Ghana is not well advanced, with a relatively low degree of value added for agricultural commodities, and very few linkages with marketing and financial services in addition to the use of simple technology. This situation is partly due to small firm sizes that make most of the firms operate below capacity or use inefficient technologies. These bottlenecks are revealed in the country's high dependence on imported goods. A study by Gyeke-Dako and others (2017) of Ghana's participation in the global value chain revealed that there is very little transformation for exports and imports, implying that there are minimal value added and limited participation along the value chain.

Constraints within the Value Chains

The value chains of both agro-processing and tourism are not well advanced, with a relatively low degree of value added. This result is partly due to the dominance of small firms along the value chain along with underdeveloped processes. Gyeke-Dako and others (2017) have shown that Ghana's participation in the global value chain is limited, as there is very little transformation for exports and imports.

In tourism, there are numerous sectors within the value chain, including accommodations, medical centers, agriculture, aviation, entertainment, and public transportation. The main challenges in this value chain are labor constraints, poor institutional arrangements, and inadequate funds to support tourism projects. As indicated in the Ghana Tourism Development Plan 2011–27, one of the main complaints by both domestic and foreign tourists in Ghana is about the poor level of the quality of services in tourism, mainly as the result of the low quality of the workforce. With the exception of the higher star-rated hotels, which make use of extensive information technology infrastructure for all services and have well-trained staffs, most hotels and tourist sites lack skilled personnel and do not have the needed software and expertise to facilitate their technical operations. The industry is mainly made up of private micro and small firms, but upskilling the workforce through training and capacity development is not prioritized.

The Potential for Future Output and Employment Growth and Demand for Labor

Both the agro-processing and horticulture, as well as tourism, have the potential for growth and employment. The government has created plans for the two sectors to be given financial and policy support, as outlined in the country's budget and development agenda. Moreover, the skill requirements of these two sectors are already abundant in the country. Ghana has a very youthful population, which can meet the needs of the two sectors.

Agro-processing is currently one of the priority sectors under Ghana's policy of developing strategic anchor industries. Activities within the sector are going to be driven by the private sector but supported by the government in land acquisition, land registration, and the provision of infrastructure. The government also intends to support the development of industrial parks. These initiatives, according to the government, are expected to boost growth through the provision of employment opportunities for youth, while enhancing the country's competitiveness.

In tourism, the government is encouraging the private sector to participate by supporting the development of various projects. Key among such projects is the upgrading of road infrastructure to various tourist sites, the development of government priority projects such as the Marine Drive Tourism Project, upgrades to various tourist sites, and the development of linkages between the tourism sector and other sectors such as agro-industry. These initiatives are expected to increase the number of international

Table 7-9. The Demographic Pattern of the Unemployed in Ghana

Demographic group	2012/13	2016/17
Gender		
Male	48.9	37.9
Female	51.0	62.1
Age (years)		
15–24	36.0	40.7
25–34	29.8	30.0
35–65	34.1	29.3
Education		
Less than secondary	76.8	62.1
Secondary	17.1	28.6
Postsecondary	6.1	9.3

Source: GLSS 6 and 7.

travelers, as well as increase visitors' lengths of stay. The National Tourism Development Plan projects that the proportion of domestic tourists will increase by 60 percent, and international travel by 15 percent, in the short to medium terms. The contribution of the tourism sector to the country's GDP is further expected to increase significantly (Ministry of Tourism 2012).

There is a large pool of unemployed—and young—labor that can be relied on to improve the agro-processing and tourism sectors. In 2016/17, more than a third of the unemployed were between 15 and 24, and more than half were between 15 and 34 (table 7-9)—an increase from 2012/13. In 2016/17, about 62 percent of the unemployed population had a basic education, and 29 percent had a secondary education.

There appears to be a declining proportion of the unemployed with a basic education and an increase in those with a secondary education. Under the current government's policy of providing free education at the secondary level, it is generally expected that average education of the total labor force of Ghanaians will gradually transition from the basic to the secondary level. This can significantly enhance the productivity of jobs and increase average wages.

Under the country's current 10-point agenda for industrial transformation, various sectors with high growth and employment generation potential have been identified as strategic anchor industries, including agro-processing. The strategy for boosting the agro-processing sector includes at least four themes: improving production efficiency; development of products; storage, processing, and transportation; and marketing.

The Government of Ghana is strongly leveraging the uptake of technology and digitization to improve administrative systems through initiatives such as the introduction of a national identification card, digital property addressing system, paperless port systems, mobile money interoperability, and land digitization with block-chain technology. Where the agro-processing sector dominates, there are attempts to establish the Ghana Design and Manufacturing Centre, which will be a center of excellence for the design, manufacturing, and technology commercialization of manufacturing activities.

Scenarios for the Future: Projecting Output and Employment Growth and Demand for Skilled Workers

As discussed, both the agro-processing and tourism sectors in Ghana display a potential for high growth and employment, spurred on by the country's (1) changing demographic patterns of the population; (2) path to economic and industrial transformation; and (3) uptake of technology and digitization.

In this section, we present projections for the country's GDP growth as well as labor demand and its skill decomposition for Ghana in 2025 and 2035. The projections for GDP are based on an annual average growth rate of about 8 percent, while the sectoral rates are based on past performance and projections (MoF 2019). The projections for employment and sectoral employment are based on two rounds of the Ghana Living Standards Survey, GLSS 5 in 2012/13 and GLSS 6 in 2016/17 (see the chapter's appendix A for assumptions underlying the projections).

The results, as seen in table 7-10, show that with annual GDP growth of 7.4 percent, employment is projected to grow at a rate of 6.9 percent (with an employment output elasticity of 0.86). The IWSS sectors are expected to grow by about 8 percent. IWSS sectors that are contributing to this growth include hotels and restaurants, finance and insurance, and trade.

IWSS sectors are expected to contribute a little above 50 percent to employment by 2035, after a projected decline from a share of 43.3 percent in 2017 to 42.1 percent in 2025. Manufacturing and other non-IWSS sectors are expected to contribute 9.3 and 37.1 percent, respectively in 2035. The annual growth in employment for IWSS sectors is estimated at 10.3 percent relative to manufacturing and other non-IWSS sectors by 2035. The IWSS sectors driving the growth in employment include agro-processing and

Table 7-10. A Growth Scenario to 2035: Projecting GDP and Employment

Sector	Value added (millions of cedi)			Employment ('000s)				Employment share (%)	
	2017	2035 (Projected)	Annual growth (%)	2017	2035 (Projected)	Added jobs (2017–35)	Annual growth (%)	2017	2035 (Projected)
Total	250,889	906,899	7.4	11,082	36,832	25,750	6.9	100	100
IWSS	122,352	472,878	7.8	4,397	25,677	21,280	10.3	48.8	52.1
Agro-processing	8,241	16,695	4.0	721	2,520	1,799	7.2	3.3	1.8
Construction	19,433	41,463	4.3	468	854	386	3.4	7.7	4.6
Export crops and horticulture	18,141	36,750	4.0	1,048	3,663	2,615	7.2	7.2	4.1
Financial and business services	22,621	180,169	12.2	183	3,965	3,782	18.6	9.0	19.9
Information and communications technology	9,254	23,444	5.3	47	102	55	4.4	3.7	2.6
Tourism	9,254	121,909	15.4	352	2,194	1,842	10.7	3.7	13.4
Trade (formal)	32,582	156,250	9.1	1,196	7,456	6,260	10.7	13.0	17.2
Transportation	2,826	9,081	6.7	382	9,293	8,911	19.4	1.1	1.0
Other IWSS services									
Manufacturing	26,860	70,413	5.5	1,273	2,324	1,051	3.4	10.7	7.8
Non-IWSS	101,677	343,661	7.0	5,412	12,370	6,959	4.7	40.5	37.9
Traditional agriculture	28,358	59,571	4.2	2,480	8,583	6,103	7.1	11.3	6.6
Government	3,679	14,219	7.8	69	97	28	1.9	1.5	1.6
Mining	25,917	144,096	10.0	164	736	572	8.7	10.3	15.9
Trade (informal)	17,092	81,967	9.1	1,952	12,164	10,213	10.7	6.8	9.0
Utilities	5,805	13,466	4.8	44	95	51	4.4	2.3	1.5
Other non-IWSS	20,826	102,963	9.3	703	1,144	441	2.7	8.3	11.4

Sources: Authors' calculations based on Ghana Statistical Service (2018), GLSS 5 and GLSS 6, and MoF (2018).

horticulture, hotels and restaurants, finance and insurance, transportation and storage, and trade. Noticeably, annual employment growth in agro-processing (7.2 percent) is expected to be double the annual employment growth of manufacturing (3.4 percent) and higher than that of non-IWSS (4.7 percent) by 2035. Employment annual growth in tourism (hotel and restaurants) is expected at a much higher rate (10.7 percent) compared with agro-processing (table 7-10).

The estimated pattern of growth and employment is expected to generate demand for high-skilled workers for the economy (table 7-11). The skills defi-nitions are based on educational level: highly skilled workers are those with a postsecondary education; skilled workers have either completed secondary school or at least have some years of secondary education; and low-skilled workers have less than a secondary education or no formal education. For instance, the overall share supply of low-skilled workers is expected to decline by about 5 percentage points between 2017 and 2035, while that for skilled and highly skilled workers is expected to increase by 3 and 2 percentage points, respectively, over the same periods. Most of the skill transformation of the workforce is expected to occur in the non-IWSS sector. Manufac-turing is expected to witness the most increase in demand for skilled workers. This notwithstanding, Ghana's economy will remain dominated by low-skilled workers.

Firm Survey Results

In order to establish whether the trends described above reflect the expe-riences of firms in the agro-processing and tourism sectors, we conducted a survey with selected firms using the Association of Ghana Industries as a sampling frame; the sample was restricted to firms in Accra and Tema (the main business hubs of Ghana). Firms in Accra and Tema are not dif-ferent from those in other regions, except for their proximity to the main ports. In all, the staffs of 15 agro-processing firms and 10 hotels and res-taurants (tourism sector) were interviewed, with managers of the firms as the main respondents. Descriptive statistics of the sample are presented in appendix table 7-A3.

Categorizing firms based on the number of workers, the survey includes one small firm, eight medium-sized firms, and six large firms, all in agro-processing. Firms in the tourism sector include two small firms, four medium-sized firms, and four large firms. The average age of employees

Table 7-11. Projected Labor Demand by Skills

	2017		
	Skill shares (%)		
Sector	Low skilled (%)	Skilled (%)	High skilled (%)
Total population	71	17	13
Total IWSS	67	20	13
Agro-processing and horticulture	93	6	1
Construction	81	15	4
Trade	78	17	5
Hotels and restaurant	78	17	5
Information and communication technology	27	40	33
Transport and storage	79	16	5
Financial and insurance	41	28	31
Real estate	61	19	20
Manufacturing (excl. agro-processing)	84	14	3
Other non-IWSS	73	15	12
Other crops	92	6	1
Cocoa	92	7	1
Livestock	82	13	5
Forestry and logging	91	4	5
Fishing	94	6	0
Mining and quarrying	82	13	4
Electricity	74	21	5
Water and sewage	73	9	19
Professional, administrative & support service	59	25	16
Public administration & defense; social security	53	28	19
Education	37	22	41
Health and social work	34	31	35
Other service activities	79	15	6

Source: Authors' calculations based on Ghana Statistical Service (2018), GLSS 5 and GLSS 6. See the appendix to this chapter for the methodology used in making the projections to 2035.

2035 (Projections)						Annual % growth, 2017–35		
Labor demand			Skill shares (%)			Growth in labor demand		
Low skilled	Skilled	High skilled	Low skilled (%)	Skilled (%)	High skilled (%)	Low skilled (%)	Skilled (%)	High skilled (%)
9,767,902	1,574,801	705,809	66	20	15	7	14	13
1,376,744	218,044	44,747	65	21	14	13	17	15
1,645,257	193,552	11,915	89	10	1	7	18	3
362,855	154,897	78,293	61	26	13	3	17	44
7,233,677	1,007,717	114,465	87	12	1	31	17	3
640,168	195,085	23,989	75	23	3	11	17	3
17,864	81,388	72,452	10	47	42	4	29	31
996,551	76,298	25,137	91	7	2	19	3	3
111,330	31,057	26,662	66	18	16	19	3	1
6,489	4,361	5,062	41	27	32	9	29	31
941,566	671,140	72,492	56	40	4	3	39	17
380,099	95,180	83,381	67	18	16	4	10	11
2,305,742	162,832	31,462	92	7	1	3	4	3
1,338,966	92,226	9,373	93	6	1	11	9	3
22,419	3,772	1,257	82	14	5	3	4	3
31,921	1,353	1,681	91	4	5	3	3	3
86,239	5,379	-	94	6	0	2	1	0
270,938	60,276	7,475	80	18	2	9	15	1
27,116	9,616	4,160	66	24	10	7	11	28
17,162	3,213	4,435	69	13	18	3	9	3
126,851	33,935	50,354	60	16	24	9	3	17
113,708	64,560	47,142	50	29	21	2	2	3
190,102	538,191	626,685	14	40	46	3	44	25
37,489	109,039	258,139	9	27	64	0	17	43
372,638	152,944	41,791	66	27	7	0	9	3

FIGURE 7-5. **Importance and Level of Skills for Youth in Agro-processing**

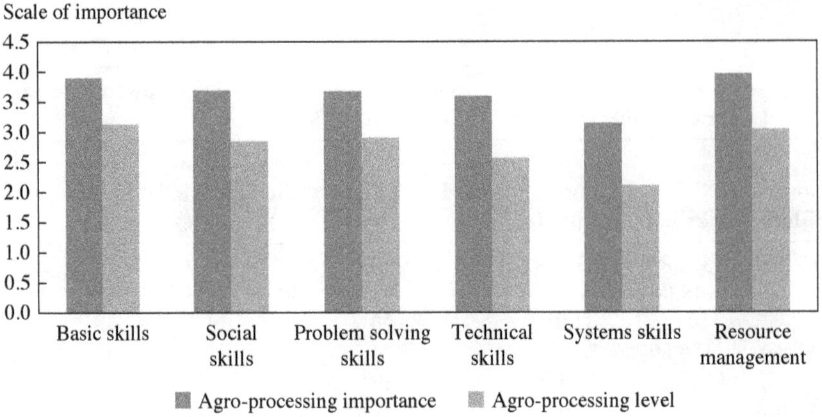

Scale of importance

Source: Authors' calculations.

in agro-processing is 18.8 years, with average total employment of 146.8 workers. Most of the workforce in agro-processing has a secondary education, confirming the moderate skill requirement. The average total workforce is 117.7 in tourism, with the majority having at least a post-secondary education.

Identifying Skills in Business

To assess the skills necessary for successful employment in these businesses, firms were asked to classify the main occupations of youth (15–24 years) workers in their organizations. The skill types include basic skills, social skills, problem-solving skills, technical skills, systemic skills, and resource management skills. Both the importance and level of the skills were ranked on a scale of 1 to 5, where 1 = not important and 5 = very important. The definitions of these skill categories were provided in the survey instrument.

Importance and Level of Skills in Agro-processing and Tourism

Details of main occupation classifications for both agro-processing and tourism are presented in the appendix. Classification of skills in occupation by level of importance and skill, as presented in figures 7-5 and 7-6, shows the differences in the relevance of skills for firms.

As shown in figure 7-5, firms in agro-processing ranked basic, social, problem-solving, technical, and resource management skills as very important. Resource management skills—developed capacities used to allocate

FIGURE 7-6. **Importance and Level of Skills of Youth in Tourism**

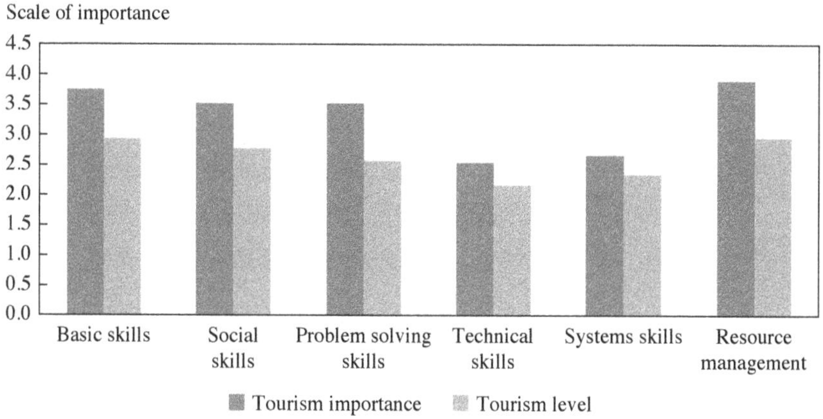

Source: Authors' calculations.

resources efficiently—include the management of financial resources, materials resources, personnel resources, and time management. With regard to tourism, the most important skills of youth workers in tourism were resource management skills, basic skills, and social skills (see figure 7-6). These same skills were ranked highest when firms were asked to indicate the current skill level for youth workers. Similar to firms in the agro-processing sector, firms in tourism indicated that the basic skills of youth workers met their requirements. Basic skills were followed closely by social skills, technical skills, problem-solving skills, and resource management skills. Systems skills of youth workers fall short of the requirement for firms in the tourism sector.

In Figure 7-7, we present the skill deficits for the different skill types.[4] In both agro-processing and tourism, there are skill deficits. However, the deficit is less severe for basic skills and social skills. Systems skills face the highest deficits in both tourism and agro-processing.

Digital Skills and Future Occupational and Skill Needs

About 85 percent of the firms surveyed required digital skills. For instance, the digital skills identified by firms in agro-processing include data management and analytics, production management, mobile transactions, and social selling. For tourism, digital skills identified include online communication and mobile transactions. For most agro-processing firms, plans for expansion/growth are in the medium term (73.3 percent). Examples of such

FIGURE 7-7. **Skill Deficits**

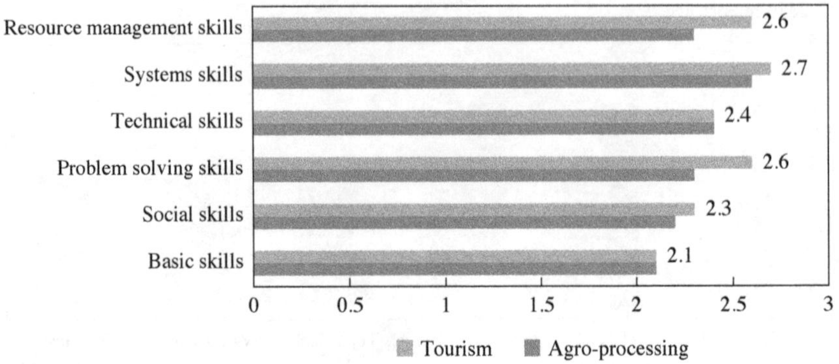

Source: Authors' calculations.

Note: The scores use this ranking: 1 = meets requirements; 5 = does not meet skill requirements.

medium-term expansion plans include increasing the sizes of factory floors, producing in other countries, introducing another line of production, gaining ownership of a farm, and exporting products to more countries.

Unlike firms in the agro-processing sector, most firms in the tourism sector did not show much interest in future expansion/growth (either in the medium or short term). The few that hinted of an expansion wanted to integrate business operations vertically. Others had plans to open more branches. Most firms in the tourism sector are also likely to employ more young workers who have at least a secondary education if their business expansion plans materialize.

The Business Environment

The survey asked the firms to indicate the business environment variables that were major obstacles to their current operations. Specifically, firms were asked to select three business environment variables and rank them from 1 to 3, with 1 representing the variable considered the most important obstacle and 3 representing the variable of least importance.

In order to measure the incidence of the obstacles, we computed a severity index. The results are presented in table 7-12. Electricity supply, access to credit, and the practices of informal competitors constitute the most significant obstacles for agro-processing firms. The top three obstacles for firms in tourism are tax rates, policies, and administration; electricity; and access to credit.

Table 7-12. Severity Index of Business Obstacles

Obstacle to Agro-processing	Agro-processing	Tourism
Electricity supply	0.8	0.3
Access to credit	0.6	0.3
Practices of informal competitors	0.6	0.1
Customs and trade regulations	0.5	0.1
Tax rates, policies, and administration	0.4	0.4
Competition from imports	0.4	0.0
Business licensing and permits acquisition	0.2	0.2
Political instability	0.2	0.1
Access to land	0.0	0.0
Uncertainty about government industrial policies	0.0	0.2
Corruption	0.0	0.2
Court delays	0.0	0.0
Crime, theft, and disorders	0.0	0.1
Labor regulations	0.0	0.1
Inadequately skilled labor	0.0	0.1
Transportation	0.0	0.1

Source: Authors' calculations.

Policy Implications: Unlocking Growth Potential and Overcoming Skill Gaps

Evidently, there is an enormous potential for growth, with attendant employment generation prospects, in the IWSS sectors (agro-processing and tourism) in Ghana. Given the country's youthful population and the need to diversify its economy away from mineral dependence through industrial transformation. Industries without smokestacks, based on their shared characteristics with traditional manufacturing, offer an important alternative in a multifaceted framework for structural transformation, the generation of productive jobs, and economic development.

The Government of Ghana's policy directives for these sectors point to the fact that they are viewed as avenues for growth and employment, due to the intensive use of the low- to medium-skilled labor that is abundant in the country's pool of unemployed youth. In agro-processing, the recent One District One Factory initiative is one such policy that focuses on higher value added along the agriculture value chain. The objective of this policy is to create employment for youth in rural and peri-urban communities in the country. In the tourism sector, the success of the Year of Return campaign in 2019, which sought to market Ghana as a tourism destination with transatlantic trade appeal, and its immediate impact of an increase in the number of tourists, is an indication of the potential inherent in the sector in Ghana.

Despite the modest growth observed in the IWSS sectors in Ghana in recent times, challenges exist that prevent the IWSS sectors from operating at their maximum potential. Overall, the constraints identified in agro-processing and tourism sectors include a lack of skilled labor, a lack of credit facilities, inadequate infrastructure, the cost of electricity, limited capacity to export, and an unfriendly regulatory environment. Skill gaps—including in systems skills, technical skills, and problem-solving skills—are predominant in the IWSS firms surveyed.

Ghana has been implementing policy reforms aimed at training young people to obtain the skills required to be productive in the economy. Principal among these reforms was the 1987 educational reform, which sought to deemphasize the grammar-school-type education at the time and introduce technical and vocational education as part of primary and secondary school curricula. Subsequently, access to education improved, but the quality of education at all levels remained unchanged (World Bank 2014). Although several other interventions have been undertaken by the government to improve access and the quality of education in the country, challenges for the educational system persist vis-à-vis access and the quality of graduates. Consequently, in 2017, the Government of Ghana launched the Free Senior High School Program for public senior high schools aimed at providing equitable access and a high-quality education, thus improving the human capital base. This policy was informed by the need for an educated workforce.

The government must prioritize and increase enrollment into technical and vocational education for hands-on employable skills to support growth and provide a pathway to sustainable employment for young people. In addition, like manufacturing, IWSS sectors' growth and development hinge on technology; and the capability of firms to upgrade their output depends on the ability of their workforce to learn and master new technology.

Special economic zones are critical for IWSS sectors, especially for those in agro-processing. Support for the private sector by the Ghana Free Zones Authority and Ghana Investment Promotion Centre is anchored in potential benefits. However, due to challenges of installing the appropriate infrastructure, the benefits have yet to be fully realized.

Overall, infrastructure, a critical component of any attempt at industrialization, must be strategically developed to facilitate diversification. As recently indicated by the Ghana Institution of Engineers, Ghana's roads and bridges, electric power, and IWSS sectors share characteristics with manufacturing—their effective functioning depends critically on the country's infrastructural base.

The downstream activities of the agro-processing value chain are constrained by the lack of proper contractual relationships, thereby exacerbating the unreliable supply of inputs. In addition, there is limited long-term access to financial services for supporting these downstream activities. The tourism value chain has weak linkages with other sectors of the economy. Firms in the sector also have inadequate financial services/incentives to encourage locals to participate or patronize their activities.

Both sectors must enhance their operations by leveraging the opportunities that exist in innovation and digitization. Typical non-IWSS sectors were observed to perform better in the exports market, but innovation and digitization provide various opportunities for the agro-processing and tourism sectors to enhance their productivity and general operations. In countries where agro-processing and tourism have been important contributors to growth, digital technologies have been important in enhancing operations—specifically with respect to various trade-related aspects of their operations. Initiatives to encourage and promote innovation and digitization need to be supported by the government, and, in the case of Ghana, both IWSS sectors have already been identified to receive priority in the current national innovation and digitization strategy.

In an attempt to address the financial needs of local firms, the government has recently set up the National Development Bank to establish an incentive-based risk-sharing arrangement for agricultural lending, strengthen the Venture Capital Fund, and also establish the Ghana Commodity Exchange. In addition, the Government of Ghana, together with the banking community, was planning to launch a GHS 2 billion credit and guarantee plan by the end of 2020. This initiative is structured to incentivize banks to lend to the private sector at discounted rates and is targeted at specific industries such as agri-businesses, hospitality, and tourism. The government has also shown a commitment to strengthening the Ghana Infrastructure Investment Fund by actively leveraging innovative financial sources to address infrastructural challenges, with a specific interest in infrastructure related to production and trade. For tourism, various programs under the National Tourism Development Project aim to address business environment challenges by improving several tourist sites, ensuring the quality in service delivery, and encouraging private participation.

Conclusion

This chapter has presented a case study of Ghana's industries without smokestacks in Africa. Its main premise has been grounded on the empirical observation that Ghana has had a trajectory of jobless growth against the backdrop of poor performance in the manufacturing sector and propelled by a low-productivity services sector. There is a need to refocus the country's attention on identifying and supporting sectors with greater employment potential. This refocusing is critical for dealing with jobless growth while charting a new course. The specific IWSS sectors identified here, based on their characteristics and the unique nature of Ghana's development challenges, are agro-processing and tourism.

This study finds that the agro-processing and tourism sectors have several characteristics that can be relied on as an alternative development strategy for Ghana, including the recently improved regulatory environment, medium- to long-term policies aimed at enhancing economic growth, and the potential of the two sectors to rely on the large unemployed labor force because of their labor-intensive nature. Some of the policies intended to promote agro-processing include the National Industrial Revitalization Program; the One District-One Factory project; and Strategic Anchor Industries. For tourism, some of the specific policies are captured in the National Tourism Development Plan (2013–27) and programs such as the Marine Drive Tourism Investment Project; the Year of Return, which commemorates 400 years of slavery; and the See Ghana, Eat Ghana, Wear Ghana, Feel Ghana campaign. The government expects these projects to be instrumental in redirecting attention to the two sectors.

Some skill gaps were observed for both the agro-processing and tourism sectors. More specifically, systems, technical, and problem-solving skills appear to be lacking, while basic, as well as resource management skills, are relatively abundant.

Some business environment obstacles were found in both sectors. For agro-processing, access to credit, electricity supply, and practices of informal competitors are the main obstacles; while for tourism, the electricity supply, business licensing and permit acquisition, and tax rates, policies, and administration were cited.

The agro-processing and tourism sectors are labor intensive, and in the unemployed pool, a large group of individuals with at least a secondary education can be relied on to develop the sectors. Third, while the technologies used by agro-processing and tourism are also labor intensive, some complementary digitalization will be needed to enhance their relevance to the changing nature of work. Fourth, even though typical non-IWSS sectors, such as traditional manufacturing, have had a high growth and exporting potential, the increasing contribution of the IWSS sectors to employment generation will be indispensable for addressing Ghana's jobless growth situation.

A more specific effort is required to address the issues of access to credit and gaps in infrastructure at important tourist sites, along with those for agro-processing, and to minimize the sector's overregulation. Finally, there is a need to increase human resource capacity to enhance efficiency in both sectors.

Appendix: Methodology for Growth Scenarios and Projections

The GDP projections were obtained based on historical values and the more recent economic growth targets using these formulas:

$$GDPt = GDPt - 1 + \left(GDPt - 1 * growth\_target \right)$$

Labor demand was forecast from two household surveys of the Ghana Living Standards Surveys (GLSS 5 in 201/13and GLSS 6 in 2016/17). The projections for 2035 were calculated based on adjusted employment elasticities and projected growth in labor productivity:

$$Lab\_ddt = Lab\_ddt - 1 + \left(Lab\_ddt - 1 * adj\_emp\_elasticity \right)$$
$$+ \left(Lab\_dd2017 * Lab\_dd\_growth \right)$$

To project skills breakdown, we rely on the growth of skills distribution between the two household surveys (GLSS 5 and GLSS 6). This was adjusted by sectoral employment elasticities from the projected employment growth. Skill definitions are based on educational level: high skilled workers are those with a postsecondary education; skilled workers have either completed secondary school or at least have some years of secondary education; and low-skilled workers have less than a secondary education or no formal education (see table 7-A1, 7-A2, and 7-A3).

Table 7-A1. Doing Business Indicators for Ghana, 2016–20

Indicator	2016	2017	2018	2019	2020	Percent change
Overall	57.0	58.0	58.4	60.4	60.0	5.3
Starting a business	83.7	83.7	84.0	84.3	85.0	1.6
Dealing with construction permits	58.5	59.2	61.9	66.2	67.6	15.6
Getting electricity	59.5	60.3	61.0	74.0	77.4	30.1
Registering property	59.2	59.3	59.3	59.3	59.4	0.3
Getting credit	60.0	60.0	60.0	60.0	60.0	0.0
Protecting minority investors	60.0	60.0	60.0	60.0	60.0	0.0
Paying taxes	66.2	66.2	66.5	66.8	56.0	−15.4
Trading across borders	43.7	52.3	52.3	54.8	54.8	25.4
Enforcing contracts	54.0	54.0	54.0	54.0	54.0	0.0
Resolving insolvency	25.0	25.3	24.8	24.9	25.4	1.6

Source: World Bank, Doing Business database, 2020.

Note: Scores are scaled from 0 to 100, where 0 represents the lowest performance and 100 represents the best performance.

Table 7-A2. Classification of Surveyed Firms

Category	Agro-processing	Hotels/restaurants
Firm size classification		
Small (5–19)	6.7%	20.0%
Medium-sized (20–99)	53.3%	40.0%
Large (100+)	40.0%	40.0%
Average age (years; total sample)	18.8	11.4
Small (5–19)	7.0	11.5
Medium (20–99)	12.3	12.5
Large (100+)	29.5	10.3
Average employment (total sample)	146.8	117.7
Small (5–19)	10.0	15.5
Medium-sized (20–99)	48.9	46.5
Large (100+)	300.2	240.0
Total workforce (average proportion)		
Presecondary	20.8	19.3
Secondary	46.9	32.9
Postsecondary	21.1	43.3
Youth (15–24) (average proportion)		
Presecondary	24.2	27.4
Secondary	70.4	58.9
Postsecondary	10.8	29.9
Degree	7.1	10.6
Postgraduate	0.0	1.1
Sample	15	10

Sources: Authors' calculations.

Table 7-A3. Main Occupations of Youth in Agro-processing and Tourism

Agro-processing	Tourism (hotels and restaurants)
Administrative workers	Administrative workers
Production workers	Waitresses
Nonproduction workers	Security staff
Cleaners	Kitchen cooks/support staff
Quality control officers	Stewards
Sales workers	Technical staff
Maintenance	Front desk
	Drivers/mechanics
	Gardeners
	Housekeepers
	Unskilled workers
	Cleaners

Source: Authors' compilation.

NOTES

1. This was set within the context of Ghana's long-term strategic vision of achieving middle-income status by 2020, through the transformation of the economy into an industry-driven one.

2. We refer to the firm distribution in agriculture and manufacturing sub-sectors to discuss the distribution for agro-processing in the absence of census data on agro-processing. Fortunately, agro-processing firms make up the majority of firms in these two subsectors.

3. Examples of such multinationals in Ghana are Nestle Ghana, Promasidor, Guinness Ghana, Accra Brewery, Cadbury, and Unilever Ghana limited.

4. Respondents were asked to rank the skill deficits from 1 to 5, where 1 = meets skill requirements and 5 = does not meet requirements.

REFERENCES

Abor, J., and P. Quartey. 2010. "Issues in SME Development in Ghana and South Africa." *International Research Journal of Finance and Economics* 39: 218–28.

Ackah, C., C. Adjasi, and F. Turkson. 2014. "Scoping Study on the Evolution of Industry in Ghana." WIDER Working Paper 2014/075. UNU–World Institute for Development and Economics Research, Helsinki.

Ackah, C. G., F. Agyire-Tettey, and F. E. Turkson. 2020. "Wood Processing in Ghana." Report 145505. World Bank.

Afful-Koomson, T., and W. Fonta. 2015. "Economic and Financial Analyses of Small and Medium Food Crops Agro-processing Firms in Ghana." United Nations University Institute for Natural Resources.

Ansu-Kyeremeh, K., L. Casely-Hayford, J. S. Djangmah, J. Nti, and F. Orivel. 2002. "Education Sector Review: Final Team Synthesis Report." Associates for Change, Accra. www.webnet/afc/research.html.

Baah-Boateng, W. 2013. "Determinants of Unemployment in Ghana." *African Development Review* 25: 385–99.

Baah-Nuakoh, A., F. E. Turkson, K. Baah-Nuakoh, and W. Baah-Boateng. 2002. "Multi Country Study on Transformation of Small firms in Africa: The Case of Ghana." Research Report, African Centre for Economic Growth, Nairobi.

FAO (Food and Agriculture Organization of the UN). 1997. *The State of Agriculture 1997.* Rome: FAO.

———. 2013. "Analysis of Incentives and Disincentives for Cassava in Nigeria." http://www.fao.org/3/a-at582e.pdf.

GAIN. 2012. "Ghana Cashew Nut Industry Is Growing." Report GH1205.

Ghana Grains Council. 2020. "Warehouse Receipt System." http://www.ghanagrainscouncil.org/en/warehouse-receipt-system/.

GSS (Ghana Statistical Service). 2018. "Annual Domestic Product." Accra.

———. 2020. "Rebased 2013–2019 Annual Gross Domestic Product." Accra.

GSS (Ghana Statistical Service). 2000. "Ghana Living Standards Survey: Report on the Fourth Round." Accra.

———. 2006. "Ghana Living Standards Survey: Report on the Fifth Round." Accra.

———. 2017a. "Ghana Living Standards Survey: Report on the Seventh Round." Accra.

———. 2017b. "The Integrated Business Establishment Survey, IBES."

GoG (Government of Ghana). 2004. *White Paper on the Report of the Education Reform Review Committee.* Accra: Government of Ghana.

———. 2014. "National Employment Policy, Ministry of Employment and Labour Relations."

Gyeke-Dako, A., A. D. Oduro, F. E. Turkson, P. T. Baffour, and E. N. Abbey. 2017. "Ghana's Participation in Global Value Chains: The Employment Effects." R4D Working Paper 2017/05.

ILO (International Labor Organization). 2007. "The 13th International Conference of Labour Statisticians, ILO Bureau of Statistics."

———. 2014. "ILO Calls for Bold Political Action to Promote Youth Employment in Africa." https://www.ilo.org/africa/media-centre/news/WCMS_234712/lang--en/index.htm.

MoF (Ministry of Finance). 2018. "The 2018 Budget Statement and Economic Policy of the Government of Ghana for the 2018 Financial Year." http://mofep.gov.gh.

———. 2019. "Ghana Is Number One Fastest Growing Economy in Africa in 2019—IMF." https://mofep.gov.gh/news-and-events/2019-04-10/ghana-is-number-one-fastest-growing-economy-in-africa-in-2019-imf.

————. 2020. "The 2020 Budget Statement and Economic Policy of the Government of Ghana for the 2020 Financial Year." http://mofep.gov.gh.

MoFA (Ministry of Food and Agriculture). 2009. "Food and Agricultural Sector Development Policy II."

————. 2015. "Medium-Term Agricultural Sector Investment Plan (META-SIP II)."

————. 2016. "Agriculture in Ghana: Facts and Figures 2015."

MoTAC. 2020. "Ghana as an Attractive Destination for Tourists." http://motac.gov.gh/index.php?Itemid=203&option=com_content&view=article&id=68&catid=2.

Ministry of Tourism. 2012. "National Tourism Development Plan (2013–2027)." http://www.ghana.travel/wp-content/uploads/2016/11/Ghana-Tourism-Development-Plan.pdf.

MoTI (Ministry of Trade and Industry). 2010. "Industrial Sector Support Program 2011–2015."

————. 2019. "Meet the Press: Presented by the Minister of Trade." http://www.moti.gov.gh/docs/Hon_Minister_Presentation.pdf.

National Communication Authority. 2019. "Quarterly Statistical Bulletin on Communications in Ghana." https://www.nca.org.gh/assets/Q4-2019-Bulletin-compressed.pdf.

Newfarmer, R., J. Page, and F. Tarp. 2018. *Industries Without Smokestacks: Rethinking African Industrialization*. Oxford University Press.

Owoo, N. S., and M. P. Lambon-Quayefio. 2017. "The Agro-processing Industry and Its Potential for Structural Transformation of the Ghanaian Economy." WIDER Working Paper 2017/9.

Page, J. 2018. "Rethinking Africa's Structural Transformation." https://www.brookings.edu/research/rethinking-africas-structural-transformation/.

————. 2019. "Addressing Africa's Youth Unemployment through Industries without Smokestacks: Framing Paper II—Industries Without Smokestacks, Firm Characteristics and Constraints to Growth."

Quartey, E. T., and S. Darkwah. 2015. "Factors Affecting the Use of Modern Technologies in Agro-processing in Ghana." *Academia Journal of Agricultural Research* 3: 99–115.

Republic of Ghana. 2012. "National Tourism Development Plan (2013–2027)." Accra.

Rodrik, D. 2014. "The Past, Present, and Future of Economic Growth." *Challenge* 57: 5–39.

Sutton, J., and B. Kpentey. 2012. *An Enterprise Map of Ghana, Volume 2*. London: International Growth Centre and London Publishing Partnership.

Turkson, F. E. 2010. "Firm Growth Dynamics in Africa: Evidence from the Manufacturing Sector in Ghana." *Journal of Business Research* 4: 141–69.

———. 2018. "How Well Does Observable Trade Data Measure Trade Friction Costs? Evidence from Member Countries within the Economic Community of West African States." *Journal for African Trade* 5: 69–86.

UN Comtade. 2020. "UN Comtrade Database."

World Bank. 2004. *Books, Buildings, and Learning Outcomes: An Impact Evaluation of World Bank Support to Basic Education in Ghana.* Operations Evaluation Department, Report 28779. Washington: World Bank.

———. 2010. *Ghana's Infrastructure: A Continental Perspective.* Washington: World Bank. https://openknowledge.worldbank.org/handle/10986/27760.

———. 2020. "Ghana Trade Summary, 2018 Data." https://wits.worldbank.org/CountryProfile/en/Country/GHA/Year/LTST/Summary.

World Bank. 2020. "World Development Indicators."

EIGHT

Kenya

Linking Manufacturing and Industries without Smokestacks to Drive Transformation

BOAZ MUNGA, ELDAH ONSOMU, NANCY LAIBUNI, HUMPHREY NJOGU, ADAN SHIBIA, AND SAMANTHA LUSENO

This chapter argues that the persistence of high unemployment—particularly among women and the youth, despite high economic growth rates in Kenya—requires the creation of a new development pathway. We show that three service subsectors—horticulture, information and communications technology (ICT), and tourism—have the potential to create a sufficient number of jobs in the future, although several constraints need to be overcome before the employment potential of these sectors can be realized.

After strong economic growth performance in the 1960s through the 1980s, Kenya's economy experienced slow growth in the 1990s and early 2000s. Then economic growth picked up, and it has remained mostly positive since 2003. In the first half of the 1990s, real gross domestic product (GDP) per capita growth averaged a negative 1.7 percent, followed by a slight increase to just over 0 percent in the second half of the 1990s. Some of the factors linked to the poor growth performance included droughts, oil price increases, aid embargoes, and ethnic clashes in 2007. Real GDP growth accelerated to an average of 2.7 percent in 2003–18. This was linked from 2003 to 2007 with economic and structural reforms under the Economic Recovery Strategy for Wealth and Employment Creation, and from 2008 onward with the implementation of Kenya Vision 2030. From 2012 to 2018, real GDP per capita remained on an upward trend, and its growth has been relatively stable.

Despite this robust economic growth, the country faces significant labor market challenges in the form of unemployment, time-related under-employment, and inactivity.[1] These challenges are more severe for youth and women, and they vary widely across both rural and urban areas. The Kenya Integrated Household Budget Survey (KIHBS) 2015/16 reveals that whereas the overall unemployment of the working-age group of the popu-lation (15–64 years) was estimated at 7.4 percent, that of women was 9.6 percent while that for the youth (15–24 years) was 17.7 percent. Time related underemployment was estimated at 20.4 percent for the overall population, and 26.0 and 35.9 percent for women and youth, respectively.[2] These statistics reveal that economic growth is yet to be fruitfully trans-lated into employment opportunities, and/or is not large enough to offer adequate jobs.

The population and labor force growth patterns suggest not only a changing age structure but also a greater need for productive employment generation. While the country's population grew from 37.7 million in 2009 to 47.6 million in 2019—thus recording an average annual growth rate of 2.2 percent—the labor force grew by a higher rate, of 3.1 percent annually, over the same period, rising from 15.8 million to 20.7 million.

Table 8-1 shows access to various types of employment based on years for which survey data are available.[3] The share of self-employed (own-account workers) has risen significantly to become the leading type of employment in Kenya. This shift saw the share of the self-employed rise from 23.9 percent in 1998/99 to 47.7 percent in 2015/16. Despite the increase in the share of formal wage employment, the economy is experiencing difficulty in gener-ating wage employment.

Family agriculture was the major source of employment, particularly for women in 1998 and 2005. A larger proportion of men (31.1 percent) than women (17.7 percent) are in formal wage employment. This is likely

Table 8-1. Access to Employment in Kenya, 1998/99–2015/26

Sector	1998/99			2005/6			2015/16		
	Male	Female	Total	Male	Female	Total	Male	Female	Total
Family agriculture (%)	39.8	61.9	50.78	38.1	53.1	45.0	21.6	18.4	20.5
Formal wage (%)	32.0	10.6	21.4	18.1	9.3	14.2	31.1	17.7	24.5
Self-employed (%)	25.2	22.7	23.9	41.8	34.4	38.4	41.2	54.4	47.7
Unpaid workers (%)	1.4	3.5	2.5	1.4	2.7	2	5.4	8.9	7.1
Apprentices (%)	0.2	0.0	0.1	0.2	0.2	0.2	0.2	0.1	0.2
Other (%)	0.6	0.1	0.4	0.2	0.3	0.2	0.5	0.5	0.5
Total (%)	100	100	100	100	100	100	100	100	100
Total (Number) '000	8,782	8,673	17,455	9,905	8,251	18,156	16,559	15,878	32,437

Sources: Estimates based on Labour Force Survey 1998/99 and KIHBS 2005/6 and 2015/16 data.

Table 8-2. Percentage of Total Employment

Sector	1991	2001	2010	2018
Agriculture (including horticulture)	47	51	60	57
Industry (including agro-processing)	13	10	7	8
Services	40	38	33	35
Total employment ('000s)	8,001	10,980	13,794	18,033

Source: World Bank (2019), World Development Indicators and Jobs Structure Tool.

to be due to inequality in terms of employability (i.e., education and skill levels), among other factors. For example, although the gap is narrowing, a larger proportion of males (47.7 percent) than females (43.6 percent) had a secondary education or higher in 2015/16 (KIHBS 2015/16). Further, fewer females enroll for science, technology, engineering, and mathematics (STEM) courses in tertiary institutions; hence, they are disadvantaged in securing job opportunities within the industrial and the emerging technology sectors.

This chapter is structured as follows. It begins by analyzing the patterns of growth in Kenya. It then compares IWSS and non-IWSS sectors on a number of measures. Next, it highlights the value chain, employment potential, and constraints of selected IWSS sectors. This is followed by a projection of output and employment growth of IWSS and non-IWSS sectors until 2030. The chapter then identifies occupational skill gaps using quantitative analysis, which is supplemented by the authors' skill deficit findings from firm surveys. It is important to note that the firm surveys are illustrative rather than representative of the sectors. The chapter concludes with sector-specific policy recommendations.

Patterns of Growth in Kenya between 1991 and 2018:
The Role of IWSS Sectors

With respect to the three broad economic sectors of agriculture, industry, and services, the share of agriculture in total employment (formal and informal) generally increased, from 47 percent in 1991, to 60 percent in 2010. Levels thereafter fell to 57 percent in 2018 (table 8-2). Relative to 2001, the industrial share declined by 2 percentage points, while the share of services employment decreased from 38 to 35 percent.

FIGURE 8-1. Correlation between Sectoral Productivity and Employment Shares

Annual change in productivity, percent

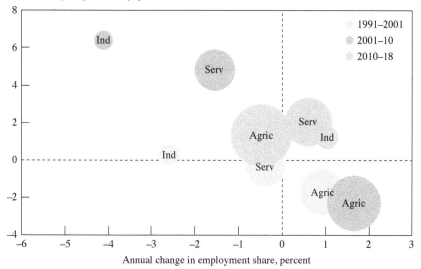

Annual change in employment share, percent

Source: World Bank (2019), World Development Indicators and Jobs Structure Tool.

The sectoral employment growth patterns demonstrate that Kenya has not transitioned to industrial economic activities, despite policy efforts to support industrialization and/or expand manufacturing activities. It could be averred that employment in agriculture has remained large due to entry barriers and few opportunities for the labor force to be absorbed in industrial activity. In figure 8-1, we examine the evolution of employment shares of the three broad sectors in relation to their productivity levels.

We note that manufacturing, and services (which are mainly IWSS sectors) have maintained relatively high productivity levels. In agriculture, the value added per worker was lower in 2018 than it was in 2001, but slightly higher than the level in 2010. On the other hand, the value added per worker for 2018 nearly doubled for industry relative to its 2001 level. For services, there was a 79.5 percent increase in value added in 2018 relative to 2001 levels. The implication of these productivity trends (and the employment levels discussed above) is that most workers have moved to lower value-adding activities, with agriculture accounting for 57.5 percent of total employment in 2018 relative to 51.5 percent in 2001. The correlation between productivity growth and employment growth is negative for agriculture, but no similar pattern is evident for industry and services.

Our overview of employment trends and structural transformation shows that between 1991 and 2018, the Kenyan economy shifted to low-productivity agriculture and away from high-productivity services and manufacturing, constraining the economy's ability to grow sustainably. Ideally, employment growth should be generated by high-productivity activities, such as those in the services sector. In the next section, we explore whether the services sectors have the potential to fulfill the role traditionally expected of the manufacturing sector: mass employment.

Sectoral Decomposition:
The IWSS Sectors in Comparative Perspective

This section focuses on output, wage employment, productivity, and skill levels in more disaggregated IWSS and non-IWSS sectors or subsectors. The discussions provide more attention to wage employment and its growth in the 2001–18 period.

Our analysis of the Kenyan data identified seven IWSS sectors: agro-processing, export crops and horticulture, tourism, information and communications technology (ICT), transportation, financial and business services, and trade and repairs. In this case study, we focus particularly on horticulture, ICT, and tourism. Horticulture, in Kenya's context, is mainly dominated by the production of flowers (largely roses, carnations, cuttings, and mixed flowers), and fruit (mainly avocados and mangoes) and vegetables, which mainly encompass fine beans and processed beans. The focus on subsectors in horticulture is based on the relative production quantities and the commodities share in the export basket. For ICT, the focus is on its role as an enabler. As an enabler, ICT supports business processes and enhances efficiency in the development agenda. Tourism is viewed as a set of integrated services, which include travel and tours, accommodations, food and beverages, souvenirs and entertainment, and transportation and excursions.

The GDP of IWSS sectors, manufacturing, and other non-IWSS sectors, are presented in table 8-3. With respect to absolute changes in GDP, the total change in IWSS was slightly lower than that of non-IWSS. The IWSS sectors with the largest absolute changes in GDP in 2018 relative to

Table 8-3. IWSS and Non-IWSS Sectors' GDP Shares, 2001–18

Sector	GDP, 2001 (millions of ksh)	GDP, 2018 (millions of ksh)	GDP share, 2001 (%)	GDP share, 2018 (%)	Absolute change in GDP (millions)	Share of change (%)	Annualized growth of GDP (%)
GDP by activity	1,178	2,730	100	100	1,552	100	5.1
Total IWSS	547	1,282	46.4	46.9	735	47.3	5.1
Agro-processing	56	140	4.7	5.1	85	5.4	5.6
Export crops and horticulture	250	478	21.2	17.5	228	14.7	3.9
Tourism	12	37	1.0	1.4	25	1.6	7.0
Information and communications technology	23	106	1.9	3.9	83	5.4	9.5
Transportation	70	178	5.9	6.5	108	7.0	5.6
Financial and business	42	152	3.6	5.6	110	7.1	7.8
Trade and repairs	94	189	7.9	6.9	96	6.2	4.2
Manufacturing	71	146	6.0	5.3	74	4.8	4.3
Other non-IWSS	560	1,303	47.6	47.7	743	47.9	5.1
Agriculture	278	523	23.6	19.2	246	15.8	3.8
Mining	5	26	0.4	0.9	21	1.3	10.2
Utilities	20	65	1.7	2.4	46	2.9	7.3
Construction	32	140	2.7	5.1	108	7.0	9.1
Domestic services	181	439	15.4	16.1	258	16.6	5.4
Government	45	110	3.8	4.0	65	4.2	5.4

Source: Construction based on data from Kenya National Bureau of Statistics, various years, "Statistical Abstract."

Note: GDP is measured in 2009 prices.

2001 were export crops and horticulture, financial and business services, and transportation. While total output expanded at an annualized rate of 5.1 percent, the respective annualized rates for IWSS, manufacturing, and other non-IWSS, were 5.1, 4.3, and 5.1 percent, respectively. The sectors with the highest annualized growth in output were mining, ICT, and construction, with respective rates of 10.2, 9.5, and 9.1 percent. Even so, these sectors began from a relatively low GDP base in 2001—which partly explains their relatively higher growth.

The relatively large increase in mining output can be linked to the production of a wider variety of minerals since recent discoveries of such minerals as titanium ore. Kenya began exports of titanium in 2014 and has begun commercial exploitation of other minerals, including niobium and rare earth metals. Although Kenya now exports crude oil, this began only after 2018. Construction has been largely driven by large investments in infrastructure, more so in recent years, encompassing roads and railways. A recent example is the construction of the Standard Gauge Railway, which hitherto is Kenya's largest infrastructure project, at a cost of $3.6 billion.

Shifting our attention to employment (see table 8-4), we note that wage employment increased by over 1 million in 2018 relative to 2001. Non-IWSS contributed 62.5 percent of this change, while the rest was contributed by IWSS (30.2 percent) and manufacturing (7.2 percent). Most of the employment within non-IWSS was in domestic services, which accounted for 64.2 percent and 62.1 percent of total non-IWSS employment in 2001 and 2018, respectively.[4] For the non-IWSS sectors, the main drivers of wage employment growth were services rather than a vibrant industrial sector. The largest absolute increase resulted from expansions in domestic services (mainly education) and government (administrative services). The increase in government's wage employment was mainly driven by the 2013 transition to a devolved governance structure that created 47 new governments. This resulted in the emergence of thousands of public sector jobs in the period 2013–18.

The absolute changes in employment were positive in all sectors except financial and business services. The IWSS sectors with the largest absolute change in wage employment in 2018 relative to 2001 were trade and repairs, ICT, and tourism, with 14.3 percent, 9.0 percent, and 3.7 percent of the total absolute change in wage employment, respectively. Outside IWSS and domestic services, the construction sector and manufacturing had relatively strong performance with respect to absolute changes in

Table 8-4. IWSS and Non-IWSS Sectors' Formal Employment, 2011–18

Sector	Wage employment, 2001 (millions)	Wage Employment 2018 (millions)	Wage employment share, 2001 (%)	Wage employment share, 2018 (%)	Absolute change (millions)	Share of change (%)	Annualized growth (%)
Total wage employment	1,599	2,670	100.0	100.0	1,071	100.0	3.1
Total IWSS	576	900	36.0	33.7	324	30.2	2.7
Agro-processing	27	31	1.7	1.2	4	0.4	0.9
Export crops and horticulture	224	230	14.0	8.6	6	0.5	0.1
Tourism	49	89	3.1	3.3	39	3.7	3.5
Information and communications technology	27	123	1.7	4.6	97	9.0	9.5
Transportation	58	91	3.6	3.4	33	3.1	2.7
Financial and business services	84	76	5.2	2.8	–8	–0.8	–0.6
Trade and repairs	107	260	6.7	9.8	153	14.3	5.3
Manufacturing	136	213	8.5	8.0	77	7.2	2.7
Other non-IWSS	886	1,556	55.4	58.3	670	62.5	3.4
Agriculture	60	74	3.8	2.8	14	1.3	1.2
Mining	5	15	0.3	0.6	10	0.9	6.5
Utilities	21	34	1.3	1.3	13	1.2	2.8
Construction	77	172	4.8	6.4	95	8.9	4.8
Domestic services	569	966	35.6	36.2	397	37.0	3.2
Government	154	295	9.6	11.0	141	13.2	3.9

Source: Construction based on data from Kenya National Bureau of Statistics, various years, "Statistical Abstract."

Note: Manufacturing excludes agro-processing.

wage employment, accounting for 8.9 percent and 7.2 percent of the total absolute change, respectively.

With respect to annual employment growth across the sectors, the total wage employment growth between 2001 and 2018 was 3.1 percent and the employment growth of IWSS (at 2.7 percent) was equal to that of manufacturing but lower than other non-IWSS (3.4 percent). The wage employment growth of IWSS was lower than the growth of the national labor force (of about 3.1 percent). Although it was expected that agro-processing and horticulture would be vibrant with respect to wage employment growth, their respective wage employment shares declined in 2018 relative to 2001. On the other hand, the wage employment shares of ICT and tourism increased, despite a decline in the share of employment for the total IWSS sectors. Annualized growth in wage employment in tourism (at 3.5 percent) was larger than the total employment growth (of 3.1 percent). In relative terms, wage employment in manufacturing was 2.8 times larger than tourism in 2001, but tourism seems to have performed better with respect to growth in wage employment—resulting in wage employment in manufacturing settling at 2.4 times larger than tourism in 2018.

Among the sectors of focus, ICT stands out as a sector with both high output and wage employment growth. Export crops and horticulture have high output growth but low wage employment growth. On the other hand, tourism—despite a relatively lower base—fares better than manufacturing in output and wage employment growth in 2018 relative to 2001. Although wage employment in manufacturing expanded by 2.7 percent, its employment share declined (from 8.5 to 8.0 percent), suggesting that, on average, wage employment in the other sectors grew faster than in manufacturing. All the other non-IWSS sectors, except utilities and agriculture, recorded an increase in wage employment.

In terms of productivity, we observe that labor productivity increased consistently for IWSS, manufacturing, and non-IWSS sectors in 2018 relative to 2001 and 2010 (table 8-5). Among the IWSS sectors, agro processing, export crops and horticulture, and financial and business services had the largest productivity in 2018. These sectors also experienced the largest growth rates in productivity, suggesting that it is worthwhile to focus on these sectors to create productive employment—which is crucial for addressing the high poverty and inequality levels in Kenya.

Table 8-6 represents the breakdown of sectoral wage employment by relative skill composition of the IWSS and non IWSS sectors—as measured

Table 8-5. Labor Productivity by Sector

Sector	Labor productivity unit		
	2001	2009	2018
Total IWSS	0.95	1.08	1.42
Agro processing	2.07	2.58	4.47
Export crops and horticulture	1.12	1.09	2.08
Tourism	0.24	0.29	0.42
Information and communications technology	0.86	1.04	0.86
Transportation	1.21	1.38	1.96
Financial and business services	0.50	1.29	2.01
Trade and repairs	0.87	0.93	0.73
Manufacturing	0.52	0.53	0.68
Other non-IWSS	0.63	0.65	0.84
Mining	0.93	0.74	1.67
Utilities	0.92	1.57	1.91
Construction	0.41	0.53	0.82
Domestic services	0.32	0.34	0.45
Government	0.29	0.32	0.37

Source: Kenya National Bureau of Statistics, various years, "Statistical Abstract."

Table 8-6. Breakdown of Sectoral Employment by Skill Level, 2018

Sector	Absolute ('000s)			Share (%)		
	Highly skilled	Skilled	Low skilled	Highly skilled	Skilled	Low skilled
Total employment	453,063	798,800	1,418,191	17.0	29.9	53.1
Total IWSS	152,639	314,999	432,358	17.0	35.0	48.0
Agro-processing	1,472	6,185	23,722	4.7	19.7	75.6
Export crops and horticulture	6,550	71,687	151,602	2.9	31.2	66.0
Tourism	16,951	38,724	33,121	19.1	43.6	37.3
Information and communications technology	93,368	22,846	7,089	75.7	18.5	5.8
Transportation	12,573	37,374	40,701	13.9	41.2	44.9
Financial and business services	43,263	18,202	14,164	57.2	24.1	18.7
Trade and repairs	54,169	113,416	92,816	20.8	43.6	35.6
Manufacturing	44,662	84,499	84,307	20.9	39.6	39.5
Other non-IWSS	264,104	425,181	867,015	17.0	27.3	55.7
Agriculture	1,846	17,240	55,027	2.5	23.3	74.2
Mining	572	1,951	12,841	3.7	12.7	83.6
Utilities	17,899	10,926	5,308	52.4	32.0	15.6
Construction	19,215	63,651	88,699	11.2	37.1	51.7
Domestic services	385,381	284,809	295,919	39.9	29.5	30.6
Government	118,859	138,005	38,145	40.3	46.8	12.9

Sources: Computations based on Kenya National Bureau of Statistics, "Statistical Abstract," 2019; KIHBS 2015/16.

by education. High-skill jobs are defined as those performed by workers with a complete tertiary education. Skilled jobs refer to employees with a secondary education, while low-skilled workers are those with only a primary education or less. This is not directly observable in the data sources used. For this reason, the KIHBS 2015/16 data were used to generate the relative shares of sectoral wage employment by skill level and relevant ISIC codes. The computed shares were applied to aggregate data from the "Statistical Abstract" published by Kenya's national statistical agency, KNBS, to estimate the distribution of wage employment across the IWSS and non-IWSS sectors. For total wage employment, the distribution is such that most wage employees (53.1 percent) are low skilled. Only 17 percent have high skills and about 30 percent are skilled.

The highest proportion of low-skilled workers is employed in non-IWSS—at 55.7 percent, followed by IWSS, at 48.0 percent; and manufacturing, at 39.5 percent. ICT turns out to be the high growth sector that requires a relatively large proportion of highly skilled workers. Other sectors requiring relatively higher skills are the financial and business services sector (57 percent) and utilities (52.4 percent). On the other hand, tourism and horticulture can absorb a relatively high proportion of workers with moderate to low level skills. Agro-processing and horticulture are the IWSS sectors with the largest share of low-skilled waged employment, at 76 percent and 66 percent, respectively. As for the non-IWSS sectors, utilities and government have the largest concentration of highly skilled and skilled employment.

Focus on Vulnerable Groups: Women and Youth

One of the attractions of IWSS compared with non-IWSS sectors is the greater ability of the IWSS sectors to exhibit inclusive growth—that is, growth that is experienced by all sections of society, especially those who have historically been underrepresented in the labor market. In our case study, we focus on two underrepresented groups: women and the youth.

Table 8-7 shows the distribution of wage employment share in 2001 and 2018 for male and female youth. Relative to 2001, the share of employment in IWSS sectors increased from 33.8 percent to 43.6 percent for males in 2018—while that of non-IWSS declined. On the other hand, females experienced a rise in the share of wage jobs in non-IWSS sectors. The share of wage jobs for IWSS sectors declined from 44.2 percent to 29.3 percent for females. The main drivers of the increase in the share of IWSS for males

Table 8-7. Share of Youth (15–24 Years) in Wage Jobs by Sex, 2001 and 2018

Sector	Wage employment share, 2001, males (%)	Wage employment share, 2001, females (%)	Wage employment share, 2018, males (%)	Wage employment share, 2018, females (%)
Total wage employment (%)	100	100	100	100
Total IWSS	33.8	44.2	43.6	29.3
Agro-processing	2.2	0.8	1.6	1.4
Export crops and horticulture	15.5	21.0	10.2	8.6
Tourism	4.0	4.3	4.2	2.6
Information and communications technology	1.2	3.0	5.0	4.0
Transportation	5.4	0.8	3.8	1.8
Financial and business services	1.3	4.4	3.1	2.9
Trade and repairs	4.2	9.9	15.6	7.9
Manufacturing	9.0	7.0	10.3	6.1
Other non-IWSS	57.2	48.8	46.1	64.7
Agriculture	9.0	1.4	6.5	5.5
Mining	0.5	0.3	0.7	0.1
Utilities	1.2	0.3	0.5	0.3
Construction	5.2	0.2	4.8	7.5
Domestic services	40.5	44.9	32.2	50.0
Government	0.7	1.6	1.4	1.2

Sources: Computations based on Kenya National Bureau of Statistics, "Statistical Abstract," 2019; KIHBS 2015/16.

were trade and repairs, ICT, financial and business service, and tourism. For females, there were increases in ICT, transportation, and agro-processing.

The share of employment in manufacturing changed marginally, with an increase for males and a decline for females. Domestic services expanded for females and declined for males. With respect to jobs by sex, a key observation is that some of the sectors with strong growth in wage employment, such as ICT and construction, are less accessible to women. This is supported by the KIHBS 2015/16, which indicated that in construction and ICT, the share of women of working age in wage jobs was 5.4 percent and 31.9 percent, respectively; see table 8-8). Women tended to dominate wage

Table 8-8. Share of Males and Females in Wage Jobs for the Working Age Group in 2015/16

Sector	Wage employment share	
	Males	Females
Agro-processing	61.4	38.6
Export crops and horticulture	37.0	63.0
Tourism	45.5	54.5
Information and communications technology	68.1	31.9
Transportation	95.9	4.1
Financial and business services	50.6	49.4
Trade and repairs	57.3	42.7
Manufacturing	71.4	28.6
Agriculture	47.0	53.0
Mining	85.7	14.3
Utilities	73.2	26.8
Construction	94.6	5.4
Domestic services	46.8	53.2
Government	75.1	24.9
Total	57.5	42.5

Source: KIHBS 2015/16.

jobs in services and agriculture, horticulture, tourism, and domestic services. These skewed shares suggest that efforts to enhance employment should pay keen attention to the sex distribution. IWSS sectors such as ICT and agro-processing would require enhanced participation of women. Other sectors that would require similar interventions include construction, manufacturing, and utilities. Overall, our findings suggest that while IWSS employment growth was slower than that of the non-IWSS sectors, IWSS has a better future employment potential based on its higher labor productivity and its absorption of low-skilled workers, particularly in the agro-processing and horticulture sectors.

Constraints on IWSS Growth

The identification of constraints that impede the ability of a country to experience sustainable growth is important in an environment where there is a limited number of resources (e.g., finance or institutional capacity).

In highlighting only the most severe constraints facing Kenya, from both economy-wide and sectoral perspectives, we hope to focus the minds of policymakers.

Constraints on Growth: The Broad Operating Environment for Firms in Kenya

We begin by identifying cross-cutting constraints that affect all sectors of Kenya's economy. We emphasize the investment climate, which encompasses infrastructure, the regulatory environment, and skills. Infrastructure, in turn, focuses on enablers, which include not only utilities (energy and water supply), but also transportation and ICT.

INFRASTRUCTURE. Limited access to reliable electricity was identified as a challenge in the Kenya Enterprise Survey 2018 (World Bank 2018), in all three sectors—that is, ICT, horticulture, and tourism. Besides the unreliable supply, the high cost of electricity was also identified by industry representatives as a key constraint. Indeed, electricity costs are higher in Kenya than in comparable countries in Africa, including Ethiopia, Nigeria, South Africa, Tanzania, and Uganda.

With respect to the ICT infrastructure, while Kenya outperforms the rest of Sub-Saharan Africa in mobile connectivity, there are still ICT-related constraints that stifle growth. A key challenge is the relatively high cost of mobile broadband services, and a large digital divide between urban and rural areas of Kenya.

THE REGULATORY ENVIRONMENT. The country's average performance in the World Bank's 2020 Doing Business rankings faltered mainly on account of three areas of business regulation, including starting a business in Kenya (it ranked 129 out of 190 countries), cross-border trade (117), and obtaining a construction permit (105). These cross-cutting constraints hamper the country's ability to improve its competitiveness, attract investments, and create more jobs. Based on stakeholder consultations, a key issue that needs to be addressed in Kenya is weak regulatory quality—especially with respect to the incorporation of competition principles in designing regulations. Kenya trails behind other middle-income countries in rules that enable a market-based economy and was ranked 72 out of 129 countries (World Bank 2020). There are concerns about monopoly behavior and the relatively strong participation of the government in some of the markets (e.g., utilities and agricultural input markets)—and its role as a regulator at the same time.

SKILLS-RELATED CONSTRAINTS. The first broad constraint is that educational achievement in Kenya is low relative to a typical middle-income country, and this is likely to be a key constraint on firm growth and access to gainful employment by youth. This can be associated with unsatisfactory education and training outcomes among the populace. A key observation is that a relatively large proportion of the working-age population (46.5 percent) has a primary education or less as its highest education level.

The second broad hurdle is that the country faces a skills mismatch between those skills demanded and available in the labor market. This has been attributed (in part) to the weak linkages between education and industry.

Constraints on Growth in Specific IWSS Sectors

The key to comprehending the constraints faced by specific IWSS sectors is to understand the value chains of the sectors. Value chain analysis provides us with an understanding of the different activities of firms across the value chains, and describes constraints along each value chain.

HORTICULTURE. The green bean value chain, like the other value chains in horticulture, consists of a wide range of actors, including farmers (i.e., both small- and large-scale farmers), traders, packing houses, canning factories, and logistics and freight establishments (figure 8-2). The small-holder and large-scale farmers sell their produce in three distinct markets for green beans: the fresh bean export market, the market for exporting canned beans, and the domestic market.

In terms of employment potential, it was estimated that of the 58,915 full-time-equivalent wage jobs generated by the value chain, 49,400 (84 percent) were on small-scale farms. The green bean value chain was estimated to account for at least a quarter of all jobs within the sector covering the exporting of crops and horticulture. About 95 percent of all the wage jobs are for the unskilled labor force. It is further estimated that 21 percent of those employed are youth, and that women make up an estimated 50 percent of all the wage jobs. The estimated jobs in the subsector can be improved if the constraints highlighted here are addressed.

A major constraint facing the actors in the subsector, especially small-holders, is the quality of road infrastructure—specifically, the feeder roads from farms to the packing houses and/or canning factories. Farmers also lack cold chain facilities for fresh horticulture. Together, these two challenges are major causes of large postharvest losses on the horticultural value chain. Indeed, it is estimated that up to about 42 percent of the output of

FIGURE 8-2. The Green Bean Value Chain, with an Inventory of Market Players

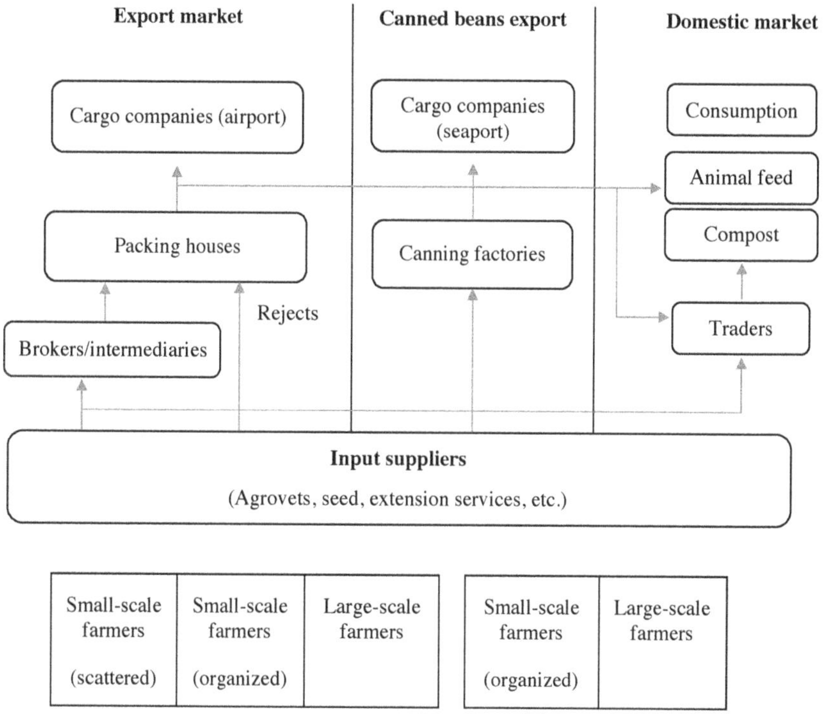

Source: Adapted from Kleih et al. (2018).

green beans is lost due to poor road infrastructure and the lack of cold chain infrastructure (Kleih et al. 2018; RSA 2015; Kok, Osena, and Snel 2019).

A related constraint is the relatively high transportation costs and inadequate options for transportation. Kenya's inland transportation costs are among the highest for comparator countries in the region. Although there is great potential in using maritime transportation, this option has yet to be properly utilized, for reasons identified by our key informants, including long transportation days to the market attributed to the lack of dedicated investment in maritime lines to the main target markets.

With respect to green beans and horticulture in general, there are constraints related to skill supply (or skill pool) and quality. In terms of the pool of technical skills, there is a general decline in the number of students registered in agricultural-related courses by an estimated 7 percentage points, from 9 percent in 2010 to 2.2 percent in 2019 (KNBS 2010, 2019). It is projected that unless there are specific interventions, the number of qualified

FIGURE 8-3. The ICT Value Chain

experts will decline—especially in farm technology, marketing, and soil and plant science.

INFORMATION AND COMMUNICATIONS TECHNOLOGY. We focus on ICT as an enabler that supports the growth of various sectors. The role of ICT in job creation may be assessed using a simplified value chain that involves core infrastructure providers that are charged with the provision of backbone hardware and software services, such as telecommunication service providers, as shown in figure 8-3. Some of the core infrastructure providers include telecommunication firms and internet service providers. The intermediary consumers/providers include finance firms, e-commerce firms, and banks. Finally, the end users are the final consumers of services offered by the intermediary consumers/providers in a value chain, and they are usually the subscribers or end users of services.

All along the ICT value chain, several jobs are created. While there are gaps in employment data, the available data indicate that between 2014 and 2019, internet service providers and telecommunication firms generated between 12,200 and 19,000 jobs at the core infrastructure provider level, while at the intermediary service level, the number of mobile money transfer agents increased, from 143,946 in 2015 to 224,108 in 2019. Even so, Kenya has not significantly translated high mobile and internet penetration at the last-mile user level into massive economic and employment opportunities, due to the constraints facing the sector.

According to the World Bank Enterprise Survey (2018), the major constraints facing the ICT sector are the political environment, tax rates, and corruption. In addition, ICT firms face broad competition restrictions, such as a lack of transparent regulatory frameworks for mobile spectrum allocation, the e-commerce ecosystem, infrastructure sharing, and mobile network virtual operators. Skill constraints within the ICT sector also hinder its progress; for example, the business process outsourcing subsector struggles to recruit individuals with specialized ICT skills. Finally, there is a low

FIGURE 8-4. The Tourism Value Chain

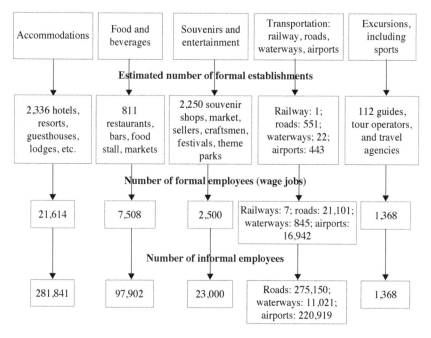

Sources: World Tourism Organization (2015); TSA Kenya.

rate of adoption of emerging technologies such as cloud computing and artificial intelligence.

TOURISM. Kenya's tourism industry has three major product lines—safari, coastal, and business and conference travel. These three lines are interrelated, and many visitors usually combine at least two of them in each visit. The tourism firms are distinguished by formality, size, and ownership. The focus of the value chain is to map an inventory of key market players (figure 8-4).

Based on information from the Tourism Satellite Account (Tourism Research Institute 2019), the contribution of tourism to employment was about 1 million individuals—if informal jobs are included. It should be noted that these numbers are comparable to those compiled by the World Tourism and Travel Council, in which the total employment was estimated at 1.06 million in 2016, accounting for 9.2 percent of total employment in Kenya (World Tourism Organization 2015). Kenya's tourism sector has over 4,000 formal establishments that offer over 70,000 direct wage jobs. In addition, over 900,000 individuals are self-employed in direct tourism-related sectors.

A major constraint faced by the Kenyan tourism sector is access to reliable electricity. According to the World Bank Enterprise Survey (2018), about 91 percent of sampled hotels and restaurants experienced electricity outages, with an average of 6.3 outages in a typical month.

Another challenge relates to the issue of taxation of establishments. Almost a third of tourism establishments (31 percent) described taxation administration as a major obstacle, and it was called a very severe obstacle by another 6 percent (World Bank 2018). In addition, tax rates were perceived as a major or very severe obstacle by over 53 percent of all tourism establishments (World Bank 2018).

The tourism sector in Kenya faces inadequate or a lack of specialized training institutions delivering graduates who have crucial, high-level, and diverse skills. Examples of these skills include film production; decision-making and problem-solving; food technology; information technology; and leadership. The World Bank Enterprise Survey (2018) shows that skills (particularly those related to technological upgrading) remain an obstacle for hotels and restaurants. About 20 percent of these businesses indicated that skilled labor power is a major or very severe obstacle to technological upgrading. A further 21 percent identified it as a moderate obstacle.

These broad and sector-specific constraints highlight the fact that Kenya faces several obstacles in achieving high growth rates. Only once these constraints are overcome can the full potential of these sectors be realized. In the next section, we compare the future employment potential of IWSS and non-IWSS sectors.

Trends into the Future:
The IWSS Sectors' Potential Growth and Labor Demand

This section outlines the projections of selected IWSS sectors to generate wage jobs on a comparative basis with manufacturing and other sectors of the economy. Job creation is estimated into the future (to 2030). To assess the current and projected employment creation potential of the respective sectors, the Jobs Structure Tools (World Bank 2018) were used to examine sectoral contributions to aggregate employment growth and productivity.[5] The resulting projections are discussed under three subheadings: overall wage employment prospects, youth wage employment prospects, and gender dimensions of employment.

The main assumption for the projections is that the prevailing sectoral growth trends from 2009 to 2018 continue to 2030 and that no major shocks will occur. There are exceptions to this growth assumption, which include that agro-processing is assumed to grow at 1.0 percent a year, which is just about equal to its growth rate between 2014 and 2018, while the tourism sector growth is revised to about two-thirds of its rate between 2009 and 2018, to incorporate the COVID-19 pandemic's shock to the industry. The totality of these assumptions is subsequently referred to as the most likely scenario in our discussions. The growth rate is computed as a geometric average growth rate between the beginning and end year $(t, t + T)$ using the compound average growth rate formula. For example, growth in economic

activity (Y) is computed as $g_{t,t+T} = \left(Y_{t+T} \big/ Y_t \right)^{\frac{1}{T} - 1}$

where $g_{t,t+T}$ = period average growth rate of value added between year t and $t + T$; Y_t = value added in year t; and Y_{t+T} = value added in year $t + T$.

Overall Wage Employment Prospects

For the most likely growth scenario, the share of total wage employment in the IWSS sectors is projected to decline from 33.7 percent in 2018 to 24.6 percent in 2030. On the other hand, the employment share of non-IWSS sectors is projected to increase from 58.3 to 67.1 percent (table 8-9). The increase in the share of non-IWSS is driven mainly by the projected large growth in domestic services, rather than by a more vibrant industrial subsector encompassing mining, utilities, and construction.

The sectoral scenario suggests that the IWSS sectors are still important for total wage employment, as are manufacturing and non-IWSS. The specific sectors projected to contribute to the largest share of wage employment in 2030 are construction (non-IWSS), manufacturing, and trade and repairs (IWSS), with respective shares of 10.8, 8.3, and 7.9 percent. The other significant sectors will be mainly IWSS sectors—including tourism, horticulture, and ICT—with shares of 5.5, 4.0, and 3.5 percent, respectively (table 8-9). Based on these wage employment prospects, the implied policy is to focus on not just IWSS but also non-IWSS and manufacturing sectors for wage employment of the working-age group in Kenya to 2030.

Additional evidence points to substantial growth in informal employment (or informalization) in some IWSS sectors, suggesting that the contribution of IWSS is potentially larger—but only if the new jobs are decent jobs. Examples include horticulture and financial services, which experienced high output growth but low or declining wage employment growth. In horticulture, the relatively low wage employment growth is partly explained

Table 8-9. The Sector Share Wage Employment (Actual 2001–18 and Projections for 2030)

Sector	Employment		Share of total wage employment, 15–64 years (%)		Share of youth wage employment (%)		Share of absolute change in employment (%)	Growth rates in employment (%)
	2018	2030	2018	2030	2018	2030	2001–18	2001–18
Total	2,669,787	6,861,936	100.0	100	100.0	100.0	100.0	3.1
Total IWSS	899,997	1,689,700	33.7	24.6	26.0	27.5	30.2	2.7
Agro-processing	31,378	35,143	1.2	0.5	1.1	0.7	0.4	0.9
Export crops and horticulture	229,839	271,476	8.6	4.0	6.5	4.3	0.5	0.1
Tourism	88,796	378,878	3.3	5.5	2.5	5.9	3.7	3.5
Information and communications technology	123,290	241,220	4.6	3.5	3.2	3.4	9.0	9.5
Transportation	90,647	106,963	3.4	1.6	2.1	1.4	3.1	2.7
Financial and business services	75,621	112,485	2.8	1.6	2.1	1.7	-0.8	-0.6
Trade and repairs	260,426	543,534	9.8	7.9	8.7	10.1	14.3	5.3
Manufacturing	213,490	566,849	8.0	8.3	6.0	8.8	7.2	2.7
Other non-IWSS	1,556,300	4,605,387	58.3	67.1	35.9	63.7	62.5	3.4
Agriculture	74,120	79,730	2.8	1.2	4.2	2.5	1.3	1.2
Mining	15,364	45,947	0.6	0.7	0.3	0.6	0.9	6.5
Utilities	34,132	39,724	1.3	0.6	0.3	0.2	1.2	2.8
Construction	171,565	739,363	6.4	10.8	3.9	9.5	8.9	4.8
Domestic services	966,110	3,310,032	36.2	48.2	26.3	50.3	37.0	3.2
Government	295,009	390,592	11.0	5.7	0.9	0.7	13.2	3.9

Source: Authors' calculations using data from KIHBS 2015/16.

Note: Youth refer to age 15–24 years.

by a large increase in nonwage jobs, resulting from a sizable expansion in small-scale producers rather than large farms. In financial services, there was a decline in the share of mainstream wage jobs amid financial innovations, which have seen a large increase in money transfers, as well as banking agents who are mainly self-employed.

Youth Employment Prospects, Assuming Historical Growth Trends

With respect to the potential to create wage jobs for youth age 15 to 24 years—the focus of this project—wage employment projections suggest that not only IWSS but also manufacturing and non-IWSS are important for creating wage jobs. Wage employment projections to 2030 indicate that the sectors with the highest potential for creating wage jobs for youth are trade and repairs, construction, and manufacturing, with shares of 10.1, 9.5, and 8.8 percent, respectively. The other sectors with the greatest potential (for youth 15 to 24), in succeeding order, are tourism, horticulture, and ICT, with respective shares of 5.9, 4.3, and 3.4 percent of total wage employment in 2030 (table 8-10).

Youth Wage Employment Prospects, Assuming IWSS Constraints Are Addressed

If IWSS sectors are assumed to grow faster than non-IWSS, based on historical trends, the outlook is likely to change. We assume that constraints are overcome and that the horticulture, ICT, and tourism sectors grow at 10 percent a year. The other IWSS sectors are assumed to grow at 5 percent—except trade and repairs, whose growth is fixed at 10 percent. Non-IWSS and manufacturing are assumed to retain the most likely growth prospects.

Under this scenario, the overriding observation is that IWSS, non-IWSS, and manufacturing remain important for youth wage job creation in Kenya. Trade and repairs (6.8 percent), construction (14.9 percent), and manufacturing (9.4 percent) are the top three job creators. The importance of IWSS is reflected by the fact that the next three most important sectors are all IWSS—horticulture, ICT, and tourism, with respective shares of 5.6, 4.7, and 3.7 percent in 2030 (table 8-10).

Gender Dimensions of Employment

The projections indicate that there will be wider gender disparities in wage employment if the prevailing growth trends persist (and no interventions

Table 8-10. Youth (15–24) Employment Across IWSS and Non-IWSS Sectors, 2018 and 2030

Sector	Employment ('000s)		Additional jobs ('000s)	Annual growth (%)	Share of total employment (%)	
	2018	2030	2018–30	2018–30	2018	2030
Overall, 15–24 years	505	1,422	917.3	9.0	100.0	100.0
Total IWSS	193	374	180.5	5.6	38.3	26.3
Agro-processing	8	9	1.0	1.0	1.5	0.6
Export crops and horticulture	49	58	9.0	1.4	9.6	4.0
Tourism	18	75	56.5	12.5	3.6	5.3
Information and communications technology	23	48	24.8	6.2	4.6	3.4
Transportation	15	18	3.0	1.5	3.1	1.3
Financial and business services	15	23	7.9	3.5	3.0	1.6
Trade and repairs	64	143	78.3	6.8	12.8	10.0
Manufacturing	44	130	85.5	9.4	8.8	9.1
Other non-IWSS	267	918	651.3	10.8	52.9	64.6
Agriculture	31	33	2.4	0.6	6.1	2.3
Mining	2	8	5.8	10.7	0.5	0.6
Utilities	2	3	0.4	1.3	0.4	0.2
Construction	29	154	125.1	14.9	5.8	10.9
Domestic services	195	711	515.1	11.4	38.7	50.0
Government	7	9	2.5	2.7	1.3	0.7

Source: Authors' calculations using data from KIHBS 2015/16.

are put in place). This will be the case for the working-age group and the youth group (15–24 years). In the aggregate, male youth are forecasted to dominate the more productive sectors—including manufacturing, construction, and trade and repairs—and their numbers are projected to be respectively 1.5, 13.8, and 1.2 times greater than females. In ICT, there will be nearly 3.0 times more males than females if present growth trends persist. The projections also indicate that there will be more females in horticulture (1.3 times more) and tourism (1.1 times more) (table 8-11).

Although the population ratio of males to females is about 1 to 1, males take up a larger share of wage jobs in the fast-growing nonservice sectors. In the aggregate, the respective ratios of females to males in wage

Table 8-11. Total Potential Youth Employment Generation in IWSS and Non-IWSS Sectors by Gender, 2030 Projections

Sector employment by activity	Youth jobs (age in years; '000s)		Youth jobs (age in years; '000s)	
	15–24 males	15–24 females	15–34 males	15–34 females
Total IWSS and non-IWSS	724.5	697.4	2,304.4	1,923.4
Total IWSS	204.9	168.9	618.0	508.9
Agro-processing	5.9	2.9	12.5	7.0
Export crops and horticulture	24.7	32.9	58.7	93.0
Tourism	36.3	38.5	107.6	137.0
Information and communications technology	36.1	12.1	123.4	65.6
Transportation	18.0	0.5	62.5	2.8
Financial and business services	6.6	16.7	31.1	39.3
Trade and repairs	77.4	65.3	222.1	164.2
Manufacturing	77.3	52.4	282.3	134.8
Other non-IWSS	442.2	476.1	1,404.0	1,279.8
Agriculture	18.4	14.9	26.9	25.5
Mining	6.7	1.5	25.2	4.8
Utilities	1.9	0.6	10.9	6.6
Construction	144.0	10.4	469.6	32.1
Domestic services	267.1	443.4	764.7	1,163.6
Government	4.0	5.2	106.7	47.3

Source: Authors' calculations using data from KIHBS 2015/16.

jobs are about 1 to 1.3 for those age 15–64 years and 1 to 1 for youth (15–24 years). The wage employment ratios are more uneven across the sectors; in the aggregate, women tend to dominate horticulture (63 percent) and to some extent agriculture (53 percent), tourism (55 percent), and domestic services (53 percent). The share of males is particularly large in the sectors associated with high productivity and high output, and employment growth, including construction (94.6 percent), ICT (68.1 percent), and trade and repairs (57.3 percent). Males also dominate manufacturing (71.4 percent) and agro-processing wage jobs, with a share of 61.4 percent. The gender shares in wage jobs suggest that efforts to enhance employment should pay keen attention to the gender distribution in sectors such as ICT, agro-processing, manufacturing, utilities, and construction.

Labor Skill Requirements and the Skill Gap

In this section, we consider labor skills requirements, the skills supply, and the skill gaps of IWSS sectors. Our broad approach encompasses several steps, including estimating sectoral employment potential; obtaining profiles of sectors' occupational requirements based on estimates of employment potential; determining skill requirements; and identifying skill gaps based on the skills requirements of the sector and the stock of skills in the target population (youth). The standardized O*NET (Occupational Network) database was used to develop a profile of occupations and analyze skill gaps, with a specific focus on tourism, horticulture, and ICT.[6] This broad approach was complemented by a mini-survey to assess the nature of skills gaps in Kenya at the firm level.

Skills are an important element in an economy and have implications for sustainable job creation for youth. Investment in human capital and strong education and training systems are drivers of economic growth and sustainable development. On the other hand, skill gaps constrain industries' ability to grow. A gap in skills may be caused by a qualitative skills mismatch, where industries do not find employable graduates even when they have the right qualifications on paper, and a quantitative mismatch, where not enough young people are educated and trained at certain levels and in fields to satisfy specific industry needs. Five skill levels were considered: primary education (level 1); postprimary education, which includes artisan-level certificates (level 2); secondary education (level 3); postsecondary education, which leads to certificates or diplomas (level 4); and tertiary education (level 5).

Skill Gaps under a Growth Scenario without Constraints

HORTICULTURE. Table 8-12 summarizes occupational categories with the largest skill gaps. The overall average skill gap for youth (15–24 years) was 6.3 years of education. This gap increased to 14.3 years for the cohort age 30–34 years. Soil and plant scientists, agricultural technicians, and nursery and greenhouse managers were some of the occupations with the largest skill gaps.

ICT. The occupations under ICT are those unique to firms classified under ISIC Rev 2 codes: 3420, printing, publishing, and allied industry; 7200, communications; 8323, data processing; and 9592, photographic studios activities. Occupations within the ICT sector demand high skills, and most fall under skill level 5. There exists a skills shortage for all occupations for all age cohorts (table 8-13).

Table 8-12. Selected Occupational Skill Gaps for Horticulture

Occupation	Modal schooling years (O*NET)	Skill gap (years)			
		15–19	20–24	25–29	30–34
Soil and plant scientists	18	−10	−10	−10	−18
Agricultural technicians	18	−10	−10	−10	−18
Biologists	18	−10	−10	−10	−18
Nursery and greenhouse managers	16	−8	−8	−8	−16
Farm and ranch managers	16	−8	−8	−8	−16
Aquacultural managers	16	−8	−8	−8	−16
First-line supervisors of landscaping, lawn service, and groundskeeping workers	15	−7	−7	−7	−15
Landscaping and grounds-keeping workers	12	−4	−4	−4	−12
Pesticide handlers, sprayers, and applicators, vegetation	12	−4	−4	−4	−12
Farmworkers and laborers, crop farmers	10	−2	−2	−2	−10
Average (for 15 occupations)		−6.3	−6.3	−6.3	−14.3

Source: Author's calculations using data from KIHBS 2015/16.

TOURISM. Occupations in food and beverages are mostly skill level 3 and below. For the sample of occupations selected for this node, there was a skill deficit of 4.4 years of schooling, with the smallest deficit being observed in the youth cohort between 20 and 24 (0 to 4 years) (table 8-14). Skill adequacies and surpluses were only observed for this cohort. Some of the skills with the largest gaps were occupational health and safety specialists (8 years), and chefs and head cooks (8 years).

For entertainment and excursions, skill gaps were computed for 20 occupations. Occupations in this node mainly require high skills (at least level 5). The average skill gap for occupations was 6.7 years for all the age cohorts, except the 20–24 group, for which it was 2.7 years. Skill adequacies and surpluses were only observed for the 20–24 cohort for six occupations. With respect to specific occupations, curators had the largest skill gap, ranging from 6 (for those 20–24) to 10 years—for the rest of the age cohorts. Other occupations with large skill gaps were poets and creative writers, talent directors, producers, and environmental restoration planners.

Table 8-13. Selected Occupational Skill Gaps in Information and Communications Technology

Occupation	Modal years of schooling (O*NET)	Skill gap (years)			
		15–19	20–24	25–29	30–34
Computer science teachers, postsecondary	18	−10	−6	−10	−10
Computer systems analysts	16	−8	−4	−8	−8
Network and computer systems administrators	16	−8	−4	−8	−8
Software developers, systems software	16	−8	−4	−8	−8
Information security analysts	16	−8	−4	−8	−8
Computer user support specialists	16	−8	−4	−8	−8
Computer network support specialists	16	−8	−4	−8	−8
Software developers, applications	16	−8	−4	−8	−8
Computer programmers	16	−8	−4	−8	−8
Web administrators	16	−8	−4	−8	−8
Bioinformatics scientists	16	−8	−4	−8	−8
Computer systems engineers/ architects	16	−8	−4	−8	−8
Average for 19 occupations		−8.75	−4.75	−8.75	−8.75

Source: Author's calculations using data from KIHBS 2015/16.

IWSS Sector Skill Deficits and Gaps (Firm Survey)

This subsection supports the analysis above by using findings from interviews at 24 firms across the three IWSS sectors to capture insights on the nature of skill gaps. An important caveat is that the IWSS survey (2020) firm data did not cover a representative number of firms in the respective sectors—that is, horticulture (3 firms), ICT (6 firms), and tourism (14 facilities). Even so, the results offer important insights on current and anticipated skill requirements and deficits.

The horticultural firms were small, medium-sized, and large, with 32, 110, and 1,200 employees, respectively. All the firms produced vegetables

Table 8-14. Selected Occupational Skill Gaps in Tourism

Occupation	Modal years of school (O*NET)	Skill gap (years)			
		15–19	20–24	25–29	30–34
Supply chain manager	16	−8	−4	−8	−8
Lodging managers	16	−8	−4	−8	−8
Meeting, convention, and event planners	16	−8	−4	−8	−8
Real estate brokers	16	−8	−4	−8	−8
Concierges	12	−4	0	−4	−4
First-line supervisors of housekeeping and janitorial workers	12	−4	0	−4	−4
Average for 20 occupations		−5.63	−1.63	−5.63	−5.63

Source: Author's calculations using data from KIHBS 2015/16.

and leguminous crops, and the largest firm also produced seeds used for propagation. The firms carry out basic value-added activities, like sorting, grading, and packaging produce for the export market. The smallest of the three firms had established an out-grower business model, while the two larger firms relied on their own production to meet their domestic and export demand. The six surveyed ICT firms ranged in size from small to large, with the largest having more than 100 employees. The firms were involved in computer programming, consultancy and support activities, software engineering, and software publishing. In tourism, firm interviews were conducted primarily in the accommodation and food and beverages segments of the tourism value chain, which account for the bulk of this chain. The establishments interviewed ranged in size from 14 employees to 260. The largest hotel was a 5-star-rated facility. The medium-sized hotels ranged from unrated (5 firms) to 3- or 4-star-rated facilities (7 firms) to 5-star-rated hotels (2 firms).

The sampled firms were asked to provide a measure of their skill deficit on a 5-point scale, ranging from 1 = meets skill requirements to 5 = does not meet skills requirements at all. The range of skills assessed for the skill deficit were lumped together in six broad categories, including basic skills, social skills, and technical skills (table 8-15).

Table 8-15. Skill Deficits by IWSS Sector

| | Skill deficit (1–5) | | |
Skill Category	Horticulture	Information and communications technology	Tourism
Basic skills	1	1.8	2.4
Social skills	1	1.7	2.0
Problem-solving skills	1	1.7	1.8
Technical skills	1	1.8	2.3
Systems skills	1	1.8	2.6
Resource management skills	1.3	2.5	2.3
Average	1.1	1.9	2.2

Source: Authors' data.

Note: The scale for deficits runs from 1 = meets skill requirements to 5 = does not meet skills requirements at all.

The skill deficit of employees in the firms surveyed in the horticulture industry can be considered low, with an average skill gap measure of about 1.1 out of 5. The firms interviewed indicate that their workers meet the skill requirements and there are no skills in deficit.

The skill deficit of ICT employees can be considered low or moderate, with an average skill gap measure of about 1.9 out of 5. The skills with a higher deficit score were resource management skills, with an average score of 2.5 out of 5. Generally, all the other skills have a score of 1.8 or less, and employees are described as meeting skill requirements in technical and problem-solving skills in banking sector technology solutions, software engineering, and in services to end users, including enterprise resource planning solutions.

Concerning the main deficit areas with respect to skills, the surveyed ICT firms indicated that although there was a potential for growth in the ICT sector, this growth would predominantly be along the lines of expanding current operations. The new occupations seem to require much higher skill levels than the current occupations available to youth in the sector. However, moderate skill gaps in a number of soft skills will need to be addressed before the true potential of the ICT sector as an engine for tackling youth unemployment in Kenya can be realized.

In tourism, the skill deficit of employees in the surveyed firms can be considered moderate, with an average skill gap measure of about 2.2 out of 5.

The skills most critically in deficit are systems skills, with an average of 2.9, followed by basic skills with a score of 2.4, and technical skills, with a score of 2.3 out of 5.[7]

Policy Implications

Although economic growth in Kenya improved in the two decades leading to 2020, this growth has yet to be translated into adequate wage employment, and/or may not have been strong enough to generate adequate wage employment. There are good prospects for improving economic growth, given that some of the key factors linked to less vibrant growth performance (e.g., droughts, oil price fluctuations, and uncertainty during election cycles) are amenable to policy interventions. A more predictable and stable electoral cycle, and an increase in the share of farmland under irrigation, will be crucial for increased and sustained investments—as well as for reduced volatility in the growth of IWSS and the overall economy.

With respect to the IWSS sectors, we found that horticulture, ICT, and tourism were among the sectors with a good potential for creating jobs. However, the potential of these sectors cannot be achieved if the constraints analyzed above are not addressed. In what follows, we focus on policies that will enable the growth of these three sectors. It is important to emphasize that sectoral growth requires multiple, complementary policies, and thus there is no single "magic bullet" policy prescription that will harness the employment potential of the sector.

Horticulture

For the employment potential of horticulture to be achieved, several constraints need to be overcome. Nontariff trade barriers—including consumer standards, such as the European Good Agricultural Practice Standard—are key impediments to the growth of horticulture. Similarly, deficits in cold chain infrastructure and declining skill pool in agriculture are key constraints. To overcome these constraints, continuous skill transfers and lending support to local producers (e.g., in leveraging consumer-driven standards) will be important. Also, initiatives to promote investments in cold chain infrastructure—for example, investing in cold collection centers and packing houses—make agricultural curricula more attractive to youth through redesign, and better marketing of agriculture to youth will help.

ICT

Although ICT is one of the more promising sectors in Kenya, especially with the onset of the Fourth Industrial Revolution, several constraints prevent the realization of the true potential of the sector. Key constraints include non-competitive market structures; lacks of comprehensive policy and legal frameworks for various ICT fields, such as e-commerce; an inadequate number of individuals with advanced ICT skills; and low rates of adoption of emerging technologies, such as cloud computing and artificial intelligence.

Policies should strive to enhance competitive markets so that costs are lowered, enabling greater access to ICT. They should also promote private sector investments in education for high-level ICT skills, attract certain skills (e.g., programming) from the Kenyan diaspora, and increase the adoption rate of emerging technologies by using these technologies on a wide scale, such as in government departments.

Tourism

The vast number of businesses involved in the Kenyan tourism value chain suggests substantial future employment potential. However, the sector faces several obstacles, including congestion at certain tourist spots, leading to the erosion of the value of natural attractions over time, limited inclusion of local small and medium-sized enterprises in the tourism value chain, and inadequate product diversification/innovation in coastal tourism. The sector could also benefit from more lodging options, which now mostly focus on international (i.e., Asian, European, or American) tourists, rather than local or regional tourists. Several policies could overcome these constraints:

- Increase the entry price for international tourists at prime tourist locations to reduce the overall number of visitors: low-impact, high cost, or "quality over quantity."
- Promote local value-added efforts by incentivizing major tourist businesses to include local small and medium-sized enterprises in their supply chain.
- Create new experiences and/or products in coastal tourism.
- Encourage tourist lodgings to create a differentiated pricing structure, with locals being charged a lower price compared with international tourists.

Conclusion

Our research suggests that Kenya has achieved a relatively diverse economy in which IWSS, non-IWSS, and manufacturing sectors all have a promising potential to create jobs. Projections indicate that all these sectors will remain significant sources of employment in the next 10 years. IWSS and manufacturing have certain advantages over agriculture, including their high productivity levels, making them instrumental in reducing poverty. IWSS sectors also have high elasticity of employment relative to growth, further cementing their key role in generating more employment relative to non-IWSS sectors.

Even so, this study observes that a large share of new jobs are nonwage jobs. This could be a result of diverse factors, including complex regulations, weak enforcement of regulations, high taxes, or even simply tax evasion. This could also be a natural response to the poor investment climate. Due to the complexity of this subject, there is a need to carefully examine how growing and expanding informality (which varies across sectors) can be turned into a positive development.

A fundamental finding is that the growth observed in IWSS and other sectors of the economy is curtailed by constraints. Some of these are binding; but if addressed, they have the potential to generate higher growth in output and wage employment. The broad area of infrastructure and regulatory frameworks stands out as important for making the economy increasingly functional and thus capable of creating jobs. A key agenda should center on identifying and eliminating regulatory bottlenecks at sector/subsector levels on a continual basis. This requires strong monitoring and evaluation through continual stakeholder engagement, and subjecting all new laws and regulations to regulatory impact assessments.

The overriding finding on skills is that skill deficits can be a constraint to growth of IWSS and other sectors. In addition, skills mismatches may prevent youth from accessing gainful and productive employment. Monitoring skills needs will be a key component of ensuring that youth are equipped for available jobs. Stakeholders—including those for industry, and for education and training institutions—need to strengthen their partnerships for skill development and enhance programs that combine on-the-job and in-class training. The education and training system needs to be tailored to produce skills demanded by the market, rather than academic credentials.

NOTES

1. Underemployment encompasses individuals whose total work hours are less than 29 (KNBS 2018).

2. This country case study mainly adopts the International Labor Organization's (2016) definition of the youth 15 to 24 years. In some cases, the study uses the broader category of 15 to 34 years to accommodate the Kenyan definition.

3. Note that the survey data are not strictly comparable with those in the annual Economic Survey, which excludes small-scale farming and pastoralist activities.

4. The domestic services sector includes these categories: (1) professional, scientific, and technical services; (2) administrative and support services; (3) education; (4) human, health, and social work activities; (5) other service activities; and (6) activities of households as employers.

5. The assumptions underlying the projections are given by Munga et al. (2021).

6. The O*NET database contains information on standardized and occupation-specific mixes of knowledge, skills, and abilities. The study focused on the occupational descriptors for tourism, horticulture, and ICT.

7. Systems skills are only required in three out of the eight occupations identified by respondents. Moreover, only some of the listed systems skills were applicable to these occupations. As a result, the deficit present in these skills may not be as practically serious as the deficit in other areas, such as basic skills and social skills.

REFERENCES

European Commision. 2018. "Green Beans Value Chain Analysis in Kenya."

ILO (International Labor Organization). 2016. *Indicators of the Labour Market, Ninth Edition.* Geneva: ILO.

Kleih, U., C. Basset-Mens, C. Allen, and A. Edewa. 2018. "Green Beans Value Chain in Kenya." Report for European Commission, DG-DEVCO. Value Chain Analysis for Development Project VCA4D CTR 2016/375-804. https://capacity4dev.europa.eu/library/vca4d-kenya-green-beans-december-2017-full-report_en.

Kok, M. G., E. Osena, and H. Snel. 2019. "Food Loss in the French Bean Supply Chain of VEGPRO-Group Kenya." Wageningen University & Research.

KNBS (Kenya National Bureau of Statistics). 1990–2020. *Economic Survey,* various years. Nairobi: Government Printer.

———. 2000–2019. "Statistical Abstract," various editions.

———. 2018. *The 2015/16 Kenya Integrated Household Budget Survey (KIHBS) Labour Force Basic Report.* Nairobi: Government Printer.

Munga, B., E. Onsomu, N. Laibuni, H. Njogu, A. Shibia, and S. Luseno. 2021. "Industries Without Smokestacks in Africa: A Kenya Case Study." AGI Working Paper 31.

RSA. 2015. "Study of the Mapping of Distributors of Fruits and Vegetables in Kenya."

Tourism Research Institute. 2019. "Tourism Satellite Account, Kenya."

World Bank. 2018. "Kenya: Enterprise Survey (ES) Ref. KEN_2018_ES_v01_M." Data set. http://www.enterprisesurveys.org.

———. 2019. "World Development Indicators, Job Structure Tool."

World Tourism Organization. 2015. *UNWTO Annual Report 2014*. Madrid: World Tourism Organization. DOI:https://doi.org/10.18111/9789284416905.

NINE

Zambia

From Mineral Dependence to Skill Development in New Sectors

ANAND RAJARAM, DENNIS CHIWELE, AND MWANDA PHIRI

This chapter contends that the combination of noninclusive economic growth and the recent increase in the overall and youth unemployment rates in Zambia entails the development of an alternative growth trajectory that accounts for Zambia's current and projected stock of skills among its youth.[1] We provide evidence that four services subsectors—horticulture and floriculture, agro-processing, tourism, and information and communications technology (ICT)—have the potential to generate a sufficient number of jobs that align with Zambia's skill profile. However, this employment potential is predicated on overcoming a number of macroeconomic and sector-specific constraints, for which we provide a number of policy recommendations.

Zambia has been attempting to transition from an economy that is historically dependent on primary sector activities, including mining, to a more diversified economy. The pace and pattern of this transition has

FIGURE 9-1. **GDP Per Capita (Constant Dollars)**
and GDP Annual Growth, 1960–2018

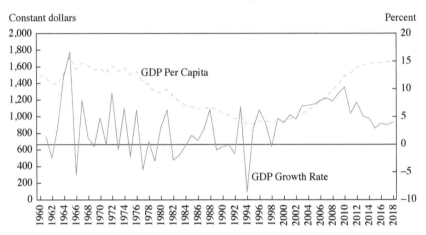

Source: Authors' construction, based on World Bank Development Indicators, 2020 (using World Bank national accounts data), and 2020 National Accounts data files from the Organization for Economic Cooperation and Development.

varied over the decades since independence: the first three decades were marked by import substitution, a strong direct role of the state in the economic sphere, and the growth of industry and services. This period also witnessed volatile gross domestic product (GDP) growth and declining per capita incomes (figure 9-1). After the introduction of multiparty democracy in 1991, structural adjustment reforms opened up the economy to import competition and marked the beginning of a more market-oriented approach to economic development.

Reforms liberalized exchange and interest rates, removed quantitative restrictions on trade, and privatized numerous state-enterprises. This pivot from a statist economy to a market-oriented one imposed drastic structural change. GDP declined sharply in 1994, but after a slow recovery, growth picked up after 2000, driven in part by a nine-year rally in copper prices. Whereas average GDP growth rates were barely 1 percent in the period 1981–90, and 1.75 percent in 1991–2000, average growth in the first decade of the 2000s stepped up to an impressive 7.5 percent, before slowing to 5.2 percent in 2011–15 and declining further in 2016–19 to about 3.2 percent.

Despite the recovery of GDP per capita, the quality of growth has been narrow and noninclusive in a number of respects—first, it has been confined to activities that are regionally concentrated in a few urban locations; and second, it has not generated employment or income-earning opportunities to enable improvement in the standard of living for the broad population. Income inequality in Zambia is very high, with the Gini coefficient of income distribution in 2015 estimated to be over 0.70 (Bhorat et al. 2018).[2] Regional inequalities across provinces, urban/rural inequalities, and inequalities across occupational groups have all widened. The poorest groups derive most of their income from agricultural self-employment, while the richest groups derive most income from wages. Those in the middle deciles derive most of their income from nonagricultural self-employment.

One reason for the poor distributional outcomes of growth is because the Zambian economy failed to create decent jobs to match the growing labor force. Table 9-1 indicates the trend in total and youth unemployment rates, both of which show a dip followed by an increase over the period 2005–18. Youth unemployment has varied between 7 and 3 percentage points above the overall unemployment rate, although the very sharp dip between 2005 and 2008 raises some concerns about whether both the level and the change are accurately measured by the Labour Force Surveys.[3] Accordingly, it becomes imperative to acknowledge definitional shifts over time, since they pose some problems for identifying trends in the labor market (see box 9-1).

While the mining boom did have a subsequent effect on employment in construction, services, and the public sector, the dip of 8–9 percentage points in unemployment between 2005 and 2008 seems exaggerated.[4] Lacking skills and experience, nearly 70 percent of employed youth were in the informal sector (46.6 percent) or household workers (22.9 percent), where conditions of employment were likely to be unfavorable. An important feature of development in Zambia has been the stunting of the formal sector and the corresponding expansion of the informal sector. By the end of the economic rebound in 2014, 84.5 percent of the employed population (4.9 of 5.8 million) worked in the informal sector. The major categories of informal sector employees were (1) own-account workers with no business registration, such as most of the small farmers in the agriculture sector; (2) employees in informal sector enterprises or in households, such as domestic workers who are "not subject to standard labor legislation, taxation, social security or entitlement to certain employment benefits"; and (3) paid or unpaid family workers.

Informal sector jobs are characterized by low earnings (implying low productivity), a lack of job security, poor working conditions, and poverty:

Table 9-1. Basic Labor Statistics, 2005–18

	2005	2008	2014	Absolute change	Annualized % change	2018
Labor market aggregates ('000s)						
Working-age population	6,202	6,716	8,150	1,434	3.3%	9,483
Employed	4,131	4,607	5,859	1,252	4.1%	2,949
Unemployed		397	470	73	2.9%	427
Labor force	4,918	5,004	6,329	1,325	4.0%	3,329
Discouraged work seekers						960
Labor force participation rate (%)			77.7	3.1	0.7	35.1
Unemployment rate (%)						
Unemployment rate (all)	16.0%	7.9%	7.4%	-0.5%	-1.1%	12.8%
Unemployment rate (youth)	23.0%	14.0%	15.0%	9.0%	6.4%	16.0%
Underemployment	—	8.2%	8.3%	0.1%	0.2%	7.1%

Source: Authors' construction based on Central Statistics Office data for 2005, 2008, 2014, and 2018 and on Labour Force Survey reports.

Note: Time-related underemployment reflects the mismatch between the hours an individual works and the hours the person is willing and available to work. Normal working hours are taken to be 40 hours. This measure depicts underutilized productive capacity of the labor force, which here, is measured as a percentage of the total employment.

Box 9-1. Technical Note: Methodological Variation in Labour Force Surveys over Time

At the time of this chapter's writing, Zambia had undertaken seven Labour Force Surveys (LFSs), covering the years 1986, 2005, 2008, 2012, 2014, 2017, and 2018. In 2017, major revisions were made to the methodological approach, including a change in the frequency of data collection from a biannual to a quarterly basis. A more significant change, however—which renders the 2017 and later LFSs incomparable with LFSs preceding 2017—are the changes in the labor force framework, the survey questionnaire, and the definition of employed and unemployed persons.

Before 2017, LFSs—namely, the 1986, 2005, 2008, 2012, and 2014 ones—were based on the 1982 Labour Force Framework adopted at the 13th International Conference of Labor Statisticians (ICLS). From 2017 onward, the LFS methodology is premised on the 2013 Labour Force Framework adopted at the 19th ICLS, which issued new guidelines for measuring and compiling labor statistics. In this new framework, the employed population now strictly includes persons engaged in work for pay or profit (including self-employed or contributing family workers); while the unemployed population must strictly satisfy the conditions of seeking a paid job and being available to take up the job. In contrast, former LFSs included in the definition of persons employed, persons in own use (consumption) production work such as "collecting firewood, growing of crops for household consumption only, fishing for household consumption" (2015 report by Zambia's Central Statistical Office).

These definitional changes have subsequently led to a significant reduction in the overall labor force population, which is defined as all persons—employed or unemployed—age 15 years or above at the time of the survey. For instance, in 2014, the labor force population was estimated at 6,329,076, while it was estimated at 3,398,294 in 2017 largely as a result of a marked reduction in number of employed persons in agriculture industries (2015 and 2018 data from Zambia's Central Statistical Office).

In addition to the conventional measures of unemployment, there is now what is defined as the national combined rate of unemployment and the potential labor force. This is the sum of the unemployed and the potential labor force populations. Whereby, the potential labor force population is defined as "all persons of working age who during the short reference period were neither in employment nor in unemployment and (1) carried out activities to 'seek employment,' were not 'currently available' but would become available within a short subsequent period established in the light of national circumstances or (2) did not carry out activities to 'seek employment', but wanted employment and were 'currently available'"—that is, discouraged workers (2018 report from Zambia's Central Statistical Office). The analysis given in this chapter is therefore made in cognizance of these methodological variations over time and the extent to which the authors reconcile these differences.

"Whereas only 5.1% of formal workers can be classified as living in extremely poor households (per capita expenditure less than the $1.90/day poverty line), 60% of informal workers live in extremely poor households by the same measure" (ILO and OECD 2018). Formal sector workers on average earned 3.2 times more than their informal sector counterparts, and 3.9 times more than household workers. Industries in the informal sector are hubs of low productivity. About 68.4 percent of the people employed in agriculture were in the informal sector. The 1994–2014 period witnessed a significant expansion of tertiary sector activities, as well as wholesale and retail trade, but much of this expansion was in the informal sector.[5]

This chapter is structured as follows. First, we examine the role of the IWSS sectors in the Zambian economy. We then compare the growth of the IWSS and non-IWSS sectors, with a special focus on women and youth. This is followed by an analysis of the constraints on four specific IWSS sectors, and a quantitative analysis of future employment growth between 2018 and 2030. We conclude the chapter with a number of policy recommendations.

Patterns of Growth: The Role of the IWSS Sectors

This section examines the structural transformation of the Zambian economy. Figure 9-2 illustrates the productivity–employment structural transformation nexus by correlating the level of relative labor productivity in 2005, with the *change* in the industry share of employment over the period 2005–18. Phrased differently, the figure allows us to assess whether labor is being released (denoted by a contraction in employment share) from industries that are least productive (i.e., in the lower left quadrant), and being absorbed (denoted by an expansion in the share of employment) in more productive industries (i.e., in the upper right quadrant) (Fox, Thomas, and Haines 2017).

We observe the following: First, employment has contracted sharply in agriculture (an industry with low productivity) and has expanded in both productive IWSS and productive non-IWSS (the upper right quadrant of figure 9-2). Second, while employment has contracted in agriculture by nearly 13 percentage points over this period, this industry still employs a considerable number of workers (57 percent of employed labor), as evidenced by the size of the bubble in the figure.

Third, the majority of IWSS (with the exception of tourism) are clustered in the figure's upper right quadrant, where relative labor productivity

FIGURE 9-2. **Correlation between Industry Productivity
and Change in Employment Share, 2005–18**

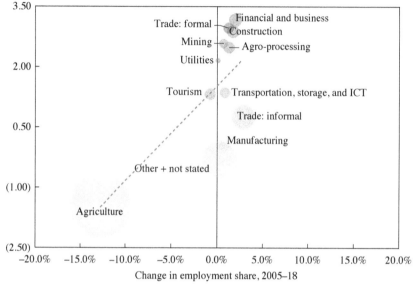

Natural Log of Relative Labor Productivity (Industry Labor Productivity /
Economy-wide Labor Productivity)

Change in employment share, 2005–18

Sources: Authors' construction based on Labour Force Survey data (2005 and 2018), gross
value-added data from ZamStats; and World Travel and Tourism Council data.

Note: ICT = Information and communications technology. Relative labor productivity is
computed as the natural log of the ratio of value added to labor of each industry divided by
economy-wide labor productivity. A ratio > 0 indicates that the industry's labor productivity is
higher than the total productivity of the economy; < 0 means otherwise. Bubble size represents
the size of employment in 2018. The dotted linear trendline shows the best fitted values.

is higher and employment is expanding. About 5.7 percentage points of
the 12.7 percent reduction of workers in agriculture over the period
2005–18 found employment in IWSS. Among IWSS, financial and business activities—the most productive in 2005—expanded employment by
2 percentage points. At the same time, workers were also reallocated to
productive formal trade and agro-processing activities, albeit to a smaller
extent. Respectively, these industries' share of employment expanded by
1.2 and 1.3 percentage points. Similarly, transportation grouped with
ICT grew their share of employment by 0.8 percentage point over this
period. Disappointingly, tourism recorded a contraction in its share of
employment (0.8 percentage point), even though the industry displays
higher relative labor productivity.

Fourth, workers were also absorbed into traditional manufacturing, whose share of employment expanded by 0.8 percentage point. Manufacturing's relative labor productivity in 2005, it appears, was only marginally above the average, so that it barely fits in the upper right quadrant. Comparatively, more workers have been absorbed into non-IWSS sectors that are relatively productive industries, such as construction and mining.

Fifth, confirming our observations about the rapid growth of the informal sector, informal trade increased its share of employment by the highest margin: 2.9 percentage points. Productivity in informal trade in 2005 appears higher than in manufacturing, but measurement issues would not warrant placing confidence in such an assessment. The share of employment in relatively very high productive industries—mining, construction, and utilities— also increased, but by 0.7, 1.7, and 0.1 percentage points, respectively.

All in all, Zambia's structural transformation has been generally positive, as evidenced by the upward-sloping linear trend line. Indeed, employment has been shifting out of low-productivity agricultural activities into more productive activities in trade, finance and business, construction, agro-processing, mining, transportation, and ICT—and even, to a limited extent, manufacturing. However, as indicated by the small size of the bubbles in figure 9-2, the IWSS sectors remain a relatively small source of employment, collectively accounting for about 8.4 percent of employment.

The experience of structural change in Zambia confirms that manufacturing has not proven to be a growth leading sector. A significant proportion of the structural change corresponding to the shrinking of agriculture appears to be driven by the absorption of labor into low-productivity activities in the informal urban services sector, a phenomenon that has been characterized as "growth reducing" (Cilliers 2018). However, the IWSS sectors have demonstrated both higher productivity and relatively high employment growth, which suggests a potential avenue for productive job creation. This is the subject of more detailed analysis in the next section.

Sectoral Decomposition:
The IWSS Sectors in Comparative Perspective

To better understand employment dynamics within sectors, table 9-2 provides a breakdown of employment across industries, which are categorized under three groups: IWSS, manufacturing (excluding agro-processing), and other non-IWSS. Labor force survey data show that non-IWSS are

Table 9-2. Employment in IWSS and Non-IWSS Sectors, 2005–18

Sector	Employment			Share of change (%)	Employment share (%)		Annual (%) growth
	2005	2018	Change		2005	2018	2005–18
Total employment	3,726,024	6,295,524	2,569,500	100	100	100	4.1
Total IWSS	114,049	550,952	436,903	17	3.1	8.8	12.9
Agro-processing	25,792	124,841	99,049	23	0.7	2.0	12.9
Horticulture	12,111	41,136	29,025	7	0.3	0.7	9.9
Tourism	98,854	118,598	19,745	5	2.7	1.9	1.4
Transportation and storage	37,468	101,333	63,866	15	1.0	1.6	8.0
Financial and business	22,347	163,397	141,049	32	0.6	2.6	16.5
Trade: formal	16,331	105,619	89,288	20	0.4	1.7	15.4
Information and communications technology		14,626				0.2	
Manufacturing (excl. agro-processing)	44,671	125,670	80,998	3	1.2	2.0	8.3

(continued)

Table 9-2. (continued)

Sector	Employment			Share of change (%)	Employment share (%)		Annual (%) growth
	2005	2018	Change		2005	2018	2005–18
Other non-IWSS	3,567,303	5,618,902	2,051,599	80	96.0	89.3	3.6
Agriculture	2,583,865	3,563,804	979,939	48	69.0	56.6	2.5
Mining	21,454	80,513	59,059	3	0.6	1.3	10.7
Construction	24,338	149,874	125,536	6	0.7	2.4	15.0
Trade: informal	198,651	516,929	318,278	16	5.3	8.2	7.6
Utilities	10,669	22,734	12,065	1	0.3	0.4	6.0
Government	21,113	76,629	55,516	3	0.6	1.2	10.4
Domestic services	41,653	63,714	22,061	1	1.1	1.0	3.3
Other**	96,091	460,492	364,401	18	2.6	7.3	12.8
Not stated	569,469	684,213	114,744	6	15.3	10.9	1.4

Sources: Authors' computations based on ZamStats Labor Force Survey data and World Travel and Tourism Council data.

** Other includes health, education, arts, entertainment and recreation, accommodations and food, and other activities, while "not-stated" are employees with missing information on the industry in which they are employed.

Note: Employment in the tourism sector is derived from World Travel and Tourism Council data. Annual employment growth rate was computed using the compound average growth rate. Before 2010, transportation and storage were classified with information and communications technology as per the ISIC Revision 3. For comparability over time, we add information and communications technology to transportation and storage in 2018. Agro-processing is taken as the sum of employment in these manufacturing subsectors: food, beverages and tobacco; textiles, clothing, and leather; wood and wood products; and paper and paper products. Employment in horticulture in 2005 is based on the ISIC Revision 3 codes 0112—growing of vegetables, horticultural specialties, and nursery products, and 0113—growing of fruit, nuts, beverages, and spice crops. Employment in horticulture in 2018 is based on the ISIC Revision 4 codes 012—growing of perennial crops and 013—plant propagation.

historically the major source of employment, as shown by the 96 percent share of total employment in 2005. Agriculture continued to shed labor as a share of total employment, declining from 69 to 57 percent between 2005 and 2018, even though nearly 50 percent of new jobs in other non-IWSS were agriculture-based. Not surprisingly, given that this period coincided with the copper price boom, construction, mining, and government employment, all grew substantially over this period, with construction in particular more than doubling its share of employment in the economy to 2.4 percent. Manufacturing employment grew by 8.3 percent and increased its employment share, but the level was just 2 percent of the total.[6]

Interestingly, employment in IWSS grew at a rate of 12.9 percent a year—well above the 3.6 percent of non-IWSS—more than doubling IWSS' share of employment over the 13-year period to 8.8 percent of total employment. Nearly one third of all new IWSS jobs in this period came from finance and business services, bolstered by the expansion in insurance and pension funds and in professional, scientific, and technical activities. This demonstrated that the higher employment creation potential of IWSS is an important finding. It suggests future potential that will require further analysis to determine whether and how it can be sustained.

Among our IWSS sectors of interest, finance and business had the fastest annual growth in employment, expanding at the rate of 16.5 percent a year, quadrupling its share of total employment.[7] Although this pace of growth in employment was closely followed by construction, a non-IWSS sector, growing at 15.1 percent, construction employment growth came at the back of the mining boom and the government's decision to spend heavily on infrastructure development. Other high performers in employment growth were agro-processing and formal trade and wholesale trade, both IWSS sectors that grew at a rate higher than 10 percent. Among the non-IWSS, mining and government also grew above 10 percent a year. Although they could only still account for only a small share of employment by 2018, it is noted that IWSS sectors were largely creating new sources of employment growth away from the performance of the mining industry. This takes into account the fact that horticulture, which in essence is a part of the agriculture sector, grew at nearly 10 percent in this period.

The employment potential of ICT activities is harder to gauge, owing to data constraints. At most, we are only able to discuss the industry's share of employment in 2018, which, at 0.2 percent, is miniscule. But this is not surprising, because ICT is in its infancy in Zambia. However, the tourism sector is a big disappointment; its share of employment contracted over the period, owing to an employment growth rate that was lower than average (1.4 percent a year). If the much-talked-about job creation potential of tourism is to be realized, it is important to obtain a deeper understanding of this sector by assessing the binding constraints it faces, and discovering how these could be resolved.

Knowing whether the movement of labor out of agriculture and into other productive activities has raised average labor productivity in Zambia – and by how much – is important to answer the question of whether the potential to raise living standards is being enhanced. Understanding which industries have the highest labor productivity is clearly important for enhancing productive job creation for the future. In table 9-3, we depict the within-industry labor productivity estimated for 2018, measured as value added per worker. IWSS displays the highest labor productivity, somewhat more than manufacturing, with other non-IWSS sectors having lowest labor productivity as a group. While IWSS labor productivity is boosted by the inclusion of ICT, most of the IWSS subgroups show higher productivity than manufacturing. Parts of non-IWSS—such as mining, utilities, and construction—are the exception, since they clearly display very high labor productivity due to their high capital-intensity. In general, the relative labor productivity of IWSS is six times greater than other non-IWSS and about four times the economy-wide average.[8]

Changes in statistical methods complicate inferences about directions of change in labor productivity through 2018, particularly regarding manufacturing and agro-processing, and the figures in general appear unreliable. In table 9-4, it appears that between 2005 and 2018, economy-wide labor-productivity increased by nearly 30 percent, driven by an increase in other non-IWSS and manufacturing labor productivity. As a result, the labor productivity gap between IWSS and manufacturing productivity particularly appears to have decreased markedly in 2018 relative to 2005, with the ratio being about 1. IWSS sectors relative to non-IWSS sectors also show a narrowing of the productivity advantage of IWSS. There is no explanation that would lead us to understand whether such a dramatic change is indeed real. While it is possible that agro-processing productivity declined and manufacturing increased, the size of the productivity shifts for these two industries may be overstated because of the methods used to rebase GDP, and the resulting effects on manufacturing and agro-processing outputs.[9] For these reasons, we report the 2018 results but do not use them to make any inferences about recent labor productivity.

Table 9-3. Labor Productivity: Value Added per Worker, in Constant 2010 Prices

Sector or productivity	Labor productivity (ZMW)		Growth, 2005–18 (%)
	2005	2018	
Economy-wide	17,188	22,188	29
Total IWSS	166,734	82,540	−50
Agro-processing	205,589	32,010	−84
Tourism	64,571	71,699	11
Transportation and storage	67,303	49,120	−27
Financial and business	410,445	86,317	−79
Trade: formal	335,138	121,442	−64
Information and communications technology	—	422,272	
Manufacturing (excl. agro-processing)	18,225	57,946	218
Other non-IWSS	11,171	14,561	30
Agriculture (incl. horticulture)	4,040	2,278	−44
Mining	226,540	185,463	−18
Construction	305,830	101,251	−67
Trade: informal	36,373	32,758	−10
Utilities	149,192	123,271	−17
Government	—	92,421	
Domestic services	—	—	
Other	12,587	15,094	20
Relative labor productivity: IWSS to other non-IWSS	15	6	
Relative labor productivity: IWSS to manufacturing	9	1	
Relative labor productivity: IWSS to total	10	4	

Sources: Authors' calculations based on ZamStats labor force and gross value-added data.

Note: The sum of IWSS excludes tourism to avoid double counting, since the tourism sector is a composite of tourism activities in various industries. We lack disaggregated gross value-added data for government and domestic activities for years before 2010. For domestic services, data were also not available after 2010. Similarly, information and communications technology cannot be disaggregated before 2010. Thus, labor productivity for some industries in some years is not computed. Agriculture includes horticulture activities due to the lack of disaggregated gross value-added data at the 4-digit level required to compute labor productivity for the horticulture subsector.

Table 9-4. Percentage Share of Employment by Education Level, IWSS versus Non-IWSS Sectors, 2005–18

Sector	Share							
	2005				2018			
	Post-secondary	Secondary	Primary	Zero or not stated	Post-secondary	Secondary	Primary	Zero or not stated
Total employment	2	23	53	23	7	42	41	10
Total IWSS	1	17	55	28	13	63	21	3
Agro-processing	1	23	52	24	6	64	27	3
Horticulture	2	23	62	13	5	52	38	5
Information and communications technology	—	—	—	—	16	72	12	0
Financial and business	1	14	56	30	23	58	16	3
Transportation and storage	1	14	53	32	5	72	17	5
Trade: formal	0	13	57	30	18	61	21	0
Manufacturing (excl. agro-processing)	2	19	58	20	7	54	35	3
Other non-IWSS	2	23	52	23	6	40	43	11
Agriculture	1	24	52	23	2	38	47	13
Mining	0	14	69	17	30	56	13	1
Construction	0	18	54	28	14	66	20	0
Utilities	6	13	45	37	35	58	7	0
Trade: informal	2	21	49	28	3	54	37	5
Government	0	21	44	36	26	62	12	0
Domestic services	2	21	44	34	0	44	52	4
Other	2	17	53	28	42	39	17	3
Not stated	2	23	55	20	0.2	26	58	23

Sources: Authors' tabulations based on ZamStats Labor Force Data.

Note: Data on workers in the tourism industry by level of education were not available.

Table 9-4 provides an overview of the education profile of employed workers in the aggregate and by industry between 2005 and 2018. While data on skills were not readily available, we use the level of education as a good proxy predictor of the capacity of workers to build their skills. In general, a higher proportion of employed workers in 2018 were educated than in 2005.

Using the highest level of education successfully completed in 2018, we find that in all IWSS, 63 percent of the employed had successfully completed some level of secondary education, having completed at least grade 7, up to a maximum of grade 12. This number is significantly higher than the 17 percent level in 2005. At the high end of the spectrum, among IWSS, the highest proportion of workers—with more than 12 years of schooling— are employed in finance and business activities (23 percent). Conversely, at the lower end, horticulture and transportation employed the lowest percentage of postsecondary workers. Manufacturing, like IWSS, shows a sharp increase in the employment of those with secondary schooling, from 19 percent in 2005 to 54 percent in 2018.

In non-IWSS, the highest level of education completed is more varied. In the aggregate, the majority of workers have a primary education. Mining and utilities demand a higher level of education, with about a third of the employed population in these industries having completed more than 12 years of schooling. Similarly, almost the majority of workers (42 percent) in other services, which includes health and education services, have a higher proportion of workers with a postsecondary education. Government employees include a quarter who have more than 12 years of education. Agriculture and domestic services, on the other hand, employ a higher proportion of workers with primary education and very few with a postsecondary education.

Exports

Trade remains an important mechanism for productivity growth that has been demonstrated empirically to hasten the process of structural transformation for countries locked in low-productivity agricultural activities. In table 9-5, we contrast the export performance of IWSS relative to manufacturing, non-IWSS, and overall exports. Under IWSS, we make an additional distinction between merchandise exports and services exports.

Zambia's exports are dominated by mining products. In large part because of the commodity super-cycle that occurred over this period and boosted copper prices and exports, the share of mining exports increased from

Table 9-5. Exports and Export Growth by Industry

Sector or growth ratio	2005		2018		2005–2018 Annual % growth
	Millions of dollars	Share (%)	Millions of dollars	Share (%)	
IWSS Total	772	32.7	1,320	13.2	4.2
IWSS services exports	506	21.5	897	9.0	4.5
Transportation	14	0.6	54	0.5	11.1
Tourism	477	20.2	801	8.0	4.1
Information and communications technology	12	0.5	36	0.4	8.8
Other business services	3	0.1	6	0.1	5.6
IWSS goods exports	266	11.3	422	4.2	3.6
Horticulture	39	1.7	16	0.2	–6.8
Agro-processing	226	9.6	406	4.1	4.6
Manufacturing non-IWSS total	82	3.5	1,043	10.4	21.6
Other non-IWSS total	1,410	59.8	7,560	75.6	13.8
Mining	1,263	53.6	7,245	72.5	14.4
Utilities	5	0.2	83	0.8	25.0
Agriculture (excl. horticulture)	143	6.1	232	2.3	3.8
Total exports (goods and services)	2,358	100	10,000	100	11.8
Ratio of IWSS exports to total exports		0.33		0.13	–6.7
Ratio of manufacturing exports to total exports		0.03		0.1	8.8
Ratio of other non-IWSS exports to total exports		0.6		0.76	1.8

Sources: Authors' construction, based on UN Comtrade data, obtained from the World Bank's World Integrated Trade Solution, http://wits.worldbank.org; United Conference on Trade and Development statistics, https://unctadstat.unctad.org; and World Travel and Tourism Council data, https://www.wttc.org/.

Note: Horticulture exports are based on the ISIC Revision 3 codes 0112—growing of vegetables, horticultural specialties, and nursery products; and 0113—growing of fruit, nuts, and beverage and spice crops. Growth rates are based on the compound average growth rate.

54 percent in 2005 to 72 percent in 2018.[10] Manufacturing exports have gained over the years, increasing from 3.5 percent in 2005 to 10 percent in 2018, with annual growth of over 21 percent. A part of this increase in manufacturing outputs can be traced to the increase in export of chemicals.[11] On the other hand, the share of agricultural exports declined from 6.1 percent in 2005 to 2.3 percent in 2018. In the aggregate, non-IWSS' share of exports increased from 60 to 76 percent.

IWSS exports have lagged non-IWSS exports by a considerable margin over this period, but this comparison may be overstated because of the choice of 2018 as the ending date, since IWSS agro-exports were significantly reduced over this period, in part due to weather conditions. Growing at well below the rate of total export growth, the share of IWSS sectors in aggregate exports declined markedly, by 20 percentage points, from 33 to 13 percent. Under services, the share of tourism exports fell by more than half, while the share of transportation and ICT exports contracted marginally, by 0.1 percentage point. Under merchandise exports, the share of horticulture and agro-processed goods also fell, from 2 percent and 10 percent to 0.2 and 4 percent, respectively. Horticulture exports have been contracting by 7 percent a year after a promising start in the 2000s.

Focus on Vulnerable Groups: Women and Youth

An important consideration of IWSS sectors is whether growth in these sectors is more inclusive than non-IWSS sectors. In our analysis, we focus on two groups that have historically been underrepresented in the Zambian labor market: women and youth.

Table 9-6 shows the change in and composition of employed females and youth in IWSS and non-IWSS sectors. Overall, it appears that the IWSS sectors have not performed as well in creating jobs for women and youth, the two critical demographics of great concern for creating an inclusive economy.

The IWSS have seen sharply lower shares of young workers, and the proportion of female workers also declined over the 2005–18 period, both in IWSS and in manufacturing, with a corresponding rise in the shares employed in agriculture. Although female employment in the IWSS sectors expanded at a rate of 9 percent, that of males was growing at an even faster rate, at 16 percent a year. Therefore, the share of women employed in IWSS appears to have declined from 52 percent in 2005 to 34 percent in 2018. The share of employment for those age 15 to 24 years declined from 37 to

Table 9-6. Percentage Shares of Employed Females and Youth, IWSS versus Non-IWSS Sectors, 2005–18

Sector	Share				Compound annual growth rate	
	Females	Youth	Females	Youth	Females	Youth
Total IWSS	52	37	34	12	9	3
Agro-processing	47	39	43	24	12	9
Horticulture	57	36	45	10	8	0
Information and communications technology			37	25		
Financial and business	50	40	39	3	14	–3
Transportation and storage	57	33	2	8	–18	–3
Trade: formal	46	36	41	12	14	5
Manufacturing (excl. agro-processing)	49	38	7	17	–7	2
Other non-IWSS	51	41	58	28	5	1
Agriculture	52	41	67	34	5	1
Mining	54	42	12	7	–2	–4
Construction	49	42	2	9	–11	2
Utilities	50	43	2	17	–16	–1
Trade: informal	49	43	59	12	9	–2
Government	50	28	40	3	9	–7
Domestic services	57	36	70	31	5	2
Other	50	46	49	9	13	0
Not stated	50	40	39	33	–1	0

Sources: Authors' tabulations based on ZamStats Labor Force data.

Note: Data on workers in the tourism industry by level of education were not available. "Youth" are defined as age 15–24 years.

12 percent in 2005 and 2018, respectively, while it grew for the 35–64 demographic category, from 33 percent in 2005 to 50 percent in 2018. While the labor force data for 2018 are relatively robust and the underlying surveys are of a better quality, the corresponding data for 2005 may not be as robust.[12] One implication is that the share of IWSS female and youth employment in 2005 is likely overestimated, so the decline in female and youth employment in IWSS by 2018 may be overstated. Nevertheless, it is likely that current trends are not expanding employment for these critical demographic groups, and Zambia will need to do more to create jobs for women and youth.

Constraints on IWSS Growth

The recognition of the most severe constraints a country faces should enable governments to prioritize overcoming these greatest hindrances to economic growth.

Constraints on Growth:
The Broad Operating Environment for Firms in Zambia

The experience of growth in IWSS and non-IWSS industries has been influenced by economy-wide constraints, as well as industry-specific constraints. Macroeconomic policies over the past decade, and the resulting high deficits and payment delays, have crowded out private sector access to credit, raised debt levels alarmingly, and caused exchange rate instability (over the past five years)—all of which have adversely affected firms' operations and profitability. Power shortages due to drought conditions, and uncertainties regarding tax policies, have also undermined investor confidence and growth.

Labor market regulations over the past five years have increasingly tilted the playing field against employers, as concerns for protecting workers have failed to take into account the impact on employers, and therefore on employment. New regulations impose significant burdens on employers by reducing flexibility, and they damage job creation, as confirmed by business surveys. Zambia introduced legislation in 2015 to address concerns about increasing the "casualization" of work, which appeared to reduce jobs of a more permanent nature to repeated casual contracts, impinging on the rights of workers. While clarifying different kinds of contracts (including consultancies and seasonal contracts), the legislation defined terms under which a repeated use of shorter-term contracts would need to be upgraded to longer-term contracts. However, the Employment (Amendment) Act also criminalized violations of the terms of the act, moving adjudication from the industrial courts to the judicial courts. A 2017 study (Masumbu and Mwenge 2017) surveyed firms across various regions to assess the effect of labor market regulations on labor outcomes. The responses identified this criminalization as a major concern for employers, as the perceived implicit ban on casual work limited the ability of firms to cope with uncertain economic conditions. High severance pay requirements for longer-term workers were also seen as disincentivizing for such contracts.

More recently, the new Employment Code Act, which came into force in May 2020, has been described by most firms as "disastrous" for their activities, raising costs and lowering labor productivity. The act has been critiqued by Zambian policy analysts as particularly inappropriate during the economic downturn, and employers have called for suspending the provisions of the act and reconsidering its approach to employment regulations (Saasa and Mwenge 2020). The study noted that the act requires all categories of employees (including those previously unprotected) to be covered, significantly expanding the scope of the law. By increasing leave entitlements, gratuity and severance payments, including management in overtime eligibility, and codifying the provision of housing assistance and medical services to employees, it significantly escalates costs to enterprises across the country. The new employment code inhibits job creation as it renders seasonal/temporary hiring extremely difficult, which particularly affects sectors such as tourism but also adversely affects many other industries. It also restricts the recruitment of expatriate staff, which will limit the acquisition of necessary skills in various industries.

Other binding constraints on economic growth in Zambia include the low quality of human capital, poor infrastructure services (electricity, water, and sanitation), and coordination failures that limit exports.[13] In a 2013 World Bank Enterprise Survey, firms in Zambia stated that they faced obstacles such as access to finance, electricity supply, and taxation. At that time, 27.5 percent of firms indicated that access to finance was their biggest obstacle, compared with a world average of 14.9 percent, and the Sub-Saharan African average of 22.2.

Constraints on Growth in Specific IWSS Sectors

Key to understanding the constraints of specific IWSS sectors is examining the value chain for each sector. Value chain analysis is potentially useful to identify each stage of production, distribution, marketing and retail, the key actors, and the linkages between them. In applying it to specific IWSS subsectors (horticulture, agro-processing, tourism, and ICT), we seek to understand the value chain for each industry, to identify likely constraints, and to assess the potential for job creation.

HORTICULTURE AND FLORICULTURE. The value chain for large scale farmers in horticulture and floriculture indicates that farms typically have contracts with European supermarkets, which determine prices and standards, and provide packaging. For example, York Farm produces organic vegetables to supply Tesco in the United Kingdom. In flower production, Khal Amazi is the major player and supplies stores in the Netherlands, the United Kingdom, Germany, and Sweden, using both passenger and cargo freight carriers. A key part of the value chain is using high-quality seeds, appropriate fertilizers, and pesticides, especially for vegetables intended for export markets, ensuring phytosanitary standards, and maintaining the cold chain. The Zambia Export Growers Association (ZEGA) is an association of farmers who export to the European Union and South Africa. ZEGA owns ZEGA Limited, a company that does cold chain management. ZEGA Limited virtually controls the entire logistics market for horticulture/ floriculture that is moved by air freight.

Air freight became a constraint for Zambian flower exporters during this period, as British Airways discontinued direct flights to Lusaka in 2013, and KLM did the same in October 2014. KLM had initiated the direct flights in May 2012, citing the robust growth of the Zambian economy, and the link to growing flower exports as the rationale. However, the stoppage of the flights in 2014 was blandly attributed to the decision to optimize the KLM network portfolio. Since Amsterdam is the global hub for the flower industry, and almost all Zambia's rose exports were to the Netherlands, the stoppage negatively affected the Zambian floriculture industry.

Further constraints faced by horticulture and floriculture are irrigation difficulties due to poor rainfall and erratic electricity supply. Floral firms have largely invested in irrigation systems to support year-round production, but costs are affected when the power supply is unreliable and power generators must be used. Firms also complain that the removal of duty exemptions has increased costs and reduced profitability. As relatively small producers, Zambian exporters are price-takers, so rising costs run into an international price constraint that squeezes profits.

AGRO-PROCESSING. Agro-processing firms process agricultural products, including horticultural produce, into other processed goods. Sugarcane and beet sugar and related products, oilcakes, beverages, and cereals are the main exports of the Zambian agro-processing sector. In this study, we looked at the agro-processing value chain for milkshakes.

Inputs into the milkshake business are imported or bought from domestic producers. Domestic logistics are conducted entirely by the agro-processing firm. Import and export logistics are conducted by a third party. The firm collects milk and milk powder in warehouses, processes them into milkshakes in production plants, and then transfers the final product to depots. From the depots, the product is distributed to domestic sellers or exported. The agro-processor provides marketing support for sellers through billboards, TV and radio advertisements, and roadshows. An increase in cost-competitive domestic production of raw materials would remove the need to import raw materials and enable an increase in domestic employment. In addition, if the quality of the milkshakes is further improved, firms could increase the export market from just Zambia's neighbors to the greater Africa region, Europe, and Asia.

Although the agro-processing sector has a lot of potential to grow in Zambia, the Zambia Development Agency (2014) states that the sector faces major constraints, such as "inadequate raw material supplies, limited access to appropriate technology, limited capacity to maintain technologies, failure by locally processed products to compete against imports, low viability of existing agro processing enterprises, and limited access to credit."

Agro-processors need a reliable supply of raw materials, with quality being a particularly important aspect for export markets. Currently, crop and livestock production can vary and be unreliable for downstream processing firms. Raw materials that are supplied in Zambia are of varying quality and quantity, partly because of fluctuations in weather and damage due to pests. While the Zambia Development Agency recommends that agro-processors should ensure implementation of appropriate standards for soil, pest, and water management, this will require staff with necessary scientific skills that are not widely available. There is an important role for public extension services to provide advice to farmers beyond what agro-processors themselves can provide.

TOURISM. In 2018, Zambia received almost 1 million international arrivals— the bulk (78 percent) of whom were from Sub-Saharan Africa, while

9.2 percent were from Europe, and 7 percent were from Asia. Business visitors were the largest group, at about 53 percent. Tourism is a sector that can provide high-value jobs to skilled and moderately skilled labor, and there is considerable underexploited potential to increase value added in this sector. According to the Zambia Tourism Agency, there are three tourism value chains in Zambia: (1) leisure tourism; (2) meetings, incentives, conferences, and events; and (3) "shopping" tourism (interview, Zambian Tourism Agency 2019).

For leisure tourists, Zambia has abundant natural assets, such as Victoria Falls and many national parks. There are several opportunities to increase employment in this sector. In particular, because the safari season runs for only six months of the year, during the other six months, lodges, other infrastructure, and labor are not utilized. To increase use in the low season, leisure tourism operators could consider offering other activities, including cultural activities, to attract tourists (Acorn Tourism Consulting 2018). Increasing the number of activities, and highlighting unique aspects of wildlife and landscapes, would encourage tourists to look at Zambia as a sole destination in itself, rather than just a short add-on destination to a South African or Botswana safari. Moreover, the northern circuit remains largely unexploited, owing to underdeveloped tourism products and weak linkages to the southern circuit.[14] This has exacerbated, in large part, the declining and short average length of stay.[15]

Zambian tour operators are not earning the producer surplus from tourists coming in from Europe, who either book online or use foreign travel agents. By looking to domestic and regional tourists, perhaps Zambian firms can earn a bigger share of revenues. However, to make this happen, Zambian firms need to invest in better technology (e.g., to make bookings, payments), need to develop their industry networks, and need to train more skilled labor (Acorn Tourism Consulting 2018).

The Zambia Tourism Master Plan 2018–23 provides a comprehensive and critical analysis and approach to addressing these issues, so as to successfully grow the tourism sector. It provides clarity and a strategy for growing the sector in a phased way, which, in the best case, could enhance international tourism revenue by $3 billion by 2038 and add 1.63 million arrivals to the current 0.98 million. But it acknowledges that this will require attention to (1) sustained clarity in policy direction toward tourism; (2) improved tourist access, including easy visa processes and air and road connections; (3) an expanded supply of suitable tourist venues, including more three- or four-star accommodations and reduced costs; (4) effective destination promotion of Zambia; and (5) perhaps most importantly, improved management of the sector, which will require a reduction of the bureaucracy, better government coordination, strengthened law enforcement, and more skilled professionals.

Zambia is seen as an expensive tourist destination; a handicap that will need to be addressed, unless Zambia adopts a focus on a high-end clientele, for whom cost may not be a consideration. Transportation connections into and within Zambia are limited and costly. It is often more expensive to fly to Zambia than other tourist destinations in Africa, such as Kenya and South Africa. Across the tourism firms surveyed, the high costs of domestic and international travel were identified as a major constraint on the growth of the sector. Additionally, the lack of a national carrier has rendered traveling to Zambia very expensive compared with other destinations, such as South Africa, Botswana, and Namibia. Internal flights are also expensive.

The potential for Zambian tourism has not been achieved for a number of reasons. In 2018, Acorn Consulting conducted an analysis to determine what is stopping Zambian small and medium-sized enterprises from attracting European customers. They named a number of constraints, including not enough differentiated products, such as activities and accommodations that meet the necessary standards of European tourists. Connectivity between different tourist areas in Zambia is poor. Domestic tourism has been significantly hampered by the poor state of the nation's roads. Although, in recent years Zambia has invested significantly in improving its road network, its road density of 9.1 per 100 square kilometers is still well below the Sub-Saharan average of 14.9 kilometers per 100 square kilometers.

A narrow range of accommodation choices also hinders the growth of tourism. In general, many hotels and lodges are luxury-rated, and there are few mid-range accommodations, the effect of which is to limit tourist options, raise costs, and reduce tourist arrivals and lengths of stay. Skilled labor is a bottleneck, a fact confirmed by the 2018 Acorn Consulting report, which notes that the quality of service staff is a constraint on the sector's development.

ICT. ICT, one of our four IWSS industries of interest, exhibits a growth rate unparalleled by non-IWSS and the overall economy; as such, we dwell on it a bit more—but on a broader level. Between 2005 and 2018, ICT expanded rapidly, on average by 18.5 percent a year, driven in large part by the adoption of modern communications technologies by businesses and government, and a rapidly growing share of the population. Financial accounts in 2017 were accessed digitally by 46 percent of the population, relative to 21 percent in 2011, a fact driven both by the adaptations of banks and financial institutions and wider access to mobile money providers in Zambia. The number of active mobile subscribers almost trebled, from 5.4 million in 2010 to 15.5 million in 2018. Similarly, mobile broadband users increased exponentially, by 2,486 percent, from less than 400,000 to more than 9 million (World Bank 2020a).

Beyond the direct output growth, ICT enables growth in other industries as well by improving productivity. The growth of mobile money, for instance—a derivative of ICT and financial services that is also proving to be a source of employment—has also been unprecedented. Between 2012 and 2018, the volume of mobile money transactions grew exponentially, by 1,644 percent, exceeding the number of transactions vis-à-vis other conventional payment forms. In tandem, the value of transactions grew by 1,807 percent—albeit, this remains below the value of transactions carried out through automated teller machines and electronic funds transfers.

Although the ICT industry has grown explosively, its past performance may not be sustained. First, skill limitations are apparent and will likely cause such growth to stall, and for dependence on foreign expertise to deepen, if not addressed through urgent action to develop a suitable digital curriculum. Second, the World Bank's (2020a) "Diagnostic Report" also pointed to the limited availability of digital entrepreneurship—the capacity to identify opportunity, design solutions, and take risks. The real challenge for Zambia, then, is with regard to upgrading digital technology skills in its population to enable full exploitation of the available infrastructure. Entrepreneurship is a skill that is not easily taught, but once the digital skills are available, there are ways in which angel investors could help develop the entrepreneurial instincts among those who show promise. While there is an incipient growth of digital enterprises—with more firms registering to provide digital services across sectors such as tourism, education, and financial services—there is also tremendous scope for expansion if skill levels are enhanced. The diagnostic report recommends that the government develop a digital transformation strategy to better exploit the potential of ICT, including promoting greater use of digital technologies and paying specific attention to the investments necessary to improve

digital skills. Relaxing this important skills constraint would help cata-
lyze rapid growth of ICT-related enterprises, and related employment for
youth in Zambia in high-productivity occupations. Prospects for attracting foreign investment and generating the exporting of ICT services will
also depend on demonstrated skills to provide reliable services in the
domestic market first, as Kenya has shown.[16]

Trends into the Future: Potential and Labor Demand

In the third section, we showed that between 2005 and 2018, the employment growth rate of IWSS sectors was greater than non-IWSS sectors. In
this section, we show that, under a number of assumptions, future employment growth is expected to be higher in IWSS sectors compared with
non-IWSS sectors.

In "Vision 2030," a document prepared in 2006, the Government of
Zambia outlined an aspirational path to become a "prosperous, middle-
income nation by 2030."[17] This scenario offered the opportunity to examine
how future growth might influence labor demand in IWSS, manufacturing, and non-IWSS sectors. "Vision 2030" provides a basis for projecting
the likely implications for sector-specific growth, and employment elasticities could then be used to estimate employment growth and skill demand
across sectors.

"Vision 2030," in its "preferred scenario," projected growth rates increasing to higher plateaus in each five-year plan period, beginning at 6 percent
and reaching 10 percent for the final decade, 2021–30. Zambia did grow at an
average rate of 7 percent over the 2004–12 period, so such a high growth rate
is conceivable, although the copper boom was a major factor in the high
growth. The 2017–21 five-year plan moderated growth assumptions to 5 percent, a more realistic target.[18] Whether these growth assumptions are realistic
or unlikely in today's postpandemic world is not relevant for the purpose of
this exercise, which is to demonstrate, for any given rate of projected GDP
growth, the potential effects on employment growth and skill requirements.

In our projection, we assume an overall GDP growth rate of 7.2 percent annually from 2018 to 2030. We also assume that IWSS sectors will
grow at 7.6 percent annually, with manufacturing and non-IWSS growing
at 10.5 percent and 7 percent, respectively.[19] With respect to labor demand,
our projections, which are described in table 9-7, are consistent with a story
of continuing structural transformation. We see a significant transition

Table 9-7. Future Projections Based on Aspirational Growth to 2030

Sector	GDP (millions)			Employment		Share of total employment	
	2018	2030 (projected)	Annual growth (%)***	2018	2030 (projected)	2018 %	2030 % (projected)
Total	139,688	323,126	7.2	6,280,898	13,626,686	100	100
IWSS*	42,080	101,183	7.6	389,571	2,601,079	6.2	19
Agro-processing	3,996	12,874	10.2	124,841	873,677	2.0	6
Tourism	8,503	23,943	9.0	118,598	700,032	1.9	5
Transportation and storage, and information and communications technology **	11,154	31,406	9.0	101,333	598,125	1.6	4
Trade (formal)	12,827	17,190	—	85,912	164,819	—	1
Financial and business	14,104	39,713	9.0	163,397	964,458	2.6	7
Manufacturing (excl. agro-processing)	7,282	24,238	10.5	125,670	424,057	2.0	3
Other non-IWSS	82,416	197,706	7.6	5,765,657	10,601,549	91.8	78
Agriculture (incl. horticulture)	8,213	15,158	5.2	3,604,940	6,196,450	57.4	45
Mining	14,932	34,663	7.3	80,513	170,941	1.3	1
Construction	15,175	48,887	10.2	149,874	432,889	2.4	3
Trade (informal)	16,933	22,694	2.5	536,636	691,803	8.5	5
Utilities	2,802	8,156	9.3	22,734	59,647	0.4	0
Government**	7,082	20,610	9.3	76,629	201,047	1.2	1
Domestic services	—	—	—	63,714	—	1.0	—
Other + not stated	17,278	47,538	8.8	1,144,705	2,848,773	18.2	21

Sources: Authors' computations, based on "Vision 2030" from the National Planning Commission.

* Sum of IWSS excludes tourism to avoid double counting.

** Before 2010, transportation and storage was classified with information and communications technology, as per ISIC Revision 3. For comparability over time, we add information and communications technology to transportation and storage in 2018.

*** Aspirational growth projections, based on "Vision 2030."

away from agriculture and toward more productive sectors, with the majority of new formal sector jobs being created in IWSS. The derived employment elasticities were 2.7 across all IWSS, 1.02 for manufacturing, 0.85 for other non-IWSS, and 0.88 for total employment.

Under these assumptions and parameters, IWSS employment shares are projected to expand from 6.2 to 19 percent of total employment by 2030, largely driven by the high employment elasticity of the category. Other non-IWSS shares decline, from 92 to 78 percent of the total. Manufacturing employment shares rise by just 1 percentage point over this period. These employment numbers are a result of the "preferred" GDP growth projection of 7 percent embedded in "Vision 2030." It demonstrates empirically the greater potential for employment creation in IWSS, given its higher employment elasticity. If actual growth rates were lower, overall levels of employment growth, and the shift in labor allocation to IWSS, would be correspondingly lower.

Table 9-8 provides a perspective on how skills demand across industries may shift over the next decade, in line with the projections of labor demand described in table 9-7. In general, the distribution of skills will shift from lower to higher skills, with a narrowing of demand for those with low skills. Within IWSS, finance and business will see the greatest demand for high skills, while agro-processing will require almost three-fourths of its workers to be moderately skilled. The numbers are similar for manufacturing, while mining will require all but 10 percent of its workforce to be highly skilled.

The overall context for Zambia is one where it is not easy to significantly expand the supply of skills in the medium term. Thus, even for moderate rates of overall economic growth in the range of 3 to 5 percent, skill constraints will be a factor limiting the ability of many sectors, but particularly the IWSS industries as well as mining and construction, to expand their output and employment. It would be important, then, for policymakers to be highly aware of this constraint and to ensure that there are as few impediments as possible to the recruitment of higher-level specialized skills from international sources. Regulations that limit the ability of firms to recruit specialized skills would be costly and should be avoided, since they will limit the capacity of firms to invest and expand overall employment. In addition, the incentive for in-service training by Zambian firms could be improved. Identifying and targeting the factors that make firms use this form of skill upgrading would improve opportunities for younger workers.

Over the longer term, Zambia urgently requires a jointly developed public–private strategy and an implementation plan for improving the supply of required skills, particularly among young as well as female workers.

Policies to Promote Employment Growth

The discussion up to this point has established the potential that Zambia needs to grow its output and employment in industries such as agro-processing, horticulture, tourism, and ICT, by noting their potential through their performance over the past 15 years. No industry shows a compelling argument, but each shows potential, which suggests that closer attention to addressing constraints may boost greater employment creation. But what policies will Zambia need to follow to significantly increase and sustain productive employment growth for its growing population?

At the time of writing, Zambia finds itself in a very difficult macro-economic predicament, having defaulted on its external debt, becoming the first African country to do so in 2020. Zambia also confronts the effects of the global COVID-19 pandemic, which has disrupted global trade and travel to an extraordinary extent and has caused producers to reconsider their supply chains. Inevitably, this economic shock will be extremely disruptive, and many firms may not survive the difficult conditions. The policies that will be required for Zambia to achieve its objective of ensuring productive employment for its population will need to take into account the extraordinary conditions that now prevail. However, there are some clear issues for policy attention within Zambia, regardless of the path the world takes to restoring normalcy.

Keeping the Macroeconomy Stable

A necessary condition for economic growth and employment generation is macroeconomic stability. Access to finance at reasonable cost, and a stable exchange rate and tax program, are essential for private investment and enterprise. These are critically necessary but not sufficient conditions for enhanced growth. But absent them, substantial employment growth on the scale required for poverty reduction will remain a goal that will be perennially out of reach. Zambia has wasted the opportunity provided by the Heavily Indebted Poor Countries' debt relief in 2005 by following a fiscally risky approach, borrowing heavily during the copper price boom

Table 9-8. Projected Labor Demand by Skill Level

Sector	2018 %		
	LS	S	HS
Total	45.6	46.6	7.8
IWSS	20.3	66.3	13.4
Agro-processing	27.4	65.9	6.6
Tourism	—	—	—
Transportation and storage / information and communications technology*	17.3	76.0	6.7
Financial and business	16.9	59.8	23.3
Manufacturing (excl. agro-processing)	36.3	56.1	7.6
Other non-IWSS	47.8	44.8	7.4
Agriculture (incl. horticulture)	53.8	43.7	2.5
Mining	13.1	56.6	30.3
Construction	19.6	66.6	13.8
Trade	36.1	58.2	5.7
Utilities	7.3	57.9	34.9
Government*	12.3	61.8	25.8
Domestic services	53.8	46.2	—
Other + not stated	46.6	34.6	18.8

Sources: Authors' own computations, based on ZamStats Labor Force Survey data.

* Before 2010, transportation and storage was classified with information and communications technology, as per ISIC Revision 3. For comparability over time, we add information and communications technology to transportation and storage in 2018.

Note: LS = low skilled; S = skilled; HS = high skilled. Level of education attained is used to proxy skills, owing to the data challenges of using occupations. Skills are defined as low skill if the highest grade completed is equal to or less than 7 but more than 1; skilled if greater than 7 but less or equal to 12; and high skilled if greater than 12. The totals do not include workers with zero years of schooling completed and workers with unstated highest level of education completed. Thus, the total does not add up to the total of workers employed in each industry. Data on workers in the tourism industry by level of education were not available.

	2030 number / % (Projected)						Annual % growth, 2018–30		
Total	LS	S	HS	LS	S	HS	LS	S	HS
9,664,253	1,056,646	4,258,715	4,348,892	10.9	44.1	45.0	2.1	9.2	16.6
9,911,928	155,635	4,437,973	5,318,319	1.6	44.8	53.7	4.2	25.1	38.7
4,058,197	265,932	3,026,315	765,951	6.6	74.6	18.9	7.2	22.0	31.7
2,240,690	31,051	1,980,511	229,127	1.4	88.4	10.2	−0.5	24.4	27.2
3,613,041	28,067	1,146,628	2,438,346	0.8	31.7	67.5	6.1	30.0	49.8
302,281	36,471	228,821	36,989	12.1	75.7	12.2	4.2	17.1	18.9
−549,956	−83,347	−235,552	−231,057	15.2	42.8	42.0	1.9	8.2	15.4
−2,573,635	−1,029,821	−1,461,797	−82,017	40.0	56.8	3.2	1.5	6.4	6.0
76,849	82	6,228	70,539	0.1	8.1	91.8	−2.9	23.3	59.0
231,309	7,575	221,192	2,542	3.3	95.6	1.1	6.4	27.3	—
162,482	22,057	128,412	12,012	13.6	79.0	7.4	5.2	17.1	16.6
30,543	97	16,823	13,623	0.3	55.1	44.6	−7.8	19.1	22.1
102,950	2,100	96,347	4,422	2.1	93.6	4.3	0.3	20.2	—
—	—	—	—	40.5	59.5	—	4.8	9.6	—
1,419,546	255,452	334,411	829,683	18.0	23.6	58.4	2.1	7.1	21.5

to build infrastructure that has rebuilt debt to critical levels. Recognition that booms are short-lived should have prompted forward-looking efforts to set up fiscal rules and finance a stabilization fund, as countries such as Chile have established. Restoring and sustaining macroeconomic stability is a deep policy and institutional challenge that will require attention if the future growth path is to achieve job creation and poverty reduction goals.

Labor Markets Need Flexibility to Create Jobs

Zambia faces a difficult task in creating jobs for its growing population, but an important part of the problem is self-inflicted. From the early years of independence, advisers have warned that the Zambian economy could not have both big increases in wages and growth in jobs, but political forces ensured that this advice was ignored (Seers 1970). First, the formal public sector continues as a privileged sector, where wage increases are not linked to labor productivity, the effect of which is to disadvantage other sectors competing for skills. Second, Zambia has a multiplicity of labor laws and regulations that are often enacted with little consultation with employers, which raise the cost of labor and limit the ability of firms to adjust the workforce during lean times (Masumbu and Mwenge 2017). These include provisions on minimum wages, severance packages, housing allowances, and a ban on "casualization." Despite firms being mandated to contribute to the National Pensions and Social Security Authority toward an employee's social protection, they are additionally required to pay two months' salary for every year completed as a redundancy package for an employee being laid off. When severance pay arises from a firm's low performance, such as during an economic downturn, these severance packages are often unaffordable and may lead to a company ceasing operations altogether. The recent Employment Code Act significantly increases the regulatory constraints on and related costs for employers, and further undermines the scope for formal sector employment growth.

Under these conditions, firms are averse to hiring labor, and incline toward less labor-intensive production technologies or avoiding investment altogether. This situation may also exacerbate a bias against younger workers, whose lower skills and lack of experience may already be a disadvantage in the job market. The rigidity of the formal labor market is a strong factor in explaining the stunting of the formal sector and the sprawling growth of the informal sector, where 70 percent of young job-seekers earn a living. Current labor market policies and institutions maroon millions of Zambians in low-productivity, informal sector occupations that cannot provide a decent living.

Instead of reforming policies to help achieve flexible labor markets, the country has unwisely sought to deepen its labor laws and regulations. While the instinct to protect workers is understandable, such policies are demonstrably hurting workers; particularly youth entering the labor market. Each of the three national development plans since 2006 has included a long list of measures aimed at protecting the fundamental rights of workers. The measures have been subsequently picked up in various legislative amendments. The culmination has been the 2019 Employment Code, which introduced a number of mandatory benefits, like a housing allowance that had been done away with in the 1990s. Coming at a time of high interest rates, unstable exchange rates, and slow business even before the COVID-19 pandemic, this new code has forced many firms to cease operations altogether and lay off workers. Amending this wrong-headed approach to labor markets will be essential for creating the enabling environment for formal sector growth and productive job creation, both in IWSS and in manufacturing, but also in non-IWSS. Any policy that has stubbornly resisted change for many decades suggests strong political interest in its retention, so we need to acknowledge the difficulty of this political economy challenge. However, the opportunity costs for millions of young Zambians of allowing narrow self-interest to prevail should be recognized and, if widely understood, may spur change.

Skill Development Should Be a Priority

Sustained improvements in productivity will require a strategy and continuous investment in developing Zambia's human capital, more so in a world where new technologies require higher skills and adaptability. This will require a solid foundation at the base of the population pyramid, where Zambia needs to ensure that primary and secondary schools provide equitable access to education for children in every region, while also enhancing the capacity of higher educational institutions to provide specialized skills to those preparing to enter the labor market in skilled positions. Recent research has shown that the distribution of teachers in Zambia is highly uneven across the provinces and even within provinces; the result of which is to limit opportunities for students in many parts of the country (Walter 2019). This built-in inequality in access to education clearly should be remedied to enable equitable growth and development. Preparing students for a world where digital technologies are the norm needs to begin at the school level, and this access to appropriate curriculums should be provided across the country. As noted in the discussion on ICT, Zambia has an immense potential to grow the industry, but it will need to make a sustained effort to develop skills broadly in the population, with an appropriate expansion of science, technology, engineering, and mathematics training. The potential for ICT services to grow is particularly dependent on skills to manage and implement the new technologies, and will require adapting curriculums, even at the school level, to facilitate such skill acquisition.

The use of training and vocational education is likely to be important to imparting skills that are required by employers, but the design of these programs should include strong collaboration with the private sector to ensure that relevant skill shortages are addressed. As noted in the discussion of value chains in tourism, Zambia wisely invested in developing its Tourism Master Plan in 2018. Effective implementation of this plan would require attention to improving the quality of training institutions, and for teaching professionals to enable a sustained upgrading of skills required by firms in the sector. Similarly, for success to be broad based and sustained in agro-processing and horticulture, a significant upstream effort will also be required to expand the availability of agronomists and other scientists who could support the increase in quality and productivity of horticulture and floriculture outputs for export.

Agriculture Productivity Is Important

Any strategy for sustained growth in Zambia must attend to the dismal and declining productivity of the agricultural sector—both because it is the livelihood of a majority of Zambians, and because a successful and growing agro-processing sector will require it. Policies to enhance agricultural diversification and growth both by smallholders and commercial farmers should not be neglected, and efforts should be made to strengthen the value chain connections to downstream agro-processors, and ultimately to domestic and foreign consumers. There is a role for the government in facilitating the collaboration and coordination with the private sector that will be necessary to make such development successful.

Transportation Connections Matter

Addressing the specific constraints faced by the IWSS industries will be another important area for policy attention. Restoring direct air connections to Europe and to other export markets appears to be another critical condition to enable horticulture, floriculture, and tourism to expand output and employment. Internal road networks are also important for domestic as well as regional and foreign trade – including tourism. Zambia has invested substantially in its road network over the past decade and some recent research by the International Growth Centre (Peng and Chen 2020) suggests that such infrastructure investment may improve the quality of life in settlements by improving access to markets, with a potential positive impact on IWSS, including agro-processing and tourism. However, it remains important to ensure good ex ante cost benefit analysis in selecting the projects, as well as transparent procurement and project implementation, to ensure that the investment provides a cost-efficient and well-maintained asset, and the benefits to the population exceed the costs.

Accurate Data and Timely Analysis Are Foundational

Given the importance of employment issues for the welfare of Zambians, there is a critical need for accurate and timely data on a range of issues related to the labor market. In particular, consistent long-term data are required on the labor force, labor force participation, employment across industries, the size and nature of formal and informal employment, unemployment and underemployment rates by age and gender, and the supply and demand for skills across industries, to name a few. In the course of undertaking this study, it became apparent that there are significant inconsistencies in the labor force and employment data.[20] Both Zambian and international researchers would benefit from attention to improving the quality, consistency, and timeliness of such data in order to enhance empirical research. In turn, the government will benefit from solid research in designing evidence-based policies for job creation and productivity enhancement. This important challenge would require a joint effort by the public, private, and academic sectors under the leadership of the government.

Conclusion

Zambia faces an immense challenge in generating productive and decent employment for its burgeoning population. Structural transformation is taking place, but at a pace and in a pattern that reveal both problems and promise. Workers leaving the declining agricultural sector, and others entering the labor market, are being forced to find livelihoods in the informal sector, largely in informal trade—a sector characterized by low productivity and low incomes. Both unemployment and underemployment disproportionately affect younger workers, whose capacity to contribute productively is being lost.

A necessary condition for any effective growth and employment generation process is macroeconomic stability. After a creditable first decade (2001–10), during which it was better managed, macroeconomic stability has steadily eroded over the past decade, to the point where Zambia defaulted on its external debt in 2020. While concerns about an unsustainable fiscal policy have been repeatedly raised by both domestic and external analysts over the past five years, the government has delayed and resisted making the necessary policy and budgetary adjustments. This delay has been costly and had rendered the objectives of "Vision 2030" unattainable. Macroeconomic stability will need to be restored and sustained in Zambia for any of the propsed interventions to improve industrial employment and growth to achieve their full potential.

The overall growth of the formal sector in recent years has also been constrained by, among other things, increasing labor market regulations that raise the cost of labor and limit the ability of firms to respond to changing market conditions. Until recently, these regulations largely applied to the formal sector, constraining its growth and exacerbating the expansion of the informal sector. Reforming labor regulations would go a long way toward creating a healthier process of structural transformation, enhancing job creation in the formal sector, and enabling workers to be employed in higher-productivity activities. Even the manufacturing sector might do better and contribute to job creation with less onerous labor regulations.

Despite this policy-induced (and, therefore, correctable) handicap, there is a promise of growth in output and employment in the IWSS sectors, notably in agro-processing, horticulture, floriculture, tourism, and ICT. In each of these industries, firms have shown the ability to exploit Zambia's comparative advantage and create productive job opportunities across different skill levels, more than other sectors. However, each of these industries also faces particular constraints that will need to be addressed, some of which are amenable to policy intervention. Logistical constraints are a hurdle for floriculture and horticulture to reach high-value export markets in Europe; but if that key constraint is addressed, there is a great potential for growth in employment, output, and exports. Agro-processing has a great potential both in the domestic market and in regional markets, but it will require the development of value chains between growers and processors, and between processors and retail shopping outlets. Tourism faces both logistical hurdles along with costs imposed by regulations.

All sectors will require investment in skills to ensure that firms are able to recruit the necessary capabilities to sustain quality and grow their markets. Nowhere is this more important than in the nascent ICT industry, where demand for digital services is strong but skill shortages are already evident. If Zambia is to develop its high-productivity services, including ICT and finance and business services, it will need to call on a deeper reservoir of skilled talent than is currently available. This implies that Zambia will need to urgently develop and implement a deep strategy of education and training to create the requisite generation of skilled technology workers to fuel and manage the expansion of this sector. Tourism, another promising sector, has the advantage that the government has developed the Tourism Master Plan, whose effective implementation—no easy task—would greatly enhance growth prospects in the sector. If these constraints are addressed, the process of productive job creation will be significantly improved and, with it, the standard of living for a growing share of the population.

The rewards to Zambia for accomplishing these necessary improvements in policies and implementation with regard to macroeconomic management, labor market regulation, and skill development would be substantial. While creating the conditions for broad-based growth across sectors, including manufacturing, it would also enable the IWSS sectors to expand output and productive employment for the burgeoning youth workforce. Structural transformation of this nature would enable important progress to the goals outlined in "Vision 2030."

NOTES

1. Contributions from S. Haria, R. Tabetando, P. Mathewson, and H. Chomba are acknowledged.

2. Research commissioned by the International Growth Centre, Zambia. The World Bank and Zambia CSO estimates for the Gini coefficient for Zambia for 2015 is 57.1, substantially lower than the estimate cited above, which is explained by the fact that Bhorat et al. (2018) use income rather than expenditures to measure inequality.

3. For more details on the methodological problems of the Labour Force Surveys, see Rajaram et al. (2021).

4. ILO data for 2012–18 suggest that unemployment rates did dip by 2 to 3 percentage points for both the 15–19 and 20–24 age groups in 2012–14 but rose sharply to about 24 percent by 2018 as economic growth slowed dramatically.

5. Arnold and Mattoo (2007) noted that while services have grown consistently over the period 1966–2002, at an annual average growth rate of 3 percent, its growth appeared impressive only relative to the low overall average GDP growth of 1.4 percent over the same period. Also, growth of services such as tourism, transport and communications, and finance and insurance, lagged behind less dynamic sectors such as community and social services, and wholesale and retail trade (p. 62).

6. Manufacturing employment grew in absolute and relative terms during a period when manufacturing's share of GDP declined. This is likely due to growth in some more labor-intensive industries relative to those that declined or grew at lower rates.

7. In some instances, we single out agro-processing, tourism, ICT, and horticulture as IWSS with the most potential for employment creation and economic transformation in Zambia.

8. Changes in statistical method between 2005 and 2018 complicate inferences about directions of change in labor productivity through 2018, so trends over this period cannot be computed. But the 2018 data is considered relatively robust so relative productivities in 2018 can be reliably estimated.

9. Agro-processing, financial and business, and formal trade became significantly less productive over the period under review. The marked reduction in labor productivity in agro-processing (84 percent) and corresponding increase in manufacturing (218 percent), are interesting to note but we suspect this is an artefact of the data. Between 2009 and 2010, we observe a step in the time series gross value-added data for manufacturing and agro-processing. Gross value added jumped by 379 percent from ZMW 963 million in 2009 to ZMW 3.9 billion in 2010 for manufacturing. Conversely, gross value added nearly halved for agro-processing from ZMW 6.3 billion in 2009 to ZMW 3.5 billion in 2010. This abrupt change is borne out of the change in the variable used to disaggregate gross value added according to manufacturing subsectors. Before 2010, ZamStats relied on the Industrial Production Index for this disaggregation. Following the rebasing of the national accounts in 2010, the Economic Census became the basis of the computation of the gross value added for manufacturing sub-sectors.

10. Most copper exports are classified as manufactured basic metals. We exclude exports of manufactured basic metals from manufacturing in order to better gauge and reflect the performance and contribution of non-mining manufactured exports.

11. Data from ITC indicate that Zambia is a major exporter of sulfuric acid and cobalt oxides, accounting for between 9-11 percent of world trade in these items in 2017.

12. The 2018 data proved to be more reliable in terms of being clearly labelled with a detailed questionnaire that was easy to follow. Further, the 2018 data had a lower share of workers with unstated economic activities.

13. "Analysis of Constraints to Inclusive Growth in Zambia," Millennium Challenge Corporation, 2011.

14. Office of the Auditor General, "Report of the Auditor General on the Performance of the Tourism Sector in Ensuring an Increase in the Length of Stay of International Tourists," 2020.

15. Office of the Auditor General.

16. "Kenya's Reputation for Quality Leads Companies to Choose Nairobi," *Financial Times*, November 1, 2019.

17. The "optimistic scenario" assumed that growth would increase steadily from 6 percent to 14 percent over the 24 years (National Planning Commission 2006).

18. See the 2017–21 Five Year Plan, https://www.mndp.gov.zm/wp-content/uploads/2018/05/7NDP.pdf.

19. Over the years 2010–18, the compound annual GDP growth rate was 4.4 percent, while IWSS grew at 4.6 percent, manufacturing at 8.1 percent and other non-IWSS at 4.4 percent. Given the assumption of GDP growth of 7.2 percent over 2018–30, the corresponding growth rates for the three categories are assumed to be 7.6 percent, 10.5 percent, and 7 percent, respectively.

20. E.g., official figures suggest that the labor force dropped from 6.3 million in 2014 to 3.3 million in 2018. Since the working-age population in 2018 was 9.5 million, this suggests that 6.2 million are considered to be "outside the labor force." Similarly, the labor force participation rate drops sharply, from 78 to 35 percent, between 2014 and 2018. Such large discrepancies need to be fully explained in order to sustain the credibility of labor data and to ensure accurate tracking of real trends. Lack of disaggregated employment data by youth age 15–24 years and by two-digit ISIC classification of economic activities also limits analysis of issues regarding youth employment.

REFERENCES

Acorn Consulting Ltd. 2018. "Zambia Tourism Sector Value Chain Analysis." CBI, Amsterdam.

Arnold, J., and A. Mattoo. 2007. "Services in the Zambian Economy." In *Services, Trade, and Development: The Experience of Zambia*, ed. A. Mattoo and L. Payton. London: Palgrave Macmillan.

Bhorat, H., N. Kachingwe, M. Oosthuizen, and D. Yu. 2018. "Growth and Inequality in Zambia." Development Policy Research Unit, University of Cape Town.

Cilliers, J. 2018. "Made in Africa: Manufacturing and the Fourth Industrial Revolution." Institute for Security Studies.

Fox, L., A. H. Thomas, and C. Haines. 2017. "Structural Transformation in Employment and Productivity: What Can Africa Hope For?" International Monetary Fund.

ILO and OECD (International Labor Organization and Organization for Economic Cooperation and Development). 2018. "Informality and Poverty in Zambia, Findings from the 2015 Living Conditions and Monitoring Survey."

Masumbu, G., and F. Mwenge. 2017. "Labor Market Regulations and Labor Market Outcomes in Zambia: A Firm's Perspective." Zambia Institute for Policy Analysis and Research, Policy Paper 4.

Millenium Challenge Corporation. 2011. "Analysis of Constrains to Inclusive Growth in Zambia."

National Planning Commission. 2006. "Vision 2030." https://www.mndp.gov.zm/wp-content/uploads/filebase/vision_2030/Vision-2030.pdf.

Peng, C., and W. Chen. 2020. "Does Paving Roads Improve the Quality of Life? Examining the Zambian Context Using AI." Working paper, International Growth Centre. https://www.theigc.org/project/the-impact-of-infrastructure-improvement-on-urban-life-quality-and-firm-output/.

Rajaram, S., et al. 2021. "Addressing Zambia's Youth Unemployment through Industries without Smokestacks." Unpublished working paper, International Growth Centre.

Republic of Zambia. 2005–18. Various Labour Force surveys. Zambia Statistical Agency.

———. 2018a. "2017–21 Five Year Plan." https://www.mndp.gov.zm/wpcontent/uploads/2018/05/7NDP.pdf.

———. 2018b. "Zambia Tourism Master Plan 2018–2023." Ministry of Tourism and Arts. https://www.mota.gov.zm/wp-content/uploads/2020/03/Zambia-Tourism-Master-Plan.pdf.

———. 2020. "Report of the Auditor General on the Performance of the Tourism Sector in Ensuring an Increase in the Length of Stay of International Tourists." Office of the Auditor General.

Saasa, O., and F. Mwenge. 2020. "Critical Assessment of the Employment Code Act." Premier Consult Ltd.

Seers. D. 1970. "Urbanization in Zambia, 1970: An International Urbanization Survey Report to the Ford Foundation."

Walter, T. 2019. "The Allocation of Teachers Across Public Primary Schools in Zambia." International Growth Centre. https://www.theigc.org/publication/the-allocation-of-teachers-across-public-primary-schools-in-zambia/.

World Bank. 2003. "Zambia Post-Privatization Study." Operations Evaluation
    Department.
———. 2017. "Jobs Diagnostic: Zambia."
———. 2018. "Enterprise Skills and Firm Performance in Zambia: Evidence
    from Structural Equation Modeling of a Skills Demand Model."
———. 2020a. "Accelerating Digital Transformation in Zambia: Digital Econ-
    omy Diagnostic Report."
———. 2020b. "Doing Business: Comparing Business Regulation in 190
    Economies."

TEN

South Africa

In Search of an Employment Escape to a Growth Path

CAITLIN ALLEN, ZAAKHIR ASMAL, HAROON BHORAT, ROBERT HILL,

JABULILE MONNAKGOTLA, MORNÉ OOSTHUIZEN,

AND CHRISTOPHER ROONEY

The Employment Challenge: Education and Skill Constraints

South Africa has been in a long-run, low-growth trap since the onset of democratic rule in 1994. Between 1994 and 2008, real gross domestic product (GDP) per capita growth was between 1 and 3 percent, with a sharp decline in 2009. Since 2010, real GDP per capita growth has been below 2 percent, with the rate of growth turning negative in 2014. The impact of this poor economic growth on the labor market has been significant: In 2018, 16.4 million individuals were employed in the South African economy, with 6.1 million unemployed, rendering the national unemployment rate 27.1 percent (table 10-1). If we include discouraged work seekers—defined as

Table 10-1. Employment Patterns and Salient Features in South Africa, 2010–18

Aspect of employment	2010	2018	Absolute change	Annualized % change
Labor market aggregates ('000s)				
Working-age population	32,007	37,907	5,900	2.1
Employment	13,061	16,394	3,333	2.9
Narrow unemployment	4,332	6,103	1,771	4.4
Narrow labor force	17,393	22,496	5,103	3.3
Expanded unemployment	6,330	8,909	2,579	4.4
Expanded labor force	19,391	25,303	5,912	3.4
Discouraged work seekers	1,998	2,806	808	4.3
Labor force participation rate (LFPR) (%)				
Narrow LFPR	54.3	59.3	5.0	1.1
Youth narrow LFPR	25.9	25.4	-0.5	-0.2
Expanded LFPR	60.6	66.7	6.2	1.2
Youth expanded LFPR	32.3	32.9	0.6	0.2
Unemployment rate (%)				
Narrow unemployment rate (all)	24.9	27.1	2.2	1.1
Narrow unemployment rate (youth)	50.5	53.4	2.9	0.7
Expanded unemployment rate (all)	32.6	35.2	2.6	1.0
Expanded unemployment rate (youth)	60.3	64.0	3.6	0.7

Sources: Authors' calculations using data from Kerr, Lam, and Wittenberg (2019).

Note: Narrow unemployment refers to individuals who are currently unemployed and who have actively looked for work in the recent past (typically in the past four weeks). Broad unemployment includes the narrow unemployed and the unemployed who are not searching for jobs (Kingdon and Knight 2005).

those who want to work but are not actively seeking employment—then a further 2.8 million unemployed are added, resulting in an expanded unemployment rate of 35 percent. This situation is particularly dire for youth age 15 to 24 years: The narrow and expanded unemployment rates for youth are substantially higher than those of the overall population, at 53.4 percent and 64 percent, respectively.

Figure 10-1 highlights the stark differences in unemployment rates between education levels. Those who have not completed secondary education face the highest unemployment rates, although this line is very close

FIGURE 10-1. **Narrow Unemployment Rates
by Education Level, 2000–2019**

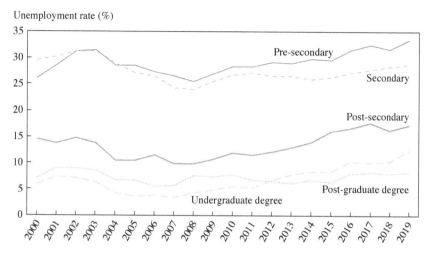

Sources: Authors' calculations using data from Kerr, Lam, and Wittenberg (2019).

to that for individuals who have completed secondary schooling. Degree holders, both undergraduate and postgraduate, generally have much lower unemployment rates, although unemployment has been increasing among even this group in recent years. Thus, addressing South Africa's unemployment will require not only an increased number of jobs but also an increased number of the *right* jobs: In short, South Africa is particularly in need of the types of jobs that can provide employment to those with lower levels of education.

It is evident that South Africa's current economic growth trajectory is not producing the volume and types of jobs required to reverse these trends in unemployment. Manufacturing, traditionally one of the largest employers of low-skilled workers, experienced an annual growth rate of less than 1 percent between 2010 and 2018. Instead, there has been a shift to services.

This chapter is structured as follows. First, we examine the sectoral patterns of economic growth in South Africa. This is followed by a comparative assessment of industries without smokestacks (IWSS) and the non-IWSS sectors. We then identify constraints on growth in four specific IWSS sectors and provide a quantitative analysis of future employment growth between 2019 and 2028. This quantitative analysis is supplemented by a firm survey, which we use to better understand the skill requirements of firms in these sectors. Based on our findings, we conclude the chapter by discussing a number of policy implications.

Patterns of Growth: The Role of the IWSS Sectors

We begin this chapter by examining the structural transformation of the South African economy. Figure 10-2 brings together output and employment growth to give a holistic picture of industry changes over time and shows the correlation between the natural log of relative productivity (measured as value added per worker), and the change in employment by industry for South Africa between 1995 and 2019. In the figure, the size of each bubble represents the sector's share of employment in 2019. The linear regression line indicates whether the structural transformation is

FIGURE 10-2. Correlation between Sectoral Productivity and Change in Employment in South Africa, 1995–2019

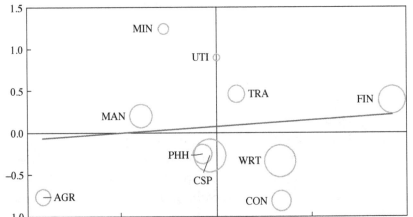

Natural log of sectoral productivity/Total productivity

Change in employment share, 1995–2019 (%)

Sources: Authors' calculations using SARB (2019).

Note: AGR = agriculture; MIN = mining; MAN = manufacturing; UTI = utilities; CON = construction; WRT = wholesale and retail trade; TRA = transportation services; FIN = financial and business services; CSP = community, social, and personal services; PHH = private households.

growth-inducing (positively sloped) or not (negatively sloped). The desired change over time would be declining shares of employment in low-productivity sectors (the lower left quadrant) and increased shares of employment in high-productivity sectors (the top right quadrant).

For South Africa, between 1995 and 2019, although the slope of the regression line is positive, the estimated coefficient is insignificant (p value = 0.72), indicating that there is no evidence of growth-inducing structural transformation. In other words, labor resources have shifted from low-productivity sectors such as agriculture to other low-productivity sectors such as community, social, and personal services, wholesale and retail trade, and transportation. To a lesser extent, employment has also shifted to higher-productivity sectors like construction, and financial and business services.

This pattern of structural transformation contrasts with what has been observed in the East Asian countries, with manufacturing in the top right quadrant—that is, a shift in labor resources to high-productivity manufacturing industries. In South Africa's case, the opposite has occurred, with manufacturing in the top left quadrant, suggesting a shift of labor away from this high-productivity industry. Shifts toward higher-productivity activities have been concentrated in the financial and business services and transportation sectors—both predominantly tertiary sectors.

These trends in productivity growth, combined with the increase in employment shares of finance and transportation, suggest that nonmanufacturing sectors—specifically, tertiary sectors—are already an important component of the South African economy. Unlike emerging economies in Asia, structural transformation in South Africa has gone straight from low-productivity agriculture to high-productivity services, with no stop at manufacturing along the way.

South Africa has bypassed the traditional Lewis model of structural transformation and begun the process of deindustrialization. In the context of this deindustrialization, this chapter explores whether other sectors that share several characteristics with manufacturing (so-called industries without smokestacks, IWSS) have the potential to fulfill the role of manufacturing in the structural transformation of an economy when manufacturing is unable to do so. We start with a detailed comparison of the composition of employment in IWSS and non-IWSS sectors in the next section.

Here, we have presented an overview of the trends in growth and structural transformation in South Africa, noting a decline in manufacturing and a shift toward services instead. The decline in manufacturing is a cause for concern, given that this sector has been widely understood to be a key driver of structural transformation in an economy. In the next section, we consider whether other sectors, which share a number of characteristics with manufacturing, have the potential to fill the role traditionally expected to be industrialization in an economy. These sectors, termed IWSS, have these shared characteristics:

1. They are tradable.
2. They have high value added per worker relative to average economy-wide productivity.
3. They exhibit the capacity for technological change and productivity growth and show some evidence of scale and/or agglomeration economies.
4. They have the ability to employ large numbers of low- and moderately skilled labor.

Sectoral Decomposition: IWSS Sectors in Comparative Perspective

Our analysis of the data identified eight IWSS sectors in the private formal sector in South Africa: agro-processing, horticulture, commercial agriculture (excluding horticulture), tourism, information and communications technologies (ICT), transit trade, financial and business services, and trade.[1] In this section, we consider employment in these IWSS sectors in comparison with the non-IWSS sectors. The non-IWSS sectors include mining, manufacturing (excluding agro-processing), construction, utilities, and community, social, and personal services. Informal, government and domestic employment are excluded from consideration in the discussion of IWSS versus non-IWSS sectors because we are concerned only with those sectors that have the potential for wide-scale expansion to absorb the labor force.[2] The discussion is restricted to employment and not GDP, as disaggregated IWSS-sector-level GDP data are not available.

We compare the numbers of jobs in IWSS sectors with those in non-IWSS sectors, noting to what extent IWSS sectors account for formal private employment in South Africa and consider the demographic of employment in the IWSS sectors (as a whole) in comparison with non-IWSS sectors. Table 10-2 shows employment in the formal private sector in the IWSS and non-IWSS sectors, as well as in individual IWSS sectors, in both 2010 and 2018.

Table 10-2. Formal Private Employment in IWSS and Non-IWSS Sectors in South Africa, 2010–18

Sector	2010 ('000)	2018 ('000)	Employment share (%) 2010	2018	Absolute ('000)	Share of change (%)	Annual growth
Total formal private employment	7,069	8,806	100.0	100.0	1,737	100.0	2.8
Total IWSS	4,627	5,873	65.5	66.7	1,246	71.8	3.0
Agro-processing	549	593	11.9	10.1	43	3.5	0.9
Horticulture	243	331	5.2	5.6	88	7.1	3.9
Commercial agriculture (excl. horticulture)	146	200	3.2	3.4	54	4.3	4.0
Tourism	669	849	14.5	14.5	180	14.5	3.0
ICT	81	74	1.8	1.3	-7	-0.6	-1.2
Transit trade	332	436	7.2	7.4	104	8.3	3.5
Financial and business services	1,421	2,020	30.7	34.4	599	48.1	4.5
Trade (excl. tourism)	1,185	1,371	25.6	23.3	186	14.9	1.8
Total non-IWSS	2,442	2,933	34.5	33.3	491	28.2	2.3
Mining	298	406	12.2	13.8	107	21.9	3.9
Manufacturing (excl. agro-processing)	873	851	35.7	29.0	-21	-4.4	-0.3
Utilities	77	124	3.1	4.2	47	9.7	6.2
Construction	525	643	21.5	21.9	118	24.1	2.6
Community, social, and personal services	667	902	27.3	30.7	235	47.8	3.8

Sources: Authors' calculations using data from Kerr, Lam, and Wittenberg (2019).

IWSS activities account for two-thirds (66.7 percent) of 8.8 million formal private sector jobs in South Africa in 2018, up from 65.5 percent of 7.8 million jobs in 2010. Two sectors account for close to two-thirds of this employment: financial and business services (34.4 percent), and trade (23.3 percent). The share of financial and business services has, however, increased from 30.7 percent, while the share of trade has declined from 25.6 percent. Horticulture and transit trade have also seen increases in their share of IWSS employment.

The importance of IWSS sectors is clear when we consider the share of change in formal private employment between 2010 and 2018, with the increase in IWSS employment accounting for 71.8 percent of the change in employment over the period. All IWSS sectors have seen an increase in employment, apart from ICT (declining at a rate of 1.2 percent a year). ICT, however, accounted for just 1.3 percent of total IWSS employment in 2019.

Non-IWSS sectors account for close to 3 in 10 new jobs in the formal private employment sector over the period 2010–18. The dominant contributor to employment growth in these sectors is community, social, and personal services, which grew at a rate of 3.8 percent a year, and accounts for just under half (47.1 percent) of the increase in non-IWSS employment over the period. It is, thus, clear that IWSS sectors became more important contributors to employment in South Africa between 2010 and 2018, with IWSS employment increasing at an average annual rate of 3.0 percent, compared with 2.3 percent for non-IWSS sectors' employment.

It is also clear that, within the IWSS sectors, one sector dominates with respect to the increase in employment: financial and business services account for close to half (48.1 percent) of the increase in employment in the IWSS sectors, growing at an annual average rate of 4.5 percent. The next fastest-growing sectors in employment are commercial agriculture and horticulture. Employment in these sectors has grown at a rate of 4.0 percent a year. Collectively, these two sectors account for 11.4 percent of the change in total IWSS employment. Tourism and transit trade have also seen considerable growth: employment in both grew at a rate in excess of 3 percent a year, accounting for 14.5 and 8.3 percent, respectively, of total IWSS employment growth over the period. Trade has grown at a relatively lower rate of 1.8 percent a year. However, it still accounts for the second-highest share of the change in total IWSS employment (14.9 percent) over the period.

Three sectors (financial and business services, tourism, and trade), therefore, accounted for three-quarters of the growth in employment in the IWSS sectors, with financial and business services being the major contributor to this growth. However, commercial agriculture, horticulture, and transit trade have also seen employment growth greater than the average growth in IWSS employment, while trade employment has been growing at a rate lower than the overall IWSS average. These trends suggest that, apart from the dominant financial and business services sector, there may be considerable employment growth potential in the IWSS sectors of tourism, horticulture, commercial agriculture, and transit trade.

Table 10-3 shows the change in and composition of employment in IWSS and non-IWSS sectors by education and skill level. In 2018, 35.3 percent of those employed in the IWSS sectors had less than a secondary education, compared with 35.2 percent of those employed in the non-IWSS sectors. Of those employed in IWSS, 42.4 percent had completed a secondary education, compared with 34.8 percent in non-IWSS. Over three-quarters (77.7 percent) of IWSS employment was, thus, accounted for by individuals with a secondary or lower level of education in 2018 (down slightly from 78.5 percent in 2010). In non-IWSS sectors, the share is 70 percent of employment (down from 72.4 percent in 2010).

Overall, our results show that IWSS sectors are more intensive in employment of individuals with lower levels of education, showing higher growth in employment for the two lower educational attainment groups than non-IWSS sectors. This trend is confirmed by our results in the lower half of table 10-3, which shows that low-skilled employment accounts for just over a fifth (20.3 percent) of all employment in IWSS sectors, compared with 16.9 percent for non-IWSS employment. Low-skilled employment is also the fastest-growing occupational category of employment across both the IWSS and non-IWSS sectors, growing at an annual average rate of 4.2 percent and 4.3 percent a year, respectively.

Skilled employment accounts for 61.3 percent of IWSS employment (down from 61.9 percent in 2010) and 64.7 percent of non-IWSS employment (down from 66.6 percent in 2009). Highly skilled employment accounts for 18.5 percent of employment in the IWSS sectors (down from 19.6 percent in 2010), and 18.4 percent of non-IWSS employment (down from 18.9 percent in 2010). This profile of employment suggests that the IWSS sectors are more intensive in low-skilled occupations. However low-skilled employment has grown at similar rates in both sectors. The profile also suggests that, while skilled employment accounts for a similar share of employment in both sectors and has seen its share decline in both sectors, the decline in share has been greater in IWSS sectors. This finding suggests that lower-skilled employment is becoming more important over time in

Table 10-3. Education Level and Occupational Structure of IWSS and Non-IWSS Workers, 2010–18

Education Level	Absolute change, 2010–18		Employment share, 2010		Employment share, 2018		Average annual growth		
	IWSS ('000s)	Non-IWSS ('000s)	IWSS (%)	Non-IWSS (%)	IWSS (%)	Non-IWSS (%)	IWSS (%)	Non-IWSS (%)	Total (%)
Total	1,246	491	100	100	100	100	3.0	2.3	2.8
By education									
Less than secondary	277	100	38.8	38.2	35.3	35.2	1.8	1.3	1.6
Secondary complete	653	184	39.7	34.2	42.4	34.8	3.9	2.5	3.5
Postsecondary	323	216	20.4	26.1	21.6	29.1	3.7	3.7	3.7
By skill level									
Highly skilled	180	78	19.6	18.9	18.5	18.4	2.3	2.0	2.2
Skilled	734	271	61.9	66.6	61.3	64.7	2.9	1.9	2.6
Low skilled	332	142	18.6	14.5	20.3	16.9	4.2	4.3	4.2

Sources: Authors' calculations using data from Kerr, Lam, and Wittenberg (2019).

the IWSS sectors. Furthermore, across all levels of skill, in absolute numbers, increases in employment have been greater in the IWSS sectors.

Although the gap between the share of low-skilled workers in the IWSS and non-IWSS sectors has decreased marginally, IWSS sectors remain more intensive in low-skilled occupations, and this intensity is increasing over time. While employment opportunities for skilled and highly skilled employment opportunities are also increasing, the shares of these skill categories are shrinking, albeit at a minimal pace. This finding suggests that IWSS sectors may be better placed than non-IWSS ones to provide jobs for the low-skilled unemployed in South Africa, while still providing jobs that can accommodate the more highly skilled among the labor force as well.

Focus on Vulnerable Groups: Women and Youth

An important consideration of IWSS sectors is whether growth in these sectors is more inclusive than non-IWSS sectors. The Organization for Economic Cooperation and Development (OECD 2018) defines inclusive growth as "economic growth that creates opportunities for all groups of the population and distributes the dividends of increased prosperity, both in monetary and non-monetary terms, fairly across society." In our analysis, we focus on two groups that have historically been underrepresented in the South African labor market: women and youth.

Table 10-4 shows the change in and composition of employment in IWSS and non-IWSS sectors by gender and age. Notably, IWSS employment is more female-intensive than non-IWSS employment, with 41.9 percent of employment in the sector accounted for by women in 2018, compared with 33.3 percent in non-IWSS sectors. The female share of employment has increased in both sectors, up from 40.3 percent in 2010 for the IWSS sectors, and from 31.7 percent for the non-IWSS sectors.

In 2018, those age 15 to 24 years accounted for 8.9 percent of employment in IWSS sectors and 5.4 percent of employment in non-IWSS sectors. The share of those age 25 to 34 in employment is also higher in the IWSS sectors than the non-IWSS sectors: 33.9 percent, in comparison with 29. 0 percent. IWSS sectors, thus, seem to be slightly more intensive in employing youth.

In terms of changes in the profile of employment over time by age, employment of those age 15 to 24 years has declined in non-IWSS sectors (at a rate of 0.5 percent a year) and has remained virtually unchanged in IWSS sectors. Employment of those age 25 to 34 years has, however, increased in both IWSS and non-IWSS sectors, with the rate of increase

Table 10-4. Demographic Characteristics of IWSS and Non-IWSS Sectors, 2010–18

Characteristic	Absolute change, 2010–18		Employment share 2010		Employment share 2018		Average annual growth		
	IWSS ('000s)	Non-IWSS ('000s)	IWSS (%)	Non-IWSS (%)	IWSS (%)	Non-IWSS (%)	IWSS (%)	Non-IWSS (%)	Total (%)
Total	1,246	491	100	100	100	100	3.0	2.3	2.8
By gender									
Male	648	290	59.7	68.3	58.1	66.7	2.7	2.0	2.4
Female	598	201	40.3	31.7	41.9	33.3	3.5	2.9	3.4
By age in years									
15–24	4	–31	11.2	7.8	8.9	5.4	0.1	–2.2	–0.5
25–34	294	63	36.6	32.2	33.9	29.0	2.0	1.0	1.7
35–65	946	454	51.2	59.0	56.4	64.6	4.3	3.5	4.0

Sources: Authors' calculations using data from Kerr, Lam, and Wittenberg (2019).

higher in the IWSS sectors (2 percent a year, in comparison with 1 percent per year for non-IWSS). The greatest growth in both the IWSS and non-IWSS sectors has been for older cohorts, with employment for those age 35 to 65 growing at, respectively, 4.3 and 3.5 percent a year for these sectors.

Overall, we have also noted that the IWSS sectors seem to be more female- and youth-intensive in terms of the current composition of employment, suggesting that these sectors may have the potential to provide greater opportunities for employment for these groups. Importantly, however, the broad IWSS sectors consists of a number of different sectors, some of which may individually be better placed to provide the type of employment required to address South Africa's widespread unemployment.

A further analysis of the composition of IWSS employment shows that across demographic, education, and skill characteristics, tourism, trade, and agro-processing are most intensive in employing women; trade, tourism, and horticulture are most intensive in employing youth; and horticulture, commercial agriculture, and agro-processing are most intensive in employing those with the lowest levels of education.[3] At this point, we refer to our initial discussion of the structural transformation of the South African economy, which suggests that South Africa was already on an IWSS-based growth path, but one that is dominated by growth in the financial and business services sector. Across our disaggregation of the broader IWSS sectors, in terms of employing women, youth, and the lower-skilled—the three groups with the worst employment outcomes in South Africa—the financial and business services sector has not been particularly intensive in employing these groups.

Overall, our findings suggest that, though South Africa is already on an IWSS-based path, there is potential for a different IWSS-based growth path that may be better suited to addressing South Africa's unemployment. A shift to other IWSS sectors that are more intensive in their employment of lower-skilled workers may be necessary to realize the full potential of the IWSS sectors in generating employment.

Constraints on IWSS Growth

Key to realizing the employment potential of these IWSS sectors is to understand the constraints that currently inhibit their growth, at both a macroeconomic and sector-specific level. The identification of the most severe constraints facing a country or sector facilitates the allocation of limited resources, such as institutional capacity and financial capital, to areas where they can have the most impact in generating higher levels of economic growth and employment.

The Broad Operating Environment for Firms

Page's (2020) growth constraints framework identifies four broad constraints facing IWSS: the investment climate, exports, agglomeration, and firm capabilities. Here, we outline a number of other overarching constraints that have an impact on the operating environment for firms, and that exacerbate constraints in the four broad areas identified by Page (2020), by giving rise to an unfavorable investment climate and limiting: export potential, the benefits of agglomeration, and firm capabilities. We note five overarching constraints that affect the operating environment for all firms:

1. *Infrastructure.* South Africa's current electricity crisis poses possibly the biggest constraint on economic growth. Eskom, the country's state-owned electricity utility, has implemented load-shedding—deliberate, planned shutdowns of power in parts of the power distribution system—to varying degrees since 2008 to prevent a complete shutdown of the system. According to Ateba, Prinsloo, and Gawlik (2019), an insufficient and unstable electricity supply has led to increased input costs and difficult industrial relations, affecting business enterprises' performance and investment plans.

2. *Fiscal pressure.* The country's proposed 2020 budget adopts a fiscal consolidation plan and suggests cuts to the wage compensation bill and poorly performing programs (National Treasury 2020). These changes will include decreased spending on infrastructure. Extreme and consistent cuts in infrastructure investments might result in lower capital stock in the long run and, therefore, lower growth (Stupak 2018).

3. *A lack of capacity and a skills mismatch.* Another reason often cited for South Africa's poor infrastructure delivery is the public sector's lack of capacity and limited technical skills and expertise for infrastructure projects (DBSA 2019). The lack of capacity acts as a headwind for infrastructure investment in South Africa, exacerbating dwindling economic growth.

4. *Labor market regulation.* According to Bhorat and Stanwix (2018), the most frequently cited constraints employers and firms face are the regulations governing firing, hiring, and other nonwage costs. The study found that South Africa, in comparison with other countries, ranks relatively high in difficulty of firing and hiring employees, and in rigidity of working hours.

5. *Corruption and political interference.* Since 1996, the World Bank's global governance indicators have shown a steady decline in South Africa's estimates of corruption control and governance effectiveness (Kaufman and Kray 2020).[4] The estimate of corruption control declined from 0.73 in 1996 to –0.02 in 2018 (Kaufman and Kray 2020). In the same period, the estimate of governance effectiveness also declined by 0.68, from 1.02 to 0.34. During the Zuma era,[5] the integrity and effectiveness of state institutions were undermined by political interference (Cilliers and Aucoin 2016). Corruption and patronage have compromised the strength of many state institutions, leading to waning international confidence.

Constraints on Growth in Specific IWSS Sectors in South Africa

Key to understanding the constraints of specific IWSS sectors is examining the value chain for each sector. Value chain analysis allows us to recognize the types of firms that operate in the sector and identify potential weaknesses (constraints) within the sector.

TOURISM. In figure 10-3, Daly and Gereffi (2017) illustrate the value chain for leisure tourism.[6] The value chain is designed from the perspective of an international tourist and has three main components: consumers (tourists), distribution intermediaries, and service providers. This illustration is intended to be representative at the broadest level: In reality, there is likely to be integration between the "distribution intermediaries" and "service provider" segments of the value chain.

Constraints on realizing the potential of tourism and its associated employment in South Africa can be thought of in terms of the three key agents involved in the value chain: consumers, intermediaries, and service providers. With respect to these components of the value chain, the tourism sector faces a number of challenges that inhibit it from reaching its full potential.

A number of factors limit the number of consumers of South African tourism (i.e., the demand for tourism), including government regulations,

FIGURE 10-3. **The Leisure Value Chain**

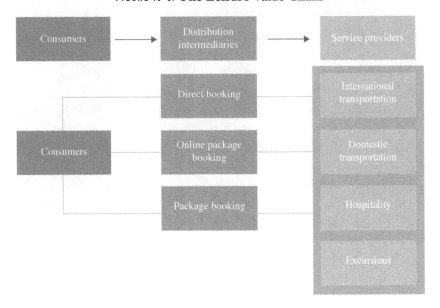

Source: Adapted from Daly and Gereffi (2017).

perceptions, and ease of access. With respect to the first, in mid-2014, the Department of Home Affairs introduced new visa regulations to reduce child trafficking (Oxford Business Group 2015). The regulations were onerous, in that they required all children under the age of 18 who were entering South Africa to have an unabridged birth certificate. In addition, for countries for which a visa is required to enter South Africa, all applicants had to appear in person during the application process to obtain the new biometric visa (Oxford Business Group 2015).

A further constraint influencing consumer demand is crime (Department of Tourism 2016). South Africa has one of the highest crime rates in the world, with many instances in the media of international tourists having been victims of crime. These stories create a negative perception of South Africa as unsafe and, as a result, deter potential international tourists.

In terms of ease of access, the country is far from many key source markets—such as the United Kingdom and Germany—which makes flights expensive. Furthermore, attracting visitors from new countries is made more difficult by the inconvenience of a lack of direct flights (Department of Tourism 2012a).

Service providers, on the other hand, contend with not only limited consumer demand but also factors that limit their ability to fulfill consumer demand. A report noted that about 30 percent of employment in the sector was difficult to fill because the skill requirements were high,[7] with the consequence that these occupational roles were not filled or filled by individuals with insufficient skills (Department of Higher Education and Training 2019). However, the report did not stipulate which specific skills were in shortage.

While there is potential to develop tourism services where they do not currently exist, a number of obstacles inhibit this growth. Although South Africa has a well-developed tourist market, the focus remains on established tourist hubs—such as Cape Town, Durban, and the Garden Route—and national parks in the North-West and Mpumalanga provinces, such as Kruger National Park (Africa Geographic Travel 2017). At the same time, rural communities have been neglected, despite the many new opportunities they could present to both local and international travelers (Department of Tourism 2012b). Development of tourist experiences in rural communities could lead to a much-needed cash injection into local, low-income economies, and could empower people who have been economically marginalized for decades.

The distribution intermediaries play an important role in connecting consumers with service providers, and constraints at this part of the value chain can have an impact on both the demand for and supply of tourism. As noted, however, it does not seem that major constraints on tourism in the country are currently being experienced at this level of the value chain. The online package booking distribution channel, in particular, has grown in recent years (Daly and Gereffi 2017).

HORTICULTURE. Figure 10-4 shows a generic fresh fruit and vegetable (FFV) value chain (adapted from Sohnen, Goldmark, and Pswarayi 2015) as an example of a typical horticultural value chain. As the figure shows, this value chain has six segments, beginning with the planting of a fruit or vegetable seed through the purchase of the final product by consumers. Not all activities are undertaken by different agents; a number of integrated firms are involved in many activities along the value chain. The different components of the chain face a number of constraints, which we outline here.

High input costs—especially for seeds and fertilizer—are a constraint for especially smaller-scale producers. There are a variety of seeds for a

FIGURE 10-4. **Horticulture: The Fresh Fruit**
and Vegetable (FFV) Value Chain

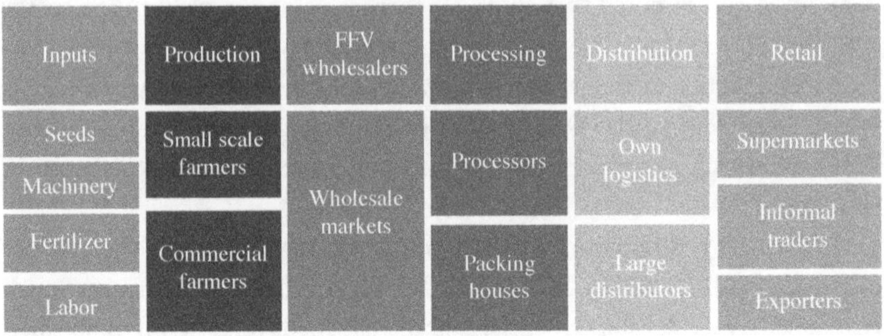

Inputs	Production	FFV wholesalers	Processing	Distribution	Retail
Seeds	Small scale farmers	Wholesale markets	Processors	Own logistics	Supermarkets
Machinery					Informal traders
Fertilizer	Commercial farmers		Packing houses	Large distributors	
Labor					Exporters

Source: Adapted from Sohnen, Goldmark, and Pswarayi (2015) and from Fernandez-Stark, Bamber, and Gereffi (2011).

particular crop, and the higher-quality seeds cost more money, which many farmers cannot afford (Harvest SA 2016). The lack of high-quality seeds ultimately affects the yield of the crops, and the profits of the farmer.

Poor infrastructure is a further constraint faced all along the value chain. On the production side, many farmers lack proper farm equipment, such as tractors and fences. However, in terms of product distribution, many farmers also do not have easy access to markets, which is crucial for developing a steady supply of customers (Harvest SA 2016). Indeed, the poor state of road infrastructure in rural areas makes it difficult for farmers to guarantee wholesalers that they will deliver their products on time.

Climate change also remains an ongoing concern for horticulture farmers, as many horticulture crops are rain-fed and therefore are susceptible to variations in the climatic conditions of the area (Harvest SA 2016). In addition, long-term land degradation caused by climate change has made the land less resilient to the changing climatic conditions, exacerbating the effects of droughts (Harvest SA 2016).

AgriSETA (2018) identified a list of "hard-to-fill" vacancies along the horticultural value chain. Employers pinpointed the insufficient number of students with the necessary mathematics and science grades to enter agriculture-related degree programs and a lack of experience among graduates for one set of horticulture occupations. For another set of horticulture occupations, employers noted that certain occupations were not seen as a career path in agriculture (e.g., market researcher), and other industries were regarded as more attractive than agriculture in certain occupations.

FIGURE 10-5. **The Agro-processing Value Chain**

Inputs	Production	Processing	Distribution	Retail
Seeds	Small scale farmers		Large distributors	Supermarkets
Machinery		Processors		Independent retailers
Fertilizer	Commercial farmers		Wholesalers	
Labor				Food services

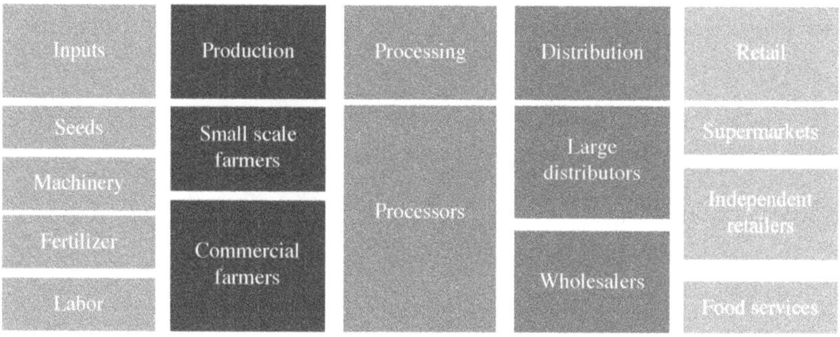

Source: Adapted from Dube et al. (2018).

AGRO-PROCESSING. In figure 10-5, we provide a generic value chain through which agricultural products are processed for further distribution and sale. The chain of activities relevant to the sector includes agricultural inputs and production, as well as distribution and retail. Notably, the key value addition of this sector is in the processing segment of the value chain—for example, processing oranges into orange juice. Our analysis of constraints, detailed below, covers the entire spectrum of the agro-processing value chain.

With respect to inputs, a key constraint is the lack of raw material supply. Firms report challenges in obtaining inputs of sufficient quality and supply (DAFF 2012). In addition, the high cost and volatility of inputs, such as animal feed, put further pressure on businesses.

The lack of access to capital is another constraint, impeding the ability of firms to expand their operations. Small firms are unable to provide enough collateral for the loans they require (DAFF 2012). Moreover, banks regard lending to the agro-processing industry as risky, due to the inherent uncertainty of variables such as weather, which can greatly affect the amount of revenue that a firm can be expected to earn.

A lack of skills is another challenge in the agro-processing sector; in 2018, the FoodBev Sector Education and Training Authority analyzed 633 firms in the sector and found that about 43 percent of firms cited a lack of skilled people as the reason they could not fill vacancies, while a further 27 percent cited an inadequate supply of suitable candidates (FoodBev 2018). Furthermore, firms cited these skill gaps existing in the sector: soft skills (e.g., communication, team, and interpersonal skills) and managerial skills. The latter skill gap arose because some individuals had earned

FIGURE 10-6. The Transit Trade (Logistics) Value Chain

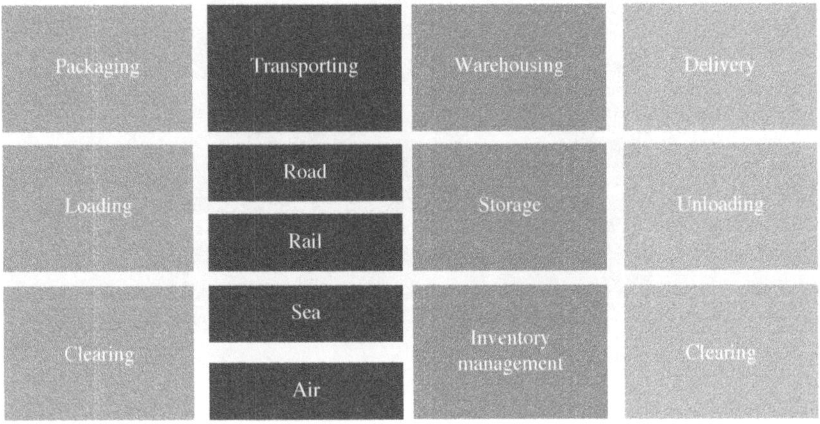

Source: National Skill Development Corporation (2010).

promotions to managerial positions, however, they did not yet have all the requisite skills (FoodBev 2018).

Firms in the sector also encounter challenges in supplying their goods to the retail market. Stringent regulations and standards are set by the retail market, which constitutes a lucrative source of income for small agro-processing firms. However, many smaller firms cannot meet the standards, due to the huge investment required (DAFF 2012), so they turn to the informal sector for their supply, which then hinders firm expansion.

TRANSIT TRADE (LOGISTICS). Figure 10-6 illustrates the components of a typical logistics value chain. Goods are first received from a manufacturer and are packaged into the correct container (Erkan 2014). Once the goods are packaged, they are transported to a warehouse using various modes of transportation. In these warehouses, the goods are repackaged in a suitable format for customers and then are finally delivered to customers, either indirectly through retailers or directly through door-to-door delivery (Erkan 2014). Our analysis highlights the current constraints the logistics sector faces along the value chain.

A key constraint on further development of the sector is the distinct lack of integration across the various logistics subsectors in South Africa. Havenga (2011) notes that South Africa has 10 departments or agencies responsible for the country's logistics system. The number of departments involved create fragmentation, a lack of accountability, and policies inconsistent with each other. Ultimately, the lack of policy coordination creates suboptimal outcomes for the logistics subsectors involved.

Related to a lack of policy coordination at the national level are two issues: a lack of standardized documentation, and no document integration (Barloworld Automotive and Logistics 2013). Both result in companies having to fill out many different forms and send them to different institutions, increasing the time they have to focus on administration rather than the movement of goods.

A key metric in the logistics industry is efficiency. Specifically, efficiency refers to the speed at which goods can be delivered to the customer. In this value chain especially, any bottlenecks along the way can have a substantial impact on the value of the goods. For example, fruits and vegetables destined for export require certain time targets to be met and, if these targets are not met, retailers will refuse to accept them, costing the farmers and other intermediaries a lot of revenue. Currently, the average on-loading and off-loading times in South Africa are long, about 4 hours (Barloworld Automotive and Logistics 2013). Furthermore, cross-border clearance takes between 24 and 48 hours (Barloworld Automotive and Logistics 2013).

Given the skills profile of common occupations in the sector, the sector also faces skills constraints. Heyns and Luke (2012), who conducted a survey aimed at determining the skill gaps within the logistics industry, found that, while operational positions were relatively easy to fill, 63 percent of strategic-level positions were difficult to fill. Furthermore, respondents were asked to rate the most important skills for logistics managers. Of the top 10 skills, 5 were behavioral/interpersonal skills (e.g., problem solving, teamwork), 3 were general management skills (e.g., ability to plan and priorities), and 2 were logistics sector-specific skills.

If both the economy-wide and sector-specific constraints are addressed, the substantial growth potential of IWSS sectors can be fulfilled. In the next section, we analyze future employment projections for IWSS and non-IWSS sectors, and provide quantitative estimates for the sectors' employment potential.

Trends into the Future: Potential Growth and Labor Demand

In this section, we show that projected employment growth will be higher in IWSS than non-IWSS sectors. In addition, we estimate that there will be a sufficient youth labor supply to take advantage of the additional employment opportunities, with the potential exception of high-skill jobs.

We employ two different analyses in this section:

1. We use the ratio of labor to value added as a measure of labor intensity to calculate a simple projection of IWSS employment (and therefore the number of new jobs) in the next 10 years *on the current growth path*;[8] and

2. We adjust these estimates to consider the potential of these sectors to generate jobs and reduce unemployment—especially youth unemployment—if these sectors were to be scaled up and enabled to grow *beyond the current growth path* (i.e., at a rate greater than the historical growth trend suggests, due to constraints on the IWSS sectors having been addressed).

For both these projections, we also note the occupational profile of the projected new IWSS jobs and consider whether the skills required for these occupations exist or are likely to exist among youth. We use ratios of labor to value added (see appendix table 10-A1) to project IWSS employment between 2020 and 2028, in the case of the current growth path and then beyond the current growth path.

Projection of Jobs on the Current Growth Path

This subsection presents simple projections of new employment in formal, private, nondomestic employment in the IWSS and non-IWSS sectors, making use of labor–to–value added ratios calculated by the authors. Constant linear growth rates across the nine main sectors at the 1-digit SIC level are applied on the basis of established trends in gross value added (GVA) in these sectors over the period 2010–18.[9] The annualized growth rate is applied to the period 2019–28 to estimate employment in IWSS and non-IWSS on the current growth trend.[10]

Table 10-5 shows the growth patterns of jobs across IWSS and non-IWSS sectors from 2019 to 2028 using these projected growth rates. It is immediately clear that, on the current growth path, the majority of employment growth will be concentrated among IWSS sectors, and that, up to 2028, IWSS employment growth will consistently account for about 78 percent of total employment growth in South Africa.

Table 10-5. New Jobs in the IWSS and Non-IWSS Sectors, 2019–28, Current Trends in Growth

Sector	Employment level ('000s)			Share of change (%)		
	2019	2023	2028	2019–23	2023–28	2019–28
IWSS	5,979	6,426	7,033	77.19	77.53	77.39
Agro-processing	598	618	645	3.53	3.38	3.45
Horticulture	335	354	379	3.24	3.18	3.21
Other agriculture	203	214	229	1.96	1.92	1.94
Tourism	864	927	1,012	10.82	10.79	10.80
Information and communications technology	76	82	90	1.05	1.06	1.06
Transit trade	444	480	529	6.19	6.22	6.21
Finance	2,066	2,259	2,527	33.47	34.13	33.85
Trade	1,394	1,492	1,624	16.92	16.84	16.87
Non-IWSS	2,965	3,097	3,273	22.81	22.47	22.61
Mining	406	406	406	0.02	0.02	0.02
Other manufacturing	858	888	926	5.08	4.86	4.95
Utilities	124	122	120	-0.28	-0.26	-0.27
Construction	652	687	735	6.20	6.07	6.12
Community services	925	993	1,085	11.79	11.78	11.79
Total	8,944	9,522	10,306	100.00	100.00	100.00

Sources: Authors' calculations based on projections using Kerr, Lam, and Wittenberg (2019) and StatsSA (2019).

South Africa is not on a manufacturing-based growth path, and services—especially financial and business services—are dominant in the country's current growth path. Indeed, on the current growth path, financial and business services can be expected to account for just over one-third of the increase in total employment over the period. The sector accounting for the second-highest proportion of new jobs is trade, with about one in five new IWSS jobs being projected to be created in this sector between 2019 and 2028. The three largest sectors in IWSS (financial and business services, trade, and tourism) collectively, then, are expected to contribute 61.5 percent of all new jobs in South Africa over the period. In contrast, non-IWSS employment growth is only expected to account for 22.6 percent of all new jobs between 2019 and 2028, with community, social, and personal services projected to be the dominant driver of the increase in employment in the non-IWSS sectors.

Overall, the evidence suggests that South Africa is already on an IWSS-intensive growth path. The IWSS sectors most intensive in the employment of low-skilled workers are horticulture, agriculture, and agro-processing. Collectively, these sectors are projected to account for just 11.1 percent of the increase in IWSS employment between 2019 and 2028, on the current growth path. Thus, while IWSS seems to be the major driver of future employment growth, the subsectors driving current IWSS growth are not those best suited for the employment of the low-skilled and youth. The current growth path will be unable to generate future jobs at the scale and skill level required for the country's labor force.

Occupational Distribution of New Jobs on the Current Growth Path

We proceed now to consider the skills profile of these new jobs on the basis of the most recently available skills profile of employment across sectors in South Africa.[11,] In table 10-5, we present both the numbers of individuals in different occupations and the number of individuals of different levels of education required for the new jobs projected in the years 2019, 2024, and 2028.

Between 2019 and 2028, we project that just over 1 million new jobs will be created in IWSS. Of these new jobs, around one in five (21.4 percent) are projected to be created for service, shop, and market sales occupations, while another 18.1 percent are projected to be created for elementary occupations. These two occupations are followed by clerks (17.6 percent of new jobs) and managers and senior officials (14.3 percent). These four occupational categories account, therefore, for just over 70 percent of all jobs projected to be created on the current growth path during that time period. Only one of these (elementary occupations), however, is a low-skilled occupation. Other lower-skilled occupations (craft workers, plant and machine operators, and assemblers) account for 13.5 percent of the projected new jobs collectively. Around one in three new jobs (31.6 percent) are thus expected to be created in the three lowest-skilled occupational categories.

Looking at the education profile, it is projected that over half of all the new jobs (57 percent) will require a completed secondary education, while 36.8 percent will require a postsecondary education. Just 6.2 percent of the new jobs will require individuals with less than a completed secondary education, which is a cause for concern, given that this group still accounts for a large proportion of the current unemployed as well as those entering the labor force each year.

Skill Gaps on the Current Growth Path

Table 10-6 shows the difference between the number of jobs required in each education category in 2028 and the number of youth who fall into these categories in the same year.[12] Of course, the gap (or surplus) does not take into account that the stock of supply here (youth) is not the only pool from which employment for IWSS will be drawn. It also does not take into account that youth will be employed in non-IWSS sectors as well. It should thus be interpreted as an indicator of whether the skills required can be drawn from the youth population alone, while bearing in mind that in reality, it will not be the case that all skill requirements will come from solely the youth population, and the youth population's skills will not solely serve the skills requirement needs of the IWSS sectors only.

The table shows that, on the current growth path, the skills required for new jobs will be available in the youth labor force in 2028. In fact, there will be a surplus of available skills at all education levels, with this surplus decreasing considerably, from over 1 million individuals for both presecondary and completed secondary, to just 33,900 for postgraduate as the education level increases. The next subsection considers how employment numbers and skill gaps can be expected to change if potentials in the IWSS sectors were to be realized.

Beyond the Current Growth Path

In this subsection, we project employment using the same methodology used in the subsection above, but instead apply a higher rate of job creation

Table 10-6. Occupational and Educational Distribution of Projected New Jobs in the IWSS Sectors, 2019–28

Occupation and education level	Employment level ('000s)			Share of change (%)		
	2019	2024	2028	2019–24	2024–28	2019–28
Occupation						
Legislators, senior officials, and managers	823	904	974	14.26	14.28	14.27
Professionals	289	321	350	5.75	5.82	5.78
Technical and associate professionals	480	530	574	8.87	8.94	8.90
Clerks	1,017	1,116	1,203	17.60	17.62	17.61
Service workers, shop, and market sales workers	1,184	1,304	1,409	21.37	21.44	21.40
Skilled agricultural and fishery workers	33	36	38	0.42	0.41	0.42
Craft and related trades workers	415	450	480	6.21	6.17	6.19
Plant and machine operators and assemblers	528	569	605	7.34	7.27	7.31
Elementary occupations[a]	1,210	1,312	1,401	18.17	18.05	18.11
Total	5,979	6,543	7,033	100.00	100.00	100.00
Level of education required						
Presecondary	475	511	541	6.30	6.18	6.24
Secondary	3,469	3,790	4,069	56.99	56.92	56.96
Postsecondary	722	793	854	12.50	12.53	12.51
University degree	1,168	1,289	1,395	21.46	21.60	21.53
Postgraduate degree	145	160	174	2.74	2.77	2.76
Total	5,979	6,543	7,033	100.00	100.00	100.00

Sources: Authors' calculations based on projections using Kerr, Lam, and Wittenberg (2019) and StatsSA (2019).

a. "Elementary occupations involve the performance of simple and routine tasks, which may require the use of hand-held tools and considerable physical effort" (ILO 2012: 337).

across four selected IWSS sectors with the potential to create jobs across the skills spectrum in South Africa. We apply higher growth rates for the four IWSS sectors of horticulture, agro-processing, tourism, and transit trade.[13]

On this higher growth path, financial and business services—the currently dominant sector in the South African economy—can be expected to account for 27 percent of the increase in total employment over the period, with this share declining from just under a third (32 percent) for 2019–23 to 25 percent for 2023–28. At the same time, tourism is expected to increase its share of the change in total employment, from 13 percent for the 2019–23 period to 24 percent for the 2023–28 period (averaging 20 percent for the full 2019–28 period). Thus, by 2028, under this scenario, tourism attains a level of job creation on par with financial and business services. Tourism, unlike financial and business services, is not concentrated in one services sector of the economy. Thus, expansion of the tourism sector can be expected to have more inclusive growth outcomes and stimulate growth in other sectors of the economy that are linked to tourism.

Table 10-7 shows the growth patterns of jobs across the IWSS and non-IWSS sectors from 2019 to 2028. Under this scenario of a higher growth path, IWSS employment growth will account for 79 percent of total employment growth between 2019 and 2023, and 84 percent of total employment growth between 2023 and 2028. For the overarching period 2019–28, then, IWSS employment growth will account for about 82 percent of total employment growth in South Africa, with this share increasing as growth increases in the four selected IWSS sectors.

On this higher growth path, financial and business services—the currently dominant sector in the South African economy—can be expected to account for 27 percent of the increase in total employment over the period, with this share declining from just under a third (32 percent) for 2019–23, to 25 percent for 2023–28. At the same time, tourism is expected to increase its share of the change in total employment, from 13 percent for the 2019–23 period to 24 percent for the 2023–28 period (averaging 20 percent for the full 2019–28 period). Thus, by 2028, under this scenario, tourism attains a level of job creation on par with financial and business services. Tourism, unlike financial and business services, is not concentrated in one services sector of the economy.[14] Thus, expansion of the tourism sector can be expected to have more inclusive growth outcomes and stimulate growth in other sectors of the economy that are linked to tourism.

Table 10-7. Employment in the IWSS and Non-IWSS Sectors, 2019–28, Higher Growth Path

Sector	Employment level ('000s)			Share of change (%)		
	2019	2023	2028	2019–23	2023–28	2019–28
IWSS	5,979	6,461	7,358	78.50	83.59	81.74
Agro-processing	598	623	674	4.04	4.75	4.49
Horticulture	335	360	433	4.02	6.84	5.81
Other commercial agriculture	203	214	229	1.77	1.40	1.54
Tourism	864	946	1,200	13.40	23.62	19.90
Information and communications technology	76	82	90	0.92	0.77	0.83
Transit trade	444	485	581	6.74	8.95	8.14
Finance	2,066	2,259	2,527	31.50	24.94	27.33
Trade	1,394	1,492	1,624	15.96	12.31	13.64
Non-IWSS	2,965	3,097	3,273	21.50	16.41	18.26
Mining	406	406	406	0.00	0.00	0.00
Other manufacturing	858	888	926	4.89	3.54	4.03
Utilities	124	122	120	-0.33	-0.19	-0.24
Construction	652	687	735	5.70	4.47	4.92
Community services	925	993	1,085	11.07	8.58	9.49
Total	8,944	9,558	10,631	100.00	100.00	100.00

Sources: Authors' calculations based on projections using Kerr, Lam, and Wittenberg (2019) and StatsSA (2019).

Horticulture is also expected to increase its share of the total change in employment considerably, from 4 percent in the 2019–23 period to 7 percent in the 2023–28 period (averaging 6 percent for the full 2019–28 period). In comparison with the current growth path, this higher share of horticulture in the change in employment suggests a more balanced, IWSS-based growth path under the higher growth path scenario, where growth in employment in the skills-biased financial and business services sector is complemented by growth in more inclusive sectors such as tourism and horticulture.

We now consider the skills profile of these new jobs on the basis of the most recently available skills profile of employment across sectors in South Africa.[15] Between 2019 and 2028, we project that about 1.4 million new jobs will be created in the IWSS sectors. Under the current growth path, this number was estimated at just over 1 million. Of these new jobs, around one in five (21.7 percent) is projected to be created in service occupations, while another one in five (20 percent) is projected to be created in elementary occupations. These two occupations are followed by clerks (16.9 percent of new jobs) and managers and senior officials (14 percent). These four occupational categories account, therefore, for 72.6 percent of all jobs projected to be created over the period on this growth path. Compared with the current growth path, the share of jobs expected to be elementary is higher (20 percent, compared with 18 percent for the current growth path). Just over a third of all new jobs (34.3 percent) are expected to be created in the three lowest-skilled occupational categories. In table 10-8, we present both the numbers of individuals in different occupations and the number of individuals of different levels of education required for the new jobs projected in the years 2019, 2024, and 2028 for the new growth path scenario.

Looking at the education profile, it is projected that over half of all the new jobs (58.6 percent, higher than the share of 57 percent for the current growth path) will require a completed secondary education, while a third will require a postsecondary education (lower than the share of 36.8 percent for the current growth path). About 8 percent of the new jobs will require individuals with a less-than-complete secondary education, higher than the 6.2 percent share of new jobs for this group of individuals on the current growth path. Thus, a greater share, and number, of jobs that can be accessed by individuals who do not have high levels of educational attainment under the new growth path scenario will emerge.

Table 10-8. Occupational and Educational Distribution of Projected New Jobs in the IWSS Sectors on a Higher IWSS Growth Path, 2019–28

Occupation and education level	Employment level ('000s)			Share of change (%)		
	2019	2024	2028	2019–24	2024–28	2019–28
Occupation						
Legislators, senior officials, and managers	823	913	1016	14.12	13.90	14.00
Professionals	289	322	355	5.28	4.37	4.79
Technical and associate professionals	480	533	588	8.36	7.33	7.80
Clerks	1,017	1,127	1,251	17.26	16.66	16.94
Service workers, shop, and market sales workers	1,184	1,319	1,483	21.43	21.90	21.69
Skilled agricultural and fishery workers	33	36	40	0.44	0.48	0.46
Craft and related trades workers	415	453	495	6.07	5.64	5.84
Plant and machine operators and assemblers	528	578	644	7.92	8.85	8.42
Elementary occupations	1,210	1,331	1,486	19.11	20.86	20.06
Total	5,979	6,613	7,358	100.00	100.00	100.00
Level of education required						
Presecondary	475	522	592	7.34	9.45	8.48
Secondary	3,469	3,835	4,276	57.74	59.25	58.56
Postsecondary	722	800	890	12.33	12.01	12.16
University degree	1,168	1,295	1,422	20.01	17.09	18.43
Postgraduate degree	145	161	178	2.57	2.21	2.38
Total	5,979	6,613	7,358	100.00	100.00	100.00

Sources: Authors' calculations based on projections using Kerr, Lam, and Wittenberg (2019), StatsSA (2019), and United Nations (2019).

Table 10-9 shows the difference between the number of jobs required in each education category in 2028 and the number of youth who fall into these categories in the same year. As noted above, the gap (or surplus) does not take into account that the stock of supply here (youth) is not the only pool from which employment for IWSS will be drawn. It also does not take into account the fact that youth will be employed in non-IWSS sectors as well. Thus, the indicator only specifies whether the skills required are available within the youth population.

The table shows that, in 2028, overall, the skills required for the new jobs on the new growth path will be available in the youth labor force. There is a surplus of available skills at all education levels, with this surplus decreasing considerably from over 1 million individuals for both pre-secondary and completed secondary to just 33,100 for postgraduate as the education level increases. Given the greater demand for labor, the surplus is lower than under the current growth path case.

These projected numbers suggest that, while increased employment opportunities may arise from overcoming sector-specific constraints, the accessibility of such opportunities depends on the availability of suitable skills. In comparison with the current growth scenario, there remains a surplus of individuals in the labor force in the higher growth scenario. However, in terms of skill requirements, there is likely to be a low proportion of youth who can take advantage of employment opportunities in higher-skilled occupations. In contrast, there will be a sufficient supply of youth for lower-skilled job opportunities.

Skill Requirements of the IWSS Sectors Beyond Qualification: Preliminary Evidence from Firm Surveys

Our quantitative analysis shows the large potential employment growth in IWSS sectors, regardless of whether the economy continues along its current growth path or on a higher growth path. However, the results also highlight the possibility of skills shortages in qualifications (and in high-skill occupations in particular). We now examine the issue of skill shortages in more detail, noting that while our quantitative analysis shows an abundant supply of low-skilled workers, we used education as a proxy for skill level. In our firm surveys, we provide a more holistic view of skills that cannot be measured using education data.

Table 10-9. Skill Gaps for IWSS Sectors with Respect to Youth, 2028 (thousands)

Sector or labor aspect	Presecondary	Secondary complete	Postsecondary	University degree	Postgraduate
Labor supply (youth labor force)	1,281.8	1,262.0	138.41	93.0	37.4
Labor demand	19.1	117.9	23.8	33.3	4.3
Legislators, senior officials, and managers	—	4.3	4.0	16.7	2.5
Professionals	—	—	0.2	6.5	1.9
Technical and associate professionals	—	1.3	3.1	9.9	—
Clerks	—	21.7	11.1	0.2	—
Service workers, shop, and market sales	0.1	42.4	1.2	—	—
Skilled agricultural and fishery workers	0.0	0.3	0.6	—	—
Craft and related trades workers	1.8	6.0	3.3	—	—
Plant and machine operators and assemblers	0.1	17.5	0.1	—	—
Elementary occupations	17.1	24.5	0.0	—	—
Sectoral skill gap	1,262.75	1,144.05	114.65	59.67	33.11

Sources: Authors' calculations based on projections using Kerr, Lam, and Wittenberg (2019), StatsSA (2019), and United Nations (2019).

Our firm survey consisted of 18 semistructured firm interviews. Fifty percent of these interviews were conducted in the tourism sector, while the remaining 50 percent were split equally across the agro-processing, horticulture, and logistics sectors.

The survey instrument used to conduct the interviews—comprising a mixture of closed-ended and open-ended questions—aims to provide measures of these factors, among others: the main occupations within the firm; the current skills profile of the firm; the expansion plans of the firm; and the future employment, occupational, and skills needs of the firm.

We were particularly interested in understanding occupational skills requirements, which can act as an input to the development of a national skill development strategy. Respondents were asked about the occupational requirements for a highly disaggregated list of soft and hard skills. The various skills are aggregated into six overarching categories, which are consistent with classifications provided by O*NET (2019b). We also classify these categories according to whether they are a "hard" or "soft" skill:

- Basic skills: skills that facilitate learning or the more rapid acquisition of knowledge (*soft skill*).
- Social skills: skills that are used to work with people to achieve goals (*soft skill*).
- Problem-solving skills: skills that are used to solve novel, ill-defined problems in real-world settings (*soft skill*).
- Resource management skills: skills that are used to allocate resources efficiently (*soft skill*).
- Technical skills: skills that are used to design, set up, operate, and correct malfunctions involving the application of machines or technological systems (*hard skill*).
- Systems skills: skills that are used to understand, monitor, and improve sociotechnical systems (*hard skill*).

Consistent with metrics used in the O*NET database (O*NET 2019a), respondents were asked to classify each skill in the above-noted categories according to two metrics: level and importance. The level of a skill refers to how complex the application of the skill is in the occupation's daily course of events.[16] A skill's level was measured on a scale ranging from 1 (lowest) to 5 (highest). On the other hand, the importance of a skill can be thought of as how critical it is that an individual has this skill in order to complete their day-to-day tasks. Importance was also measured on a scale of 1 (not important) to 5 (critically important).[17]

Respondents were asked to estimate the severity of the skill gap of youth hires for each skill category. In other words, respondents would consider a category of skills—for example, basic skills—and compare the required level of these skills with the level of the skill exhibited by youth hires in the firm. The skill deficit rating is measured on a 5-point scale, with a rating of 1 indicating that most employees met the skill requirements and a rating of 5 indicating that most employees did not meet the skill requirements and that there was a critical gap present for the relevant skill. Where a skill was not identified as applicable to a certain occupation, respondents did not provide an estimate of the skill gap.

In what follows, we provide a summary of the results from our surveys. A more detailed analysis is given by Allen and others (2021).

In terms of the types of jobs that could be created by our four target industries, our results suggest that the industries could cater to different sections of the unemployed youth population. While the tourism and horticulture sectors provided the most scope for catering to low-skilled individuals, agro-processing and logistics cater to higher-skilled individuals. The weighted average level and importance of soft skill requirements are presented in figure 10-7.

These results paint a slightly different picture of the formal educational requirements, and instead indicate that the horticulture sector requires the second-highest level of soft skills of all sampled IWSS sectors—a finding likely driven by the sector's need for many laboratory technicians and plant pathologists, and that does not necessarily take away from the sector's high employment potential for unskilled youth in roles requiring less specialized skills, such as farm workers, operators, and plant extractors. The tourism sector still presents a potential employment opportunity for low-skilled workers, with a low aggregate level of soft skills required.

In terms of job growth, the results are more heterogenous. Although a total of about 458 jobs were expected to be created across all 18 interviewed firms in the next five years, the number of jobs per firm differ greatly by industry. Interviewed firms in the agro-processing industry showed the highest job creation potential over the next five years, with

FIGURE 10-7. Average Level and Importance of Soft Skills by IWSS Sector

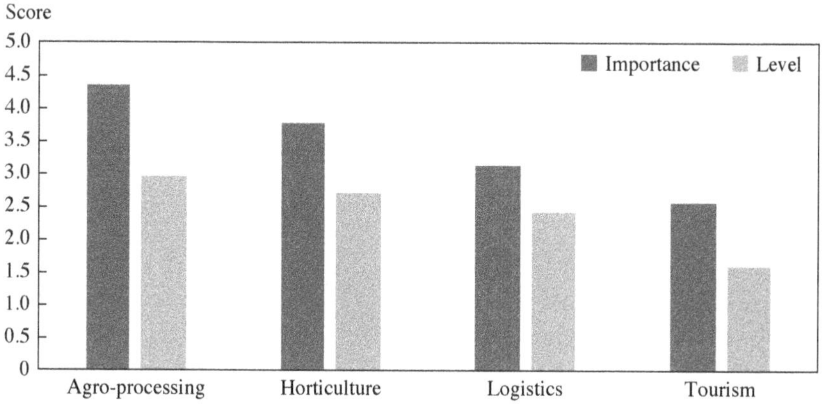

Source: Authors' data.

Note: Averages are calculated by weighting responses according to the proportion of jobs in the interviewed firms represented by the response.

62 jobs per firm, while the interviewed horticulture firms project to create about 6 jobs per firm. This job growth pattern is heavily skewed toward semiskilled occupations, which agrees with the findings in the data given above.

However, high deficit scores in certain key skill groups (basic, social, and resource management skills) suggest that finding youth to fill the positions that are created may be challenging. Assuming that unemployed youth have similar, if not greater, skill deficiencies than employed youth, the soft skill deficits found in this section are a cause for concern for the employability of future youth. A particular deficit that appeared across all industries was that of basic skills. Given that basic skills include those skills that should be developed in the early stages of formal education—for example, reading, mathematics, and active listening—it may be worthwhile to more carefully monitor the South African education system to ensure that it upholds education standards to those required by firms.

Table 10-10 presents a summary of the incidence of job creation and skill deficits across the interviewed IWSS firms. From the first row of the table, it is clear that the majority (42 percent) of new jobs are projected to be created in the agro-processing sector, with the overwhelming

Table 10-10. Incidence of Job Growth and Skill Deficits in the IWSS Sectors

Growth or deficit	Agro-processing	Horticulture	Logistics	Tourism	All
Share of jobs created	0.42	0.04	0.21	0.33	1.00
From existing occupations	0.38	0.04	0.20	0.26	0.88
From new occupations	0.04	0.00	0.01	0.07	0.13
Average skill deficit (out of 5)	1.70	3.20	1.80	2.29	1.98

Source: Authors' data.

Note: Numbers may not add up correctly due to rounding.

majority of these jobs being in occupations that currently exist within the firms. Across the 18 interviewed firms, a total of 448 jobs were expected to be created, with 96 percent of these occurring in sectors that present with relatively low skill deficits of between 1.7 and 2.29 out of 5.[18] Only 4 percent of jobs projected to be created by these firms are in the horticulture sector, which presents the highest aggregate skill gap of employed youth.

An important finding is the degree of heterogeneity across the firms, and across industries more generally, a trend that should be taken into account when designing policies for increasing employment in the sector. The differences between and within sectors must be recognized and understood so that appropriate actions can be taken to grow the sector and for youth to be able to access employment in them.

Policy Implications and Conclusion: Unlocking Growth Potential and Overcoming Skill Gaps

In prescribing policy options for the IWSS sectors, and specifically for the four industries focused on in this study, we emphasize that these industries are heterogeneous and, as such, there is no single policy prescription or magic bullet that will unlock growth for these sectors. Rather, a coherent plan, with multiple policies that complement each other, will unlock the growth potential of the IWSS sectors. Thus, this section explores these four high-level, interrelated recommendations for enabling growth and job creation in the IWSS sectors:

1. Facilitating an enabling operating environment in which firms can thrive across the economy.
2. Crafting and implementing policies that focus on enabling the growth of specific IWSS sectors and addresses the specific constraints faced by different IWSS sectors.
3. Developing relevant skills that will support the growth of the IWSS sectors.
4. Ensuring that all policies grow the economy and that the IWSS sectors are inclusive.

Facilitating an Enabling Operating Environment to Promote Economic Growth

The country-level constraints on economic growth discussed in the fourth section—particularly infrastructure, fiscal consolidation, labor market regulation, and corruption—must be addressed to facilitate an enabling operating environment for firms to grow so that employment can be generated. Here, we propose changes that can be made to facilitate an operating environment. We focus specifically on infrastructure development and government spending challenges. In terms of infrastructure, we focus on three policy options:

- Increase institutional capacity at the municipal level, especially in the engineering and town-planning fields;
- Increase the amount of money for the maintenance, rehabilitation, and upgrading of existing infrastructure; and/or
- Increase transnational infrastructure development to facilitate better economic integration between South Africa and its neighbors.

In relation to government spending, our main policy prescription is that the South African government needs to move to a zero-based budgeting approach, which will require each government department to justify its budget each year, rather than use the previous year's departmental budget as a starting point for budget negotiations.

Focused Policies That Enable the Growth of Specific IWSS Sectors

TOURISM. Both our quantitative analysis and the firm survey of the tourism sector demonstrated that the sector has the potential to generate many new jobs, especially low-skilled ones that can benefit youth. However, for the employment potential of the sector to be achieved, several constraints need to be overcome. These include:

- Negative perceptions of South Africa as a tourist destination and the lack of ease of access to South Africa; and
- The concentration of tourism experiences in South Africa, and particularly the lack of inclusion of individuals from disadvantaged backgrounds within the service provider segment of the value chain.

Given that the tourism sector requires many different parts to work together, private–public cooperation is vital to secure the future of the tourism industry. Indeed, this is the underlying thrust of the policy recommendations provided by Saunders (2019), outlined here:[19]

- *Actively develop and promote tourism markets in less established areas.* Active development of and marketing for less-developed tourist regions will increase growth in the sector and include more previously disadvantaged individuals.
- *Enhance crime-prevention strategies, especially in tourist hotspots.* The tourism industry and the country's South African security apparatus—including the South African Police Service, the metro police, and the private security industry—must be coordinated more closely.
- *Develop and implement a world-class e-visa system.* An easy-to-use interface, support for multiple languages, nononerous documentation requirements, and quick turnaround times for visa applications will increase ease of access to South Africa as a tourist destination.

HORTICULTURE. We have shown that horticulture has many job opportunities for low-skilled youth. However, numerous constraints faced by firms undermine investment in the sector, and consequentially the ability of the sector to generate jobs. Key constraints include:

- Insufficient financial support for farmers; and
- Inadequate infrastructure, which inhibits production and distribution from farmers to wholesalers and to retailers.

To overcome these constraints, Lemmer (2017) outlines a few major policy recommendations that, if enacted, would enable growth of the sector. These include:

- *Implement comprehensive water infrastructure development.* As South Africa is one of the driest countries in the world (World Wildlife Fund 2020), policymakers should increase support for projects that expand the storage capacity of South Africa's dams, maintain the upkeep of water irrigation schemes, and more efficiently utilize its current water reserves.
- *Allocate sufficient financial aid to the agriculture sector in order to mitigate shocks.* The development of affordable, specialist insurance products that cover natural disasters is necessary.
- *Partially subsidize input costs for emerging farmers.* High input costs act as a barrier to entry for new market entrants; thus, the government should partially subsidize these high input costs to encourage new entrants into the industry.

AGRO-PROCESSING. While overall employment in manufacturing decreased between 2010 and 2018, formal private employment in agro-processing increased, indicating the resilience of the sector. When more favorable economic conditions return, we expect faster growth in the agro-processing sector. However, for the substantial employment potential to be reached, decisive action needs to be taken to address key constraints faced by the sector:

- High costs and a lack of access to capital, and
- A lack of support for small and medium-sized enterprises in particular.

Owoo and Lambon-Quayefio (2018) discuss a number of policies that helped the Ghanaian agro-processing sector grow and may also be applicable to the South African agro-processing sector:

- *Create a comprehensive incentives program for imported agro-processing equipment and inputs.* Incentives could take the form of reduction of the value-added tax and import duties and the introduction of an export-processing zone.

- *Increase coordination between the public and private spheres vis-à-vis relevant technology.* The government must facilitate technological transfer between publicly funded research institutions and the private sector, which can utilize these inventions.

LOGISTICS. While the results of our study suggest that job opportunities for low-skilled youth will be limited, for youth who obtain the requisite education, there are multiple job opportunities along the logistics value chain. For these opportunities to be realized, however, constraints faced by the sector must be overcome. These include:

- The lack of integration within the sector;
- The lack of a coherent national policy framework for the sector; and
- Inefficiencies along the value chain.

In 2019, the governor of the Saudi Arabian General Customs Authority, His Excellency Ahmed Alhakbani, outlined these key lessons that other countries could learn from Saudi Arabia (Sivalingum 2019):

- *Take an integrated approach to the logistics sector.* In South Africa, this move would require a coherent national strategy for the sector as well as mechanisms to ensure that the sector is integrated with others in the economy.
- *Eliminate regulations that increase the difficulty of doing business and adopt technologies that make businesses more efficient.* In transforming Saudi Arabia's logistics sector, technology was the key—most clearance procedures are automated, and the government has developed an integrated electronic platform that makes 135 services easily available to customers.
- *Cooperate with global organizations to reduce the number of obstacles that hinder the free flow of goods through the country.* Although South Africa has a number of free trade agreements (FTAs) with key trading partners, it still lacks FTAs with three of its five biggest trading partners: China (1st), the United States (3rd), and Japan (5th) (Workman 2020), and concluding FTAs with these countries must be a priority.

Developing Skills to Support the Growth of IWSS Sectors

Overall, the projected skill gaps for the current and higher IWSS growth path scenarios suggest that there will be a large labor surplus of youth for roles in the IWSS sectors. However, for occupations that require either an undergraduate or postgraduate university degree, there may be challenges in finding youth specifically with these educational qualifications. To ensure a sustainable supply of individuals educated at the required levels, Asmal and others (2020) suggest that there be a demand-led approach to the attainment of qualifications through collaboration between employers and postsecondary educational institutions.

Providing better qualification support is not enough, however, because soft skill gaps exist as well in different sectors and occupations, as demonstrated in the firm surveys. Possible measures to increase the number and intensity of soft skills, according to Lapm (2016), include these:

- Including compulsory courses on public speaking and written and verbal communication in all postsecondary schooling courses;
- Promoting a culture of volunteerism at secondary schools and at postsecondary educational institutions;
- Encouraging extracurricular teamwork activities; and
- Developing mentorship and ongoing training programs for new trainees.

Promoting Inclusive Growth:
Policies Must Be Cognizant of the Most Vulnerable

When considering the policies described above, policymakers must consider the differing effects that such policies can have on underrepresented groups, such as women and youth, and should incorporate the needs of these groups into national development strategies. With respect to gender, while a number of IWSS sectors employ a considerable number of women, their access to employment in different occupations along value chains is variable. For example, the Department of Tourism (2016b) notes that, despite women accounting for much of the employment in the sector, many of these women are in low-skilled occupations, with women constituting only 40 percent of managerial positions and 20 percent of general management roles.

Policies need to incorporate channels through which those who are still excluded from participation in the economy (e.g., women and youth) are consciously targeted. For example, this may mean ensuring that tourism is developed in areas where there are currently no established tourism markets, or ensuring that women or youth are actively targeted and supported to obtain the skills that are required in the IWSS sectors and are linked to employment opportunities in those sectors.

In this regard, the legal environment can be used to achieve socially inclusive outcomes: Affirmative action measures in relation to hiring practices, equal pay for equal work, and higher education opportunities are all policy levers available to policymakers—some of whom are already integral to South Africa's labor legislation. However, it is ultimately important that there is buy-in from all sectors of society to achieve inclusive growth.

In conclusion, the set of policies that we have presented indicate that overcoming economy-wide and sector-specific constraints will require a sustained effort from several different stakeholders for an extended period. Collaboration between the private and public sectors will be crucial to unleash the employment creation potential of the agro-processing, horticulture, logistics, and tourism sectors—and to ultimately achieve a more inclusive growth trajectory that provides better prospects for employment of youth in South Africa.

Appendix Table 10-A1. Ratios of Sectoral Labor to Value Added at the 1-Digit SIC Level, 2018

Sector	Ratio of labor to value added 2018
Agriculture	11.57
Trade	7.72
Transportation	3.66
Financial and business services	3.92
Average	6.72
Mining	1.82
Manufacturing	4.63
Utilities	2.26
Construction	13.78
Community services	7.80
Average	6.06
Average (excluding community services)	5.62

Sources: Authors' calculations using data from StatsSA (2017; 2019) and Kerr, Lam, and Wittenberg (2019).

Note: Employment figures by sector are publicly available from official data sources in the form at both the 1-digit and 3-digit Standard Industrial Classification (SIC) level. For the purpose of calculating labor–to–value added ratios, employment data for all quarters of 2018 has been used (Kerr, Lam, and Wittenberg 2019), in conjunction with the most recent 2018 GVA figures (in 2010 prices). The averages are simple averages.

NOTES

1. Transit trade refers to "the business connected with the passage of goods through a country to their destination" (*Free Dictionary*, 2019).

2. In the remainder of this chapter, employment refers only to formal, private sector employment.

3. See Asmal et al. (2020).

4. Estimate of governance (ranges from about –2.5 (weak) to 2.5 (strong) governance performance).

5. Jacob Zuma was the president of the Republic of South Africa from May 9, 2009, until his resignation on February 14, 2018.

6. Leisure tourism accounts for 66.0 percent of South Africa's tourism GDP, compared with 34.0 for business tourism (World Travel and Tourism Council 2020).

7. The sector combined the culture, arts, tourism, hospitality, and sports subsectors.

8. A technical explanation of the computation of labor–to–value added ratios is given by Asmal et al. (2020).

9. Given that this was a particularly poor period for economic growth across most sectors in the country, it may be that projections based on these rates may not represent the growth potential of the sectors.

10. The base year is 2018, as this is the latest year that we have GVA data and all Quarterly Labour Force Survey data for the entire year.

11. This is based on an average of the shares of employment for each occupational and education group across all quarters of 2018. Here, we make an assumption that the occupational employment profile in the different sectors will remain constant over time. In reality, however, it is likely that in many of these sectors skill requirements will become higher. Therefore, any skill requirements and gaps estimated here should be interpreted as a lower bound. That is, the skill requirements for many sectors may be higher in the future, and thus an estimate based on the current occupational distribution of employment may be an under-estimate of the skill requirements the skill gap calculated in the next section. The methodology is further detailed by Asmal et al. (2020).

12. A technical explanation for the estimation of skill gaps is given by Asmal et al. (2020).

13. While the previous section made use of GVA growth rates to project employment, in this section we make use of the employment growth rates implied by the GVA growth rates we used before as a basis for the analysis. This is because we are unable to apply a sector-specific GVA growth rate to the IWSS sectors, as we do not have access to sector-level GVA data. This essentially means that the new growth path projections scale up the employment creation projections of the previous section for the four IWSS sectors according to the new growth path scenario laid out here.

14. While all financial and business services employment can be found in one services sector, tourism employment is found in multiple services sectors

including trade, community services, and financial and business services. The type of skills required in these service sectors is typically lower than the type of skills required in the financial and business service sector.

15. As noted above, this is based on an average of the shares of employment for each occupational and education group across all quarters of 2018. Here, we make an assumption that the occupational employment profile in the different sectors will remain constant over time. In reality, however, it is likely that in many of these sectors skill requirements will become higher. Therefore, any skill requirements and gaps estimated here should be interpreted as a lower bound. In other words, the skill requirements for many sectors may be higher in the future, and thus an estimate based on the current occupational distribution of employment may be an underestimate of skill requirements and, consequently, the skill gap calculated in the next section.

16. E.g., mathematics may be classified as a low-level skill for a receptionist, while it would be classified as a high-level skill for a professor of mathematics at a university.

17. It is important to note that there is not necessarily a correlation between the importance of a skill and the level of a skill; e.g., a receptionist taking telephone messages for their superior may not require a high level of active listening—however, it is essential that this skill is present in order for the individual to complete their daily tasks. In this case, the "active listening" skill would present as low-level, but high-importance.

18. Recall that the scale used in measuring skill deficits codes 1 as "meeting skill requirements."

19. Saunders was a special adviser to the previous tourism minister, Derek Hanekom.

REFERENCES

Africa Geographic Travel. 2017. "South Africa's Top Tourist Attractions." https://africageographic.com/blog/south-africas-top-tourist-attractions/.

AgriSETA. 2018. "Horticulture Sub-Sector Skills Plan." https://www.agriseta.co.za/downloads/HORTICULTURE%20FINAL%20v02.pdf.

Allen, C., Z. Asmal, H. Bhorat, R. Hill, J. Monnakgotla, M. Oosthuizen, and C. Rooney.(2021. "Employment Creation Potential, Labor Skills Requirements and Skills Gaps for Young People." Brookings African Growth Initiative Working Paper 65.

Asmal, Z., H. Bhorat, S. Culligan, H. Hofmeyr, J. Monnakgotla, M. Oosthuizen, and C. Rooney. 2020. "Skills Supply and Demand in South Africa." Labour Market Intelligence Programme.

Ateba, B. B., J. J. Prinsloo, and R. Gawlik. 2019. "The Significance of Electricity Supply Sustainability to Industrial Growth in South Africa." *Energy Reports* 5: 1324–38.

Barloworld Automotive and Logistics. 2013. "Meeting the Challenges of Transportation in South Africa." https://blog.barloworld-logistics.com/blog/2013/11/19/meeting-the-challenges-of-transportation-in-south-africa.

Bhorat, H., and B. Stanwix. 2018. "Wage Setting and Labor Regulatory Challenges in a Middle-Income Country Setting: The Case of South Africa." World Bank, Washington.

Chisoro-Dube, S., R. das Nair, and N. Landani. 2019. "Technological Developments for Increased Market Access and Participation in Fresh Fruit Value Chains." Industrial Development Think Tank.

Chisoro-Dube, S., and P. Mondliwa. 2019. "South Africa Is Missing Out on Fresh Fruit Export Growth. What It Needs to Do." https://theconversation.com/south-africa-is-missing-out-on-fresh-fruit-export-growth-what-it-needs-to-do-124391.

Cilliers, J., and C. Aucoin. 2016." Economics, Governance and Instability in South Africa." *Institute for Security Studies Papers* 293: 1–24.

DAFF (Department of Agriculture, Fisheries, and Forestry). 2012. *Agroprocessing strategy.* https://www.nda.agric.za/doaDev/sideMenu/AgroProcessing Support/docs/DAFF%20agro-processing%20strategy.pdf.

———. 2019. "Processed Food and bev. Trade SA." https://www.daff.gov.za/doaDev/sideMenu/internationalTrade/docs/tradeFacilitation/Processed %20Food%20and%20Bev%20Trade%20SA%202019-20.pdf.

Daly, J., and G. Gereffi. 2017. "Tourism Value Chains and Africa." UNU-WIDER Working Paper 17/2017. UNU-WIDER, Helsinki.

DBSA (Development Bank of Sothern Africa). 2019. "Infrastructure: New Opportunities for Funding Set to Resolve Backlogs, Aid Delivery." Financial Mail special report.

Department of Higher Education and Training. 2019. "Skills Demand and Supply." http://www.dhet.gov.za/SiteAssets/Report%20on%20Skills%20Supply%20and%20Demand%20in%20South%20Africa_%20March%20 2019.pdf.

Department of Tourism. 2012a. "National Tourism Sector Strategy." https://www.tourism.gov.za/AboutNDT/Branches1/Knowledge/Documents/National%20Tourism%20Sector%20Strategy.pdf.

———. 2012b. "Rural Tourism Strategy." https://www.tourism.gov.za/AboutNDT/Branches1/domestic/Documents/National%20Rural%20Tourism%20Strategy.pdf.

———. 2016. "National Tourism Sector Strategy." https://www.tourism.gov.za/AboutNDT/Branches1/Knowledge/Documents/National%20Tourism%20Sector%20Strategy.pdf.

Dube, S., R. das Nair, M. Nkhonjera, and N. Tempia. 2018. "Structural Transformation in Agriculture And Agro-Processing Value Chains." South Africa: Industrial Development Think Tank.

Erkan, B. 2014. "The Importance and Determinants of Logistics Performance of Selected Countries." *Journal of Emerging Issues in Economics, Finance and Banking* 3: 1237–54.

Fernandez-Stark, K., P. Bamber, and G. Gereffi. 2011. "The Fruit and Vegetable Global Value Chain: Economic Upgrading and Workforce Development." Duke Center on Globalization, Governance & Competitiveness.

FoodBev (Food and Beverage Manufacturing Sector Education and Training Authority). 2018. "Food and Beverage Manufacturing Sector Education and Training Authority Sector Skills Plan (2018–19) Annual Update." http://www.foodbev.co.za/wp-content/uploads/2018/06/SSP.pdf.

Harvest SA. 2016. "Facing the Facts: Challenges and Constraints Facing Small-Scale Agricultural Productivity in South Africa." https://www.arc.agric.za/arc-iscw/News%20Articles%20Library/Challenges%20and%20constraints%20for%20small-scale%20farmers.pdf.

Havenga, J. 2011. "Trade Facilitation Through Logistics Performance: The Enabling Role of National Government." Centre for Supply Chain Management, Department of Logistics, University of Stellenbosch.

Heyns, G., and R. Luke. 2012. "Skills Requirements in the Supply Chain Industry in South Africa." *Journal of Transport and Supply Chain Management* 6: 53–68.

ILO (International Labor Organization). 2012. *International Standard Classification of Occupations, ISCO-08, Volume 1: Structure, Group Definitions and Correspondence Tables*. Geneva: ILO.

Kaufmann, D., and A. Kraay. 2020. Worldwide Governance Indicators, 2020 Update. Data set, World Bank.

Kerr, A., D. Lam, and M. Wittenberg. 2019. Post-Apartheid Labour Market Series (PALMS), Version 3.3. Data set. DataFirst, producer and distributor, Cape Town.

Kingdon, G., and J. Knight. 2005. *Unemployment in South Africa, 1995–2003: Causes, Problems and Policies*. Global Poverty Research Group Working Paper 10. Swindon, UK: Economic and Research Social Council.

Lapm, E. 2016. "Helping Youth Improve Soft Skills for Job Success." https://recruiterbox.com/blog/helping-youth-improve-soft-skills-for-job-success.

Lemmer, W. 2017. "Policy Interventions Essential to Optimise South Africa's Agricultural Output. https://www.bizcommunity.com/Article/196/358/169164.html.

NSDC (National Skill Development Corporation). 2010. *Human Resource and Skill Requirements in Transportation, Logistics Warehouse and Packaging Sector*. New Delhi: NSDC.

National Treasury. 2020. "Budget Review 2020." http://www.treasury.gov.za/documents/National%20Budget/2020/review/FullBR.pdf"http://www.treasury.gov.za/documents/National%20Budget/2020/review/FullBR.pdf.

OECD (Organization for Economic Cooperation and Development). 2018. "Opportunities for All: OECD Framework for Policy Action on Inclusive Growth." Inclusive Growth Initiative Policy Brief.

O*NET. 2019a. O*NET Online. Data set.

———. 2019b. "O*NET Resource Centre." https://www.onetonline.org.

Owoo, N., and M. Lambon-Quayefio. 2018. "The Agro-Processing Industry and Its Potential for Structural Transformation of the Ghanaian Economy." In *Industries Without Smokestacks: Industrialization in Africa Reconsidered*, ed. R. Newfarmer, J. Page, and F. Tarp. Oxford University Press.

Oxford Business Group. 2015. "New Visa Rules a Barrier to Expanding South African Tourism Sector."https://oxfordbusinessgroup.com/overview/challenge-growth-new-visa-rules-prove-be-barrier-sector-expansion.

Page, J. 2020. "Industries without Smokestacks: Firm Characteristics and Constraints to Growth." Africa Portal. https://www.africaportal.org/publications/industries-without-smokestacks-firm-characteristics-and-constraints-growth/.

SARB (South African Reserve Bank). 2019. Economic and Financial Indicators Data set.

Saunders, G. 2019. "A foundation for South African Tourism Growth." https://www.bizcommunity.com/Article/196/373/196445.html.

Sivalingum, Z. 2019. "Enhancing Logistics Performance to Drive SA's Economic Growth: Lessons from Saudi Arabia." https://www.bizcommunity.com/Article/196/389/197841.html.

Sohnen, E., L. Goldmark, and T. Pswarayi. 2015. "Leveraging Labor Market Assessment Tools to Address the Youth Unemployment Challenge." Available at http://marketlinks.org/.

Statistica. 2021. "Fresh Fruits." https://www.statista.com/outlook/cmo/food/fruits-nuts/fresh-fruits/worldwide.

StatsSA (Statistics South Africa). 2017. "Input-output tables for South Africa, 2013 and 2014."

———. 2019. "GDP P0441." Data set.

Stupak, J. M. 2018. "Economic Impact of Infrastructure Investment." Congressional Research Service. https://fas.org/sgp/crs/misc/R44896.pdf.

United Nations. 2019. "World Population Prospects: The 2019 Revision." Database. Department of Economic and Social Affairs, Population Division.

Workman, D. 2020. "Top South African Trading Partners." http://www.worldstopexports.com/top-south-african-import-partners/.

World Travel and Tourism Council. 2020. "South Africa: 2020: Annual Research, Key Highlights."

World Wildlife Fund. 2020. "Water Doesn't Come from a Tap." https://www.wwf.org.za/ourwork/water/.

ELEVEN

Policies to Create Productive Jobs in Africa

Unleashing Industries without Smokestacks

CHRIS HEITZIG, RICHARD NEWFARMER, AND JOHN PAGE

E ngaging the full power of Africa's young labor force in the process of development is a major challenge across the continent. As this book has shown, employing Africa's young labor force requires integrating them into both traditional growth-driving sectors like manufacturing, as well as agro-processing, horticulture, and export crops; information and communications technology (ICT); business and financial services; and other industries without smokestacks (IWSS). The case studies have described in detail how IWSS sectors are at the center of efforts across the continent to accelerate growth, increase trade, and create new jobs.

Policy has an important part to play in shepherding Africa's economic transformation. This chapter lays out policies that emerge from the case studies to create jobs in the transformation process, and in the IWSS sectors in particular. To set the stage, the chapter begins with a brief summary of key trends emerging from the case studies and then a look ahead at prospective job creation over the next 10 to 15 years. It then considers policies on both the demand side of the labor market (those spurring overall growth) and the supply side (those developing skills). It also advances specific policies to promote IWSS. It concludes by pointing to ways the international community can support Africa's transformation.

Revisiting the Main Findings of the Case Studies

The case studies have sought to document the rapid expansion of "modern" sectors that we have termed IWSS in their respective economies and to assess their potential for growth and job creation. Common patterns run through the case studies. On one hand, the manufacturing sectors in African economies look different from those in the rest of the world. The sectors tend to be smaller and less productive than in other parts of the world and be characterized by a few large firms in a sea of many small firms (Rodrik 2022). Still, the manufacturing sector is creating new jobs at a fast clip; in six of the eight case studies, the share of the labor force employed in manufacturing has been growing since 2000. Yet, unlike the IWSS sectors, growth in employment has not translated to concomitant growth in output. In many case study countries (Rwanda, Zambia, Kenya, Ghana, and Senegal), we observe a decline in manufacturing's share of total value added, despite a rise in manufacturing's share in employment. Much of the labor absorption in Africa's manufacturing sector has gone into small manufacturing enterprises and, while creating jobs, has not raised productivity substantially (Diao et al. 2021).

Conversely, however, IWSS sectors have been more productive than other sectors in the economy and have attracted a substantial majority of labor leaving traditional agriculture in the case studies. Consequently, IWSS sectors are creating jobs at a fast rate and are expected to create a significant share of new jobs in the coming decades. While many IWSS sectors—such as ICT, tourism, and wholesale trade—stand out in their job creation potential, it is the highest-productivity sector, financial and business services, that is the fastest employment-creating IWSS sector in five of the eight case study countries. The case studies also note a sharp rise in the IWSS share in overall output. In countries like Ethiopia and Uganda, this rise in output share has been greater than the rise in the employment share, which implies increases in IWSS sector productivity over time.

Unlike the growth paths of now-developed economies, in which employment has flowed from agriculture to industry and then to services, the countries studied in this volume have seen employment flow from agriculture directly into services. This has raised questions subsequently explored by the case studies, such as whether a services- *and* manufacturing-led growth model is viable. It is helpful to review key trends emerging from the case studies, which are presented here by income group.

The Low-Income Countries

The low-income countries featured in this book—Ethiopia, Rwanda, and Uganda—have important differences from the middle-income countries. Of course, they are poorer, with an average gross domestic product (GDP) per capita of $775. But they are also larger, have lower unemployment rates, and are more reliant on women and youth in the labor force.

These characteristics provide an important context for the main findings about the low-income countries. In the low-income countries, the IWSS sectors tend to have lower employment and value-added shares. High-productivity agricultural sectors and retail trade tend to be less developed in the low-income countries. The IWSS sectors tend to have high productivity in these countries, and the gap between productivity in the IWSS sectors and other sectors tends to be large relative to middle-income countries. Rapid structural transformation could partly explain the large productivity gap, and indeed there is some evidence for this in the case studies of low-income countries, where a disproportionate share of productivity growth is from more productive sectors attracting labor. Individual country experiences illustrate these commonalities, albeit with considerable variation.

ETHIOPIA. Ethiopia has undergone significant economic transformation over the last several decades. The case study notes that labor is leaving subsistence agricultural sectors at a rapid rate, and is joining a diverse range of economic activities, from both high-productivity agricultural IWSS sectors and nonagricultural IWSS sectors to manufacturing. The result is impressive growth in productivity, at a rate of more than 5.3 percent per year. Productivity growth has channeled much-needed improvements to individual livelihoods. In 2000, Ethiopia was the poorest country in Africa, according to the World Development Indicators' GPD per capita. By 2017, Ethiopia had jumped 15 places, to 16th.

IWSS sectors have been the focal point of this productivity growth. Despite employing only about 10 percent of the labor force in 2017, IWSS sectors were responsible for 59 percent of the country's productivity growth from 2000 to 2017. IWSS sectors have had less success in Ethiopia absorbing labor; the IWSS share of employment rose only a few percentage points over the study period. Tourism and construction have nonetheless been a bright spot in this regard. Thanks to the promotion of United Nations Educational, Scientific, and Cultural Organization's World Heritage Sites—such as Aksum, Simien Mountains National Park, and the Rock-hewn Churches of Lalibela—annual tourist arrivals have grown nearly ninefold over the last two decades, with the employment share of tourism doubling. The tourism sector has had important linkages with the transportation sector, whose flagship air-carrier, Ethiopian Airlines, has become a Star Alliance member and one of the largest airlines in the world in countries served. Unfortunately, the civil war, ignited in 2021, coming on the heels of the COVID-19-pandemic-driven recession in tourism, seemed likely to undermine these gains and entail a huge social cost.

RWANDA. The extent of structural transformation into IWSS sectors in Rwanda has been impressive. Employment elasticities have exceeded 1, and have been in a broad array of sectors, especially in agro-processing, construction, and retail trade. Structural transformation into the IWSS sectors has supported strong growth rates of about 8 percent annually. As in the other low-income countries, IWSS sectors have a big productivity premium over the rest of the sectors, including manufacturing. ICT and financial and business services are the two most productive sectors in Rwanda, though together they only account for about 1 percent of employment. Construction, tourism, and transportation each employ more than 2.5 percent of the population and are notably more productive than the economy as a whole.

The case study reveals that, in Rwanda, IWSS have accounted for a major share of employment increases since 2000. Growth in IWSS sector exports has outpaced growth in non-IWSS sectors, with the strongest growth coming from tourism, horticulture, and agro-processing. These sectors, like manufacturing, display high average productivity, contribute a large portion of exports, and employ a relatively skilled labor force. IWSS sectors in Rwanda are about twice as productive as the economy as a whole. High-employment growth sectors include agro-processing, horticulture and export agriculture, business and financial services, tourism, and construction. These sectors employed only 5 percent of the population in 2000, but more than tripled in size, to 16 percent, by 2017.

UGANDA. At nearly one-fifth of the labor force, Uganda has the highest employment share in IWSS of any of the low-income countries studied. Employment in IWSS sectors is very evenly distributed across a range of IWSS sectors—including agro-processing, construction, export crops and horticulture, financial and business services, tourism, retail trade, and transportation—with each accounting for between 1.9 and 3.3 percent of the labor force. Importantly, IWSS sectors have also increased their output significantly over the last two decades and now account for nearly half of annual GDP in Uganda. Chief among these is financial and business services, which accounts for 11.5 percent of Uganda's GDP, followed closely by ICT, at 10.6 percent.

Despite averaging 5.4 percent growth over the period 2008–18, there has been limited creation of productive jobs. Most of these jobs have tended to be in the services sector, in sectors like financial and business services and retail trade. IWSS sectors have been an especially welcome source of job creation in Uganda, given the manufacturing sector's inability to create jobs over the last 10 to 15 years. The challenge in the coming decades is to ensure that high-quality job creation keeps pace with Uganda's high population growth rate. In this vein, IWSS sectors have shown a potential to create high-quality jobs alongside manufacturing, in no small part due to their tradability. In 2017, for example, horticulture products and agro-processed goods amounted to a combined one third of Uganda's total exports.

The Lower-Middle-Income Countries

With the exception of Kenya, the lower-middle-income countries that were studied tend to have smaller labor forces than the low-income countries described previously. They also have more diversified economies than their low-income counterparts. Whereas traditional agriculture accounts for 63.1 percent of the labor force in the low-income countries, it employs just 40.1 percent in the lower-middle-income countries. The primary beneficiary of this diversification away from traditional agriculture has been IWSS sectors, which employ on average 25.3 percent of the labor force, compared with just 16.4 percent in the low-income economies. Manufacturing's share in employment is also higher: 5.8 percent versus 3.4 percent.

Despite IWSS sectors employing about 9 percentage points more of the labor force than the low-income countries, they are responsible for only about a 2-percentage-points higher share in output. The more important point, however, is not that output has not risen one-to-one with employment, but that IWSS sectors have been able to employ large swaths of workers while still remaining productive. This pattern has unfortunately not been true for manufacturing sectors, which, while having success in creating jobs in most of the case study countries, have also seen their share of GDP decline.

GHANA. Ghana has had more success diversifying its economy than any other case study outside Africa, its recent macroeconomic travails notwithstanding. An estimate of only one-fifth of its workforce is employed in traditional agriculture. Almost 40 percent of workers are employed in IWSS sectors, while another 11.5 percent are employed in manufacturing. The mining sector employs about 1.5 percent of workers, and is highly productive, accounting for 10.3 percent of GDP. Diversification has gone hand-in-hand with strong growth. From 2001 to 2018, Ghana averaged an annual growth of real per capita GDP of 3.6 percent, the highest of any of the lower-middle-income case study countries and the fourth-highest in Africa over this period.

The two largest IWSS sectors in terms of production are retail trade and financial and business services, which account for 13 and 9 percent of GDP, respectively. Both have a higher productivity than the economy-wide average. Modern agricultural sectors like agro-processing and horticulture are excellent sources of jobs, but are not as productive as other IWSS sectors (or even sectors like manufacturing or mining). In addition to improving its macroeconomic management, an important challenge for Ghana in the coming decades will be its ability to guide service-sector workers in IWSS and non-IWSS from low-productivity, own-account workers to employment in productive firms with connections to international markets.

KENYA. Kenya stands out from other African economies in many ways. It is an innovative economy whose population has widely adopted mobile phones, digital finance, and other technologies. It has relatively strong mobile internet connectivity and is an important seller of coffee, tea, and flowers in international markets. It is the third-largest country in Sub-Saharan Africa by GDP, after showing 28 straight years of positive GDP growth from 1992 to 2020. Despite this positive growth and despite a significant economic transformation between 1980 and 2010, Kenya's structural transformation stalled in the 2010s, with employment and GDP shares in IWSS and manufacturing showing minimal growth, if any. During this same period, however, overall output growth was the highest of any case study, resulting in strong within-sector productivity gains.

Moreover, this country case study identified horticulture, tourism, and ICT-based services as among the most promising IWSS sectors. The horticulture sector accounted for at least 20 percent of the value of all annual exports between 2014 and 2018. Horticulture features a labor-intensive production process, solid backward and forward linkages with other sectors, and strong policy support from the government. This combination of factors makes it a particularly important subsector for the creation of wage jobs. In addition, Kenya's tourism industry has a contribution (including indirect linkages) to GDP estimated at 5 to 12 percent. The sector is an important interaction point with the global economy. Finally, ICT is an important source of quality employment in Kenya, representing about 4.5 percent of wage employment and 0.8 percent of overall employment, which is the highest share of any of the case studies. The sector continues to demonstrate strong growth, expanding 7.3 percent in 2018.

SENEGAL. In contrast to the rest of the continent, Senegal experienced sluggish growth in GDP per capita from 2002 to 2013—averaging just 0.4 percent growth per year—yet it grew at 3.6 percent per year from 2014 to 2018, a time when many African economies were reeling from commodity price shocks. In 2014, the Senegalese government launched the Emerging Senegal Plan. This plan is built on three strategic areas: (1) structural transformation of the economy and growth; (2) human capital, social protection, and sustainable development; and (3) governance, institutions, peace, and security. Strategic area 1 has been a boon for IWSS sectors, whose employment share grew by as much as 5 to 10 percentage points in just five years.

Between 2010 and 2017, as the case study confirms, movement of labor from agriculture into manufacturing, historically a major employer of moderately skilled labor, was absent, and IWSS sectors—including agroprocessing, tourism, and horticulture—are absorbing a significant share of the labor released by the decline in agriculture. IWSS have recorded both higher than average productivity growth and an increasing employment share. Horticulture and tourism have been doing well in output growth. Between 1999 and 2019, horticulture increased its value added more than four times. Tourism nearly tripled its value added. Overall, IWSS sectors are doing better than manufacturing at generating jobs per unit of value added. In manufacturing, the employment elasticity with respect to value added is 0.88. It reaches 0.97 for horticulture and 0.96 for tourism. Projections indicate that IWSS sectors in Senegal will be home to two-thirds of jobs created between 2017 and 2035, and manufacturing will only create 2 percent of jobs.

ZAMBIA. After struggling initially after the introduction of structural adjustment programs in the 1990s, a strong period of economic growth from 2000 to 2011 accelerated Zambia into lower-middle-income status and was seen by many as an example of success for other poor countries. Yet Zambia has struggled to diversify its economy away from mineral resources, especially copper, and has the highest mining share in GDP of any of the case study countries. Zambia also has the lowest share of employment in IWSS sectors (12.8 percent) of any of the eight case studies and is nearly 4 percentage points below the low-income country average. The result has been a vulnerability to changes in commodity prices, particularly for the IWSS sectors with linkages to mining (transportation, tourism, construction, etc.).

The other side of the coin of low IWSS employment is IWSS' tremendous productivity: IWSS' share in output, at nearly 54 percent, is the highest of any case study country except South Africa. In this sense, Zambia is akin to many of the low-income countries, with a large gap in productivity between IWSS sectors and the rest of the economy. Construction and retail trade are among the most productive IWSS sectors, accounting for a combined 19.5 percent of GDP.

Despite a dependence on minerals and low IWSS employment share, Zambia has made considerable progress since 2005 in growing IWSS sectors that are at various stages of maturity. Zambian horticulture firms have developed close partnerships with European supermarkets, which import flowers and organic vegetables. In 2018, Zambia eclipsed 1 million international tourist arrivals, a roughly even split between business and leisure travel. Tourism firms, although smashed by the COVID-19 pandemic recession, could well resume their high growth rate by expanding their online sales presence, as many tourists book travel online via foreign travel agencies. Tourism firms should take advantages of linkages with Zambia's fastest-growing sector: ICT. Nearly 50 percent of the population has access to digital financial accounts. Zambia is home to nearly 15 million mobile phone subscribers, a majority of whom have access to the internet through their devices.

Upper-Middle-Income Countries

While South Africa is the only upper-middle-income country featured in this volume, it is sensible to categorize it separately given its important structural differences from other case study countries. Global estimates of the relationship between the size of IWSS sectors and wealth are strongly positive, and South Africa is no exception. At $6,373, South Africa boasts the highest GDP per capita of any of the case study countries and, at 54.6 percent, has the highest employment share in IWSS. Importantly, IWSS sectors in South Africa are also responsible for 63.8 percent of the country's GDP, offering evidence that the sector can employ significant shares of the population while also remaining productive.

SOUTH AFRICA. South Africa has been in a long-run, low-growth trap since the onset of democratic rule in 1994. The case study further finds that South Africa is on a path of structural transformation driven by a shift toward IWSS. The tertiary sector accounted for almost 75 percent of employment growth between 1980 and 2018. Manufacturing's share of GDP declined from 17.3 percent in 1980 to 13.5 percent in 2018. Agriculture accounted for only 2.6 percent of GDP in 2018. The financial and business services sector experienced the largest increase in GDP share over the period (a 9 percentage point increase). Shifts toward higher-productivity activities have been toward the financial and business services and transportation sectors. These tertiary sectors have absorbed labor in the place of a declining manufacturing sector. In fact, between 2010 and 2018, IWSS sectors such as agro-processing, horticulture, tourism, and financial and business services have become increasingly important contributors to employment. The increase in IWSS employment accounted for about 72 percent of the change in employment over the period. Three sectors—financial and business services, tourism, and trade—accounted for three-quarters of growth in employment. These trends suggest that there may be considerable employment growth potential in tourism, horticulture, commercial agriculture, and transit trade.

South Africa's recent growth, the case study notes, has been uneven at best. While economic growth has resulted in modest reductions in household poverty levels, it also has ushered in era of high-income inequality; according to the World Bank, South Africa has among the highest Gini coefficients in the world (World Bank 2022). The labor market is the primary driver of the rise in inequality. South Africa's unemployment rate and, more specifically, its youth unemployment rate—at 29 percent and 56 percent, respectively, in 2018—were considerably higher than comparable upper-middle-income countries and have been on a clear upward trend since 2008. The case study concludes with a salient question relevant to many case studies: "The question for South Africa is not whether there is a role for IWSS in the economy, but rather which particular IWSS sectors have the potential to address South Africa's unemployment crisis." For South Africa, these sectors appear to be tourism and horticulture.

The future of economic growth for South Africa, as with all the case studies, will necessarily involve competitive IWSS sectors working in concert with sectors outside IWSS.

Looking Ahead: Job Creation in the Coming Decade

Driven by high, if declining, fertility rates, the rapid growth of Africa's labor force indicates that the informal sector will expand for decades ahead, even under the best IWSS scenarios. The country studies use different methodologies to develop scenarios for growth to map the relative expansion of the IWSS, non-IWSS, and manufacturing sectors. Chosen to take advantage of government scenarios, the time horizons vary from 2028 (South Africa), to 2030 (Uganda and Zambia), to 2035 (e.g., Rwanda, Senegal, and Ghana), and the overall economic growth rates differ, sometimes on the basis of government aspirations and other times based on historical averages, so the specific country numbers are not strictly comparable.

In spite of their differing assumptions, the country studies' base case scenario assumptions collectively suggest that the IWSS sectors are likely to be growing at a more rapid rate than the economy as a whole. If the numbers envisioned in these illustrative scenarios materialize, the projections indicate that over the next decade or so, somewhere between one-third and two-thirds of new jobs created will likely be in IWSS sectors in a majority of the countries.

The results of the country studies suggest that while IWSS sectors create many new jobs with a higher productivity than traditional agriculture, the types of jobs created in the IWSS sectors are varied and may cater to different segments of the labor force. While the agro-processing, export agriculture and horticulture, transportation, and construction activities provide the most scope for absorbing low-skilled individuals, tourism, ICT-based activities, and finance offer higher-skilled individuals prospects for increased employment. This is consistent with the findings of Nayyar and others (2021), who noted quite different employment patterns for segments of the service sector.

As governments turn increasingly to IWSS sectors to push the pace of economic change, several countries have undertaken projects that have a positive impact on women's employment in sectors such as tourism. In Ghana, the proposed Tourism Development Project will target women-owned small and medium-sized enterprises (SMEs) in the tourism sector by providing SME business development services. Direct jobs in the tourism sector are expected to rise from 305,628 in 2019 to 380,000 in 2030 and 419,562 by 2035. The indirect jobs supported by the tourism industry and related sectors are projected to increase from 764,000 in 2019 to 895,000 in 2027. In Kenya, employment projections to 2030 indicate that the sector with the highest potential for creating good-wage jobs for youth is trade and repairs. Other sectors with potential are tourism, horticulture, and ICT. Among female youth, the most important wage employment sectors are export crops and horticulture, trade and repairs, and construction. In Senegal, IWSS sectors are doing better than manufacturing in generating jobs per unit of value added. The employment elasticity with respect to value added in manufacturing is 0.88. It reaches 0.97 for horticulture and 0.96 for tourism. Horticulture and tourism have been doing well in output growth. Between 1999 and 2019, horticulture increased its value added more than four times, and tourism nearly tripled its value added.

In part because IWSS jobs are highly productive, it follows that their skill content would be generally higher. Indeed, in four of the eight countries we were able to map education of the labor force—a proxy for skill requirements—into job categories. Assuming jobs with education levels of some high school and tertiary were adequate proxies for "skilled" workers, IWSS activities generally employ a higher percentage of skilled workers on average than manufacturing (32 percent vs. 23 percent) and non-IWSS activities (19 percent), as shown in table 11-1. This pattern held for all the countries but Ghana. Among IWSS activities, sectors employing a higher-than-average share of high-skilled workers include agro-processing, tourism, ICT, and business services.

Looking to the future, it is also evident that for these countries, IWSS sectors will make greater demands on those workers with higher levels of

Table 11-1. Skilled Employment and Projected Employment by Sector

Sector	Skilled worker share (%), 2017					Projected CAGR in skills (%)				
	Ghana	Rwanda	Senegal	Uganda	Avg.	Ghana	Rwanda	Senegal	Uganda	Avg.
Total	16.9	16.8	38.2	14.3	21.6	6.3	8.5	7.4	5.2	6.8
Total IWSS	15.9	31.9	45.7	34.5	32.0	5.7	12.9	11.4	5.7	8.9
Export crops & horticulture	8.2	10.0	23.2	1.0	10.6	4.7	18.6	21.1	0.7	11.3
Agro-processing	7.0	79.0	34.0	28.0	37.0	8.1	8.7	11.0	7.5	8.8
Construction	19.0	26.3	35.4	6.0	21.7	5.5	14.1	5.1	16.2	10.2
Tourism	22.0	51.5	53.4	79.2	51.5	6.0	12.0	8.4	4.2	7.6
Information & communications technology	73.0	76.0	92.5	91.0	83.1	11.1	14.1	2.4	5.4	8.3
Transportation	21.0	27.0	74.5	18.0	35.1	1.3	12.9	3.8	8.5	6.6
Financial & business services	56.4	59.0	94.0	86.9	74.1	-0.5	10.6	17.7	4.8	8.1
Trade (formal, excl. tourism)	42.6	5.0	68.9	23.0	34.9	3.7	14.5	14.5	1.0	8.4
Other IWSS services		20.8	76.9	26.0	41.2		7.0	7.2	1.4	5.2
Manufacturing (excl. agro-processing)	16.8	26.0	38.2	10.1	22.8	7.1	11.8	4.0	9.6	8.1
Non-IWSS	17.6	13.9	35.5	9.2	19.1	6.4	5.0	4.6	4.4	5.1
Traditional agriculture	7.1	10.0	19.7	1.0	9.4	-2.3	4.5	4.2	6.3	3.2
Mining	17.2	9.0	69.4	4.0	24.9	5.1	18.2	1.4	4.0	7.2
Utilities	27.5	65.0	84.3	51.0	56.9	10.3	3.4	2.8	4.2	5.2
Trade (informal)	17.9	4.0	42.4	10.0	18.6	4.7	3.2	8.3	3.0	4.8
Other non-IWSS	37.0	27.7	66.7	46.9	44.6	11.1	7.1	1.6	2.9	5.7
Government	44.4	81.0	93.0	95.0	78.4	7.4	3.5	3.1	4.9	4.8

Sources: Authors' calculations using data from the country case studies.

Note: CAGR = compound annual growth rate.

education. Though all projections have to be taken with a grain of salt, the demand for skilled labor in the IWSS sectors is likely to outpace even manufacturing and non-IWSS sectors (table 11-1), a conjecture borne out in the impressionistic surveys for the case studies.

This background sets the stage for looking at policies that affect the labor market in the future. Let us consider first those policies affecting the demand for labor, and then those that affect the supply of labor, notably skills. In each section, the role of the IWSS sectors plays an important role.

Demand-Side Problems and Policies: Overcoming Economy-Wide Constraints on Job Creation

Harnessing the full power of Africa's young labor force to propel growth is a central challenge facing the continent. The case studies have shown that the policy focus necessary to meet this challenge includes but goes beyond developing the manufacturing sector. Indeed, the studies have shown that increasing the pace of productivity growth requires investing in a broad array of activities, in people, and in the organization of the development process.

The Big Driver of Labor Demand: Recovering from the Serial Shocks After 2020

Because the strongest determinant of the demand for labor is the growth of the economy, policy must prioritize economy-wide solutions to problems that constrain growth. The recession resulting from the COVID-19 pandemic dragged down the global economy and cut economic growth short in 2020. Just as green shoots of strong recovery began to blossom in 2021, the omicron variant of the COVID virus hit, stalling global recovery, particularly in China. Then, in early 2022, Russia invaded Ukraine, unleashing a second shock of rising food and energy prices. Rising prices then led high-income countries to raise interest rates dramatically.

The scene in the rearview mirror was not pretty. Much like other regions, Africa suffered devastating human losses in 2020. Per capita incomes contracted for the second time in this century; health status, whether measured by nutrition indicators or mortality, worsened; and many of the gains in poverty reduction were erased—at least temporarily, if not permanently.

Virtually all countries emerged from the serial shock with lower international reserves, higher fiscals deficits, and greater indebtedness, and a new adjustment imperative: the need to reduce fiscal deficits.

The IWSS sectors, a bright spot in trend growth prepandemic, turned out to be the main conduits of the recession caused by the global pandemic. Tourism, a major source of foreign exchange for many African countries, virtually stopped (Page 2021). The effects were twofold: on one hand, the willingness of potential tourists, particularly those from rich northern countries, evaporated in the face of travel risks; on the other hand, many governments in the region temporarily closed their borders as part of lockdown efforts. Tourist arrivals to African countries in 2020 fell by 72 percent (World Bank 2023).

Similarly, in the long wake of the pandemic, restrictions on cross-border movement in Africa reduced export earnings from agro-processing. Border closings backed up trucks for days and created queues miles long. Mobility indices show reductions in traffic of more than 40 percent for the last 10 months of 2020 (see World Bank 2023). But this shock was relatively short lived, and surging agricultural prices soon favored export agriculture.

The IMF forecast the region's growth to decline to 3.6 percent in 2023, down from 3.9 percent in 2022 after the strong rebound of 2021. Regional averages mask considerable variation across the continent. The low-income countries in this volume—Ethiopia, Uganda, and Rwanda—were predicated to average 6.0 percent in 2023. The middle-income countries—Kenya, Ghana, Senegal, and Zambia—will grow somewhat more slowly, at 5.4 percent, with wide variation, because of slow growth in Ghana and a sharp recovery in Senegal. The region's largest economy, South Africa, will likely drag down the regional average because of power outages and weak global demand. Near-term growth remains shackled by the need to fight inflation through restrictive monetary and fiscal policies, constraints on external finance, and the prospect of weak global growth, dragged down because of the continuing conflict in Ukraine. Some of these constraints might ease marginally in 2024–26, with regional growth projected to surpass 4.0 percent in 2024 and beyond, and thus create much stronger demand for labor (see IMF 2023).

Circumventing near-term constraints to speed faster growth in labor demand requires efforts over the medium term to *accelerate exports, invest in infrastructure*, and *augment firms' capabilities*. In each, IWSS plays a role.

FIGURE 11-1. In Sub-Saharan Africa, Export Growth Drives GDP—Providing Foreign Exchange to Fuel Increased Investment (10-year periods since 1980)

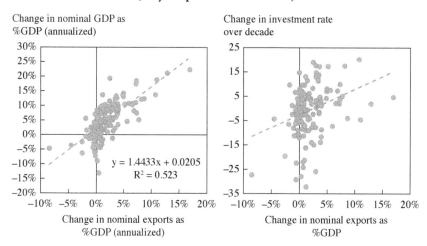

Source: Lea (2023).

Accelerating Export Growth

Exports are a key driver of growth. Export growth is strongly correlated with overall growth (figure 11-1). As Africa emerged from the serial shocks, its debt levels—already having increased steadily in the decade after the financial crisis—surged to an average of 55.5 percent of GDP across the region, up from 37.6 percent in the 2011–19 period (IMF 2023). Access to foreign exchange to finance investment has become a greater imperative for the region. Indeed, because it provides foreign exchange for imported capital goods, export growth is also associated with higher investment rates (see Lea 2023).

While the IWSS sectors were a channel for the pandemic-driven recession, it was precisely because they had been a main driver of export development and job creation for the prior decade of growth in Africa. Exports from IWSS sectors have nonetheless played an increasingly important role in overall trade in Sub-Saharan Africa (see chapter 1). In Rwanda, for example, exports of goods and services in IWSS sectors account for 61 percent of overall trade—$1.3 billion of $2.1 billion. In recent years (2011–17), IWSS exports have grown at a considerable rate of 15 percent a year, increasing their share of overall exports from 59.8 percent to 61.1 percent. The exporting of services has played a particularly important role: the share of IWSS services in overall trade increased from 43 percent to 46 percent from 2011 to 2017. At $438 per year, tourism account for almost half of Rwanda's IWSS services exports. Meanwhile, IWSS goods exports are concentrated in coffee and tea (8 percent of total trade).

Despite the strong performance of IWSS goods sectors in trade, the duty drawback, tariff exemption, and value-added-tax reimbursement programs remain complex and poorly administered. Export procedures—including certificates of origin, quality and sanitary certifications, and permits—are burdensome. Reforms to improve the institutional framework of trade logistics—including customs and standards—have not been implemented in many countries analyzed in this volume. In Ghana, for example, documentation requirements, customs procedures, and inefficient port operations exacerbate high trade costs. In Uganda, the days needed to clear customs and obtain import licenses increased between 2006 and 2013, and regional political feuds that result in sporadic border closures and nontariff barriers limit the country's prospective benefits from regional integration.

In Kenya, poor export performance reflects specific constraints, including poorly functioning tariff exemption programs. Several coordination problems affect the horticulture, ICT, and tourism sectors. For example, respondents indicated that in horticulture, there was little collaboration among exporters to consolidate shipments, combined with little export promotion or advertising. There is limited branding of export products, despite opportunities to leverage fair trade certification and emphasize the role of small farmers and women in the production of horticultural products. In ICT, a failure to comply with foreign certification processes and difficulties in establishing a local presence in external markets was identified as a constraint on the capacity to offer ICT products and technical support. In Rwanda, cumbersome export procedures limit the growth of the horticulture sector.

Nontariff barriers, permit requirements, and standards in importing countries create obstacles to trade in agro-industrial products in Uganda and restrict the reach of products such as dairy to neighbors. At the same time, horticulture exports—dominated by coffee, tea, and cut flowers—account for about 21 percent of Uganda's export basket and are almost exclusively export to the high-income markets of the North. For these, delays, high transportation costs and burdensome export procedures constrain horticultural exports. Similarly, service exports are hampered by regulatory and other barriers. Even though services amount to nearly one-fifth of its foreign exchange earnings in the pre-COVID years, the World Bank's Services Trade Restrictiveness Index indicates that Africa's barriers are significantly higher than average, and are a detriment to services export development.

The Challenge Ahead: Spurring Exports to Create Jobs

The case studies provide limited evidence that governments have developed a package of trade and exchange rate policies, public investments, regulatory reforms, and institutional changes aimed at creating an "export push" that would raise growth to a new and sustained high plateau. Because individual firms face high fixed costs in entering export markets, countries risk that they will export too little unless public policies are put in place to offset the costs to first movers. To deal with these externalities, African governments need to develop a package of trade and exchange rate policies, public investments, regulatory reforms, and institutional changes to increase the share of nontraditional exports in GDP. Tariffs on intermediates and capital goods can place exporters at a disadvantage relative to global competitors. One option to address antiexport bias is to create an effective free trade arrangement for exporters through various mechanisms to eliminate or rebate tariffs on intermediate and capital inputs used in export production. Export procedures—including certificates of origin, quality and sanitary certification, and permits—can be burdensome. These institutional failures fall disproportionately on IWSS sectors such as horticulture and agri-business.

The exchange rate influences the relative attractiveness of producing for the domestic or foreign market, and a competitive real exchange rate has underpinned most prolonged episodes of rapid export growth. Hausmann and others (2004) and Rodrik (2008), among others, have argued that countries at early stages of economic transformation might even try to maintain an undervalued exchange rate over some period to establish beachheads in foreign markets. At a minimum, macroeconomic policy should strive to avoid overvaluations that stifle nontraditional exports (see Eichengreen 2008).

To foster dynamic service sectors that can drive exports, Nayyar and others (2021), in their seminal study, focus on what they call the 4Ts: trade, technology, training, and targeting. *Trade* is essential to expand access to larger markets and scale economies, requiring reductions in barriers to services exchange, harmonizing regulation, and developing common policies for data. Policies to access *technology* are crucial, including digital technologies and platforms, improving internet services, and increasing firm capabilities. Expanding *training* in technical skills across the board (see below) is a sine qua non. They also suggest *targeting* specific services activities for development in any given country, pushing available infrastructure and skills at the margin to move into higher-value-added services (see Nayyar et al. 2021).

Investment in Infrastructure

Export development, particularly regional trade and trade in tasks associated with service exports, has greatly increased the importance of trade logistics and infrastructure services. Limao and Venables (2001) find that an improvement in communication and transportation infrastructure from the median score on the World Bank's trade logistics index survey to the highest 25th percentile is associated with a decrease in transportation costs of 12 percent and an increase in trade volumes of 28 percent. Beyond exports, by one estimate, the current infrastructure deficiencies in Africa exacerbate a loss of about 2 percentage points per year in GDP growth (NEPAD, AU, and AfDB 2011). Reliable electrical power may be the greatest single constraint. The quality of electricity service is ranked as a major problem by more than half the firms in more than half the African countries in the World Bank's Investment Climate Assessments. Transportation follows as a close second.

These facts echoed through the case studies. In Kenya, for example, a reliable supply of power and the high cost of electricity pose challenges not only to firms in IWSS sectors but also to firms across the economy. Limited access to reliable electricity was identified as a challenge in ICT, horticulture, and tourism. About 89 percent of ICT firms reported electricity outages (averaging 3.5 outages monthly) and 91 percent of tourism establishments (mainly hotels and restaurants) experienced outages—averaging 6.3 electricity outages a month. A lack of feeder roads has been a major cause of large postharvest losses in the horticultural value chain (estimated at 42 percent). A key challenge for tourism is the difficulty of accessing natural and wildlife assets due to poorly maintained roads within the national parks. Prime tourism offerings are also affected by congestion. Zambia, which depends on hydropower for building its energy generation capacity, has experienced serious shortages over the past half decade because of declines in rainfall.

Both connectivity and high-speed data transmission are critical for exporting a wide range of services and IT-intensive exports. Connectivity is also important to IWSS sectors such as tourism and horticulture. Travelers attach importance to internet access and communication infrastructure. While Kenya outperforms the rest of Sub-Saharan Africa in mobile connectivity, there are still ICT-related constraints that stifle growth. Although the government set out to position the country as a leading business process outsourcing (BPO) destination, this is yet to be matched by a world-class BPO infrastructure.

In Rwanda, the government has committed to develop horticulture by earmarking sites for horticultural cultivation, investing in agricultural land information systems and irrigation facilities, and developing a cold chain system. ICT-enabled services in Rwanda have received a policy focus under the National ICT Strategy and Plan. The second phase of the plan (2006–10) centered on establishing a world-class communications backbone infrastructure. The government has also emphasized the tourism sector by supporting improvements in tourism infrastructure. Substantial investments have been made in Kigali International Airport, the Kigali Convention Centre, and the national airline carrier.

Several constraints inhibit the expansion of the horticulture sector. In South Africa, the high costs of seeds and fertilizer are a constraint, especially for smaller-scale producers. Poor infrastructure is a further constraint. Many farmers do not have easy access to markets. The poor state of road infrastructure in rural areas makes it difficult for farmers to guarantee wholesalers that they will deliver their products on time. In Senegal, high costs and poor quality of most infrastructure services are major causes of the country's poor performance in exports. In Ghana, the lack of cold storage facilities has been a major constraint on exports of highly perishable agro-industrial and horticultural products. Zambia's horticulture and floriculture industries were badly affected when KLM and British Airways discontinued flights to Europe in 2014.

According to enterprise survey data from Uganda, electricity is a major obstacle to firms' competitiveness. In a typical month, firms reported about 9 outages, resulting in losses of about 16 percent of total sales. The high cost of internet connectivity and mobile phone services makes information exchange between small-scale firms, agricultural traders, agro-processing plants, and global markets cumbersome and expensive. According to the 2017–18 Uganda National Information Technology survey, over 76 percent of respondents reported the high cost of an internet subscription as a key limitation on internet use. Although Uganda's road density is among the highest in Sub-Saharan Africa, the quality of the roads is low.

The challenge ahead is to secure infrastructure finance to create jobs. Governments in Africa—responding to the critical role that infrastructure plays in raising productivity—need to focus on mobilizing new sources of finance. Yet going into 2024–25, nearly all countries face mounting pressures to accommodate rising interest payments; and, with fiscal headroom exhausted in response to the serial shocks, programs of fiscal consolidation is the order of the day for most countries. Too frequently, these programs end up cutting public investment—at precisely the moment when it is needed most. At the same time, external sources of finance are tightening (IMF 2023).

Firms' Organization and Capabilities

The creation of "good jobs"—those with higher remuneration and greater productivity—is highly correlated with formal wage labor. As Fox and Ghandhi point out in chapter 2 of this volume, most new jobs in Africa are informal and/or are self-employment. Bringing workers together in a firm structure creates the opportunity for productivity gains through specialization typically not available through self-employment.

Bandiera (2021) has shown that formal wages and salaried labor are highly correlated with levels of income—as it is in the eight country studies. Key to raising productivity and creating good jobs is increasing the number, average size, and capabilities of formal firms. Creating opportunities for the self-employed to form firms, and for small and medium sized enterprises to become large firms, is one secret for increasing labor productivity (Cian et al. 2018).

Enhancing firms' capabilities, the knowledge and working practices used by firms in the course of production and in developing new products, is another. Capabilities in the agro-processing industry in Ghana are not well advanced. The industry has a relatively low degree of value added to agricultural commodities and very few linkages with marketing and financial services. In addition, firms use simple technologies. Ghana's participation in the global value chain shows that there is very little transformation to exports. Surveys conducted in Senegal found that most businesses feel they lack the technological and managerial skills needed to succeed on the international market. Although they want to export, they do not believe that they will meet the price and timeliness requirements imposed by demanding international buyers.

The Senegal study also indicates that not only do they experience a lack of adequate information, but, more significantly, firms do not believe they have the necessary technical mastery of production. Indeed, Maloney and others (2021) have shown for a much larger group of firms in other countries that access to technology is critical for firms to develop and raise their levels of productivity.

Regulation of business is particularly important for ensuring environmental, health, and safety standards; but, where they constitute a policy barrier to competition, they may have adverse effects. Competition is essential to firm-level productivity. Senegal's decline in IT-enabled services provides an example of the costs of a monopoly controlling the price and quality of access to the backbone infrastructure (English 2018). A lack of competition in transportation markets—often a product of regulation— is associated with higher trucking costs. Reforms of the regulatory environment that promote competition are an essential complement to other investment climate reforms. In Ethiopia, the transportation sector is highly regulated. Permits and licenses require extensive red-tape and are prone to corruption. In Kenya, the business regulatory environment is complex. The Kenya Enterprise Survey 2018 indicates that 8.6 percent of firms' senior management time is spent on complying with government regulations. Horticulture is affected by nontariff barriers, which represent a key constraint, especially for small-scale farmers. The ICT sector lacks a comprehensive policy and legal framework for e-commerce, and firms have identified several regulatory constraints. Some of the main constraints reported include business licensing and permits, bureaucracy, and corruption. A key issue is weak regulatory quality, especially with respect to incorporating competition into the design of regulations. In Ghana, tourism businesses are subject to standards and regulations under the Ministry of Trade and Industry. Lengthy, expensive, and complicated visa procedures and policies that limit the expansion of air travel are obstacles to the continued expansion of tourism.

Foreign investment is another channel that can enhance firms' capabilities in IWSS and other activities. The UN Conference on Trade and Development estimated that flows of foreign direct investment (FDI) to all developing regions peaked in 2015 and thereafter began a secular slowdown, a contraction that was even more pronounced in low-income countries. This pattern was mirrored in Sub-Saharan Africa, where FDI flows peaked at about $45.5 million, only to fall steadily downward, to $29.6 billion in 2020. While much of this can be explained by the decline in petroleum prices, the sudden contraction of global commerce has affected both manufacturing and IWSS.

The Challenge Ahead: Spawning Firms, Increasing Firm Size, and Building Firm Capabilities

Capabilities are mainly embodied in people and in working practices, so they are difficult to codify and measure. Bloom and Van Reenen (2007) find that better management practices are strongly correlated with several measures of productivity and firm performance. Management training can be used to improve firm-level productivity, though studies cast doubt on the effectiveness of classroom-based training (see Valerio et al. 2014). Organized efforts to acquire good management or working practices could take the form of collective action by firms. Alternatively, a public-private partnership could be formed to seek out information on good practices and make it available as a public good. The success of the Fundación Chile— a public-private partnership—in helping to establish Chile's world-class wine and salmon export industries has been widely documented. Initiatives of this type might be undertaken at a lower cost, and with a greater share of the cost borne by the private beneficiaries, than training.

Creating an attractive environment for foreign investment – along with domestic investment – is a key challenge for all of Africa. FDI is one— and some would argue, for countries at low levels industrial development, the most important—way of introducing higher-capability firms into an economy. The foreign investor can bring the technology, managerial knowledge, and working practices it has developed elsewhere.[1] Once higher capabilities have been introduced, their potential benefit will depend on the extent to which the technical knowledge and working practices held by the firm are transmitted to other firms. Buyer-seller relationships along the value chain are effective ways to transfer both technological knowledge and better working practices. Removing barriers to foreign entry can increase competition, reduce costs, and extend access to a broader range of services. FDI is a particularly important channel for the transfer of know-how and technology, as foreign firms introduce new types of services that may be better suited to the needs of clients.

Supply-Side Problems and Policies: Skill Constraints on Job Creation and Skill-biased Growth

The supply of labor entering Africa's labor market is rapidly increasing and will continue to grow well into coming decades. Understanding ways that skills can be developed—and better harnessed—to deal with the changing nature of growth itself is a crucial issue for policymakers.

Skill Deficiencies, Allocation, and Mismatches as Constraint on Productivity Increases

The importance of education and skills—human capital—for growth and economic transformation is well analyzed in the literature.[2] Although Africa has had considerable success in expanding access to education, nearly 60 percent of African 15- to 24-year-olds have only completed primary school and only 19 percent have gone beyond lower-secondary school (Filmer and Fox 2014). Beyond this, even at higher levels of education, too many graduating students are not equipped with skills that match employers' demands, a mismatch that exacerbates relatively high levels of unemployment among secondary and tertiary graduates (Fox and Gandhi 2021). Educational quality is an issue at all levels. Learning assessments show that most primary students in Africa lack basic proficiency in reading at the end of second or third grade. Employer surveys report that African tertiary graduates are weak in problem solving, business understanding, computer use, and communication skills. In Uganda, for example, feedback from employers indicates that current training programs are failing to equip trainees with practical skills and job-relevant competencies.

These skill gaps and mismatches are likely to be particularly acute in an IWSS-led growth path. To get a qualitative reading of the skills requirements and deficiencies in IWSS sectors, some of the case studies conducted an informal qualitative survey of a few firms on the importance of various skills to be employable and productive in IWSS. Countries indicate high importance across all the six skill groups: basic, problem solving, resource management, social, systems, and technical skills. The only exceptions were social and systems skills in the logistics sector. Importantly, the ICT sector stands out as the sector for which skills requirements are quite high.

Skill shortages are prevalent across most IWSS sectors, but with variations. In the logistics sector, the skills shortage is less severe. Soft skill gaps exist in different sectors and occupations, and youth, including those who are employed, often lack both formal qualifications and soft skills. For example, in Kenya firms reported that IWSS sectors faced a mismatch between skills demanded and skills available in the labor market, which was partly attributable to weak linkages between education and industry. The lack of skills in ICT is frequently cited as one of the factors limiting the growth of BPO. In agro-processing and horticulture, inadequate skill levels, especially among small-scale producers, result in a large share of substandard outputs. Firms also reported skills deficiencies in appropriately trained and qualified personnel in the tourism sector. About 20 percent of hotels and restaurants indicated that a lack of skilled staff members was a severe obstacle to growing their business. At least 5,000 new graduates with tourism qualifications are needed annually, compared with only 3,000 produced. The tourism sector has only a limited number of specialized training institutions in the region. Some of the most needed skills are customer service; decision-making and problem-solving; food technology; information technology; leadership; oral, written, and interpersonal communication; and time management.

In Rwanda, about 31 percent of workers in IWSS sectors are either high-skilled or medium-skilled workers as defined by educational attainment. The financial, business services, and ICT sectors require the most education. IWSS sectors with the highest share of low-skilled workers are formal trade, export crops, horticulture, and maintenance and repairs. Lacks of adequate knowledge of proper crop cultivation, fertilizer use, pest management, and postharvest handling limit the growth of the horticulture sector. Other challenges to horticulture include gaps in the knowledge and skills required to cultivate high-yield varieties, and inadequate quality management. Limited basic education in rural areas also may impede technological adoption, even when it is offered through agricultural extension. To improve employment prospects, the Rwandan government approved a project to upskill 30,000 youth for careers in the tourism and hospitality sector in 2018. Major initiatives under the program include support for programs of technical and vocational education and training that offer tourism-related courses and short courses to improve service delivery for hotel staff.

Ghana's National Tourism Development Plan identifies the poor quality of tourism services as a major complaint made by both domestic and foreign tourists. Except for the higher-star-rated hotels, most hotels and tourist sites lack skilled personnel. Currently, there is no clear national policy framework for tourism training and development. The large informal sector of the tourism industry has been similarly neglected. Failure to make use of IT infrastructure is a constraint on the development of the tourism sector.

Senegal faces significant occupational skills gaps in three IWSS sectors—horticulture, tourism, and agri-business. The lack of skills is most acute in tourism, followed by horticulture and agri-business. In South Africa, despite low formal qualification requirements for many of the jobs done by youth, high deficit scores in key skill groups—such as basic, social, and resource management skills—suggest that finding youth to fill the jobs created by IWSS may be challenging. A skill deficit that appeared across all IWSS industries was that of basic skills—skills that should be developed in the early stages of formal education. Soft skill deficits were also noted and limit the employability of youth. Firms surveyed indicated an increasing reliance on digital skills for the majority of their occupations. These stories, though anecdotal and perhaps unrepresentative, illuminate the importance of establishing programs in close collaboration with domestic private sectors to upskill the labor force, starting with reforms for basic and secondary education (see Arias, Evans, and Santos 2019).

Skill-Biased Growth and the Risks of Unequal Growth

Africa experiences very high levels of inequality when compared with other regions (Bhorat and Naiboo 2017).[3] The serial shocks and ensuing fiscal tightening may well have intensified inequality by undermining educational progress in much of Africa, with particularly adverse effects on low-income groups. In Uganda, for example, the COVID-19 pandemic forced the closure of schools for two years. Beyond this, trends toward greater inequality may be more structural. As more become integrated into the global economy, international market forces tend to pull up the salaries and wages of the most skilled Africans toward international levels. At the same time, product and technology markets typically introduce both a skill bias and a capital intensity to production. Baldwin (2019) highlights the "phenomenal advance" in digitization and deepening integration of world markets, a process he christened "Globotics," that is, the merger of globalization with robotics.

Technological advances in the global economy, while contributing to growth, have been driving worsening inequality in labor markets around the world. Qureshi (2020) underscores the role of technology in labor markets:

Digital technologies and automation have shifted demand toward higher-skill levels. Globalization has exerted pressure in the same direction. Demand has shifted, in particular, away from routine, middle-level skills that are more vulnerable to automation. . . . Job markets have seen an increasing polarization, with the employment share of middle-skill jobs falling and that of higher-skill jobs, such as technical professionals and managers, rising.[4]

How these forces will play out in developing countries generally and in Africa in particular remains to be seen. The recent emergence of generative artificial intelligence compounds the uncertainty. However, the country studies analyzed in this volume point out that both IWSS and manufacturing create strong demand for skilled workers. If skill levels are proxied by educational attainment, and "skilled workers" are assumed to be those with at least a primary school degree, in all countries for which we have information, save for Ghana, both IWSS and manufacturing employ more skilled workers than non-IWSS sectors. This is despite the fact that the non-IWSS sectors include both public sector employment and mining, both activities that employ many more skilled workers in their respective labor forces. Employment growth in the IWSS sectors as well as manufacturing is, if anything, likely to intensify this pattern.

Investing in Skills: Improving Labor Productivity and Offsetting Unequal Growth

Because of the rapid growth in population and the labor force of Africa, informal employment in both the rural and urban sectors is likely to be a feature of Africa's growth pattern for years to come. For the bottom half of the income distribution in virtually all African countries, labor skills are the most important asset poor Africans possess, so programs to expand their productivity is central to reducing poverty and offsetting market-driven tendencies toward inequality. Access to education and skills constitute a central determinant of economic opportunity for Africans.

A first-order priority—as Arias, Evans, and Santos (2019) recommend—is building universal foundational skills—investments in the early years as well as basic literacy and numeracy—though investments to promote school readiness, including through investments in maternal health, child nutrition, and early stimulation during the first 1,000 days of life and the early years. Beyond this, improving access to basic education with decisive interventions to close large and persisting learning gaps is necessary through improvements in school quality. Improving foundational skills also require interventions, such as second chance and adult literacy programs, to support those who missed out on critical early learning opportunities. Many countries in Africa as well as in other regions have expanded access without assuring effective teaching and thus school quality. Countries will have to find simultaneous ways to build more high schools and improve the quality of education provided by becoming more efficient in the use of resources. Those countries in the region with the biggest gains in enrollment boast free education. Ethiopia, Lesotho, and Malawi have leveraged cash transfer programs targeted to poor families as part of a strategy to increase enrollment and offset other indirect costs, including the opportunity cost of school; the results have been overwhelmingly positive (Arias, Evans, and Santos 2019).

There are skill deficits, especially among the young—particularly in soft skills and digital skills—that may limit the job-creating potential of IWSS. A demand-led approach to qualifications, through collaboration between employers and postsecondary educational institutions, can be effective in addressing these skill gaps. Programs that focus on focus on digital skills training and development for young girls and women to make them more employable could have a high, equalizing payoff. Because skill requirements differ across sectors, businesses must be consulted on a regular basis. Nationally representative surveys, which typically only ask firms about the distribution of employees across skill levels, could be expanded to include questions about areas of skill deficiency and how they affect their plans. To address digital and soft skill deficits, employers can develop mentorship and training programs for new trainees. Such programs are also a way in which the specific skills required in a sector can be learned. Mentors can teach life-skills to young people and highlight areas of strength and areas for improvement. Because mentors are usually people who hold more senior positions at a company, they can help new trainees to understand the skills required to reach such a position.

Over the medium term, however, redressing the skill-intensive bias in African growth will require more than simply expanding the supply of skilled workers. Fiscal policies are particularly important. Lustig (2018) points out that net fiscal incidence is typically mildly progressive among low-income countries, but relatively small—as in the case of Uganda, because the taxes and spending of the government as a share of national income are relatively low. Although the tax system across the continent is generally regressive, the increasing share of direct taxation in the total revenues observed in several countries has reduced inequality. Moreover, increases in well-targeted social expenditures in South Africa, Ethiopia, and a few other nations could mitigate income inequality. On the spending side, spending on social services is nearly always progressive (Odusola 2017).

Spending levels, however, are not the only determinant of effectiveness. Even more important is increasing the effectiveness and efficiency of expenditures. In Uganda, for examples, surveys show that teacher absenteeism amounts to an astronomical 27 percent of class time (Akseer and Karamperidou 2020). In an age of rapid technological progress, and where technology holds the key to productivity increases, countries can ill afford to neglect education and do so at the peril of reducing growth—and falling further behind.

Policies to Enable IWSS to Support Job Creation

The country studies suggest that sector-specific public actions on both the demand and supply sides of the labor market interact to accelerate growth. To illustrate the power of drilling down on sector-specific obstacles to growth, this section highlights efforts that could be made in the focus IWSS sectors covered in the case studies—agri-business and horticulture, tourism, ICT enabled services, and financial and business services, as well as other IWSS sectors.

Agri-Business and Horticulture

Investments to improve trade logistics are essential to export success in agro-processing and horticulture—as is the skills and knowledge dissemination associated with agricultural research and extension. Vulnerability to excess costs is particularly acute for processing activities because these frequently operate on small margins relative to the production of traditional exports. The global value chains characteristic of horticulture are demanding of logistics. Horticultural exports are perishable and particularly vulnerable to delays in shipping. As we saw in the case of Ethiopia, the underlying infrastructure in getting cut flowers to the airport is critical to success. Zambia's experience underlines the critical need for direct flight links to destinations markets for the growth in flower exports and other highly perishable products. Kenya's flower-growing region is well connected by road to Kenya's international airport, whereas Ethiopia's flower-growing region in the past has had poor road connectivity, resulting in a 40 percent spoilage rate. Skilled labor is very important to produce and deliver high-quality horticulture products. Shortages of skilled labor in flower production and marketing constrain the growth of Ethiopia's cut flower industry, for example. In Rwanda, adequate knowledge of proper crop cultivation, fertilizer use, pest management, and postharvest handling limit the growth of the horticulture sector. Other challenges for horticulture include gaps in the knowledge and skills required to cultivate high-yield varieties, and inadequate quality management.

Tourism

Adequate tourist-related infrastructure is a necessary condition for fully leveraging tourism's potential. Infrastructure constraints associated with air travel and road quality can limit the growth of the sector. Connectivity to the internet and communication infrastructure are also important considerations for travelers to Africa. Such logistical challenges restrict end-market upgrading opportunities in a number of countries. A workforce that has the skills needed to interact with tourists and to provide the many services that are inputs into the production of high-quality tourism is essential. Lack of skills consistently emerges from the country studies as a constraint on tourism development. Management, organization, communication, and computer skills are critical. In Zambia, the low quality of training at tourism-related institutions diminishes the effectiveness of the 700 students who graduate each year. In Kenya, about 20 percent of hotels and restaurants indicated that skilled labor power was a major or very severe obstacle to growth. In Ghana, there is no clear national policy framework for tourism training and development. Although there are international programs designed to teach these skills, Africa only has two schools that have earned certification from the UN World Tourism Organization. A study conducted by Acorn Consulting to assess impediments to Zambian tourism SMEs from attracting European customers and found a number of constraints, including poor connectivity between different tourist attractions and a sparce/inefficient domestic road. Despite significant investments in recent years, Zambia's road density of 9.1 per 100 square kilometers remains well below the Sub-Saharan average of 14.9 kilometers per 100 square kilometers.

ICT-Enabled Services

Not surprisingly, ICT-based services may be the most sensitive IWSS sector to infrastructure constraints. Backbone infrastructure is essential to exploit opportunities in first-generation IT-enabled services. Most African countries lack adequate backbone infrastructure. The cases of Kenya, Rwanda, and Senegal show that high-speed data transmission is critical for exporting a wide range of services, and especially for IT-intensive exports.

More broadly, governments need to revamp their innovation systems to encourage the creation of local technologies, adaption of imported technologies, and research and development. This is particularly important in agriculture, where new varieties hold the promise of enormous productivity gains. With COVID-19, pharmaceutical technologies have dramatized the importance of moving swiftly to create new capacities. Maloney and others (2021) provide a list of practical measures that would accelerate innovation and accelerated technological adaption in Africa and other developing countries.

ICT-enabled services depend on high-level skills—often those obtained at the tertiary level. The ability to hire university graduates at a fraction of the cost in Europe or the Arab Gulf was the initial impetus for many IT-enabled startups, but there remains a substantial supply-demand gap in the high-end talent pool in the IT workforce. A lack of skills in ICT is frequently cited as one of the factors limiting the growth of BPO in Kenya. Computing design skills, cybersecurity, and programming languages were identified as having the largest skills gaps. There is also a need to promote private sector–led skills development initiatives in high-level ICT skills such as programming. Senegal's ranking among the top 50 potential suppliers of outsourcing services has fallen significantly in the last five years, due to declines in the quality and quantity of human resources (English 2018). The growth of ICT in Zambia has been facilitated by the growth of digital infrastructure, digital financial services, and digital platforms, but is constrained by shortages of skills and entrepreneurship. Training for young people in digital skills should facilitate a greater employability in ICT-related work.

With the advent of generative artificial intelligence, the rising importance of e-commerce, and increase in digital activities, the role of ICT skills to command these activities assumes a heightened importance. A recent Brookings study developed an index of the gap in digitalization facing African countries relative to the Group of Twenty countries, comprising four dimensions: infrastructure (e.g., telecommunication), entrepreneurship (e.g., venture capital), finance (e.g., digital payment systems), public participation (e.g., online government services), and required education.[5] The gap between African countries and the frontier is imposing (figure 11-2). Moreover, the study finds very little improvement over time. If African countries are to seize the opportunities opened up by the emergence of ICT technologies, they cannot afford to overlook the importance of investments in science, technology, engineering, and mathematics education and the mastery of digital technologies.

FIGURE 11-2. **Digitization Index Gap, 2017**

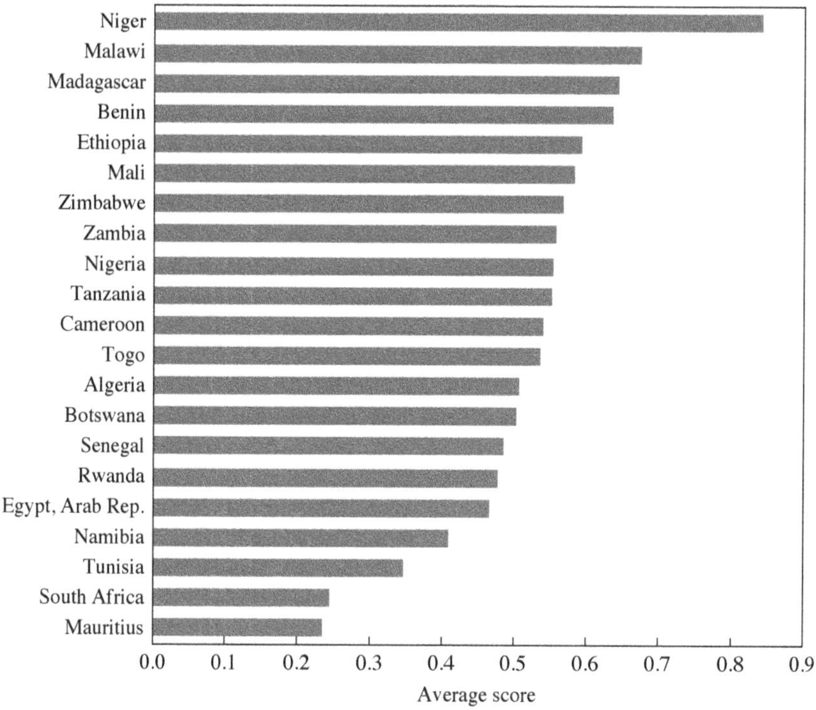

Source: Bhorat et al. (2023).

Financial and Business Services

More efficient financial services have positive spillovers to nearly every sector. More efficient financial services not only involve adopting digital solutions that improve accounting and access to financial instruments, but they also mean deepening and expanding the financial instruments available to businesses. Even nonfinancial businesses need access to an array of insurance and hedging products that help them make prudent investments. Firms also need to have affordable access to different currencies to finance trade and investment. The case studies serve to second points raised by Nayyar and others (2021) that financial services are high-productivity and high-wage, and are correlated with levels of per capita income. As jobs in the financial services sector tend to be skills oriented, governments should ensure that their youth enter the labor markets with skills demanded by the sector.

Other IWSS Sectors

Other IWSS sectors—such as transportation and logistics services, formal retail and wholesale trade, and even construction—are promising sectors in their own right. They also have important linkages with the sectors discussed above. An efficient and properly functioning transportation and logistics system drives competitiveness, particularly in an era of tightly integrated global supply chains. The small size of Africa's economies and the fact that many are landlocked make regional approaches to infrastructure, customs administration, and regulation of transportation in trade corridors imperative. Regional economic communities need to act by strengthening trade facilitation, improving services regulation, and investing in interconnected physical infrastructure. Road interconnections within regional economic communities may offer a way to close the infrastructure constraint to transportation. The issues extend beyond needed investment to policy. A lack of competition in transportation markets represents a significant barrier to integrating markets in regional groupings. Competition in the trucking industry plays a major role in price determination and therefore in trade. Lack of competition is associated with higher trucking costs. The most common anticompetitive regulations are discriminatory prices on transit permits; different axle-load regulations, discriminatory road use charges for foreign-registered vehicles, taxes at borders, and prohibition of sabotage.[6]

At the other end of the services spectrum, retail and wholesale trade in Africa absorbs a huge pool of new entrants into the labor market but has low productivity. It is decidedly local: more than 70 percent of food, beverage, and personal care products are purchased from small, independent shops rather than supermarkets (Ivers et al. 2022). The formal sector of trade, for our purposes designated an IWSS sector, is notably higher in productivity than the self-employed, informal sector. Large retailers and wholesalers, often foreign owned, are increasingly high tech and create jobs with relatively higher productivity and wages. Even SMEs can participate in deploying some new technology, whether it is laptop computers to manage inventories or accounting or cell phones to manage deliveries or collect mobile money payments. Policies should be aimed at equipping SMEs with the logistical and digital solutions (e.g., e-commerce and mobile money) they need to meet the changing needs of their communities as well as tap into. These solutions can help employees in the formal trade sector tap into regional and domestic markets if the opportunity arises.

Like trade, construction emerges in the case studies as a dynamic sector of job creation, most unskilled. Its growth is a direct result of rising investment rates associated with the growth of other IWSS sectors and the rest of the economy. Over the last five years, real estate and transportation have been among the sectors that have garnered the greatest value of construction projects across the continent (Deloitte 2022). Ample attention has been given to China as the continent's largest builder of construction projects; but domestic firms are responsible for the second-largest number of projects and, given their expanding share of projects built, could surpass China in this decade. Despite being one of the largest IWSS sectors and its promise for growth, construction in Africa faces impediments. These range from constraints on investment financing to weak bureaucratic processes that created delays in obtaining construction permits that open the way to corruption. Governments would be wise to find ways to expedite these processes, improving public procurement, and engaging the private sector in financing growth-promoting projects. Governments should pay special attention to domestic and region firms, as African firms themselves will play an important role in building African infrastructure.

With policies that drive the growth of these IWSS sectors, along with manufacturing and other activities, these studies show that opportunities for productive job creation are abundant.

The International Community Can Help: Resources, Remedies, and Research

As Africa emerges from the serial shocks of the events of 2020 to 2023, the international community can actively help recovery and accelerate the region's growth during the remainder of the decade. Three ways are particularly important.

First, as African countries confront the postserial shock need for fiscal budget tightening, the international community can ease adjustment pressures by providing increased access to finance growth. The cost of private borrowing on international capital markets has increased dramatically. Borrowing on private markets has also grown rapidly, and countries from Angola to Zambia have issued sovereign Eurobonds (IMF 2023). At the same time, donor finance has remained virtually flat for the last half decade—and itself is under strain because of responses from the countries that belong to the Organization for Economic Cooperation and Development to the Ukraine refugee crisis have placed a hold on normal development finance and on mobilized new sources of finance, including public-private partnerships and private borrowing. Nonetheless, the international community can mobilize several forms of external investment finance: bilateral development assistance, grant and concessional lending from multilateral development banks and the international financial institutions, greater access to nonconcessional windows of the multilateral development banks, redistribution of quota arrangements, grants from the growing (if still relatively small) private foundations, and public guarantees for private finance as well as innovative forms of public-private partnerships. Because development assistance to Africa is at risk with the demands to provide humanitarian and development resources to Ukraine and Eastern Europe, mobilizing necessary resources will require an extraordinary political effort in the high-income countries (Heitzig and Newfarmer 2022).

Second, ending the COVID-19 pandemic was especially important because it permitted the reactivation of IWSS activities, tourism in particular and services in general, along with a general recovery. This underscores the importance of providing access to vaccines that will protect the health of Africans against any new variants, Ebola and Marburg, and other pandemics that are likely to occur in the future. Africa has the lowest vaccination rates in the entire world—with only one in five of its citizens having been vaccinated (Africa Center for Disease Control 2022). The longer Africans remain underprotected and without adequate research and public health, the more likely it is that they will be affected by future pandemics—with risks to the whole world.

Third, promoting the generation and dissemination of knowledge holds the ultimate key to productivity growth. This volume also suggests several areas where knowledge dissemination and new research could shed light on economic transformation in Africa. Much research has already gone into increasing productivity in agriculture, but the pressures of climate change point to the need to accelerate the transition to new, higher-value-added crops and more efficient techniques for production. Agro-processing, which is linked inextricably to production in agriculture for inputs, is an activity that Africa could harness to drive growth; identifying promising, new unique products, new technologies and new markets, often as part of newly forming value chains, is a priority. Services remain understudied as a source of productivity growth but have been shown in this study to be central to Africa's growth path. Improvements in telecommunications have created whole new activities—and opened up new possibilities, ranging from telecommuting and remote service supplying to new forms of back-office services supply. Likewise, identifying new ways to promote new services exports—including tourism and tourism-related activities in the age of pandemics, business services, and cross-border financial services—requires more study. Evaluating programs that promote goods and services exports will be increasingly important to policymakers to identify successful approaches. In all the trade areas, the role of regional agreements, including the African Continental Free Trade Agreement, will be crucial. Finally, improving the quality of education to increase labor skills is as— or perhaps more—important as investments in expanding quantity, yet work on organizing education and motivating teachers has yet to produce a definitive menu of modalities. This includes for youth and women. Remote learning holds enormous promise, yet the determinants of access and effectiveness remain largely unknown. This list is only suggestive. The agenda of new questions is as large as the process of economic transformation in Africa itself.

Conclusion: Realizing the Promise of Transformation

Economic transformation is happening in Africa. This volume has sought to highlight the potential of industries without smokestacks—nontraditional activities and services that share characteristics with conventional manufacturing—to drive economic development alongside manufacturing. The eight case studies we have presented have revealed that many sectors in addition to manufacturing enjoy productivity growth and job creation potential that exceeds both manufacturing and other sectors, such as mining and utilities. Because several activities in agriculture have the opportunity to adopt new technologies (including in the organization of business and value chains), and because services are now tradable, new industries without smokestacks offer an opportunity to accelerate growth through an acceleration of economic transformation. Doing so, however, will require persistent attention to policies. Improving their business climate through investments to improve competitiveness is no less important to propel IWSS-led growth than it is for other sectors. Investing in programs to raise skill levels—from basic education through tertiary levels—is essential, not only to relieve the skill constraints and mismatches to growth but also to offset the unevenness of a technology-biased growth path that would otherwise lead to greater income inequality. Realizing the promise of the new opportunities for economic transformation is a central challenge facing Africa's policymakers—and their supporters in the international community.

NOTES

1. For a survey of the relevant literature, see Harrison and Rodriguez-Clare (2010).

2. Woldemichael and Shimeles (2019) point out that human capital formation is positively correlated with growth in labor productivity, both within-sector productivity growth and between-sector growth. This correlation is particularly strong at Africa's relatively early stage of development, though it begins to dissipate at levels of developments of today's high-income countries. Poor countries—and those at Africa's level of development—have much to gain from investments in education, health, and nutrition. See Woldemichael and Shimeles (2019) and the World Bank (2019).

3. Shimeles and Nabassaga (2017), using Gini coefficients as a measure of inequality, found that income inequities had remained stubbornly high over time, particularly since 1990. Odusola (2017) noted that 10 of the 19 most unequal countries globally are in SSA and seven outlier African countries are driving this inequality. Although the average unweighted Gini for Sub-Saharan Africa declined by 3.4 percentage points between 1991 and 2011, a clear bifurcation in inequality trends existed across countries in the region. Some 17 countries, mainly resource-poor agricultural economies, experienced declining inequality, while, on the other hand, 12 countries, predominantly resource-rich countries, mainly in South and Central Africa, recorded a rise in inequality. Using the ratio of income in the top 10 percent to the lowest 50 percent as a measure of inequality, Chancel and others (2019) found that inequality in Africa was more than three times that of Europe and substantially greater than the United States. Growth in GDP appears to have had a mild equalizing effect. A 1 percent rise in economic growth reduces inequality by 0.45 percent—with higher impact from manufacturing and agriculture than services (Odusola 2017).

4. These findings are echoed by a World Economic Forum (2020) study, which was based on a survey of business leaders around the world. It concludes: "In the absence of proactive efforts, inequality is likely to be exacerbated by the dual impact of technology and the pandemic recession."

5. See Bhorat et al. 2023 as well as Viviers et al. (2021) and Parry (2023).

6. This entails using foreign-registered vehicles for the domestic movement of merchandise.

REFERENCES

Africa Center for Disease Control. 2022. "COVID-19 Dashboard."

Akseer, S., and D. Karamperidou. 2020. "Time to Teach: Teacher Attendance and Time on Task in Primary Schools in Uganda." UNICEF Office of Research, Florence.

Arias, Omar, David K. Evans, and Indhira Santos. 2019. *The Skills Balancing Act in Sub-Saharan Africa: Investing in Skills for Productivity, Inclusivity, and Adaptability* Washington: World Bank.

Baldwin, R. 2019. *The Globotics Upheaval: Globalization, Robotics, and the Future of Work*. Oxford University Press.

Bandiera, Oriana. 2021. "Organizing Development." Lecture and presentation to London School of Economics and International Growth Centre, November 29.

Bhorat, H., L. Signé, S. Asmal, J. Monnaksootla, and C. Rooney. 2023. *Digitization and Digital Skills Gaps in Africa: An Empirical Profile*. Brookings.

Bloom, N., and J. V. Reenan. "Measuring and Explaining Management Practices Across Firms and Countries." *Quarterly Journal of Economics* 122: 1351–1408. https://doi.org/10.1162/qjec.2007.122.4.1351.

Chancel, L., D. Cogneau, A. Gethin, A. Myczkowski, and A. S. Robilliard. 2023. "Income inequality in Africa, 1990–2019: Measurement, Patterns, Determinants." *World Development* 163: 106–62. https://doi.org/10.1016/j.worlddev.2022.106162.

Cian, Andrea, Marie Caitriona Hyland, Nona Karalashvili, Jennifer Keller, Alexandros Ragoussis, and Trang Thu Tran. 2018. *Making It Big: Why Developing Countries Need More Large Firms*. Washington: World Bank.

Coulibaly, B., D. Gandhi, and A. Mbaye. 2019. "Job Creation for Youth in Africa: Assessing the Potential of Idustries without Smokestacks." Africa Growth Initiative Paper 22. Brookings.

Deloitte. 2022. "Africa Construction Trends Report." Deloitte Africa.

Diao, X., M. Ellis, M. McMillan, and D. Rodrik. 2021. *Africa's Manufacturing Puzzle: Evidence from Tanzanian and Ethiopian Firms*. NBER Working Paper 28344. Cambridge, MA: National Bureau of Economic Research.

Eichengreen, B. 2008. *The Real Exchange Rate and Economic Growth*. Commission on Growth and Development, Working Paper 4. Washington: World Bank.

English, E. P. 2018. "Senegal: A Service Economy in Need of an Export Boost." In *Industries Without Smokestacks: Rethinking African Industrialization*, edited by R. Newfarmer, J. Page, and F. Tarp. Oxford University Press.

Fox, Louise, and Dhruv Ghandi, 2021 "A Survey of African Employment Outcomes and Implications for Youth" Unpublished paper, Brookings.

Hallward-Driemeier, Mary, and Gaurav Nayyar. 2017. *Trouble in the Making? The Future of Manufacturing-Led Development*. Washington: World Bank.

Hanson, G. H. 2021. Who Will Fill China's Shoes? The Global Evolution of Labor-Intensive Manufacturing. NBER Working Paper 28313). Cambridge, MA: National Bureau of Economic Research.

Harrison, A., and A. Rodriguez-Clare. 2010. "Trade, Foreign Investment, and Industrial Policy for Developing Countries." In *Handbook of Development Economics, Volume 5*, ed, D. Rodrik and M. Rosenzwig, Amsterdam; Elselvier.

Hausmann, R., U. Panizza, and R. Rigobon. 2004. *The Long-Run Volatility Puzzle of the Real Exchange Rate*. NBER Working Paper 10751. Cambridge, MA: National Bureau of Economic Research.

Hausmann, R., D. Rodrik, and C. Sabel. 2008. "Reconfiguring Industrial Policy: A Framework with an Application to South Africa." Harvard University Center for International Development Working Paper 168 and Harvard Kennedy School Faculty Research Working Paper RWP08-031.

Heitzig, C., and R. Newfarmer. 2022. "Aid to Ukraine Should Not Come at Africa's Expense." Project Syndicate.

Ivers, Lisa, et al. 2022. "The Future of Traditional Retail in Africa." Boston Consulting Group.

IMF (International Monetary Fund). 2023. *Regional Economic Outlook–Sub-Saharan Africa: The Big Funding Squeeze, April*. Washington: IMF.

Lea, Nick. 2023. "Africa's Foreign Exchange Constraint." FCDO Internal Paper, London, March 23.

Limao, N., and A. Venables. 2001. "Infrastructure, Geographical Disadvantage, Transport Costs, and Trade." *World Bank Economic Review* 15: 451–79. https://doi.org/10.1093/wber/15.3.541.

Lustig, N. 2018. "Fiscal Policy, Income Redistribution, and Poverty Reduction in Low- and Middle-Income Countries." In *Commitment to Equity Handbook: Estimating the Impact of Fiscal Policy on Inequality and Poverty*, edited by N. Lustig. Brookings.

Maloney, W., et al. 2021. "Bridging the Technological Divide: Firm-Level Adoption of Technology in the Post-COVID World." Unpublished paper, World Bank.

Nayyar, Gaurav, Mary Hallward-Driemeier, and Elwyn Davies. 2021. *At Your Service? The Promise of Services-Led Development*. Washington: World Bank. http://hdl.handle.net/10986/35599.

NEPAD (New Partnership for Africa's Development), AU (African Union), and AfDB (African Development Bank). 2011. *Program for Development of Infrastructure in Africa*. Tunis: African Development Bank.

Newfarmer, R., J. Page, and F. Tarp. 2018. *Industries Without Smokestacks: African Industrialization Reconsidered*. Oxford University Press.

Odusola, A. 2017. "Fiscal Policy, Redistribution and Inequality in Africa." In *Income Inequality Trends in Sub-Saharan Africa: Divergence, Determinants and Consequences*, ed. A. Odusola, Giovanni Andrea Cornia, Haroon Bhorat, and Pedro Conceição. New York: United Nations Development Program.

Page, J. 2018. "Threats to Job Creation: Tourism and COVID-19." Viewpoint in *Foresight Africa* 2021, Brookings.

Parry, Ali. 2023. *Employment Effects of Digital Developments in Africa: Emerging Trends and the Way Forward*. Cape Town: AOSIS Books.

Qureshi, Z. 2020. "Inequality in the Digital Era." In *Work in the Age of Data*. Madrid: BBVA.

Rodrik, D. 2008. "The Real Exchange Rate and Economic Growth." *Brookings Papers on Economic Activity* 2: 365–412.

———. 2013. "Structural Change, Fundamentals, and Growth: An Overview." Institute for Advanced Study.

———. 2016. "An African Growth Miracle?" *Journal of African Economies* 27: 10–27.

Rodrik, D., X. Diao, and M. McMillan. 2019. "The Recent Growth Boom in Developing Economies: A Structural-Change Perspective." In *The Palgrave Handbook of Development Economics*, ed. M. Nissanke and A. Ocampo. New York: Palgrave Macmillan.

Shimeles, A., and T. Nabassaga. 2017. "Why Is Inequality High in Africa?" Working Paper 246, African Development Bank.

Valerio, A., B. Parton, and A. Robb. 2014. *Entrepreneurship Education and Training Programs around the World: Dimensions for Success*. Washington: World Bank.

Vellos, R. 2016. "Sub-Saharan Africa Sovereign Bond Issuance Boom." Blog post. http://blogs.worldbank.org/opendata/print/sub-saharan-africa-s-sovereign-bondissuance-boom.

Viviers, Wilma, Ali Parry, and Susara J. Jansen van Rensburg, eds. 2021. *Africa's Digital Future: From Theory to Action*. Cape Town: AOSIS Books.

Woldemichael, A., and A. Shimeles. 2019. "Human Capital, Productivity, and Structural Transformation." Working Paper 329, African Development Bank, Abidjan.

World Bank. 2019. *World Development Report 2019: The Changing Nature of Work*. Washington: World Bank.

———. 2022. "World Bank, Poverty and Inequality Platform." World Bank.

———. 2023. *World Development Indicators*. Washington: World Bank.

World Economic Forum. 2020. *Future of Jobs Report, 2020*. Geneva: World Economic Forum.

Index

www.ingramcontent.com/pod-product-compliance
Lightning Source LLC
Chambersburg PA
CBHW020829040525
26124CB00001B/2